Replenished Ethnicity

Replenished Ethnicity

MEXICAN AMERICANS,
IMMIGRATION, AND IDENTITY

TOMÁS R. JIMÉNEZ

UNIVERSITY OF CALIFORNIA PRESS
Berkeley   Los Angeles   London

University of California Press, one of the most distinguished
university presses in the United States, enriches lives around the
world by advancing scholarship in the humanities, social sciences,
and natural sciences. Its activities are supported by the UC Press
Foundation and by philanthropic contributions from individuals
and institutions. For more information, visit www.ucpress.edu.

University of California Press
Berkeley and Los Angeles, California

University of California Press, Ltd.
London, England

Library of Congress Cataloging-in-Publication Data

Jiménez, Tomás R. (Tomás Roberto), 1975–.
    Replenished ethnicity : Mexican Americans, immigration, and
identity / Tomás R. Jiménez.
        p.   cm.
    Includes bibliographical references and index.
    ISBN 978-0-520-26141-9 (cloth : alk. paper)
    ISBN 978-0-520-26142-6 (pbk. : alk. paper)
    1. Mexican Americans—Cultural assimilation.   2. Mexican
Americans—Race identity.   3. Mexicans—Cultural assimilation—
United States.   4. Mexicans—Race identity—United States.
5. United States—Emigration and immigration—Social aspects.
I. Title.

E184.M5J56   2010
305.868'72073— dc22   ·   2009032533

Manufactured in the United States of America

19 18 17 16 15 14 13 12 11
10 9 8 7 6 5 4 3 2

For my mother, whose grandparents crossed an ocean; and my father, who crossed under a wire.

Contents

Illustrations

Preface

My experiences as a fourth grader in Santa Clara, California, mark my own introduction to the topic of this book. I sat at a table with my best friend, Tony, and another good friend, Celena. One fall morning, a new student, Isidro, joined us. He had dark skin, straight brown hair, brown eyes, and a slight frame. Isidro was painfully shy and spoke just enough English to tell us that he was from Mexico, but he did not say much more than that. Our teacher might have thought that Isidro would be particularly comfortable at our table, since Tony, Celena, and I all came from Mexican ancestry. Tony's father was a Mexican immigrant from Acapulco, Celena's great-grandparents came from central Mexico, and my father came to the United States from the Mexican state of Jalisco at a very young age. I recall the three of us—Mexican Americans—staring at one another, not knowing quite how to respond to Isidro. Sure, we were of Mexican descent, but we were born in the United States, came from middle-class homes, and spoke English as our native and only language, all of which made it difficult for us to relate to him. We nonetheless did our best to make Isidro feel welcome. I do not recall what happened to Isidro, only that he remained in our class for less than a month.

Our small table was a microcosm of the Mexican-origin population in the United States. Like the quartet of fourth graders at that table, the Mexican-origin population is unique in its vast internal diversity. It is made up of individuals who come from many different waves of immigration, while others descend from Mexicans who were in what became the southwestern United States in 1848. Among individuals who claim Mexican ancestry are immigrants (like Isidro), children of immigrants (like Tony and me), and grandchildren and great-grandchildren of immigrants (like Celena).

Not until graduate school did I fully appreciate the larger significance of that childhood experience. I entered graduate school with an interest in questions of immigration and ethnic identity. Some of the first readings I did on this topic dealt with the descendants of European immigrants. This literature makes clear that "white ethnics" have become so integrated into U.S. society that ethnicity has become a symbolic part of their identity, one that they can invoke optionally and without consequence. White ethnics represent what most consider a "classic" assimilation story: each generation born in the United States improved on the fortunes of the previous generation on its way into the U.S. mainstream. As I thought about the European experience of assimilation, I began to wonder how this story might compare with the descendants of early Mexican immigrants, whose ancestors came to the United States decades ago. Was ethnicity a symbolic and optional part of their identity?

At first blush, the answer to this question seemed to be an unequivocal no. Popular perceptions and social science research suggested that people of Mexican origin are anything but a part of the U.S. mainstream and that being of Mexican descent is a significant handicap to mobility. I found the reasoning behind these assessments less than satisfying, however. Much of what I read argued that Mexican Americans are entirely different from the descendants of European immigrants. Mexicans, the research suggested, were originally integrated into the United States through colonization and have experienced persistent racial discrimination, preventing upward mobility and the symbolic and optional nature of ethnicity that might come with that mobility. Other social science research on the Mexican-origin population ignored distant, or later-generation, Mexican-American descendants of immigrants altogether, focusing exclusively on more recently arrived immigrants and their children.

I thought that the factors shaping the Mexican-origin experience in the United States laid out in my early readings (conquest, a history of discrimination, intergenerational mobility, residential mobility, intermarriage, etc.) must play a role in the Mexican-American experience today. But I also believed that scholars of both European-origin assimilation and the Mexican-origin population have underappreciated an additional variable: ongoing Mexican immigration, or "immigrant replenishment." The generational diversity among people of Mexican origin is a direct result of virtually continuous Mexican immigration to the United States for the last hundred years. In contrast, mass European immigration ended more than eighty years ago, and the white-ethnic descendants of the European immigrants seldom, if ever, encounter new immigrants of the same ethnic origin. If being a later-generation white ethnic means having a symbolic and optional ethnic identity, then what happens to ethnic identity when newcomers from the ethnic homeland continually replenish a group, as occurs with Mexican Americans?

I set out to answer this question by interviewing later-generation Mexican Americans in Garden City, Kansas, and in Santa Maria, California. I spent hundreds of hours talking to Mexican Americans, as well as to community leaders and rank-and-file residents in general. I also spent months living in each locale in order to understand better what it means to be a later-generation Mexican American in these two places. What follows is what I learned from my interviews and observations. I discovered that Mexican Americans have experiences that are somewhat similar to their European-descended counterparts. They are well-integrated members of their respective communities, and, in many ways, the classic story of assimilation applies. I also found that immigrant replenishment is an ingredient that is lacking in white ethnics' experience of U.S. society but is crucial for understanding what it means to be Mexican American. I learned that Mexican immigration makes ethnicity a more important part of identity for the people I interviewed, even as they become more integrated into U.S. society. I found that Mexican immigration makes ethnicity simultaneously more rewarding and more costly for Mexican Americans. In the end, I learned that ongoing Mexican immigration, more than the variables embedded in standard explanations of racial conflict and assimilation, shapes what it means to be Mexican American in the United States today.

Acknowledgments

This book began as my PhD dissertation in the sociology department at Harvard University, but I started studying the issues I address in these pages while I was an undergraduate at Santa Clara University. Alma M. García, my adviser and mentor, encouraged me to pursue graduate school and supported me along the way. At Harvard, I was fortunate to have a wonderful dissertation committee that guided this work. Mary Waters, my adviser, deserves special thanks. I benefited from her intellectual and professional guidance, and her knack for injecting a sense of calm and normalcy into what often seems like a chaotic endeavor. Any of the good ideas that I developed in this work are a result of Mary's ability to make me feel comfortable discussing interpretations of my data and brainstorming theoretical points, no matter how off the mark they might seem at first. Every scholar should be as lucky as I have been in finding an adviser and colleague like Mary. Katherine Newman went above and beyond the call of duty in guiding my intellectual and professional development. As an athlete for much of my life, I have had many great coaches. Kathy is among the best. She is an electrifying motivator. I left every discussion I had with her feeling energized and I benefited enormously from her detailed feedback. Lawrence Bobo was instrumental in helping me develop into a sociologist, and I profited from his encouragement and support in getting the ideas from my dissertation into publication. He has been unyielding in his intellectual and professional guidance, and I am very grateful to him.

While at Harvard, Irene Bloemraad, Monica McDermott, and Mario Small were especially instrumental in helping me formulate the ideas for this research, and they provided invaluable advice from beginning to end. I also benefited from excellent input from friends and colleagues: Audrey Alforque Thomas, Patricia Banks, Bayliss J. Camp, Cybelle Fox, Yvonne Gastelum, Gabriella González, June Han, Luisa Heredia, Xiaojiang Hu, Devon Johnson, Karyn Lacy, Dongxiao Liu, Freda B. Lynn, Ezell Lundy, Ian MacMullen, Helen Marrow, Richard Mora, Eduardo Mosqueda, Helen Marrow, María Rendón, Wendy Roth, and Chris Wheat.

My dissertation became a book while I was on the faculty at the University of California, San Diego, where I had many wonderful colleagues who offered feedback on my writing and gave me much support. I am especially grateful to John Skrentny, who provided indispensible advice, encouragement, and humor when I needed it most. I simply cannot thank John enough for his mentorship. David Fitzgerald deserves special thanks for reading multiple drafts of the manuscript and offering his keen insights. April Linton provided sound technical advice, and I benefited from several conversations with her. Marisa Abrajano, Amy Bridges, Zoltan Hajnal, Isaac Martin, and Eric Van Young provided excellent feedback on parts of the manuscript. While I was at UCSD, a fellowship from the Center for Comparative Immigration Studies (CCIS) and the Center for US-Mexico Studies (US-MEX) gave me the time to complete the writing. Wayne Cornelius and Takeyuki "Gaku" Tsuda at CCIS, and René Zenteno at US-MEX were wonderful hosts and colleagues. Several other colleagues at UCSD deserve special thanks: Amy Binder, Mary Blair-Loy, Steve Epstein, John Evans, David Gutiérrez, Jeff Haydu, Rebecca Klatch, and Kwai Ng.

Tamara Kay, Wendy Roth, Lynn Ta, and Rebecca C. Franklin deserve special thanks for providing helpful feedback on complete drafts of the manuscript. Suzanne Knott and Robin Whitaker also deserve thanks for applying their fantastic editing skills to this project. I would also like to thank my editor at the University of California Press, Naomi Schneider, for her support from beginning to end and for working so efficiently to see the manuscript through to publication.

I benefited from conversations with colleagues and friends who asked tough questions and encouraged me to provide a richer analysis: Richard Alba, Frank Bean, Susan Brown, Prudence Carter, Cynthia Duarte, Nancy Foner, Mario T. García, Thomas Guglielmo, Michael Jones-Correa, Jennifer Lee, Peggy Levitt, Paolo Parigi, Gregory Rodríguez, Mark Sawyer, Peter Skerry, Marcelo Suárez-Orozco, Edward Telles, Jessica Vasquez, Roger Waldinger, and Loïc Wacquant. Cheri Minton, Cherie Potts, and Pat Steffens provided helpful and very reliable technical assistance.

This research was made possible by several grants: a National Science Foundation Dissertation Improvement Grant (SES grant 0131738), the Harvard University Multidisciplinary Program on Inequality and Social Policy, funded by National Science Foundation (IGERT grant 9870661), the Minority Affairs Division of the American Sociological Association, and a grant from the Harvard University Graduate Society. I am also grateful to the American Sociological Association and Harvard University for their generous financial support throughout my graduate training. An Irvine Fellowship from the New America Foundation gave me valuable financial support. At New America, Gregory Rodríguez helped me hone my arguments by pushing me to test my ideas outside academic circles.

Doing fieldwork always requires help from "gatekeepers" and guides. In Garden City, Donald Stull was especially helpful in enabling me to make initial contacts. Dennis and Lanette Mesa served as my surrogate family and housemates. There is no way to thank them for their overwhelming generosity. They hold a place in my heart that is bigger than they may ever know. Martin Segovia was also incredibly helpful both in my fieldwork and in providing friendship to a stranger in his town. In Santa Maria, Roberto and Darlene Jiménez, my aunt and uncle, opened their warm and loving home to me. They gave me every bit of support—

emotional and otherwise—that I could have hoped for. The love and respect I have for them is boundless. Also in Santa Maria, John Jiménez, Rogelio and Arlene Flores, Caroline Martínez, and Gina Rodríguez were extremely generous in helping me get to know the city.

This book is possible only because of the kindness of the many individuals who allowed me to interview them. I am overwhelmed by how giving my respondents were to me—a complete stranger who came to their homes with a tape recorder and a list of questions. In addition to sharing their stories, some were especially hospitable and invited me to stay for dinner or even sent me away with food. Others contacted me to say "hello" at some later date. Getting to know these individuals was the most enjoyable and enriching part of this project, and I am forever grateful to them.

I know no person more fortunate than I am to have such a loving and supportive family. My brothers, Francisco ("Pancho") and Miguel; my sisters-in-law, Lori and Susie; my nephews, Carlo and Dario; and my niece, Camille, provided lots of support and encouragement. My partner in life and best friend, Nova, has been with me since the beginning of this project. She has stuck with me through four states, three time zones, and the District of Columbia. Throughout, she offered wise counsel and abundant encouragement. Her effervescent spirit and unconditional love never fail to show me just how good life can be. She sees in me many qualities that I sometimes fail to see in myself. I've concluded that anything good that she sees is a reflection of what she has added to me.

Finally, my mother, Laura, the granddaughter of four Italian immigrants, and my father, Francisco, an immigrant from Mexico, have provided me with all the support, stability, love, and encouragement that a son could hope for. They tried to instill in me the ambition, humility, compassion, respect, and graciousness that the immigrant experience taught them. I hope that this book reflects well on their efforts. I dedicate it to them.

ONE

Introduction

Sitting just southwest of Manhattan less than a mile from the Statue of Liberty is the most renowned symbol of U.S. immigration: Ellis Island.[1] During the period of heavy European migration, which lasted from roughly 1880 to 1920, twenty-four million migrants came to the United States from countries such as Ireland, Italy, Poland, Hungary, Austria, and Russia, seeking religious and political freedom and economic opportunity. Half of them passed through Ellis Island before venturing on to other destinations in the industrializing United States. But a series of events conspired to all but end the great European migration. World War I, restrictive immigration laws passed in 1917, 1921, and 1924, the Great Depression, and World War II slowed European migration to less than a trickle. The rapid decline of migration from Europe meant that a large facility to process immigrants was no longer necessary, so Ellis Island closed in 1954.

During the ensuing decades, Ellis Island stood as an abandoned and decaying relic of U.S. immigration. Looters pilfered what remained in the crumbling buildings, and vandals defaced the property. Pollution and the harsh weather in the New York Harbor deteriorated the ornate exterior of the main building. As Ellis Island lay empty and forgotten, the children and grandchildren of those who passed through it came of age. Many moved out of the ethnically concentrated neighborhoods in which they had grown up, attended college, contributed to war efforts, joined the American middle class, and married individuals outside their ethnic group. As these processes unfolded, the fears about racial contamination that had been prominent in public debates just a few decades earlier and the inability of southern and eastern European immigrants to assimilate disappeared. By the 1980s the grandchildren of these European immigrants were adults, and their assimilation into American society appeared complete. Their ethnic ancestry was scarcely a determinant of their opportunities and life chances. Their ethnic identity entered a "twilight" (Alba 1985).

Today, boats filled with people still arrive at Ellis Island, but they are not brimming with poor, tired immigrants. Instead, they carry tourists who come to visit what is now a National Park Service Monument and an immigration museum. The buildings are no longer dilapidated: the brick and stone Beaux-Arts façades are immaculately clean, the tiled floors and ceiling shine, and a fresh coat of paint blankets the interior. Many visitors come to Ellis Island hoping to recapture part of their family's past in the research center, where computers provide access to a massive database listing the names of immigrant ancestors who where processed there. Some visitors are so inspired by their visit that they pay a fee to have their immigrant ancestors' names inscribed on the American Immigrant Wall of Honor. As a visit to Ellis Island suggests, the immigrant experience is a distant influence for descendants of early European immigrants. The often difficult journey of their immigrant ancestors is now largely imagined through family trees or lives only in pictures and museums, like the one at Ellis Island. Indeed, Ellis Island represents an American dream fulfilled.

More than twenty-eight hundred miles southwest of Ellis Island is an equally notable immigrant gateway: the border crossing between San Diego, California, and Tijuana, Mexico. Like Ellis Island, the San Diego–Tijuana crossing has a prominent place in the history of U.S. immigration. As some European immigrants poured into the United States through Ellis Island at the beginning of the twentieth century, Mexican migrants journeyed through Tijuana (and many other cities along the border). In 1910, there were roughly 222,000 Mexican-born individuals living in the United States. By 1930, the number of Mexican immigrants had swelled to 617,000, or 4.3 percent of the total foreign-born population (González Baker et al. 1998: 87). The passage of these early Mexican immigrants differed significantly from that of their European counterparts. Many traversed the land on foot or by train or in some cases arrived by river, but they did not cross an ocean. Early Mexican immigrants did not pass through processing facilities, and most were never required to show documentation when crossing into the United States or back into Mexico.[2] Nonetheless, these Mexican immigrants, like their European contemporaries, immigrated in search of a better life.

What has become of the later-generation descendants of early Mexican immigrants? We know that some of the children and grandchildren of these immigrants moved out of ethnically concentrated neighborhoods, joined the military, intermarried, and experienced socioeconomic mobility, though to a more modest degree than descendants of European groups. We also know that American society discriminated against the descendants of these early Mexican immigrants because of their ethnic origin. And we know that many of these descendants voiced their grievances about this treatment during the Chicano civil rights movement of the 1960s and 1970s.

What we do not know as well is how ethnic identity plays out in the lives of later-generation Mexican Americans.[3] Has their ethnic identity entered a twilight? Is their ethnic origin an important part of their identity? This book explores these questions by examining what it means to be Mexican American—a descendant of the earliest Mexican immigrants—in the United States today.

Contrasting the contemporary scene at the San Diego–Tijuana border crossing to the one found at Ellis Island suggests an answer to these questions. A trip to the San Diego–Tijuana crossing reveals no museums, exhibits, ancestral research center, or monuments honoring the early Mexican immigrants. The San Diego–Tijuana crossing is the busiest border crossing in the world. Thousands of people—workers, tourists, migrants, and smugglers—cross each day. Hundreds of cars line the highway leading through the main passage point, and U.S. Customs and Border Protection agents inspect vehicles for contraband and unauthorized migrants.[4] Heavy metal fences and Border Patrol agents guard the area surrounding the main border crossing thoroughfare, and stretching east and west, a tall (and in some places multilayered) fence separates the two countries. Along some portions of the border, large stadium lights illuminate patches of open space where migrants may attempt to cross. Border Patrol agents roam these areas in jeeps and all-terrain vehicles searching for drugs, unauthorized crossers, and those who smuggle either of these. In more remote areas of the border east of San Diego, white wooden crosses memorialize individuals who have died attempting the trip north. These remote areas are also where organized "civil defense corps," like the Minutemen, monitor the border. For descendants of early waves of Mexican immigrants, the scene at the San Diego–Tijuana border does not represent a nostalgic look into America's past. And to many in the United States, Mexican immigration is seen as a threat to the nation's future.

Mexican Americans, unlike their later-generation European counterparts, live in a society in which emigration from their ethnic homeland is prominent. Although many Mexican Americans are several generations removed from their immigrant origins, thousands of immigrants from Mexico—representing 31 percent of all foreign-born individuals in the United States today—continue to enter this country (Migration Policy Institute 2008). Equaling the force of this demographic dominance are fiery debates about the social, economic, and political changes to the United States resulting from the influx of Mexican newcomers. The intensity of these debates is a function of not just the large number of Mexican immigrants but also their characteristics: they are generally poor, have little formal education, and concentrate in low-wage, low-status jobs, and the majority—54 percent—are in this country without legal authorization (Passel 2006).

Drawing on interviews and participant observation with later-generation Mexican Americans in Garden City, Kansas, and Santa Maria, California, I show in this book that these Mexican immigrants significantly shape what it means to be a later-generation Mexican American. Although later-generation Mexican Americans display a remarkable degree of social and economic integration into U.S. society, ongoing Mexican immigration, or immigrant replenishment, sustains both the cultural content of ethnic identity and the ethnic boundaries that distinguish groups. Mexican Americans' everyday experiences reveal that their ethnic identity is connected to contemporary Mexican immigration in ways that make that identity simultaneously more beneficial and costly than it would be without the ongoing immigration. Immigrant replenishment provides the means by which Mexican Americans come to feel more positively attached to their ethnic roots. But it also provokes a predominating view of Mexicans as foreigners, making Mexican Americans seem like less a part of the U.S. mainstream than their social and economic integration and later-generation status might suggest. Mexican Americans are not systematically excluded from full participation in American society. But the large presence of Mexican immigrants prevents Mexican Americans from being fully regarded as part of the quilt of ethnic groups that make up the "nation of immigrants." In practice, the core of the nation is composed of descendants from immigration waves that ended long ago.

IMMIGRATION, ASSIMILATION, AND THE PLACE OF MEXICANS

Explaining the experiences of Mexican Americans has proven difficult for scholars. The uniqueness of the Mexican-origin population in the United States relative to virtually any other ethnic group explains much of the difficulty. Unlike true immigrant groups, the first Mexicans in the United States were a colonized people whose presence here was not of their choosing. In 1848, the United States and Mexico signed the

Treaty of Guadalupe Hidalgo, ending the U.S.-Mexican War. The treaty stipulated that Mexico cede much of what is today the American West and Southwest to the United States for eighteen million dollars. Under the treaty, the estimated fifty thousand Mexicans who lived in the southwestern territory became U.S. citizens.[5] These individuals represent the first significant presence of the Mexican-origin population in the United States and, indeed, the first Mexican Americans.

The Treaty of Guadalupe Hidalgo also established a border stretching over two thousand miles along the southwestern portion of the United States, a second source of exceptionalism. The length of the border and the close geographical proximity of the United States to Mexico means that people of Mexican origin do not have to travel far to come to the United States, nor do Mexicans in the United States have far to go to visit their ethnic homeland. Many Mexicans traveled regularly between the two countries in the years after Guadalupe Hidalgo, and many continue to make frequent trips back and forth (Roberts, Frank, and Lozano-Ascencio 1999; Smith 2005a). Although some European migrants traveled back to their country of origin (Wyman 1993), distance, cost, and inconvenience of travel mitigated the ease of doing so.

It was not until the early part of the twentieth century—more than fifty years after the Treaty of Guadalupe Hidalgo was signed—that the first major wave of Mexican immigration began and has continued virtually uninterrupted to the present day. The number of Mexican immigrants entering the United States has increased in each succeeding decade, with the exception of the 1930s (for reasons I discuss in the next chapter), and the number of unauthorized Mexican immigrants in the United States has increased precipitously in the most recent decades (Massey, Durand, and Malone 2002; Passel 2006). No other group has a history of significant immigration that spans the periods of the great European migration, the post-1965 immigration, and the period in between,[6] and Mexicans are certainly the only group whose presence in the United States stems from both colonization and immigration. Figure 1 vividly shows the historical distinctiveness of Mexican immigration relative to selected European-origin immigrant populations. What is especially noteworthy is that Mexican immigration continued after European immigration declined.

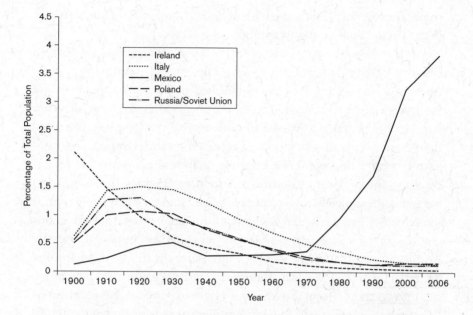

Figure 1. Number of foreign born from Mexico and selected European countries as a percentage of the U.S. total population, 1900–2006. Sources: U.S. Decennial Census; U.S. Census Bureau, American Community Survey.

After 1970, the foreign-born Mexican population spiked, while the number of foreign-born individuals from European countries continued to descend.

The exceptional nature of the Mexican-origin population also stems from the size and characteristics of its foreign-born population. No other group constitutes a greater share of immigrants in the United States today. According to estimates based on the 2006 American Community Survey, Mexican immigrants make up nearly 31 percent, or 11.5 million, of the total U.S. foreign-born population. The next largest foreign-born population comes from China and accounts for only 5.1 percent of all newcomers (Migration Policy Institute 2008). Furthermore, levels of unauthorized Mexican migration are high. Demographer Jeffrey Passel (2008) estimates that 59 percent of the total unauthorized U.S. population comes from Mexico, and more than half of all foreign-born Mexicans are in the United States without authorization.

The exceptional characteristics of the Mexican-origin population—a colonized group *and* an immigrant group; an old immigrant population *and* a new one; part of the established native-born population *and* the foreign-born population—make it difficult to explain the Mexican-American experience using existing theoretical perspectives. The more than eighty years of social science research on immigration, race, and ethnicity offer important but unstable analytical platforms for understanding the Mexican-American experience. Theories of assimilation have either completely missed people of Mexican origin or been applied too narrowly to a particular segment of this population. Interpretations emphasizing racialization resulting from colonization have too easily dismissed assimilation for ideological reasons, downplayed evidence of assimilation among Mexican Americans, and not considered how ongoing immigration affects the Mexican-origin experience. Newer theories of assimilation recognize Mexican-immigrant replenishment as significant, but the application of these theories in survey research conceives of assimilation as too static to fully appreciate how immigrant replenishment affects intergenerational change in ethnic identity. A fuller understanding of the Mexican-American experience emerges by attending to the implications of ongoing Mexican immigration for ethnic identity formation.

Classical Foundations: Built without Mexicans

The intellectual foundations of the study of immigration and ethnic change were built without considering the Mexican-origin experience; thus, discussions about how later-generation descendants of earlier immigrants experience American society rarely include Mexican Americans. Instead, in such discussions people of European origin most often come to mind. The weak attachment, if any, that later-generation descendants of European immigrants have to an ethnic identity is more or less taken for granted. These individuals commonly describe themselves as "European mutts"—people whose ancestors have intermarried to such an extent that they trace their ethnic roots to multiple strands (Lieberson and Waters 1988). People who descend from the great European migration scarcely experience discrimination based on their racial or ethnic identity, and their ancestry does not systematically determine the types of opportunities they enjoy (Alba 1990). Ethnicity holds a symbolic place in their identity, and ethnic attachments are characterized as "a nostalgic allegiance to the culture of the immigrant generation, or that of the old country; a love for and pride in a tradition that can be felt without having to be incorporated in everyday behavior" (Gans 1979: 9). Indeed, they can invoke any particular strand of their ethnic identity when they choose, should they feel a little more ethnic on any given day, or deemphasize their ethnic identity in order to feel part of a larger collective not defined in ethnic terms (Waters 1990).

This was not always the case. Southern and eastern European immigrants who came to the United States at the end of the nineteenth and beginning of the twentieth centuries by no means enjoyed ethnicity as an optional part of their identity. In recent years, historians of European immigration and race have muddied the often taken-for-granted position that these immigrants and their descendants had an easy time assimilating because they were white. A closer look at the history of assimilation reveals that many European-origin immigrants occupied an inferior racial status. Their legal status as "white" entitled even "swarthy" ethnic groups, such as the Italians, to full participation in American society, unlike blacks, who were legally barred from it (Guglielmo 2003). Many people in the early twentieth century wondered, nonetheless, if European immigrants could ever be assimilated (Higham 1963; Jacobson 1998; Roediger 1991, 2005). Yet European immigrants and their descendants struggled down the long and bumpy path of assimilation and, after several generations, came out "white" at the other end (Ignatiev 1995; Jacobson 1998; Roediger 1991, 2005).

Sociologists were among the closest observers of this process from its early stages and laid the foundation for the way that immigration, race, and ethnicity came to be understood for much of the twentieth century. Robert E. Park, Thomas Burgess, and W. I. Thomas, part of "the Chicago School of Sociology," took great interest in the European immigrants who flooded into mostly East Coast and midwestern cities, such as Chicago. They took seriously the idea that urban life shapes how immigrants encounter American society, and their early studies focused on the role that spatial location plays in how people from different ethnic groups interact (Park, Burgess, and McKenzie 1925; Wirth 1928). Their studies of immigrants in urban centers laid the groundwork for theories of assimilation. As sociologists Richard Alba and Victor Nee (2003) point out, early definitions of assimilation characterized the process not as forced homogenization but as the convergence of groups that became incorporated into a common way of life. Yet early thinking about assimilation is most often associated with Park's "race-relations cycle" (1950), which posited four irreversible stages of race relations, which begin with contact between groups, are followed by competition, give way to accommodation, and conclude with assimilation.

Assimilation, sociologists discovered, took generations to unfold, and the end of this process would be most evident among the third generation. Lloyd Warner and Leo Srole's (1945) study of "Yankee City," a New England town with large numbers of European immigrants, identified generation as the key temporal marker of assimilation. They noted gains made in occupational status from the first generation to the second and argued that all groups were moving ahead, though perhaps at a different pace. They emphasized that the pace of assimilation varied by skin color, with darker-skinned groups (such as Sicilians and Greeks) experiencing slower assimilation than lighter-skinned groups. Nonetheless, assimilation came to be thought of as an inevitable and irreversible process that progressed linearly from generation to generation.

If the Chicago School built the foundation for how we think about assimilation, sociologist Milton Gordon constructed the house. Gordon's (1964) landmark work argues that assimilation is a multidimensional process wherein "structural assimilation," or the entrance of immigrants into primary-group relationships with the host society, leads to "identificational assimilation," or the assumption of a sense of "peoplehood" (81). According to Gordon, once structural assimilation takes place, all other forms of assimilation, including identificational assimilation, follow (70).

By the late twentieth century, the third- and fourth-generation descendants of southern and eastern European immigrants came of age and reached the end of the long and rocky path of assimilation. At the end of this path was the symbolic (Alba 1990; Gans 1979) and optional (Waters 1990) nature of ethnic identity that we see among white ethnics today. Indeed, the story about American assimilation theorized by Park, Warner, and Srole and by Gordon seems to have applied for European groups.

Unfortunately, the Mexican-origin experience did not form part of the empirical basis for early formulations of assimilation theory, though Mexican immigration was certainly a part of an earlier period of immigration most often associated with European groups. During the 1910s, Mexican immigrants accounted for 4 percent of all arriving immigrants. As European immigration slowed in the 1920s, the proportion of foreign-born Mexicans rose to 11 percent (González Baker et al. 1998: 88).[7] With their analytical lens squarely focused on eastern and midwestern cities, sociologists largely ignored the experiences of Mexican immigrants and Mexican Americans in the Southwest.[8] Had they included the Mexican-origin experience, the canonical accounts of assimilation might have been formulated differently. The history of the Southwest for much of the nineteenth and twentieth centuries is fraught with systematic exclusion of Mexican Americans from mainstream U.S. society (Meier and Ribera 1993). Though Mexican Americans were legally considered white, their socioeconomic mobility, patterns of residential location, and maintenance of ethnic identity did not evince a pattern of assimilation that mirrors that of European-origin groups (Grebler et al. 1970).[9]

Classic assimilation theory is also ill fitted for explaining the Mexican-American experience, because it posits assimilation as an inevitable and mostly irreversible process. Embedded in claims of the inevitability of assimilation is the assumption that immigration eventually stops, as it did for European-origin groups beginning in the late 1910s and the 1920s, and so each new generation born in the United States has less contact with immigrants of the same ethnic ilk. The diminished contact that later-generation white ethnics have with immigrants from their ethnic homeland most certainly contributed to the development of a symbolic form of ethnic identity and the weakening salience of

European-origin ethnic categories. But this was never an explicit part of the theory. Mexican immigration, in contrast, has shown no such cessation; thus, the "Mexican" category remains a prominent part of the ethnic landscape that later-generation Mexican Americans negotiate.

Mexicans and the Changing Lens of Race and Ethnicity

By the time scholars did pay close attention to ethnic Mexicans, a second and even third generation had been born in the United States. Given what scholars knew about European-origin assimilation in the 1960s and 1970s, they might have been spurred to apply a similar interpretation to the second- and third-generation Mexican Americans. But at that time assimilation did not appear to be turning out the same way for Mexican Americans as it was for European-origin groups. Mexican-American assimilation was slower paced and more uneven (Grebler et al. 1970). Interpretations of the Mexican-origin experience were also colored by the ethnic politics of the time. The civil rights movement and the subsequent ethnic pride movements of the 1960s and '70s refocused the lens through which scholars saw race and ethnicity, bringing to national attention the experiences of nonwhite groups, particularly African Americans, but also Mexicans Americans, Puerto Ricans, Asian Americans, and Native Americans. In both scholarly and popular circles, *assimilation* became a dirty word. The mostly descriptive theory that the Chicago School put forth came to be seen as a worldview that prescribed a hollowing out of nonwhites' culture, forcefully supplanting it with a homogeneous white-dominant culture. This understanding of assimilation cut against the grain of the major tenets of the ethnic pride movements and a nascent multicultural ideology that followed.

The changed understanding of racial and ethnic relations and the slow progress of Mexican Americans led a new generation of scholars to reject assimilation as a way of explaining the experiences of ethnic Mexicans. Inspired by Marxist revolutions in Latin America and the thinking of black and Chicano activists, scholars turned abroad for models describing the relationship between the Mexican-origin population and American society, identifying colonialism as a fitting analogue

(Gutiérrez 2004). "Internal colonialism" (Blauner 1969) became a popular concept for understanding relations between nonwhite groups and whites. The perspective posits that this relationship is characterized by a colonial-like situation in which white colonizers and colonized nonwhites (Mexicans included) "are intermingled so that there is no geographical distance between the 'metropolis' and the 'colony'" (Barrera 1979: 194).

It was also during this time that the first generation of Mexican-American historians emerged from graduate school. These Chicano historians focused on the United States' annexation of Mexico in 1848 as the central event shaping the Mexican-origin experience. They emphasized the ensuing history of discrimination experienced by people of Mexican origin, viewing the present-day Mexican-origin population as inheritors of a legacy of colonization (Acuña 1972; Almaguer 1975; Barrera 1979; Camarillo 1996; Griswold del Castillo 1979). They argued that Mexican Americans' status as second-class citizens was a direct outcome of their colonized status in U.S. society and that Mexicans were not experiencing assimilation, but rather racial subjugation in a castelike social system. Their interpretations provided a necessary modification of previously dominant historical accounts that either left out Mexicans altogether or painted them as uncivilized obstacles to American progress.

The way that the Mexican-origin population came to be understood both inside and outside the academy affirmed its place as an aggrieved minority group. After the 1960s, this view came to be the taken-for-granted way of understanding the Mexican-origin population, and its germination among policy makers did not take long. As sociologist John Skrentny (2002) shows, members of Congress and the White House pushed to broaden the reach of race-based civil rights policies to include Mexican Americans despite a modest Mexican-American lobby. The notion that people of Mexican descent were an American minority also became evident in the everyday lexicon related to race and ethnicity, in media portrayals, and in race-based programs. Indeed, Mexicans are commonly listed among African Americans, Native Americans, other Latino groups, and (occasionally) Asian groups as aggrieved minorities that suffer discrimination and blocked entrance into America's social, political, and economic mainstream.

This perspective is reflected in more recent writing about people of Mexican descent and about later-generation Mexican Americans in particular. Anthropologist John Ogbu (1991) distinguishes between voluntary minorities—"immigrant minorities [that] have generally moved to their present societies because they believed that the move would lead to more economic well-being, better overall opportunities, or great political freedom" (8)—and involuntary immigrants—"people who were brought into their present society through slavery, conquest or colonization" (9). Zeroing in on the annexation of the American West and Southwest from Mexico, Ogbu asserts that Mexican Americans constitute an involuntary minority, whose presence in the United States follows from this experience.

Similarly, Gilda Ochoa's (2004) study of the relationship between Mexican Americans and Mexican immigrants in La Puente, California, adopts a "power-conflict" perspective, which links whites' historical treatment of Mexicans to their position in U.S. society today. Ochoa argues that conflict between Mexican Americans and their immigrant brethren is rooted in the internalization of the very assimilationist ideology and policies that stripped early Mexican-American generations of their culture. What emerges from Ochoa's account is not a story of assimilation like the European immigrant experience, but one of conflict and struggle for power and equality.

Colonization may have set the stage for the unequal treatment of ethnic Mexicans during the late nineteenth and much of the twentieth centuries, but very few Mexican Americans are the direct descendants of the estimated fifty thousand original colonized Mexicans. The overwhelming majority of Mexican-descent individuals trace their roots to voluntary migration. In fact, had there been no migration from Mexico in the twentieth century, the Mexican-origin population in the United States would be only a small fraction of its current size, perhaps 14 percent (Edmonston and Passel 1994). And so the question is whether the original colonized condition is so pervasive and institutionalized that subsequent Mexican immigrants and their descendants continue to suffer from its legacy.

The evidence suggests that it is not. Part of the problem with seeing the Mexican-origin population as a colonized group that has suffered from an unshakable second-class status is that this view ignores inter-generational differences among people of Mexican descent and thus glosses over evidence pointing to very real improvement in the standing of Mexican Americans over time (see Jiménez and Fitzgerald 2007). Since Mexican immigration has such a long history, ethnic Mexicans vary in how far back they can trace their origins in United States. Many trace their roots back multiple generations, while others have recently arrived from Mexico. A focus on generational differences shows that, over time, far too much intermarriage (Rosenfeld 2002), residential mobility (Brown 2007), interethnic contact (Brown 2006; Telles and Ortiz 2008), and socio-economic mobility (Alba 2006; Smith 2003, 2006; Telles and Ortiz 2008) have occurred for Mexican Americans to be seen as a group relegated to the margins of American society.

Assimilation for Mexican Americans?

Recognizing the shortcoming in interpretations of the Mexican-origin experience that rely too heavily on the effects of colonization, more recent scholarship has turned back to assimilation theory, adjusting its tenets to explain the experiences of contemporary immigrants and their descen-dants, and of ethnic Mexicans in particular (Brubaker 2001). Recent thinking about assimilation differs from previous scholarship in the way it conceives of the social, political, and economic trajectories that immigrants and their descendants follow. Whereas the canonical view of assimilation implied a linearly upward path into the American main-stream, some scholars now think of assimilation as having multiple tra-jectories, including a "downward" path (Gans 1992). Demand for highly skilled labor in today's hourglass economy may hinder opportunities for upward social mobility among less-skilled immigrants.[10] More recent thinking about assimilation also posits race as a key variable determin-ing assimilation patterns. Discrimination against nonwhite immigrants, such as Mexicans and West Indians, derails their entrance into the main-stream, pushing them into a racialized position in American society (Waters 1999). Thus, some sociologists conceive of assimilation as a "segmented" process, in which immigrants and their children assimilate into one of many segments of U.S. society, depending on the context of their reception, their relative human capital, and the social capital embedded in their coethnic community (Portes and Rumbaut 2001; Portes and Zhou 1993).[11]

Unlike earlier accounts of assimilation that largely eschewed the Mexican-origin population, segmented assimilation places Mexicans at center stage. In fact, Mexicans have come to be seen as an exemplary case of segmented assimilation. When the theory has been applied to Mexican Americans, analyses have emphasized how the long history of Mexican immigration and discrimination has created an entrenched and hostile context of reception for the contemporary second generation. According to segmented assimilation, this negative reception, combined with the low levels of parental human capital and the adoption of an "oppositional" orientation toward the U.S. mainstream, lead the Mexican-American second generation on a steep, downward path of assimilation into a potential "rainbow underclass" (López and Stanton-Salazar 2001; Portes and Rumbaut 2001).[12]

What about later-generation Mexican Americans? This question is particularly important, because two generations constitute a short time frame for gauging the full extent of assimilation, which has always unfolded over the course of multiple generations. The experiences of later-generation individuals are a much better indicator of group assimilation. Empirical studies show that later-generation Mexican Americans are not part of an underclass, as segmented assimilation might predict. Like internal colonialism, segmented assimilation offers a far too pessimistic interpretation of the Mexican-American experience. Later-generation Mexican Americans appear to have made considerable social, political, and economic progress, even if it is more modest than that of later-generation white ethnics (Smith 2003, 2006; Telles and Ortiz 2008).

Some scholars who are looking beyond the second generation maintain that earlier versions of assimilation are nearly as applicable today as they were in the past. They have called into question the taken-for-granted notion that the Mexican-origin population is radically different from European groups. In their resuscitation of assimilation theory, sociologists Richard Alba and Victor Nee (2003) argue that the major principles of the canonical view are still at play for today's immigrant groups, including Mexicans and Mexican Americans, partly because anti-discrimination laws provide a more level playing field for today's immigrants as compared with the past. For Alba and Nee, Mexican-American assimilation is happening, although at a slower pace than among their white counterparts. Similarly, sociologists Marta Tienda and Faith Mitchell are cautiously optimistic in concluding that "there are many signs that Hispanicity will become a symbolic identity rather than that of a disadvantaged minority" (2006: 15). Indeed, a large body of research shows that people of Mexican origin make significant progress from one generation to the next concerning income and education, though later-generation individuals still lag behind their white counterparts (Alba et al., forthcoming; Reed et al. 2005; Smith 2003, 2006; Telles and Ortiz 2008; Tienda and Mitchell 2006). Another key yardstick of assimilation is intermarriage, which more than any other indicator captures the rigidity of social boundaries between groups. Mexican intermarriage rates appear to be relatively high and increase with each generation born in the United States (Macias 2006; Perlmann and Waters 2004; Rosenfeld 2002). If patterns of labor-force participation are any indication, the Mexican-American second generation does not conform to a strict definition of an underclass (Waldinger and Feliciano 2004; Waldinger, Lim, and Cort 2007). Assessing the assimilation prospects of more recent Mexican immigrants, Frank Bean and Gillian Stevens (2003) echo this view. They argue that because most Mexicans enter the United States without authorization, they are at a disadvantage that requires more than the typical three generations to overcome. Nonetheless, they believe that assimilation is the predominant trend for descendants of Mexican immigrants.

Other observers of later-generation Mexican Americans have a much less sanguine assessment of their progress. In a sweeping longitudinal study of intergenerational assimilation among Mexican Americans in Los Angeles and San Antonio, sociologists Edward Telles and Vilma Ortiz (2008) draw on data collected from respondents in 1965 and 2000, as well as from the original respondents' children in 2000, to reveal complex and often counterintuitive assimilation patterns. Central to their analysis are patterns of educational attainment. They show a clear pattern of educational advancement between parents and their children, suggesting some degree of assimilation. But they also find a decline when comparing individuals of different status in genera-tion since immigration: fourth-generation Mexican Americans in Los Angeles and San Antonio have, on average, fewer years of education than third-generation Mexican Americans. Other measures of assimi-lation, such as English-language use, intermarriage, and contact with non-Mexicans, suggest a story of slow-paced assimilation. Yet racial and ethnic identity is clearly an important part of life for Mexican Americans in their study: large numbers of third- and fourth-generation individu-als identify themselves as "Mexican," some cultural practices survive, discrimination is still a prominent part of their lives, and most live in neighborhoods with a Hispanic majority. In the end, the relatively low socioeconomic attainment of later-generation Mexican Americans, which explains the slow pace of assimilation in social and political life, leads Telles and Ortiz to rather bleak conclusions. In their data they see a population that has assimilated in some dimensions of life but has not experienced assimilation where it counts most: in educational attainment. Since education is a linchpin for virtually all dimensions of assimilation, Telles and Ortiz conclude that racialization best character-izes their experiences: "Although they have lost some ethnic cultural attributes like language, most fourth-generation Mexican Americans in our study experience a world largely shaped by their race and ethnicity" (2008: 265).

Telles and Ortiz convincingly show that Mexican-American and European-origin assimilation have not proceeded on the same track. However, they also show clear signs of assimilation in a number of dimensions, including education, in which, on average, Mexican Ameri-cans are going to school longer than their parents. And so the picture of Mexican-American assimilation may not be as bleak as they conclude. Given the very dark history of discrimination that people of Mexican-origin have faced and immigration's continual restocking of the U.S. Mexican-origin population with targets of anti-Mexican nativism, the evidence of assimilation that Telles and Ortiz and others document (Alba 2006; Smith 2003, 2006), however modest, should perhaps be regarded as significant.

These more recent versions of assimilation theory illuminate the importance of intergenerational change among people of Mexican origin but still provide limited insight into the processes that explain Mexican-American ethnic identity formation. As survey research shows, intergenerational distinctions among people of Mexican origin are particularly important, because the population is a vast mix of individuals of different status in generation since immigration. This mix has implications for processes of assimilation that survey data cannot fully capture, however. Whether those who study the data believe that Mexican-American assimilation is proceeding at a slow pace or is marked by exclusion across generations, their analyses imply a process of assimilation that is overly static. Assimilation in this survey research is conceptualized as a process that takes place on a metaphorical set of narrow escalators. Beginning with the immigrant generation, each new generation born in the United States rides on a stair ahead of the previous, and assimilation is thought to be taking place so long as the escalator and those who ride it proceed on an upward slope until they reach the top floor, where ethnic distinctions in most realms of life have faded. Understanding ethnic identity formation, a key dimension of assimilation, requires a more dynamic conceptualization of assimilation. It is more like a large and wide staircase, where individuals with different generational statuses may be positioned in front of, in back of, or next to one another. As they negotiate this assimilation staircase, these individuals interact, influencing one another's ethnic identity. Given the long history of Mexican immigration to the United States, understanding the ethnic identity formation requires a method and theoretical model that explain how the different actors on this staircase shape the ethnic identity of later-generation Mexican Americans. In particular, a complete understanding of Mexican-American ethnic identity must account for how Mexican immigrants, who continually step onto the staircase anew, affect the ethnic identity of the Mexican Americans who have been climbing it for several generations.

MEXICAN-AMERICAN ETHNIC IDENTITY AND
THE PRIMACY OF IMMIGRANT REPLENISHMENT

Understanding Mexican-American ethnic identity formation involves more than the "usual suspect" independent variables that explain assimilation and ethnic identity formation: socioeconomic status, residential location, language ability, and intermarriage (see Waters and Jiménez 2005). A critical but often overlooked variable shaping ethnic identity formation is the duration of an immigration wave. Canonical accounts of assimilation took the cessation of immigration as a given, and the effects of a *lack* of immigrant replenishment were thus never an explicit part of the theory. Internal colonial theory ignored generational differences altogether, positing people of Mexican descent as a single race group that suffered from a legacy of colonialism. Clearly, vast differences exist in the ethnic identity of foreign-born Mexicans and later-generation Mexican Americans. The theory of segmented assimilation points to how a history of immigration has soured the societal context of reception for today's second-generation Mexican Americans (Portes and Rumbaut 2001), but the narrow focus on the children of Mexican immigrants leaves us with little clue as to how ongoing immigration shapes the ethnic identity of those most generationally distant from the immigrant point of origin. Accounts of assimilation among later-generation Mexican Americans emphasize the importance of ongoing immigration for the collection and analysis of survey data, but they do not suggest *how* ongoing immigration shapes a key dimension of assimilation: ethnic identity formation. When scholars have recognized ongoing immigration to be a key feature distinguishing the Mexican-origin population from other immigrant groups, they have merely asserted that immigration patterns affect ethnic identity (Alba and Nee 2003; Massey 1995; Telles and Ortiz 2008), or they have wrapped claims about its effect in polemic assertions about immigration restriction and American identity (Huntington 2004b).

This book shows *how* the ethnic identity formation of later-generation Mexican Americans is shaped by ongoing immigration, while also considering the factors that other research has identified as central to the Mexican-origin experience: race, class, a history of colonization, the proximity of the border. The book sets out to accomplish two broad goals. The first is to show how the duration of an immigration wave shapes assimilation. In doing so, I borrow Alba and Nee's definition of assimilation, which they describe as "the decline of an ethnic distinction and its corollary social and cultural differences" (2003: 11).

I argue that assimilation processes have much to do with the duration of an immigration wave. When immigration ceases, so too does abundant access to the ethnically linked symbols and practices that immigrants bring with them fresh from the homeland. These symbols and practices change over time, waning in salience and acquiring form and meaning heavily influenced by life in the United States. The ethnic distinctiveness of groups also declines when immigration stops. Without a substantial number of immigrants, groups come to be defined less by the foreign-born members and more by U.S.-born individuals, who, over the course of generations, generally enter the U.S. mainstream. Indeed, others have thoroughly shown that among groups who are not being replenished by substantial numbers of immigrants, ethnic symbols and practices become less important to people's lives, and ethnic distinctions decline such that ethnicity becomes a symbolic, optional, and inconsequential part of identity (Alba 1990; Gans 1979; Waters 1990).

When immigrants continually replenish the native-born coethnics, as has occurred with the Mexican-origin population, access to the symbols and practices that epitomize the expression of ethnicity is abundant. These symbols and practices are available through personal interactions with those who are generationally closer to the immigrant point of origin, through institutions, and through the mass media. Immigrant replenishment also adds to the ethnic distinctiveness of a group. Foreign-born members are highly distinguishable from the mainstream because of their cultural and socioeconomic characteristics, and they come to define what it means to be a member of the ethnic group for both group members and nonmembers. Immigrant replenishment thus makes ethnicity less symbolic, less optional, and more consequential for all members of the replenished group.

The consequences of replenishment depend in large part on the status that the replenishing immigrants occupy in U.S. society. If the immigrant group occupies a low status in the host context—as is the case with the largely poor, laboring, and unauthorized Mexican-immigrant population—then those who are members of the ethnic groups being replenished may experience status degradation. If, on the other hand, the status of the immigrant population is high—as with some highly skilled Asian-origin groups—then the status of the previously arrived members of that ethnic group rises through their affiliation with the high-status immigrants. Ethnic groups may be negatively recognized in some dimensions of society but positively recognized in others, resulting in immigrant replenishment's production of uneven effects on status. An ethnic group may, for example, be positively recognized for its work ethic and cultural vibrancy but also negatively recognized because of its low levels of education and perceived lack of assimilation.

In the case of later-generation Mexican Americans, the perpetual influx of Mexican immigrants for the past hundred years is a central factor shaping ethnic identity formation. Mexican Americans' daily lives do not evince unbreakable exclusion or second-class citizenship. Instead, Mexican Americans exhibit a significant degree of socioeconomic assimilation, particularly considering the history of discrimination they have endured. They are in many ways well integrated in the social, political, and economic dimensions of American life. Yet they do not experience the sort of symbolic and optional form of ethnic identity witnessed among European-origin individuals, because ongoing Mexican immigration makes Mexican ethnicity a vibrant part of the ethnic landscape.

Ethnic identity is consequential to Mexican Americans in both beneficial and costly ways. On one hand, Mexican immigration makes ethnicity enjoyably salient to later-generation Mexican Americans. Mexican Americans have ample opportunities to celebrate their ethnic origins through language, food, music, and holidays—aspects of ethnicity seen as pleasurable in an age of multiculturalism. Furthermore, the immigrant-driven growth of the Mexican-origin population gives greater clout to the Mexican-origin population in U.S. society, which often positively recognizes ethnicity in politics and popular culture.

On the other hand, Mexican Americans experience the costs of ethnic identity in a context of poor, largely unauthorized Mexican-immigrant replenishment. People of Mexican origin are racialized as an undesirable foreign group, sharpening the ethnic boundaries that Mexican Americans encounter in daily life. Furthermore, Mexican immigrants inform what it means to be an "authentic" person of Mexican descent. Mexican Americans are often unable to deploy the requisite ethnic symbols and practices that would allow them to live up to a norm of ethnic authenticity determined by Mexican immigrants.

For later-generation Mexican Americans, today's immigration is seen through the lens of the immigrant experience within their own family, coloring their view of whom should be allowed in or kept out. Decisions that Mexican Americans make about everything, from the types of organizations they join to where they live and where they send their children to school, highlight the importance of immigration to their ethnic identity.

A second goal of this book is to understand better the place of the Mexican-origin population in the U.S. racial and ethnic landscape. Previous scholarship has portrayed this group as an aggrieved minority that has experienced blocked mobility and exclusion from the U.S. mainstream. But Mexican Americans have experienced far too much assimilation to be regarded as such. Others have described the Mexican-origin experience as that of an ethnic group that is gradually assimilating into U.S. society.[13] But Mexican ethnicity remains much too highly salient for such a conclusion to be entirely valid. Neither of these characterizations fully describes the Mexican-origin population. Instead, the Mexican-origin population is best described as a permanent immigrant group that, because of ongoing immigration, perpetually deals with the turbulent process of assimilation.

The place in the racial and ethnic landscape is illuminated by conceptualizing ethnicity as a narrative. Stephen Cornell argues that "ethnic categories are categories of collective life stories" (2000: 45) created through the selection, plotting, and interpretation of certain events that are seen as common to the experiences of a group of individuals. Groups select events that may be big or small, episodic or quotidian, historical or ongoing. These events are plotted "in causal, sequential, associational, or other ways" and are linked to a particular ethnic group (43). Events are then interpreted, imbued with significance, and subject to claims about the extent to which they and the way they are plotted define the group.

The result of this process is the construction of a narrative that "captures the central understanding of what it means to be a member of the group" (42). Put another way, an ethnic narrative is an account that group insiders (and outsiders) tell about who "we" (and "they") are.

The narrative approach to ethnicity is useful for understanding Mexican-American ethnic identity and how the greater immigrant population affects it, because, as Cornell points out, it is "event-centered." Immigration is perhaps *the* defining event in the Mexican-American narrative, because it is both a past event *and* a present event. Immigration structures how the Mexican-American narrative is written from the outside in and, to a large degree, from the inside out.

Because Mexican immigration has been a nearly continuous feature of U.S. society for the last hundred years, immigration is a significant event that can be plotted at virtually any point in the Mexican-American narrative, helping to define people of Mexican origin as a poor and largely undesirable foreign group. The ethnic identity of Mexican Americans is constructed through their attempts to reconcile their own life experiences as ethnic Mexicans with a prevailing narrative of Mexicans as foreigner. At times, Mexican Americans' experiences and life circumstances conform to this dominant narrative, because they too trace their roots to immigrant origins. But their experiences also conflict with the dominant narrative, since they are, in fact, Americans whose generational roots extend deeply into U.S. soil. Their narrative cannot be simply characterized as that of an aggrieved minority group struggling with a racialized status, nor can it be seen as that of an immigrant ethnic group passing through linearly related stages of assimilation. Precisely because immigration is an important part of both their historical *and* their present-day experience, immigration and the struggles associated with immigration and assimilation have become central to what it means to be Mexican American.

GETTING TO KNOW MEXICAN AMERICANS

If the aim of this book is to take into account how the various dualities that define the Mexican-origin population shape ethnic identity, then the experiences of those most distant from the immigrant generation are the most revealing. I start from the premise that time in the United States matters in how groups experience American society. Although immigrants and the young second generation have garnered much attention from researchers and the media (García 2003; Hondagneu-Sotelo 1994; Huntington 2004b; López and Stanton-Salazar 2001; Rumbaut and Portes 2001; Smith 2005a), their experiences are not what provide the best purchase on how to understand the Mexican-origin population. The time that immigrants and the second generation have spent in the United States is too limited to tell the full story. If, in fact, the Mexican-origin experience is closer to that of an aggrieved minority that has experienced persistent exclusion, then the experiences of later-generation Mexican Americans will tell the tale. But if the case is that the Mexican-origin experience is really an immigrant ethnic group that has experienced assimilation from one generation to the next until ethnicity becomes a symbolic and optional part of identity, then the descendants of the earliest Mexican immigrants will reveal as much.

I began the research for this book by hypothesizing that the continual influx of Mexican immigrants plays a critical role in Mexican-American ethnic identity formation. I also began from the premise that other factors illuminated in the existing research—race, class, level of residential segregation, generation, and the history of relations between the Mexican population and American society—shape Mexican-American ethnic identity. In order to test my assumptions, I wanted to conduct research in a location that had both a large Mexican-American and a large Mexican-immigrant population and in a second location that had only a large Mexican-American population but no or only a few Mexican immigrants. These criteria led me to search for a place that has received a steady influx of Mexican immigrants over the course of the twentieth century and a second locale where the patterns of Mexican immigration were more similar to the temporally compressed European migration. Locating the former was relatively easy, since many places in the American West and Southwest have received a steady flow of Mexican immigrants. I chose to do this portion of the research in Santa Maria, a small city on the central coast of California. Santa Maria's agricultural economy has always attracted Mexican immigrants. Because of its long history of Mexican migration, Santa Maria has large Mexican-American and Mexican-immigrant populations.

Identifying a location where Mexican immigration patterns resembled the European case proved to be far more difficult. An ideal locale would have been one in which Mexican immigration was compressed in a short period of time from the end of the nineteenth century to beginning of the twentieth century and where Mexican immigrants either did not travel or traveled in very small numbers after that. I could not locate nor am I aware of such a place. Garden City, Kansas, offered the closest approximation of what I was looking for. As with patterns of European migration, Garden City received a large influx of Mexican immigrants in the first third of the twentieth century, followed by a long immigration hiatus. This hiatus ended in the early 1980s, when the largest beef-packing plant in the world opened its doors near Garden City, precipitating a resurgence of Mexican immigration. Compared with Santa Maria's continual influx of immigrants, Garden City's pattern is best described as interrupted.

I expected the different historical patterns of Mexican immigration to yield significant differences in Mexican Americans' ethnic identity, but I found this not to be the case. Some differences existed, and I report them where relevant. But the heavy influx of Mexican immigrants to both cities in the last twenty years suppresses the differences I expected to discover. What emerges is not as much an account of how local patterns of immigration shape Mexican-American ethnic identity as an account of how Mexican ethnic identity throughout the United States is affected by massive contemporary Mexican immigration.

I interviewed 123 later-generation Mexican Americans—60 in Garden City and 63 in Santa Maria—during 2001 and 2002.[14] I interviewed Mexican Americans whose ancestors have been in the United States since before 1940, who are of Mexican descent on both their mother's and father's side of the family, and who have lived in the same city for most of their lives. I chose people whose families have been in the United States since before 1940 because I was interested in finding a population that roughly paralleled the later-generation European-origin Americans who have been studied in other research on ethnic identity (Alba 1990; Waters 1990). The people I interviewed ranged in age from fifteen to ninety-eight. Whenever possible, I interviewed family members from different generations in order to learn how their experiences vary across generations and within families. I also made efforts to talk to people from a wide range of occupations and educational backgrounds in order to understand how social class may shape Mexican-American identity and interactions with Mexican immigrants. I found interview respondents by using a snowball sampling technique. I relied on a few key informants in each city to recommend several initial respondents, who then suggested names of other potential respondents.

I asked the Mexican Americans I interviewed about the importance of their ethnic ancestry in their daily lives and about how, if at all, they participate in various activities related to their Mexican background. I also asked them a set of questions about their perceptions of the influence that Mexican immigrants have on their lives. Finally, I asked them multiple questions about their opinions and attitudes toward Mexican immigrants and Mexican immigration. A copy of the full interview protocol can be found in appendix C.

When I was not conducting interviews, I spent my time becoming integrated into life in Garden City and Santa Maria. I lived with an established Mexican American family in each city, and members of these households were valuable "gatekeepers" to respondents, informants, organizations, and local history. I joined local gyms, volunteered in an ESL class, attended sporting events, frequented local establishments, spent time with civic organizations, attended conferences for local organizations, participated in organized recreational activities, and attended city council meetings. My time living in each city provided many occasions to gather observational notes. Casual conversations with Mexican Americans, Mexican immigrants, and non-Mexicans whom I encountered in my daily life proved to be rich opportunities for data collection and informed the in-depth interviews. I also designed opportunities to take field notes in order to understand the daily lives of my respondents. I spent time observing in the major high school in each city, in selected respondents' workplaces, and during my interactions with respondents before and after interviews. In the high schools, I observed student interactions in the classroom, between classes, and during free periods. I attended key city government meetings in order to understand how Mexican Americans and Mexican immigrants participate in local politics. Since the workplace is an important arena of interaction among respondents, immigrants, and whites, I "shadowed" several respondents throughout their workday, paying close attention to Mexican Americans' interactions with both Mexican immigrants and non-Mexicans.

I also interviewed key informants, including local civic leaders, elected officials, teachers in the high schools, and individuals who work in local industries, such as beef-packing in Garden City and agriculture in Santa Maria. These interviews provided valuable information that I used to contextualize my in-depth interviews and participant observations. The interviews also allowed me to understand better the social position of Mexican Americans in the community. Combined, the interviews and observations provided a full picture of the Mexican-American experience in these two cities. I refer readers interested in a more detailed explanation of the research methodology to appendix A.

My analysis focuses on the way in which the identities of the people I interviewed are tied to ethnicity. For the majority of my respondents, ethnicity is not necessarily their only social identity or even the most important one. Much of their daily lives is marked by uneventful encounters with family, friends, coworkers, and strangers in which their ethnic origins are minimally important. Nonetheless, plenty of "ethnic moments and events" contribute to the construction of a larger ethnic narrative to which the people I interviewed link a significant part of their identity.

This is by no means an exhaustive study of Mexican Americans. Rather, it provides an in-depth understanding of a particular group of Mexican Americans who are, broadly speaking, middle class and live in cities in predominantly rural areas. Its aim is to help readers better understand the complexity of the Mexican-origin population and the dynamic nature of immigration, race, and ethnicity in the United States.

In this book I explore several dimensions of Mexican-American ethnic identity. In chapter 2 I contextualize the book with a historical overview of Mexican immigration and assimilation. There I also provide a more detailed introduction to Garden City and Santa Maria, including a history of Mexican immigration and a demographic snapshot.

In chapter 3 I take up the question of Mexican-American assimilation. Using both ethnographic data and the existing survey research, I show that later-generation Mexican Americans are not relegated to the margins of American society, nor have they experienced unshakable marginalization. Though they have not caught up with native-born whites in most measures of economic mobility, people of Mexican origin have experienced an appreciable degree of structural assimilation as measured by education, occupation, residential location, and intermarriage. The structural assimilation of Mexican Americans has also weakened the hold that ethnicity has on how parents raise their children. Over time, the use of the Spanish language diminishes, ethnic customs play a decreasingly important role in family life, and the ties that Mexican Americans have to family in their ethnic homeland diminish.

In chapter 4 I explore how the presence of a large Mexican-immigrant population shapes the practice of ethnicity among Mexican Americans. The continual influx of Mexican immigration provides ready access to ethnically linked symbols and practices that prevent the recession of ethnicity into the distant background of social life. Mexican Americans access ethnically linked symbols and practices through interactions with Mexican immigrants and second-generation Mexican Americans that range from serendipitous encounters to romantic partnerships. Institutions—churches, schools, restaurants, and grocery stores, as well as popular culture—also provide access to things Mexican. Informing Mexican Americans' desire to access these "ethnic raw materials" is a multicultural ideology that makes a strong attachment to an ethnic identity more desirable and even rewarding in U.S. society today.

In chapter 5 I move away from the practice of ethnicity to look at the boundaries that distinguish ethnic groups from one another. Mexican-immigrant replenishment sharpens ethnic boundaries between Mexican Americans and non-Mexicans, as well as intragroup boundaries that knife through the Mexican-origin population. The foreignness of Mexican ethnicity created by the recent and heavy influx of Mexican immigrants reinforces intergroup boundaries between Mexican Americans and non-Mexicans, as well as intragroup boundaries among people of Mexican descent, making ethnicity far more than a symbolic, inconsequential, and optional part of their identity.

In chapter 6 I explore Mexican Americans' opinions about immigration and their perception of how the Mexican-immigrant population affects their own lives. When asked about their opinions of Mexican immigration and Mexican immigrants themselves, the overwhelming majority of respondents expressed accommodating views. They are much more ambivalent in their beliefs about how immigrants from their ethnic homeland shape how others view later-generation Mexican Americans, noting both the threat that poor, mostly unauthorized immigrants pose to their status and the increased social, political, and economic clout that comes from the growth of the Mexican-origin population.

In chapter 7 I examine how Mexican Americans translate their ethnic identity into action, paying close attention to whether they work toward unity with or division from their immigrant coethnics. The chapter shows that Mexican Americans are not inclined to participate in visible displays of either solidarity with or division from their coethnic immigrants. Instead, most reach out to Mexican immigrants in their everyday lives, although some seek to create social distance from an immigrant population that they see as a threat to their own social standing.

In the concluding chapter I provide a discussion of the theoretical and empirical contributions of the book. I return to the book's central findings to show that the Mexican-origin population is best characterized as a permanent immigrant group whose large immigrant population makes immigration and the struggles associated with assimilation defining events in the group's narrative. Immigration also significantly defines the relationship between the Mexican-ethnic narrative and a larger national narrative, which is based on immigration as a past event. I also show how attending to the extent and nature of immigrant replenishment provides for a more complete theoretical understanding of assimilation.

TWO Mexican Americans

A HISTORY OF REPLENISHMENT
AND ASSIMILATION

[Mexican emigration to the United States is made up,
  mainly, of unskilled labor, a great population turning
  to the United States for wages better than it can
  procure in its own country.]

—Manuel Gamio,
  Mexican Immigration to the United States (1930: ix)

The Mexican anthropologist Manuel Gamio opens his book on Mexican immigrants in the United States with the observation quoted above and goes on to describe in great detail the patterns of Mexican migration, the experiences of Mexican migrants, and the social, political, and economic factors shaping them. While much has changed since Gamio conducted his study in the 1920s, his observations ring true more than three-quarters of a century later. In fact, many of his observations are applicable to virtually any point in time during the last hundred years. As figure 2 shows, the continuing relevance of Gamio's observations owes to the constancy of Mexican immigration since the early twentieth century. This chapter covers both the broad historical contours of Mexican-American history nationwide and the more specific histories

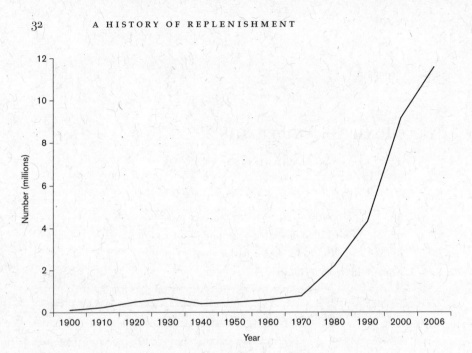

Figure 2. Number of foreign-born Mexicans in the United States, 1900–2006. Sources: U.S. Decennial Census; U.S. Census Bureau, American Community Survey.

of Garden City, Kansas, and Santa Maria, California, the two cities that are the focus of this book. What will be clear by the end of the chapter is that later-generation Mexican Americans inherit a social context that has been shaped in large part by the replenishment of a Mexican-immigrant population.

THE FIRST MEXICAN AMERICANS: 1848–1909

The first people of Mexican-origin in the United States were not immigrants at all. In the mid–nineteenth century Manifest Destiny urged American expansion westward, and the movement of American settlers into Mexican territories precipitated a war between the United States and Mexico that raged for nearly two years. The war came to an end with the signing of the Treaty of Guadalupe Hidalgo in 1848. In addition to ending the war, the treaty stipulated that Mexico cede the present-day American West and Southwest to the United States. The estimated fifty thousand Mexicans who remained in the former Mexican territory after the United States annexed it became U.S. citizens according to provisions in the treaty (Jaffe, Cullen, and Boswell 1980, cited in Massey, Durand, and Malone 2002). They were the first Mexican Americans. The treaty also stipulated a new U.S.-Mexico border, the establishment of which meant that from 1848 on, any Mexican national crossing this border northward would be entering a country that would regard her or him as a foreigner.

Despite their status as American citizens, the first Mexican Americans were treated as impediments to U.S. expansion. As more white settlers moved west into the newly annexed territory in search of gold and land, it became increasingly clear that Mexican Americans would not enjoy U.S. citizenship on equal grounds, despite provisions in the Treaty of Guadalupe Hidalgo guarantying their rights as citizens. They were second-class citizens who became socially, economically, and politically displaced. Growing numbers of whites overwhelmed a Mexican-American population that was soon forced into isolated barrios (Camarillo 1996; Gutiérrez 1995). Economic conditions for Mexican Americans quickly deteriorated. They became absorbed into a diversified market economy, radically unlike the pastoral economy that they had known prior to 1848. This new economic structure left Mexican Americans with the least desirable jobs and whites with the highest paid, most desirable positions. While Mexicans were once prominent landowners, white settlers displaced them, using a legal system that Mexican Americans found to be confusing and prohibitively expensive. Before long, Mexican Americans saw their landholdings reduced to a fraction of the territory they once owned (Gutiérrez 1995: 26–27). Although circumstances varied among states, Mexican Americans in many areas of the Southwest lost political power to federally appointed white leaders, machine politics, and exclusionary political tactics that left Mexican Americans on the margins of the political process (Griswold del Castillo and de León 1997; Gutiérrez 1995).

EARLY MEXICAN IMMIGRATION: 1910–1929

The decades immediately following the Treaty of Guadalupe Hidalgo were relatively quiet along the U.S.-Mexico border. Movement between the two countries was local and largely within communities located near the new border that ostensibly cut through them. But as the twentieth century dawned, political and economic changes in Mexico and the United States activated Mexican migration. In Mexico, President Porfirio Díaz's liberal economic policies helped a few wealthy landowning hacendados to accumulate massive swaths of the land, leaving the country's rural farming campesinos unable to eke out a living. As Mexico's population grew, the working-age population competed for few jobs, wages were depressingly low, and the Díaz regime made matters worse by enacting policies that continued to help hacendados at the expense of campesinos (Cardoso 1980). Meanwhile, in its zeal to promote trade with the United States, the Díaz regime began to develop the northern part of Mexico, especially the area near the border. Mexican states in the country's north prospered. Poor campesinos in the central part of Mexico began migrating north, seeking employment opportunities, better wages, and a lower cost of living. Aiding this internal migration was the construction of railroad lines that connected the northern and southern regions. As rail lines stretched out across Mexico, U.S. railways expanded southward, eventually connecting with Mexican tracks (Cardoso 1980). With the connection of U.S. and Mexican rail lines, the internally mobile Mexicans now had a way to migrate internationally more easily. Before long, Mexicans migrated to the American Southwest and Midwest to take advantage of abundant job opportunities in the expanding agriculture, mining, and railroad industries.

Mexico provided a seemingly unending and ideal supply of cheap labor. Industrialists, agriculturalists, and politicians in the United States idealized Mexican laborers, not only because of their work habits and their willingness to take backbreaking jobs, but also because they were seen as a temporary population and therefore as a source of minimal social disruption (Ngai 2004). Prior to Mexicans, Chinese and Japanese workers had dominated low-wage labor in much of the Southwest and especially in California. But growing antipathy for Chinese workers had led the U.S. government to restrict Chinese immigration with the signing of the 1882 Chinese Exclusion Act. When Japanese immigrant laborers took their place, similar nativist sentiment took hold, and the U.S. and Japanese governments signed the "Gentlemen's Agreement" in 1907, through which Japan agreed to stop issuing passports to Japanese citizens who wished to immigrate to the United States (Cardoso 1980). With China and Japan cut off as labor supplies, Mexico became a preferred and convenient source of labor. By the early 1900s, the use of Mexican labor was well established and expanding. When workers were needed, burgeoning industries often sent recruiters, or *enganchadores* (those who "hook," or indenture), into Mexico to coax workers northward (Massey, Durand, and Malone 2002). Soon, Mexican laborers became the backbone of the growing southwestern economy.

Political events in Mexico and the United States further spurred Mexican migration. In 1910, economic disparities in Mexico reached new heights, sparking a revolution that pitted poor, landless Mexicans against the Díaz regime, which was all too friendly to the aristocracy. Conditions in Mexico became deplorable for campesinos, as starvation, unemployment, and social upheaval swept through the war-torn country. Thousands of Mexicans fled to the United States in the revolution's wake. As the Mexican Revolution raged on, the United States experienced a labor shortage resulting from large troop deployments to the battlefields of World War I. American firms thus increasingly looked to Mexico to fill jobs in industries throughout the Southwest and Midwest (García 1996). Even as the number of Mexican migrants grew, Americans focused their nativist ire primarily on the large numbers of southern and eastern European immigrants settling mostly on the East Coast and in parts of the Midwest. Congress passed a head tax and literacy test in 1917, helping to limit an already slowing influx of European immigrants. Lawmakers recognized the need for Mexican immigrant labor and thus exempted Mexican agricultural workers from the 1917 provisions (Cardoso 1980; Ngai 2004).

By the time the Mexican Revolution reached a conclusion in 1920, sentiment against European immigrants in the United States was coming to a boil. Americans became increasingly weary of the European newcomers, who were regarded as inferior, uncivilized, racially distinct, and unassimilable (Higham [1955] 1963). In a dramatic move that would change American immigration patterns for the next forty years, Congress enacted the National Origins Quota Act of 1924. The law imposed strict quotas that were effective in bringing about a precipitous decline in European immigration.[1] The 1924 law did little to counteract the influx of Mexican immigrants, however. Although the U.S. Border Patrol came into existence that same year, it did not immediately restrict the influx of the Mexican immigrant population. The Border Patrol was ostensibly put in place to provide border security between inspections stations, but the growing U.S. economy and its accompanying need for Mexican labor counteracted the Border Patrol's efforts to limit crossings (Massey, Durand, and Malone 2002).

As Mexican immigration proceeded apace, the entire Mexican-origin population continued to live as second-class citizens. The racial and ethnic order that began to form after the Treaty of Guadalupe Hidalgo had crystallized by the end of the 1920s. Mexican Americans throughout the Southwest lived in segregated neighborhoods, attended segregated and substandard schools, and experienced limited access to social, political, and economic opportunities. In some areas of the Midwest and Texas, Mexican Americans lived under a Jim Crow–like system of segregation: they were barred from certain sections of movies theaters, were refused service at restaurants, were kept out of barber shops and hair salons, and were prevented from voting. Some established Mexican Americans feared that the influx of Mexican immigrants contributed to the second-class citizenship of the entire Mexican-origin population. As historian David Gutiérrez (1995) points out, Mexican immigration reinfused Mexican-American culture but also spurred concerns among Mexican Americans that coethnic newcomers would further sour whites' perceptions of the Mexican-American population, depress their wages, and compete with them for housing and jobs. Despite sharing a common ethnic origin and language, interactions between Mexican Americans and Mexican immigrants were often marked by conflict. Immigrants saw Mexican Americans as *pochos*, "faded" or "bleached ones," who lacked a true homeland and a strong sense of Mexican culture. Summarizing the effect of the influx of Mexican immigration on Mexican Americans during this period, Gutiérrez writes, "As increasing numbers of Mexican immigrants entered their communities, Mexican Americans were compelled to reconsider the criteria by which they defined themselves" (1995: 67).

THE DEPRESSION YEARS: 1930–1941

As the 1920s came to a close, so too did an economic boom and the influx of immigrants. The Great Depression put an end to economic expansion in the United States, ushering in a decade of stark economic conditions. Where immigration from Europe was concerned, the Depression, combined with the 1924 quotas, virtually sealed the United States to European migrants. Mexican immigration experienced a similar fate during these years. Economic insecurities and soaring unemployment created a strong nativist reaction to Mexican-immigrant labor. In response, industries that had relied on Mexican immigrant workers during the previous two decades now looked to hire U.S.-born workers. Federal authorities also responded to Americans' fears about competition for jobs by working closely with state and local officials to coordinate massive repatriations of Mexican immigrants. Thousands of foreign-born Mexicans were forcibly sent back to Mexico, and in some cases U.S. citizens of Mexican descent were deported as well (Gutiérrez 1995; Ngai 2004). Many other immigrants voluntarily returned to Mexico as economic conditions worsened. The 1930s were the only decade in the twentieth century that saw a net decline in the number of Mexican immigrants in the United States.

A declining flow of Mexican immigration and mass repatriation during the 1930s also brought about a shift in the balance of the Mexican-origin population from mostly foreign-born to a U.S.-born majority. In 1920 foreign-born Mexicans constituted nearly 66 percent of the Mexican-origin population. But by 1930, only 43 percent had been born in Mexico, and that proportion shrank to just 35 percent by the end of the decade (see figure 3).

The 1930s marked the birth of what historian Mario T. García calls the "Mexican-American generation" (1989). The burgeoning Mexican-

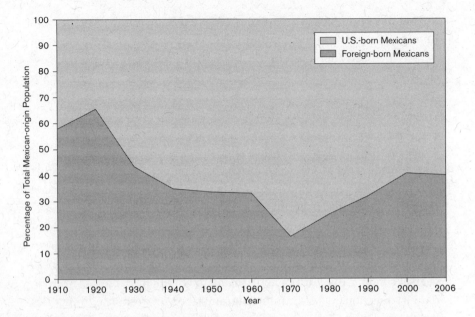

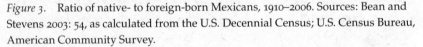

Figure 3.   Ratio of native- to foreign-born Mexicans, 1910–2006. Sources: Bean and Stevens 2003: 54, as calculated from the U.S. Decennial Census; U.S. Census Bureau, American Community Survey.

American population saw itself as firmly planted in the United States and began to assert its American identity loudly. During this decade several organizations emerged in order to improve the situation of Mexican Americans. Perhaps the most prominent was the League of United Latin American Citizens (LULAC). Made up of mostly Mexican-American middle-class individuals, LULAC endeavored to make Mexican Americans part of the U.S. mainstream. In order to accomplish the integration of its members, LULAC put a great deal of distance between itself and coethnic immigrants and even took an official stance against Mexican immigration (Gutiérrez 1995: 85). Not all Mexican-American organizations adopted these distancing strategies, however. The Congress of Spanish-Speaking Peoples, which also worked to improve conditions for the Mexican-origin population, explicitly linked the plight of Mexican Americans and Mexican immigrants and worked for equality for both

(Gutiérrez 1995: chapter 3). Whatever their tactics, these organizations and the Mexican-American leaders that guided them made it clear by the end of the 1930s that Mexican Americans intended to push against the tide of discrimination in order to achieve full participation in U.S. society. Events in the ensuing decade made the Mexican-origin population simultaneously more American and more foreign.

WORLD WAR II, THE BRACERO PROGRAM, AND THE "G.I. GENERATION": 1942–1960

In the early 1940s, the United States was enmeshed in yet another war. Like World War I, World War II created a labor vacuum, because thousands of U.S. service members fought overseas. The shortage of workers was especially pronounced in agriculture. Responding to growers' fears about a labor shortfall, the United States and Mexico negotiated the Emergency Farm Labor Program, better known as the "bracero program." Under the agreement, American growers could apply for a specified number of workers for a period of time, and employers had the exclusive use of the contracted labor (Calavita 1992). What was initially designed to be a temporary, wartime fix for labor shortages soon turned into a lengthy guest-worker program. When World War II ended, growers pleaded with lawmakers to extend the program, arguing that a steady supply of labor was needed during the postwar economic expansion. Congress obliged the powerful agricultural lobby, extending the program on a year-to-year basis in the late 1940s (Calavita 1992; Massey, Durand, and Malone 2002).

The bracero program proved to be laden with problems, the most significant of which was its precipitation of unauthorized Mexican immigration. Both Mexican migrants and employers found loopholes that allowed them to bypass the bureaucratic morass that governed the program. Some unauthorized migrants found employers who preferred to hire migrants directly rather than deal with the cumbersome process of issuing a contract through the federal government. But the U.S. government itself also played a direct role in unauthorized immigration. The

Border Patrol loosely monitored the southern border, especially during harvest season, and Congress helped short-circuit any would-be effort to control Mexican migration by limiting the allocation of resources for the Border Patrol (Calavita 1992). Congress also prohibited the prosecution of employers who hired unauthorized workers.

The bracero program satisfied growers' need for a large and readily available labor force, but rank-and-file Americans became dissatisfied with increased numbers of Mexicans and began pressuring government officials to do something about it. In order to satisfy simultaneously nativist calls for immigration restriction and the growers' need for workers, the U.S. attorney general initiated a drive to remove unauthorized workers and replace them with legal Mexican labor. Under Operation Wetback, as the drive was called, the Bureau of Immigration and Naturalization Services (INS) and state and local authorities deported thousands of Mexican immigrants.[2] In 1954, the peak year for Operation Wetback, the INS detained over one million migrants, the first time apprehension reached such a level (Massey, Durand, and Malone 2002: 37). The INS's efforts to expunge Mexican immigrants seemed less than sincere, however. Even as apprehensions rose, the number of contracts given to migrants climbed dramatically (Calavita 1992: 55). After Operation Wetback ended, the bracero program carried on with little fanfare. The U.S. government continued to expand the program but did so quietly. The highly visible, though ineffective efforts by the U.S. government to limit immigration provided the illusion of an orderly border, satisfying the citizenry's desire for limited immigration, while the powerful agriculture lobby continued to receive the supply of workers it desired (Massey, Durand, and Malone 2002).

Meanwhile, Mexican Americans increasingly asserted their belonging in U.S. society during the 1940s and 1950s. Significant Mexican-American integration began to take shape, as educational and occupational opportunities previously closed to Mexican Americans opened, and a small Mexican-American middle class emerged (García 1989). For many, entrance into the American mainstream meant creating distance from the growing Mexican-immigrant population. Mexican Americans held sympathetic views of braceros, but the predominant sentiment was that braceros stymied Mexican-American progress by making all people of Mexican origin appear foreign in the eyes of U.S. society. Organizations like LULAC, the Mexican American Movement (MAM), and the American G.I. Forum, a Mexican-American veterans and civil rights group, all took official stances in opposition to the program for this very reason (Gutiérrez 1995; Ngai 2004).

The events of World War II proved to be significant for Mexican-American assimilation, however. Hundreds of Mexican-American G.I.s fought overseas in World War II, many of whom returned home as decorated war heroes (Rivas-Rodríguez 1999). But the Mexican Americans of the "G.I. generation" (Camarillo 1971) found that their status as veterans was incongruous with how American society greeted them upon their return. The unequal treatment that they experienced prior to the war remained in place after the war's end (Avila 1997). Responding to this treatment, a group of Mexican Americans in Texas formed the American G.I. Forum in 1948 to advocate for Mexican-American civil rights. The organization rapidly expanded throughout the Southwest and Midwest and initiated anti-discrimination lawsuits, voter-registration drives, and campaigns to end educational segregation (Ramos 1998). This new generation of Mexican-American leaders experienced significant success in creating social, political, and economic opportunities for Mexican Americans.

Integration remained rocky for other Mexican Americans, however. A growing Mexican-American second generation found itself in the precarious position of identifying with neither their parents' "old-world" ways nor a white-dominated U.S. mainstream culture. As with the second generation from other immigrant groups (Child 1943; Foote Whyte 1943), the Mexican-American second generation adopted styles and orientations that portrayed a sense of rebelliousness against both their immigrant parents and the American host society that largely rejected them. Some among the second generation became part of a pachuco subculture, noted for a distinctive style of speech that combines English and Spanish and for donning zoot suits and wide-brimmed hats (Alvarez 2008; Gutiérrez 1995: 125). Historians frequently cite the Sleepy Lagoon case and the Zoot Suit Riots as emblematic of the precarious position of the Mexican-American second generation. The Sleepy Lagoon case involved the 1942 conviction of Mexican-American youths for crimes related to the murder of another Mexican-American teen found dead in Los Angeles' Sleepy Lagoon, a popular swimming hole. The all-Anglo jury convicted seventeen Mexican-American youths on the basis of flimsy evidence in a trial heavily tinged with racial overtones (Griswold del Castillo and de León 1997: 88). The following year, the Zoot Suit Riots broke out in East Los Angeles, further underlining the struggles of the Mexican-American second generation. The riot primarily involved U.S. servicemen seeking out and beating Mexican-American pachucos, but when the riot finally ended more than a week later, the Los Angeles police arrested several pachuco victims for disturbing the peace (Gutiérrez 1995: 124).

Many other Mexican Americans appeared to be following a more conventional path of integration, however. It was during the 1950s in particular that many Mexican Americans saw dramatic improvement in the social and economic circumstances. Sociologists Leo Grebler, Joan Moore, and Ralph Guzman's (1970) landmark study of the Mexican-American population shows intergenerational improvements in educational attainment and occupational status and an increase in interethnic marriage, suggesting that barriers to assimilation were waning for some in the middle of the twentieth century. Nonetheless, lingering gaps between whites and Mexican Americans remained, suggesting that full integration was far from complete.

Even as Mexican Americans forged diverging paths of integration, thousands of Mexican-born coethnics continued entering the United States. Figure 2 shows that the decline in Mexican immigration during the 1930s resumed its upward pattern in the 1940s and 1950s, such that by the end of the 1950s, Mexican Americans were once again being heavily replenished by migrants from their ethnic homeland.

THE CHICANOS: 1961–1975

The 1960s was a decade during which the United States radically redefined itself, which included dramatic changes to its immigration laws. As the civil rights movement gained steam, lawmakers began to reconsider the immigration policy of the previous forty years. With the passage of the Civil Rights Act of 1964 and the Voting Rights Act of 1965, policy makers saw the restrictive immigration laws that were passed in 1924 as racist and in need of reform. In 1965, Congress passed liberal amendments to the Immigration and Nationality Act. The amendments allocated visas more equitably across countries. Instead of applying different quota levels to countries, a quota of 20,000 persons per year was placed on all Eastern Hemisphere countries, and a total hemispheric cap was set at 170,000 immigrants per year. The 1965 amendment also placed the first-ever cap on immigration from Western Hemisphere countries, which included Mexico, allotting a total of 120,000 visas per year to all the hemisphere's countries, with no preference system stipulating a per-country limit. A certain preference system was central to the 1965 law, however—one based on family reunification and occupational skills. Policy makers believed that family reunification would mostly open up avenues to European immigrants who had relatives already in the United States. In reality, the 1965 law ushered in a new era of immigration, Mexican immigration in particular. Europe had mostly found political and economic stability by the 1960s, while American economic and political involvement in Latin America and Asia helped spur immigration from these regions.

People of Mexican origin also began to redefine themselves during the 1960s. A new generation of Mexican Americans who called themselves "Chicanos" emerged. This Chicano generation took its cues not from the Mexican-American generation that preceded it but from the civil rights, black pride, and anti-war movements of the 1960s. Chicanos saw the previous generation's efforts to work within the system as outmoded and ineffective. Instead, the Chicano generation sought to change the social order, calling on all people of Mexican descent to express pride in their ethnic origins rather than try to blend into a homogeneous white mainstream.

Whereas previous generations of Mexican-American activists sought to distance themselves from Mexican immigrants, Chicano activists saw all people of Mexican descent—American and Mexican-born—as belonging to a unified *raza*, or people. Chicano activists viewed the struggles of

Mexican Americans and Mexican immigrants as intimately tied, since all people of Mexican descent, regardless of time in the United States, suffered oppression and second-class citizenship. Chicanos traded in the "Americans all" slogan, popular among their parents' generation, for "somos todos Mexicanos" (we are all Mexicans). In reality, the Mexican-immigrant population occupied but a small place on the Chicano social and political agenda, and perhaps for good reason. The second and third generations from previous waves of Mexican immigrants numerically overwhelmed the first generation. In 1970, near the apex of the Chicano movement, the foreign-born Mexican population made up just 16 percent of the total Mexican-origin population in the United States (see figure 3). At no other point in the twentieth century did the Mexican-immigrant population constitute a smaller share of the overall Mexican-origin population.

Chicano activists also sought to recapture a history and culture that they saw as having been suppressed and distorted by white dominance. The Chicano generation coalesced around the adoration of Mexican culture, including language, music, art, and food, particularly as these things related to their indigenous heritage. Chicano activists frequently invoked Aztlán, the area now known as the U.S. Southwest, from which the descendants of the Aztecs are believed to have come. While a small number advocated that Chicanos should take back this land from the United States, most Chicano activists thought of Aztlán as a symbol of their efforts to reclaim an identity and history that they believed had been stolen from them through white hegemony.

In practice, several loosely connected fronts constituted what came to be known as the Chicano movement. The primary and most vocal front in the movement came from the burgeoning Chicano-student population. Chicano college and high school students became especially attuned to their ethnic identity and the inadequacies of educational institutions to meet their needs. Their efforts to change the system included school walkouts and the formation of student organizations on college and university campuses throughout the Southwest. Though they differed in name, these student organizations shared the goal of helping to raise the status of Mexican Americans through education and by increasing the number of Mexican Americans on college and university campuses (Muñoz 1989). The high point of the Chicano student movement came in 1969, when Chicano activists met in Denver and Santa Barbara to define Chicano nationalism and autonomy more formally, to create a plan for establishing Chicano studies courses, to establish Chicano studies departments and programs in high schools and colleges, and to encourage Chicanos to participate in community activism away from college campuses (Muñoz 1989).[3]

The Chicano movement also reached into formal politics. Dissatisfied with the two-party system, Mexican Americans in Texas formed La Raza Unida Party (LRUP). LRUP worked within the mainstream political structure to win formal political representation for Mexican Americans and won several local elections in Texas (Gómez-Quiñones 1990). But when LRUP went national, it lost considerable influence because of the difficulties of breaking into a system dominated by two parties but also because of internal divisions, scant resources, and the absence of an ideological core (Gómez-Quiñones 1990; Muñoz 1989). The political considerations of Chicano activists were not just local. They also took on national issues, namely, the Vietnam War. The overrepresentation of Mexican-origin service members among the combat-killed was seen as part of a larger oppressive system and as symbolic of the repression that the movement aimed to transform. From 1969 to 1971, Chicano activists orchestrated several large marches in Los Angeles to protest the Vietnam War and to publicize the high number of Chicano casualties. The best known of these protests, the National Chicano Moratorium, took place in 1970. The protest was marred by violence between protesters and police, resulting in the death of three activists, including the popular Mexican-American journalist Rubén Salazar.

Though not explicitly part of the Chicano movement or illustrative of the movement's ideological stances, perhaps the best-known and most enduring front was the United Farm Workers Union (UFW), led by César Chávez. The UFW organized farmworkers and staged nonviolent boycotts and strikes throughout the Southwest, bringing better wages and working conditions to farmworkers, the majority of whom were Mexican immigrants (see Griswold del Castillo and García 1995). Likewise, Reies

Tijerina's La Alianza de Pueblos Libres (Alliance of Free Peoples) was not an explicit part of the Chicano movement. However, his efforts to help the first Mexican Americans in New Mexico—those incorporated under the Treaty of Guadalupe Hidalgo—to regain the land taken from them by the U.S. government and land corporations after the 1848 treaty remain part of the Chicano movement's narrative.

The Chicano movement produced a legacy still evident today. Notable among the organizations born out of the Chicano movement are the National Council of La Raza, a powerful advocacy group based in Washington, D.C., the Mexican American Legal Defense and Education Fund (MALDEF), a Mexican-American civil rights organization, and Movimiento Estudiantil Chicano de Aztlán (MEChA),[4] a student organization with chapters in high schools, colleges, and universities throughout the Southwest. The Chicano movement's thrust did not appeal to all Mexican Americans. Many felt uncomfortable with the ideology and methods of change that the movement espoused and preferred to stay on the sidelines. These Mexican Americans instead sought integration into American society through more conventional and less collectivist means.

DE FACTO GUEST WORKERS: THE 1970S AND EARLY 1980S

The Chicano movement lost much of its momentum by the early 1970s. Its leaders increasingly moved into mainstream politics and on to other endeavors. Yet the movement defined a generation of Mexican Americans who saw themselves as inheritors of a legacy of racial discrimination (Haney López 2003). The understanding that the Chicano generation had of itself significantly shaped the way the country understood the Mexican-origin population. In policy circles, the Mexican-origin population increasingly became defined as a minority. This designation included people of Mexican origin under policies and programs born out of the civil rights movement, such as the Voting Rights Act and affirmative action policies (Skrentny 2002). The movement also shaped educational institutions by bringing about high school and college courses focusing on the Mexican-origin population, as well as Chicano studies programs and departments in colleges and universities across the country. Many of the first scholars to populate these positions were newly minted Mexican-American PhDs who themselves were Chicano-movement veterans.

The radical social and political changes ushered in during the 1960s reverberated into the 1970s in other ways. Amendments to the Immigration and Nationality Act, signed into law in 1965, began to affect patterns of Mexican immigration significantly in the 1970s. The liberalization of immigration laws opened the legal pathway for immigration from much of the world but placed legal restrictions on Mexican immigration. For the first time, Mexican immigrants had to compete with other Western Hemisphere countries for a limited number of visas. This limit ultimately spurred the beginning of massive influxes of unauthorized Mexican migrants. Although the bracero program ended in 1964, the demand for cheap labor in agriculture continued. Without a guest worker program and with more competition for visas, American agriculturalists increasingly turned to the practice of hiring unauthorized Mexican migrants. Many unauthorized workers found work in the United States with the aid of former bracero program participants, who remained north of the border after the program's end. Veteran braceros anchored social networks that connected Mexican migrants to jobs and housing in the United States (Massey 1987). What eventually developed was what Douglas Massey and his coauthors (2002) call "a de facto guest worker program." Mexican migrants could clandestinely cross the border with relative ease, find work, return home, and repeat this cycle. Further easing the entrance of unauthorized Mexican migrants was the Border Patrol, which loosely guarded the southern border during the harvest season in order to ensure that growers had a sufficient supply of labor. By the mid-1970s, Mexican migration developed a circular pattern: migrants came north when work was plentiful but were able to cross back and forth between Mexico and the United States with relative ease (Massey, Durand, and Malone 2002).

The 1970s brought even more restrictions on Mexican immigration. In 1976, a struggling economy spurred Congress to impose a limit of twenty-thousand per country (excluding family reunification) on the number of visas available to Western Hemisphere countries, including Mexico. With legal pathways to migration choked, unauthorized immigration was the only option for Mexican workers who wished to work in the U.S. economy, which increasingly depended on their labor.

MEXICAN IMMIGRATION BOOM AND THE GROWING MEXICAN-AMERICAN MIDDLE CLASS: 1980-PRESENT

As the 1980s began, a large and steady number of Mexican migrants continued to flow into the United States, and many Mexican Americans displayed significant social, economic, and political ascendancy. An increasing but still small number of Mexican Americans entered colleges and universities, and many others entered the middle class through blue-collar jobs (Ortiz 1996). Emblematic of Mexican-American advancement was the 1981 San Antonio mayoral election of Henry Cisneros, a Harvard-educated, Mexican-American politician from Texas. Cisneros's election was considered a major breakthrough for Mexican Americans in Texas, particularly because of the long and often ugly history of relations between Mexican Americans and whites in that state. Just one year later, eight southwestern Latinos were elected to the U.S. House of Representatives (Yinger 1985: 32). Intermarriage, considered the ultimate yardstick of assimilation, was on the rise for Mexican Americans during the late 1970s and early 1980s, further suggesting that significant Mexican-American integration was taking place (Cazares, Murguía, and Frizbie 1985; Murguía 1982; Valdez 1983; Yinger 1985).

Overshadowing Mexican-American integration was the growing Mexican-immigrant population that continued to arrive from south of the border. Mexican immigration grew steadily, in large part through unauthorized movement, but also through the recruitment of workers by U.S. industries. In response to fears about growing unauthorized immigration and economic insecurity and concerns about national security, Congress passed a landmark immigration bill: the 1986 Immigration Reform and Control Act (IRCA). The new legislation included three major provisions: it granted amnesty to all unauthorized immigrants who had been living in the United States for the previous five years; it imposed fines on employers who knowingly hired unauthorized workers; and it dramatically increased the Border Patrol's budget. Initially, IRCA seemed to keep the promise of its creators to give the United States a "fresh start" with immigration. But it was soon clear that the law came with dramatic and unintended consequences. Far from stemming unauthorized Mexican immigration, IRCA's provisions, the growing economic integration between the United States and Mexico, and the significant efforts to secure the border combined to spur unauthorized immigration. Roughly 2.3 million formerly unauthorized Mexicans were granted amnesty under IRCA. Many formerly unauthorized Mexican immigrants who had established themselves in the United States could now come out of the legal shadows (Chavez 1998) and more deeply (and legally) plant their roots. Newly legalized Mexican migrants were now in a better position to serve as resources for Mexicans hoping to come to the United States. Furthermore, legalized Mexicans no longer had to stay near the border for fear of apprehension, and many used their newfound freedom to travel to new immigrant gateways to act as pioneering migrants in establishing new destinations for Mexican immigrants in areas outside the American Southwest, particularly in the Midwest and the South (Durand, Massey, and Charvet 2000; Zúñiga and Hernández-León 2005).

Just when those legalized under IRCA began to become citizens, the United States and Mexico became even more economically tied because of the enactment of the North American Free Trade Agreement (NAFTA) in 1994, which removed virtually all barriers to free trade among the United States, Mexico, and Canada. As a consequence of economic integration, NAFTA spurred a flow of labor, driving millions of Mexican immigrants to move northward. Further "pushing" Mexican migrants into the United States was a virtual collapse of the Mexican economy in 1994. Inflation and a precipitous decline in the value of the Mexican peso left many Mexicans with few economic options but to migrate (Massey, Durand, and Malone 2002).

Paradoxically, even as Mexico and the United States become more economically integrated, the United States sought to clamp down on Mexican migration. Beginning in the early 1990s, U.S. lawmakers turned to the border as the focus of immigration policy. They initiated a policy of "prevention through deterrence," under which the U.S. Congress along with the Clinton administration moved to militarize heavily trafficked areas of the border. This militarization was most evident in Operation Hold the Line in El Paso in 1993 and Operation Gatekeeper in San Diego a year later. By constructing fences, employing the latest surveillance technology, installing stadium lights, and manning the border with thousands of Border Patrol agents, these two initiatives and others like them successfully curtailed traffic through El Paso, San Diego, and other urban centers along the border (Cornelius 2005). Far from stopping unauthorized entry altogether, the militarization of these urban entry points only redirected migrant traffic through more remote areas, mostly in the Arizona and New Mexico deserts (but also across rivers), where apprehension was less likely.

These new routes have made crossing more expensive and deadlier. Navigating the often dangerous desert terrain requires the use of coyotes, or immigrant smugglers, whose fees have grown more expensive as demand for their services have increased.[5] What is more, the new routes have been literally killing migrants. Increasing numbers of Mexican migrants have died of dehydration and hypothermia during their journey through the desert and across often treacherous rivers (Cornelius 2005; Eschbach et al. 1999; Massey, Durand, and Malone 2002).[6]

The growing cost and danger associated with crossing the border have actually contributed to an increase in the Mexican-immigrant population by creating a disincentive for migrants to cross back into Mexico once on the northern side of the border. Whereas migration followed a circular pattern prior to the militarization of the border, it is now simply too expensive and too dangerous for migrants to sustain a life of circular migration (Massey, Durand, and Malone 2002: 128–33). Increased border surveillance has effectively kept unauthorized migrants in, not out. Much like individuals legalized under IRCA, these newer Mexican migrants are tied to family, friends, and acquaintances in Mexico, who ultimately rely on connections north of the border to aid subsequent migration. With markedly different wages in the United States and Mexico, migration becomes the only viable option for Mexicans' economic mobility, pushing thousands of migrants northward into an economy that depends on their labor. The cumulative result of U.S. immigration policies, economic integration, and the instability of the Mexican economy has been a dramatic increase in the number of unauthorized Mexican immigrants living in the United States. Demographer Jeffrey Passel (2008) shows that this number increased from 4.7 million in 2000 to 7 million in 2008, and slightly more than half of all Mexican immigrants are in the United States without documentation.

The focus of politics and the media is squarely on the plight of poor, unauthorized Mexican migrants, but emerging from earlier waves of Mexican immigration is a growing middle class whose life hardly resembles that of their foreign-born coethnics (Agius 2008; Rodriguez 1996). The most visible representations of this group of Mexican Americans can be seen in the politicians, school principals and superintendents, business owners, lawyers, law-enforcement officials, and other professionals found throughout the West, Southwest, and Midwest (Macias 2006). Many among this growing middle class are children of the Chicano movement, who have parlayed their college degrees into professional jobs and are now passing their class status to their children (Alba 2006; Macias 2006; Reed, Hill, Jepsen, and Johnson 2005; · Smith 2003; Smith 2006). In the late 1990s and the early part of the new millennium, news reports were quick to note the growth the Latino population and its concomitant cultural influence, even as they cast a spotlight on the foreign and unauthorized status of the Mexican-origin population. The growing (mostly unauthorized) influx of Mexican immigrants often masks the internal diversity among people of Mexican origin, and as sociologist Mary Waters puts it, the integration of later-generation Mexican Americans has emerged "behind the scenes" (1998: 108).

Immigration, then, has been a prominent and relatively permanent feature of the Mexican-origin experience throughout the twentieth century and into the new millennium. As table 1 shows, the long history of Mexican immigration has created a Mexican-origin population that is today a mix of immigrant generations. Among people of Mexican descent are individuals whose ancestors were in the American Southwest when it was still Mexico, the descendants of braceros, IRCA-amnesty recipients, and individuals coming across the border today.

Table 1.   Generational Distribution of the Mexican-origin
          Population in the United States, 2007
          (INCLUDES PERSONS WHO SELF-IDENTIFIED AS
          "MEXICAN AMERICAN," "CHICANO," OR "MEXICANO")

Generation	Number	Percent of Total
First	11,366,615	39
Second	6,703,388	23
Mixed (2.5)*	2,623,065	9
Third or later	8,452,098	29
Total	29,145,166	100

SOURCE: Calculated from the March 2007 Current Population Survey.

  *Mixed generation (2.5) refers to U.S.-born individuals who have one
U.S.-born parent and one Mexican-born parent.

As historian David Gutiérrez (1995) has shown, Mexican Americans have always had to consider a sizable Mexican-immigrant population in forming their ethnic identity. In the contemporary period, Mexican Americans negotiate a U.S. society in which their ethnic group is largely defined by the immigrants within it. However, as table 1 shows, nearly three in ten trace their roots in the United States back three generations or more. Academic studies, news media, and popular culture focus the overwhelming majority of their attention on the Mexican-immigrant population and the young second generation, seemingly forgetting about later-generation Mexican Americans who have been continually replenished by new waves of immigrants.

MEXICAN AMERICANS IN GARDEN CITY, KANSAS, AND SANTA MARIA, CALIFORNIA

The diversity within the Mexican-origin population is particularly evident in the two cities in which I conducted research for this book: Garden City, Kansas, and Santa Maria, California. These cities are not Mexican-American metropolises in the way that Los Angeles and San

Antonio are, nor are they the first cities that spring to mind in most conversations about the Mexican-origin population. Garden City and Santa Maria nonetheless are instructive in revealing the experiences of Mexican Americans and the critical factors shaping those experiences. In particular, Garden City's and Santa Maria's Mexican-American populations show how immigrant replenishment shapes what it means to be Mexican American. As the following historical overview of these cities shows, Garden City has experienced an interrupted pattern of Mexican immigration, whereas Santa Maria has experienced a more continuous pattern of Mexican immigration. These diverging patterns of immigrant replenishment distinguish the Mexican-American experience in Garden City from that in Santa Maria to some degree, although the heavy influx of Mexican immigrants in the last two decades has made the experience more similar than different.

Garden City, Kansas

Garden City is located in southwestern Kansas, sitting as a near island in a vast sea of corn, soy, and wheat fields. Far from any metropolitan center, Garden City is located 215 miles west of Wichita and 309 miles east of Denver, Colorado. With a total population of 28,451 in 2000, Garden City is, however, the seat of Finney County. Southwestern Kansas is renowned as the setting of classic Western films but is much less known as a destination for immigrants. More recently, Garden City and other midwestern and southern small towns have garnered attention from scholars and the media as "new immigrant gateways" (Massey 2008; Stull 1990; Zúñiga and Hernández-León 2005). These new immigrant gateways are distinguished from more established immigrant destinations by the relative recency and rapid growth of their immigrant populations (Waters and Jiménez 2005).

Yet to call Garden City a new immigrant gateway is not entirely accurate. Kansas—especially southwestern Kansas—has a history of Mexican immigration that dates back a hundred years. Although the first Mexican immigrants came to Garden City at the time of its founding in 1872 (Oppenheimer 1985), substantial Mexican immigration to

Garden City first took place between 1910 and 1930. These pioneering migrants came to Kansas both to escape the tumult of the Mexican Revolution and to work in the expanding railroad and sugar beet industries. They laid railroad tracks for the likes of the Santa Fe Railway Company, whose lines ran through many midwestern towns (García 1996). After the tracks had been laid, many settled in Garden City, laboring on railroad-line maintenance or working in the booming sugar beet industry.

The influx of Mexican immigrants to Garden City in the first half of the twentieth century did not last much beyond 1930. The Great Depression wiped out jobs, and native-born Americans increasingly greeted Mexican immigrants with disdain and hostility. As employment grew scarce, some Mexican immigrants returned to Mexico voluntarily, and government officials forcefully repatriated many others (García 1996). Not long after the Depression, the sugar beet industry disappeared as changing technology and market forces reduced the feasibility of raising and processing the crop. The Depression, followed by the demise of the sugar beet industry, reduced Mexican immigration to Garden City to a mere trickle (Stull 1990). Although the bracero program created a surge in Mexican immigration between 1942 and 1964, very few of these guest workers went to Kansas, and the state "faded into obscurity" (Durand, Massey, and Charvet 2000: 7) as a destination for Mexican immigrants during the bracero program era. After the 1930s Garden City and the rest of Kansas experienced a long hiatus of Mexican immigration that would last for more than four decades.

The introduction of the beef-packing industry precipitated the end of this hiatus. In 1980, Iowa Beef Processors opened the world's largest beef-packing plant nine miles outside Garden City. Three years later, Val-Agri purchased an idle plant on the outskirts of Garden City (Stull 1990). When the plants opened, few potential employees were in Garden City because unemployment was already very low. Initially the beef plants employed some locals but also a number of people from outside the area, including a handful of Mexican and Southeast Asian immigrants. The steady and relatively high-paying work in the beef plants became attractive to immigrants, who quickly dominated the plant workforce and swelled Garden City's foreign-born population in a matter of a few years (Broadway 1994).

The high demand for workers and the large immigrant population in the industry are linked to the nature of the work itself. Beef-processing plants operate on narrow profit margins and run production lines at a dizzying pace in order to increase the volume of production. Workers wield sharp knives and in some cases large motorized equipment to cut, slice, and pull various parts of the cow carcass as it moves along the processing line. The work is incredibly dangerous. High injury rates plague the beef industry—skin punctures, lacerations, and repetitive stress injuries are all too common. Injuries take their toll on the workforce, leading to high turnover and the need for a steady supply of new and willing workers (Gouveia and Stull 1995; Griffith 1995). Reluctant to take work that is dangerous, poorly paid (relative to the risk involved), and low in status, most native-born Garden City residents are happy to reserve beef-plant work for immigrants.

The strategies that plants have employed to hire new workers, combined with the unintended consequences of federal immigration policy, have contributed to the "Latinization" of the beef industry. Plants provide cash incentives for those who recruit workers so long as recruits stay on the job for an extended period. Mexican immigrants are eager to recruit coethnics to work in plants, and over time the labor force has become dominated by Mexicans. Anthropologist Donald Stull (2001) shows that in 1990 the proportion of Latino plant employees at the Iowa Beef Packing (formerly Iowa Beef Processors) and ConAgra (formerly Val-Agri) beef plants were 58 percent and 56 percent, respectively.[7] By 2000, that proportion had increased to 77 percent and 88 percent.[8]

At the policy level, another factor contributing to the "Latinization" of beef-plant labor is the passage of IRCA in 1986. When legalization for many Mexican immigrants finally took effect in the early 1990s, newly legalized Mexicans had the freedom to travel beyond the border states. Many of these immigrants moved to new immigrant gateways, such as Garden City, where growing industries like beef packing provided steady employment (Durand, Massey, and Charvet 2000; Massey, Durand, and Malone 2002). Beef packing has sparked a dramatic increase in the num-

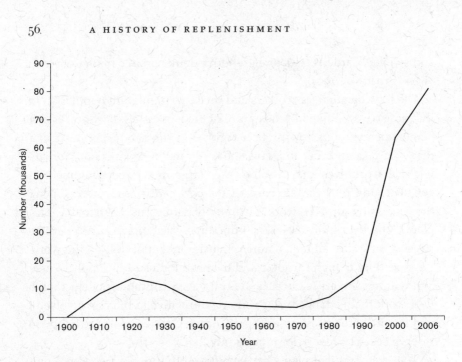

Figure 4.   Number of foreign-born Mexicans in Kansas, 1900–2006. Sources: U.S. Decennial Census; U.S. Census Bureau, American Community Survey.

ber of Mexican immigrants living in Garden City since 1980. According to U.S. Census figures, between 1980 and 2000 the Mexican-immigrant population in Finney County increased by 1,470 percent, from 468 to 7,349.

The historical pattern of Mexican immigration to Garden City can be characterized as interrupted. The demand for labor created by the railroad and sugar beet industries in the United States and growing civil unrest and low wages in Mexico created a first wave of Mexican immigration, which was followed by a nearly forty-year hiatus. But the beef-packing boom in Garden City and federal immigration policies that pushed Mexican immigrants out of more traditional immigrant destinations and into Garden City (and other new immigrant destinations) punctuated this immigration hiatus with a resurgent wave of Mexican immigration. Figure 4 provides a visual illustration of this interrupted pattern of Mexican immigration to Kansas.

Table 2. Racial and Ethnic Composition of Garden City, Kansas, 2000

Race/Ethnicity	Number	Percent of Total
White (non-Hispanic)	14,169	49.8
Mexican origin	9,865	34.7
Non-Mexican Hispanic	2,627	9.2
Black/African American	351	1.2
Asian	1,003	3.5
Total population*	28,451	100.0

SOURCE: 2000 U.S. Census.

*The entries in the "Number" and the "Percent of Total" columns do not add to the totals shown because individuals selecting the categories Native Hawaiian/ Pacific Islander, American Indian/Alaska Native, and Other, as well as those individuals selecting two or more race categories, have been excluded from these tabulations. None of these categories makes up more than 1 percent of Garden City's total population.

Today, Garden City has two Mexican-origin communities who trace their roots to two different waves of Mexican immigration. One community is linked to an immigration wave that came to Garden City in the early part of the twentieth century to build the railroads and tend to the sugar beet fields. The other Mexican-origin community has a much more recent history rooted in beef-plant labor.

Immigration has changed the demographic makeup in Garden City to look much more like traditional immigrant gateways found on the coasts. Garden City's population is primarily composed of Hispanics and whites.[9] Non-Hispanic whites account for slightly fewer than half of Garden City's 28,451 people, and the Mexican-origin population constituted more than a third of the city's population in 2000. (See table 2.) The number of African Americans and Asians in Garden City is rather small.

Garden City's Mexican-origin population is also internally diverse. People of Mexican origin are roughly evenly divided between those who were born in the United States and those who were born in Mexico.[10] (See table 3.)

Table 3.   Mexican-origin Population by Nativity
in Garden City, Kansas, 2000

	Number	Percent of Total
Total U.S.-born Mexican	4,998	50.7
Total foreign-born Mexican	4,867	49.3
Total Mexican origin	9,865	100.0

SOURCE: 2000 U.S. Census.

Dotted in and around Garden City are reminders of the ways in which Mexican immigration has transformed the city. Restaurants, nightclubs, and grocery stores catering to the Mexican immigrants can now be found throughout the town. A trip to Dillon's, the major local grocery store, provides a glimpse of these changes. The aisles in Dillon's feature a vast array of Mexican food and ingredients used in Mexican cooking, piñatas, and produce labeled in both Spanish and English. It is now common to hear Spanish being spoken throughout the city, and the grammar schools have more Latino students than whites.

Some residents of Garden City describe the town as "cosmopolitan" because of the large percentage of nonwhites who reside there. But even though Garden City is more cosmopolitan than other similar-sized cities in Kansas and the Midwest, it retains a small-town feel. Long-time residents all seem to know one another, and they commonly carry on long conversations during chance encounters. Local gossip spreads like wildfire, and even if Garden City residents do not know an individual, they are likely to know something about that individual.

Santa Maria, California

Santa Maria is a small city located on the central coast of California, about seventy-five miles north of Santa Barbara. With a total population of 77,423, Santa Maria sits at the northern edge of Santa Barbara County in the heart of the agriculturally rich Santa Maria Valley. Surrounding Santa Maria are sprawling fields of strawberries, broccoli, lettuce, cauliflower, and celery plants that supply fruits and vegetables to much of the country as well as the rest of the world.

As the city's Spanish name suggests, the Mexican-origin population has a long history in the area. The first Mexicans in Santa Maria, in fact, date prior to the formation of California as a state. A handful of Mexicans lived in the Santa Maria Valley prior to the signing of the Treaty of Guadalupe Hidalgo in 1848. However, the first large Mexican-immigrant population did not appear until the beginning of the 1900s. Mexican immigration to California at the beginning of the twentieth century followed a pattern similar to that found in Kansas. The Mexican Revolution pushed migrants out of Mexico, and the need for laborers in California's rapidly expanding agricultural industry pulled the first large wave of immigrants to California. Up until the very early part of the twentieth century, Chinese and Japanese workers filled many of the agricultural jobs in California, but then exclusionary legislation disallowed further immigration from China and Japan. With a significant supply of labor cut off, California turned to Mexicans as the preferred labor source, partly because they were seen as temporary workers who could easily return home (Camarillo 1996; Ngai 2004). Also similar to early Mexican immigrants in Kansas, many in California built railroad lines from Mexico to California, crossing the border to work for American railroad companies (Camarillo 1996). World War I spurred further demand for Mexican immigrants, since the male working-age population was fighting overseas in large numbers. When the war ended and the United States began to shut the door on European immigration in the 1920s, the door to Mexican labor remained open. A booming agricultural economy in California meant that growers needed a source of labor, and Congress structured the immigration laws to ensure that Mexican farm labor could fill this need (Ngai 2004). Even as the European immigrant population came to a halt in Santa Maria in the 1920s, Mexican immigration to the region continued until the Great Depression, when thousands of Mexican immigrants were repatriated to Mexico (along with many deported Mexican Americans)

(Gutiérrez 1995). Like the United States as a whole, Santa Maria saw a significant decrease in the Mexican-immigrant population during the 1930s.

The 1930s would be the only decade during which the number of Mexican immigrants declined in Santa Maria. World War II, like World War I, drained California of its workforce. The state's industries once again turned to Mexico for labor. Beginning in 1942, the bracero program helped fill the void. Whereas relatively few Mexican immigrants ventured to Kansas during this time, hundreds of thousands came to California, including Santa Maria, where the agricultural industry continued expanding. Sociologists Durand, Massey, and Charvet (2000) show that between 1950 and 1960 the total share of bracero-era Mexican immigrants going to California swelled from 34 percent to 42 percent.

Santa Maria remained a popular destination for Mexican immigrants well after the bracero program ended. Between 1975 and 1985 the Santa Maria Valley saw the expansion of labor-intensive specialty crops, which created added demand for manual labor (Palerm 1994, 1997). Whereas many of these crops were once risky seasonal products, advances in biotechnology had turned them into low-risk, high-yield crops. Advances in harvesting technologies created a demand for more laborers. As a result, the Santa Maria Valley witnessed what anthropologist Juan-Vicente Palerm calls the "Mexicanization" of California agriculture (1992). The demand for labor in agriculture was met with a supply of Mexican workers made possible by sociological artifacts of the bracero program. What developed in the Santa Maria Valley, similar to other areas of California, was a de facto guest worker program made possible by chain migration that former braceros initiated. Changes in agriculture, combined with this de facto guest worker program, guaranteed that Mexican immigration to Santa Maria would remain constant throughout the 1970s and 1980s. Further sparking an increase in immigration to Santa Maria were the unintended consequences of federal immigration policy related to IRCA and the fortification of the U.S.-Mexico border.

In contrast to the interrupted pattern of Mexican immigration to Garden City over the course of the twentieth century, Mexican immigration to Santa Maria was relatively constant over this period. With

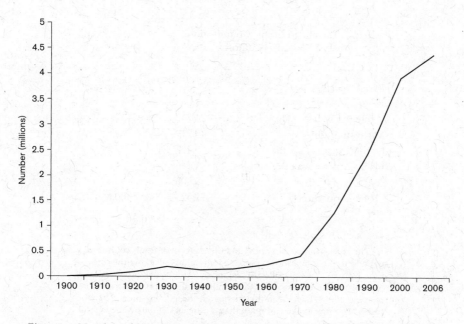

Figure 5. Number of foreign-born Mexicans in California, 1900–2006. Sources: U.S. Decennial Census; U.S. Census Bureau, American Community Survey.

the exception of the 1930s, Mexican immigration to Santa Maria has increased in each successive decade. Figure 5 displays this pattern in California.

Like Garden City, Santa Maria is primarily a Latino and white city. In contrast to the population of Garden City, however, the population of Santa Maria is composed of a majority of Mexican-origin people, who constitute just over half. Non-Hispanic whites, on the other hand, make up less than one-third of Santa Maria's population, and African Americans and Asians make up just a small fraction of the city's population. (See table 4.)

Despite different patterns of immigration, the demographic profile of the Mexican-origin population in Santa Maria is similar to that of Garden City. Table 5 shows the makeup of the Mexican-origin population in Santa Maria in 2000. Of the nearly 40,719 people of Mexican-origin in the city, slightly more than half were foreign-born.

Table 4.   Racial and Ethnic Composition
           of Santa Maria, California, 2000

Race/Ethnicity	Number	Percent of Total
White (non-Hispanic)	24,742	32.0
Mexican origin	40,719	52.6
Non-Mexican Hispanic	5,477	7.1
Black/African American	1,246	1.6
Asian	3,406	4.4
Total population*	77,423	100.0

SOURCE: 2000 U.S. Census

*The entries in the "Number" and the "Percent of Total" columns do
not add to the totals shown because individuals selecting the categories Native Hawaiian/Pacific Islander, American Indian/Alaska
Native, and Other, as well as those individuals selecting two or more
race categories, have been excluded from these tabulations. None of
these categories makes up more than 1 percent of Santa Maria's total
population.

The influence of the Mexican-origin population on Santa Maria is
unmistakable. Spanish can be heard in virtually every area of the city,
Mexican restaurants are found throughout town, and small strip malls
catering to the Mexican population sprinkle the city's landscape. The
broadcasts of multiple Spanish-language radio stations dot the airwaves
and can often be heard blaring out of cars. Spanish-language newspa-
pers and magazines are prevalent in retail stores. A quick glance in the
local phone book reveals that Spanish surnames dominate: Martínez,
Fernández, García, and similar names far outnumber any non-Spanish
last names.

Santa Maria has clearly outgrown its rural roots but still occasionally
shows flashes of the small-town feel so prominent in Garden City. While
the fruit and vegetable fields that surround the city suggest a rural setting, changes in Santa Maria's interior evince the suburban sprawl found
throughout California. The city's reach creeps north and east in the form
of housing developments in various stages of completion, strip malls
with large national chain stores are cropping up, and population growth

Table 5. Mexican-origin Population by Nativity
in Santa Maria, California, 2000

	Number	Percent of Total
Total U.S.-born Mexican	20,097	49.4
Total foreign-born Mexican	20,622	50.6
Total Mexican origin	40,719	100.0

SOURCE: 2000 U.S. Census.

has required that the city construct a third public high school (though only two existed during my time there). Residents of Santa Maria make no claims to being particularly cosmopolitan or international, however. For most residents, the existence of a Mexican-origin population, and Mexican immigrants in particular, seems mostly unremarkable, because Mexican immigration has been a feature of Santa Maria life for a long time.

Although comparing figures 4 and 5 side by side shows some difference in the patterns of twentieth-century Mexican immigration to Kansas and to California, the dramatically smaller size of Kansas complicates any direct comparison. Figure 6 provides a "normalized" basis for comparison by presenting the total number of Mexican immigrants as a percentage of Kansas's and California's respective total populations in 2000. Even in this normalized comparison, California did in fact experience continued immigration in the middle of the twentieth century while the number of Mexican immigrants in Kansas declined.

The differences in historical patterns of Mexican immigration compelled me to select these two cities as research sites. I began with the premise that these differences would yield differences in how later-generation Mexican Americans experience U.S. society. My interviews and observations show this to be true to some degree, but far less so than I had anticipated. In the end, the significant replenishment that both cities have experienced in the last twenty years has diminished the differences that I expected to find between them. The ways that

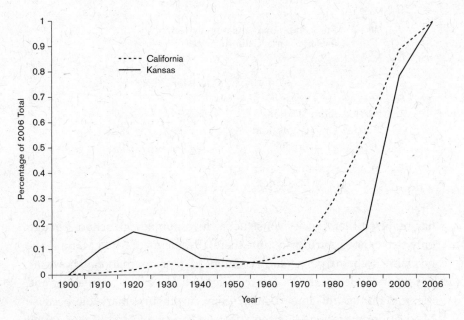

Figure 6. Number of foreign-born Mexicans in Kansas and California as a percentage of the 2006 total, 1900–2006. Sources: U.S. Decennial Census; U.S. Census Bureau, American Community Survey.

immigrant replenishment influences Mexican-American ethnic identity make Garden City and Santa Maria more similar than they are different. What emerges from my research is a story about what it means to be Mexican American in these two cities today and how Mexican immigration shapes Mexican American ethnic identity.

This cursory history of the Mexican-origin population highlights two important themes. First, this population has been almost continually restocked by immigrants for the last hundred years. Mexican immigration was prevalent at the tail end of a period of heavy European migration (1880–1920) and during a period described as a "hiatus" of American immigration (1930–65), and Mexico is the largest contributor of immigrants in the current era (1965–present). No other ethnic group has experienced immigrant replenishment for as long or on as large a scale.

The second theme emerging from this chapter relates to assimilation. Over the last hundred years people of Mexican descent have perpetually struggled for integration into American society. Though the collective approaches they have employed have varied over time—mostly in accordance with prevailing ideologies about integration—the challenges of assimilation have been a defining feature of the population over the course of the twentieth century and into the twenty-first. As the chapters that follow will show, these two themes are intimately tied in the lives of Mexican Americans today.

The large and perpetual influx of Mexican immigrants has piqued concerns that people of Mexican origin are not following a path of assimilation traveled by other immigrant groups. Immigrant replenishment makes Mexican-American assimilation radically different from that of other groups, but it does not justify the worst fears about their prospects in U.S. society.

THREE Dimensions of Mexican-American Assimilation

The dramatic immigration-driven growth of the Mexican-origin population has spawned a groundswell of concern about the group's assimilation. Some argue that Mexican immigration threatens the United States by contributing to the onset of a polyglot nation in which enduring ethnic attachments come at the expense of a larger American national identity. Political scientist Samuel Huntington's polemic book *Who Are We?* provides an elaborate articulation of these fears. He argues that the persistent influx of Mexican immigrants has contributed to confusion about the American national identity so crucial to the prosperity of the republic. In an excerpt of the book published in *Foreign Policy* magazine, Huntington writes, "The persistent inflow of Hispanic immigrants threatens to divide the United States into two peoples, two cultures, and two languages. Unlike past immigrant groups, Mexicans and other

Latinos have not assimilated into mainstream U.S. culture, forming instead their own political and linguistic enclaves—from Los Angeles to Miami—and rejecting the Anglo-Protestant values that built the American dream. The United States ignores this challenge at its peril" (2004a: 30).

Huntington is not alone in his concerns about Mexican-origin assimilation. While scholars may not agree with his conclusion that Mexican immigration constitutes a threat to national identity, they have argued that something is amiss with the assimilation of the Mexican-origin population. Their concerns are rooted in both the characteristics of today's Mexican immigrants and the U.S. society to which they migrate. Some argue that Mexican-origin assimilation is diminished by Mexicans' low "quality," a crude term referring to their low levels of human capital (Borjas 1999). Other scholars point to poverty and racism as a one-two punch that knocks the Mexican-American second generation off course and onto a steep, downward path of assimilation into a "rainbow underclass" (López and Stanton-Salazar 2001; Portes and Rumbaut 2001). If assimilation is an endpoint reached when ethnic groups achieve parity with third-generation whites on an array of outcomes, their situation may look no better after the second generation. According to some analyses, wages and educational attainment stagnate among people of Mexican origin after the second generation (Bean et al. 1994; Livingston and Kahn 2002; Ortiz 1996; Telles and Ortiz 2008; Wojtkiewicz and Donato 1995), a pattern that runs contrary to the classical story of assimilation, in which the third generation fares much better than the previous two. Whether observers believe that a discriminatory American society or people of Mexican origin themselves are to blame for these patterns of assimilation, many have reached a tacit consensus that, empirically, the Mexican-origin population is not following the path of assimilation blazed by earlier waves of immigrants.

Others scholars have called this conclusion into question, however. They emphasize that assimilation is not an endpoint reached when Mexican Americans reach socioeconomic parity with their white counterparts. Rather, assimilation is a process that takes place as long as each new generation born in the United States improves on its parents' social, political, and economic fortunes (see Jiménez and Fitzgerald 2007). From this perspective, Mexican Americans show clear signs of assimilation, and differences in assimilation patterns between people of Mexican origin and other immigrant groups are a matter of pace, not direction (Bean et al. 2007). Using a combination of generations from the immigrant point of origin and birth cohort as temporal measures, scholars have shown that each new generation of Mexican Americans born in the United States does in fact improve on the educational attainment and wages of the previous generation, though the third generation has not quite caught up to native-born whites (Alba 2006; Reed et al. 2005; Smith 2003, 2006). To be sure, some Mexican Americans, including those whose families have been in the United States for multiple generations, end up a the bottom of the socioeconomic ladder in what appears to be an underclass (Dohan 2003). Still, most studies suggest that Mexican Americans are not doomed to end up in an underclass, even if they do have a slower climb into the social and economic mainstream (Perlmann 2005; Waldinger and Feliciano 2004; Waldinger, Lim, and Cort 2007). Marriage patterns among people of Mexican descent also point to a population that is neither permanently mired in poverty nor socially isolated. Mexican Americans display relatively high intermarriage rates that resemble a story of progressive social integration rather than a tale of unshakable racism (Macias 2006; Perlmann and Waters 2004; Rosenfeld 2002).

Which of these two scenarios—downward assimilation or intergenerational progress—do later-generation Mexican Americans in Garden City and Santa Maria reflect? Do they face blocked mobility that has left them stuck on the social and economic margins? Or have they been moving ahead, improving on the fortunes of the previous generation? Do they display separatist tendencies and hold steadfastly to their ethnic roots? Or does ethnicity make up only a minor part of their social identity as they blend into the U.S. mainstream?

I take up these questions in this chapter by examining the general patterns of assimilation among Mexican Americans in Garden City and Santa Maria. My aim is not to settle the empirical debate about Mexican-origin assimilation outlined above. My ethnographic data simply do not allow me to undertake such an ambitious endeavor. Instead, this chapter has a more modest, but nonetheless important, mission of providing a context for my analysis of Mexican-American ethnic identity formation in the rest of the book. I treat assimilation as a process—not an endpoint—that is measured by examining how each successive generation fares relative to its parent generation. Emphasizing the process of assimilation among Mexican Americans makes sense when looking at socioeconomic indicators, because ongoing immigration means that people of Mexican descent trace their roots in the United States to different waves of immigration and may therefore be at different stages in the assimilation process. Furthermore, assimilation where ethnic identity is concerned is a continually unfolding process that is shaped and reshaped by economic, political, and social conditions that structure everyday interactions (Yancey, Erickson, and Juliani 1976). As these conditions change, they perpetually remake ethnic identity.

I show that Mexican Americans in Garden City and Santa Maria display clear signs of assimilation. They are by no means socially isolated, nor are they relegated to the political and economic margins. Mexican Americans remain behind native-born whites in their socioeconomic progress, but each generation born in the United States has advanced beyond the previous one on an array of measures, a remarkable pattern given the history of severe discrimination visited on them for much of the twentieth century. Contrary to the fears of some, Mexican Americans in Garden City and Santa Maria are not ethnic nationalists. Instead, ethnicity's hold on how parents raise their children weakens over time.

The assimilation of Mexican Americans bears some resemblance to the assimilation of European-origin groups when viewed from canonical approaches to the study of assimilation. But the canonical account does not tell the full story of the Mexican-American experience today. As this chapter begins to suggest (and as the next chapters more fully elaborate), the large coethnic immigrant population restocks the access that Mexican Americans have to the "ethnic stuff" that ethnicity contains, making the Mexican-American experience radically different from that of white ethnics.

A few notes are important to keep in mind before proceeding. Though most analyses of assimilation use generation as a temporal gauge, I use birth cohorts to organize my analysis and discussion. For social scientists of immigration, *generation* refers to the birth distance since the immigrant point of origin. Immigrants make up the "first generation," the offspring of immigrants are the "second generation," the "third generation" is composed of the grandchildren of immigrants, and so on. Colloquially, most people use a second understanding of *generation* to refer to people born during a particular period of time. According to this usage of the term, the historical events that define different generations inform well-known monikers: "the greatest generation," "baby boomers," "generation X," "the millennials," et cetera. This second usage of *generation* is what social scientists refer to as a birth cohort—a group of people born during the same time period, generally running twenty to twenty-five years.

One of the sample-selection criteria for respondents was that their family had been in the United States since 1940 or before. As the historical overview in the previous chapter shows, the majority of Mexican immigrants entering the United States prior to 1940 came in the 1910s and 1920s, and very few entered in the 1930s. Because of this historical pattern of immigration, most later-generation Mexican Americans trace their immigrant origins in the United States to the 1910s and 1920s; thus, a tight correlation between birth cohort and generation exists for the people I interviewed. The oldest cohort of respondents (ages fifty-six and over) tended to be second generation, the bulk of the middle cohort (ages thirty-six to fifty-five) was third or fourth generation, and the youngest cohort (ages fifteen to thirty-five) tended to be fourth generation or more, or a combination of generations (e.g., third and fourth generations). Although generation is an important aspect of assimilation, because it captures factors shaping ethnic change internal to a group, using birth cohort also measures the effects that historical circumstances have on ethnic change (Alba 1988; Jiménez and Fitzgerald 2007; Waters and Jiménez 2005). Since I am interested in how historical circumstances and generational status shape Mexican-American ethnic identity formation, the use of birth cohorts as a temporal measure is a convenient way to capture both of these effects.

A second important methodological note relates to the extent to which my sample of Mexican Americans is representative. The people I interviewed were not part of a random sample and thus should not be understood as statistically representative of Mexican Americans in Garden City, Santa Maria, or other cities and regions in the United States. That said, the patterns of assimilation I report among my respondents are consonant with findings from survey research that employs statistically representative samples, suggesting that I selected a sample whose experience of assimilation resembles that of Mexican Americans nationwide.

Finally, readers should keep in mind that Garden City and Santa Maria are, respectively, rural and semirural cities, so there may be a "small-town" effect in the findings I report from these two places. The effect may show up in a number of dimensions of assimilation in which the size of a particular locale matters. The small size of these communities may limit the array of residential options, occupational mobility, and schooling options compared with those available to Mexican Americans in metropolitan areas (see Duarte 2008; Telles and Ortiz 2008). Nonetheless, the picture of Mexican-American assimilation that emerges from this chapter largely parallels research done on Mexican Americans in metropolitan areas.

STRUCTURAL PROCESSES OF MEXICAN-AMERICAN ASSIMILATION

Social scientists still rely on a core group of assimilation measures that the earliest scholars of immigration employed: socioeconomic status, residential location, civic life and social cliques, and intermarriage.[1] These measures of assimilation generally fall under what Milton Gordon (1964) called "structural" processes of assimilation. According to Gordon, structural assimilation takes place when immigrant groups enter "fully into the societal network of groups and institutions" of the host society (70). Scholars generally regard structural assimilation as a good thing. When structural assimilation takes place, race, ethnicity, and immigration status decline in their importance for determining full participation in U.S. society. Mexican Americans in Garden City and Santa Maria have experienced a good degree of structural assimilation, though it has not come easily or quickly.

Socioeconomic Assimilation

My Mexican-American respondents in Garden City and Santa Maria do not represent a group whose socioeconomic fortunes are bogged down by diminished opportunities and persistent discrimination. Instead, they showed marked socioeconomic improvement over time. The path to upward mobility did not proceed in a smooth, straight line, however. The oldest respondents (ages fifty-six and up) achieved socioeconomic advancement above their mostly immigrant parents, but significant barriers limited their climb up the socioeconomic ladder. Several of the respondents from the oldest cohort did not finish high school, but a number of others either did complete high school or received a GED. Some of these oldest respondents spoke very little or no English when they were young and had difficulties navigating a school system that was intolerant of people like them. While their mostly immigrant parents passed their drive for a better life on to their children, they had little human capital—income and education—to bequeath. Many respondents from the oldest cohort recalled working with their parents to help make ends meet when they were not in school. For the oldest Mexican Americans in Garden City, this meant putting in long hours in the sugar beet fields and factory. The oldest cohort in Santa Maria spent their after-school time and summers laboring in the fields alongside their parents.

If their parents' socioeconomic status did not give them much of a push up the ladder of mobility, discrimination made their climb even more labored. Members of the oldest cohort recalled numerous instances of blatant discrimination on the basis of their ethnic origin. Teachers sometimes placed them in the back row of classrooms, assuming that they were less intelligent because of their limited ability to speak English. Others faced strict punishment for speaking Spanish or were placed in classes for the mentally challenged for the same reason. Such experiences were seared into the memory of Paul Sánchez, a seventy-seven-year-old retired dairy worker in Garden City, who attended school only through the fifth grade:

I quit because when I went to school, I knew nothing but Spanish. That's all we spoke at home—my mom and my grandma and the rest of the family. And at school they told us, "No Spanish allowed!" You can't even speak Spanish, not even on the playground. And if you did, they would send you to the principal's office, and they would give you two or three whacks. And I got many a whack because I wouldn't give up my language.

Some among the oldest cohort of Mexican Americans recalled especially caring teachers who helped counteract some of this discrimination. But the efforts of a few, well-intentioned teachers were overwhelmed by an educational system that was stacked against people of Mexican origin.

Despite significant barriers in education, members of the oldest cohort of Mexican Americans moved from poverty into the lower middle class, primarily through blue-collar occupations. The oldest cohort in Garden City and Santa Maria, many of whom were retired by the time of my research, concentrated in blue-collar and semiprofessional jobs, including operating heavy equipment, doing clerical work, driving delivery trucks, managing offices, nursing, owning liquor stores, doing custodial work, and working as barbers. These jobs enabled them to afford the trappings of the middle class—homeownership, occasional vacations, a sound retirement—although not much more. These trends in Garden City and Santa Maria mirror Mexican-American occupational mobility in places like Los Angeles, where early cohorts of Mexican Americans established occupational niches in unionized, blue-collar jobs that helped them move into the lower middle class (Ortiz 1996). Their entrance into that class was hard fought. Respondents in both cities recalled that very few, if any, Mexican Americans worked "downtown" (i.e., in white-collar jobs), although some Mexican Americans eventually broke into white-collar work after surmounting significant obstacles. Gilbert Mariano, a seventy-year-old retired salesman in Garden City, recalled the type of discrimination that faced many Mexican Americans when they applied for jobs:

Now people have a better chance to have a better job because of the opportunities that you have now. Then, you didn't have the opportunity, period. I was putting in job [applications] all over. I used to go to Dodge City, Liberal—any place to apply for a job, just to get a decent job. But anyway, this one guy, I talked to him, and he said, "You know, [Gil], when you applied for a job here, after you left, that application went in file 13."

TRJ: *What is file 13?*

R: *Trash can.*

Having forged ahead into the lower middle class, the oldest cohort of Mexican Americans passed on their modest socioeconomic gains to their children, who made up the middle cohort of respondents (ages thirty-four to fifty-five). The middle cohort included no high school dropouts, several college graduates, and even graduate-degree recipients. The Santa Maria sample, however, included far more respondents with college, graduate, and professional degrees compared with respondents in Garden City. Santa Maria's larger size provides more opportunities for professionals, and the city's close proximity to two major public universities allowed middle-cohort individuals to live at home while attending school, making college a lot more affordable. Their experiences seem to mirror those of individuals nationwide. As sociologist Ruth López-Turley (2009) shows, high schools students are more likely to apply to college when colleges and universities are in close proximity to their homes. Garden City, on the other hand, has a junior college but no nearby colleges or universities. The middle-cohort Mexican Americans who did attend college often traveled well outside Garden City and seldom returned. I did not interview these Mexican Americans precisely because they no longer lived in Garden City. Respondents in Garden City nonetheless spoke proudly of siblings, other relatives, and Mexican-American friends who had graduated from college and even professional schools, only to stay in larger cities (such as Denver, Kansas City, and Wichita) that offered more opportunities to pursue professional careers.

The socioeconomic assent among the middle cohort of Mexican Americans was aided by historical events. By the time the middle cohort came of age, opportunities expanded for Mexican Americans across the country. The oldest cohort of respondents had largely been shut out of the mainstream in Garden City but had successfully pressured local officials to change an existing exclusionary code of treatment. As a result, the middle cohort in Garden City grew up during a time that provided a much larger array of educational and occupational opportunities than those that had existed for the oldest cohort. Consider the relatively positive school experiences of Donald Mercado, a forty-seven-year-old manager of a nonprofit organization, compared with those from the oldest cohort in Garden City:

When I got into athletics, I had a teacher early on who noticed that I was always wanting to do something. Like, I would be looking at the clock, and he said, "You can't be a clock watcher all of your life. [. . .] I believe you are better than what you are doing. [. . .] I think you can be a great athlete. And you need to stop watching the clock and put more emphasis upon the right-now and look toward the future." So I always had good people. And they were Anglo people that were always trying to push me onto a good track of higher learning, or at least higher aspirations than what I had for myself.[2]

Relations between Mexican Americans and whites in Garden City were by no means smooth during this time, but they improved dramatically from the previous time period during which the oldest cohort came of age. The importance of timing is also evident in the educational advancement of the middle-cohort respondents in Santa Maria. They entered their teens and twenties during the 1960s and 1970s, when a "minority rights revolution" was sweeping the country (Skrentny 2002). Affirmative action programs flourished on college campuses, and Mexican Americans began to attend college in unprecedented, though still modest, numbers. Among this first significant wave of Mexican-American college students were several middle-cohort Mexican Americans I interviewed in Santa Maria, many of whom went on to earn advanced degrees in education, law, and medicine.

The middle cohort in both Garden City and Santa Maria had converted their educational gains into advances in class status. Most of this cohort had obtained semiprofessional jobs, many as salespeople and clerical workers, and they enjoyed membership in Garden City's middle class.

While many of these Mexican Americans occupied jobs that require only a high school degree, the modest cost of living in Garden City, combined with reasonably high salaries, had enabled them to afford a solidly middle-class lifestyle. Similarly, the middle-cohort Mexican Americans in Santa Maria had cashed in on the educational advances they had made beyond those of their parents. This middle cohort of Mexican Americans had leaped into Santa Maria's middle class through a combination of blue-collar, semiprofessional, and even professional occupations. Among Santa Maria's middle cohort were judges, politicians, lawyers, engineers, doctors, architects, and small-business owners. My Santa Maria respondents also constituted a sizable middle class that included law-enforcement officers, teachers, and bankers.

Within the youngest cohort of respondents, those of ages fifteen to thirty-four, socioeconomic assimilation had proceeded apace. Many were away at college during the time of my fieldwork, but a few had graduated and moved back to Garden City and Santa Maria, where they occupied professional positions as teachers, clergy, and law enforcement officers. The teenagers I interviewed were among the most successful and active students in the school. These high achievers included a homecoming queen, a school newspaper editor, star athletes, cheerleaders, club leaders, student-body officers, and honor-role students. This high level of participation mirrors the "Mexican-American-identified" students in sociologist María Eugenia Matute-Bianchi's (1986) oft-cited analysis of Mexican-origin high school students in California. Matute-Bianchi found that the most active and successful Mexican-origin students in school were those who, like my respondents, were U.S.-born (often of U.S.-born parents) and who were regarded by others in the school as the most "Americanized" (i.e., did not speak Spanish). Because a good number of individuals from the youngest cohort were still in school, I cannot be certain of their occupational fortunes. However, their continuation in school, combined with the high occupational aspirations they articulated, suggests that they will at least equal and likely surpass the middle cohort's socioeconomic standing.[3] As these young respondents looked ahead, they did not see the obstacles to socioeconomic advancement that had faced previous cohorts of Mexican Americans. Instead, they saw a much more open future, one in which their ethnic origin is not likely to bar them from opportunities.[4]

The intergenerational socioeconomic advancement that Mexican Americans experienced in Garden City and Santa Maria is not unique to these two cities. Rather, it seems to reflect the experiences of Mexican Americans nationwide. Economist James P. Smith's (2003, 2006) analyses of U.S. Census data show that when cohort and generation are taken into account, Mexican Americans exhibit significant improvement in educational attainment and wages with each successive generation and cohort. For example, Smith shows that Mexican immigrants born in the years 1920–24 achieved an average of only 6.22 years of education. The next generation, born in 1945–49, nearly doubled the previous generation's educational attainment, with 11.61 mean years of education. In the third generation of Mexican Americans, born from 1970–74, the average education attained was more than a high school degree, with 12.29 means years (see Smith 2003: table 2). During this same overall period of time, Mexican Americans narrowed their education deficit compared with the education attained by native-born whites, going from a shortfall of more than four years to less than one year in the third generation. Similarly, Richard Alba (2006) employs survey data that allow for direct comparison between children and their parents. Alba finds that each successive cohort of Mexican Americans improves on the educational attainment of its parents' cohort by an average of 2.5 years, though the third generation still lags behind non-Hispanic whites by 1 to 1.5 years. (The gap is smaller among women.)[5] Edward Telles and Vilma Ortiz (2008) show a more mixed picture of educational attainment among Mexican Americans in San Antonio and Los Angeles. Similar to Smith's and Alba's findings, Telles and Ortiz's findings show that Mexican Americans go to school longer and get better jobs than their parents. However, they find that Mexican-American educational attainment lags behind that of native-born whites regardless of cohort. Furthermore, fourth-generation Mexican Americans actually attain fewer years of education than same-aged second- and third-generation Mexican Americans. Likewise, they find a pattern of decline in occupational status when comparing generations. Telles and Ortiz conclude that these findings contain no evidence of assimilation, particularly when considering that the fourth generation from the immigrant point of origin has fared less well than the second and third generations.

My data do not allow for a direct comparison of findings. But my interviews and observations of Mexican Americans' lived experiences reflect a more positive picture. The gains that Mexican Americans in Garden City and Santa Maria have made on their parents' socioeconomic position should be regarded as a remarkably positive trend, even if they still have not reached full parity with native-born whites. Considering their very humble immigrant origins and the high level of systematic discrimination that people of Mexican origin in Garden City and Santa Maria faced for most of the twentieth century, the socioeconomic glass appears to be half full for the people I studied, and indeed for Mexican Americans nationwide.

Residential Assimilation

Another important barometer of assimilation relates to where people live. When individuals live in heavily segregated neighborhoods, they tend to have minimal contact with members of other racial and ethnic groups. Segregation can be born of discrimination embedded in housing policies and the practices of real estate agents, lenders, and exclusionary covenants (Massey and Denton 1993). But immigration adds a voluntary component to segregation. Newly arrived immigrants often concentrate in neighborhoods with their coethnics, where they have access to a host of resources available through ethnically based social networks, or what sociologists call "social capital." In these ethnic neighborhoods, immigrants find jobs, social support, housing, and a setting in which they can use their native language to conduct the business of daily life (Portes and Bach 1985). This is not to say that neighborhoods with heavy concentrations of immigrants are "desirable." Quite the contrary. Poor immigrants move into neighborhoods they can afford, and for low-wage migrants this means that they often wind up in blighted areas.[6]

According to canonical theories of assimilation, the descendants of immigrants do not remain in these ethnic neighborhoods. Instead, each new generation born in the United States lives in a neighborhood in which fewer members of its ethnic group reside. Both the discriminatory boundaries that preclude nonwhites from living in certain neighborhoods and the benefits of living near coethnics fade over time. This spatial assimilation hypothesis (Massey 1985), as sociologists call it, posits that increasing socioeconomic mobility, longer residence in the United States, and temporal distance from the immigrant generation lead to declining residential concentration for any particular ethnic group. The spatial assimilation hypothesis is based on an urban-suburban model that does not entirely apply to Garden City and Santa Maria, neither of which is located in or near an urban center. Nonetheless, if we take the spatial assimilation hypothesis to suggest that over time race and ethnicity become diminishing factors in determining people's ability to choose their place of residence, then the experiences of Mexican Americans in Garden City and Santa Maria tend to conform to the main thrust of the hypothesis.

Mexican-origin residents (including immigrants) appear to be more spatially isolated than whites in Garden City and Santa Maria, but Mexican Americans tend to live in middle- and upper-middle-class neighborhoods. In Garden City the oldest Mexican barrio occupies an area of the city near the railroad tracks, where the first Mexican Americans settled. A good number of Mexican Americans from the oldest cohort remain in this neighborhood and live alongside newly arrived Mexican immigrants. The concentration of the earliest Mexican-American community was the clear result of housing discrimination. Gilbert Mariano was one of the first Mexican Americans to move north of the tracks in Garden City, and his move was anything but easy:

I went to one real estate agent, and all he was showing me was the slums [. . .] that was the only thing he was showing me, just nothing. So then I went to another real estate agent, and he showed me [the house we are in now]. I think that was the only one. I can't remember. Anyway, he showed us this one, and we liked it. [. . .] [Our new neighbors] thought we were [. . .] a bad family. But it turned out after a while they find out that I was the right person to be in here, because everything just went their way. And we were the only Mexican people here within six or eight blocks.

While many of the older respondents still resided south of the tracks, their children and grandchildren lived in newer and larger homes on the north side of town. These neighborhoods tend to be middle-class and ethnically mixed. One area of Garden City into which Mexican Americans have not moved is the country club. Located on the outskirts of town on a pristine eighteen-hole golf course, the Southwind Country Club contains the largest homes in Garden City. This is the neighborhood in which Garden City's professional elite resides, but it has not seen the entrance of Mexican-American professionals, because they are so few in number. With this exception, ethnicity does not appear to be a factor determining where Garden City's Mexican Americans live.

In Santa Maria, patterns of spatial assimilation are similar to Garden City. The first Mexican-American community in Santa Maria hardly lived in the city at all. They often resided in migrant labor camps made up of old army barracks and tents. It was members of the oldest cohort of respondents, most of whom are second-generation Mexican Americans, who moved into town. Their initial move out of the fields found them on Santa Maria's west side—particularly the northwest—where many lived alongside a growing Mexican-immigrant population at the time of my research. But their residential concentration in the northwest did not persist into the next cohort. Large numbers of middle-cohort respondents in Santa Maria, like their Garden City counterparts, moved out of the predominantly Mexican neighborhoods where they had lived as children and into more affluent sections of town where whites predominate. These Mexican Americans owned homes in newer housing developments and an ample number of Mexican Americans lived in Orcutt, an upper-middle-class subsection south of Santa Maria.

If a departure from the spatial assimilation hypothesis occurs among Mexican Americans, it is because of the rapid spatial assimilation of newer immigrants, which allows upwardly mobile Mexican Americans to reside increasingly in neighborhoods alongside some of their more successful immigrant coethnics (see Myers 2007). Telles and Ortiz similarly note that among Mexican Americans in San Antonio and Los Angeles, "immigration has clearly changed the residential experiences of later generations of Mexican Americans from 1965–2000 by re-Mexicanizing many of their neighborhoods but also increasing Asian composition" (2008: 168). Still, spatial assimilation appears to be taking place among

Mexican Americans in metro areas with large Mexican-immigrant populations, even if it is often delayed until the third and fourth generations (Brown 2007).[7]

Civic Life and Social Cliques

Assimilation also has wider civic and social components. Assimilation entails full participation in a civic and social life not exclusively defined by race and ethnicity. Mexican Americans in Garden City and Santa Maria have experienced significant integration into a larger civic and social life in both cities; they are not "bowling alone," as political scientist Robert Putnam (2000) might put it. The oldest cohort of respondents were just as civically minded as the middle and youngest cohorts, but exclusionary practices had left them on the margins of a civic life dominated by whites. Members of the oldest cohort of respondents had created their own parallel civic organizations, which included *mutualistas* (mutual aid societies), the American G.I. Forum, and LULAC. These organizations served as centers of Mexican-American civic life for much of the 1950s, '60s, and '70s, but their success in tearing down the discriminatory boundaries has enabled later cohorts of Mexican Americans to enjoy fuller participation in a civic society previously closed to people of Mexican origin.

Today, Mexican Americans in Garden City and Santa Maria are members of both ethnically based organizations, such as LULAC and the American G.I. Forum, and nonethnic clubs and organizations, including the Elks Lodge, the Knights of Columbus, the municipal swimming pool board, the hospital board, Big Brothers Big Sisters, the YMCA, the Chamber of Commerce, Veterans of Foreign Wars, Little League, Boys and Girls Club, VFW, 4-H, the California Teacher's Association, Kiwanis, local Democratic and Republican party associations, church organizations, and the Special Olympics. The tendency to join was also prevalent among the youngest cohort of respondents in each city. As I mentioned above, they were some of the most involved students in school, participating in athletics, the performing arts, the school newspaper, 4H, and cheerleading. Mexican Americans' high level of civic participation may partly be a function of the high level of social capital exhibited in small towns and cities, especially relative to larger metropolitan areas (Putnam 2000: chapter 12). Whatever "small-town effect" might be driving civic participation in these two cities does little to change the larger point: Mexican Americans are part of the civic mainstream.

Mexican Americans also increasingly play a central role in formal politics. Garden City elected its first Mexican-American mayor in 1973, and from 1990 to 2001 four Mexican-American mayors served a total of five terms. During my time in Garden City, two of the five members of the city commission were Mexican American, and one was a Mexican immigrant. Santa Maria's Mexican Americans have made similar political gains, although their ascent has been more contentious. The political might of the Mexican-origin population remained low up until the mid-1990s, when the first Mexican Americans in more than three decades were elected to the city council. The election of these city council members came amid (or perhaps in response to) a Mexican American Legal Defense and Education Fund lawsuit against the city for violation of the Voting Rights Act. The plaintiffs argued that the at-large election of city council members in Santa Maria prevented neighborhoods with large Mexican-origin populations from having adequate representation in city government. Some among the Mexican-American leadership argued that the established conservative, white leadership in Santa Maria orchestrated the election of three Mexican Americans to the city council in order to deflect criticism and to render the lawsuit impotent. They further claimed that the three, despite their ethnic origin, hardly represented the interests of Santa Maria's Mexican-origin population and instead did the bidding of wealthy farmers and white residents. My data do not allow me to test these claims. Aside from the political leanings of these Mexican-American politicians, the ethnic makeup of Santa Maria's city council suggests that formal politics is hardly closed to people of Mexican origin.

Theories of assimilation suggest that as Mexican Americans move out of barrios and gain upward mobility, they should also have more meaningful contact with non-Mexicans. In order to understand the extent to which Mexican Americans in each of the sample cities have meaning-

Table 6. Average Proportion of Interpersonal Network Made Up of Non-Mexicans (%)

	Garden City	Santa Maria
Oldest cohort (56 and older)	38.0	39.0
Middle cohort (36–55)	42.2	46.0
Youngest cohort (15–35)	47.6	37.3
All respondents	42.7	40.6

SOURCE: Data collected from Garden City and Santa Maria respondents.

ful interactions with non-Mexicans, I asked each respondent to list the ethnic background of the five individuals with whom he or she was most likely to discuss important matters. Sociologists commonly ask this question on surveys in order to understand the characteristics of an individual's "interpersonal network" (see Marin 2004).[8] The diversity of an individual's interpersonal network indicates the extent to which that individual has meaningful contact with people who do not share the same ethnic origin. Table 6 lists the average proportion of individuals not of Mexican origin in each respondent's interpersonal network for the total sample in each city and by cohort.

Respondents in both cities had interpersonal networks made up of a significant proportion of individuals not of Mexican origin, most of whom were white. On average, this proportion was more than 40 percent. The interpersonal network of each successive cohort in Garden City shows an increase in the average percentage of individuals who were not coethnics, although this percentage curiously decreased for respondents in the youngest cohort in Santa Maria. The decline among young Santa Maria respondents may reflect the large pool of coethnics from which they chose their interpersonal networks. (Recall that 52 percent of Santa Maria's population is of Mexican origin.) But the pattern could also reflect their choice of family members when reporting the individuals in their interpersonal network. Since young respondents most often lived with their parents, they were more likely to report family members when asked to list the people with whom they discussed important matters. Even with this liberty to name family members for their interpersonal networks, the youngest Santa Maria respondents still averaged nearly two non-Mexican individuals among the five individuals named, which suggests that this cohort had a great deal of meaningful social interaction with non-Mexicans, despite the pattern of decline.

Furthermore, data for the overall sample are on par with findings from survey research that employs representative samples. Telles and Ortiz show that a quarter to a third of second-, third-, and fourth-generation Mexican Americans report having "none or few" Mexican friends (2008: 174). Sociologist Peter Marsden (1988) shows that 38 percent of the individuals that Hispanics listed as members of their interpersonal networks in the 1985 General Social Survey were non-Hispanics.[9] Likewise, sociologist Susan Brown (2006) demonstrates that native-born people of Mexican descent in Los Angeles County are far more likely to have diverse interpersonal networks than their immigrant counterparts, net of other factors. The reflections of Bob Fernández, a fifty-two-year-old graphic designer in Santa Maria, aptly summarize these findings and overall patterns in Garden City and Santa Maria:

You know, for the most part I would venture to say that the people I run around with, we're all the same. Matter of fact we were out the other night with a group and, oh my gosh, we had a cross-section there: two Jews, myself, and Jane was white. Jerry Shaw and Doug were white. Rosa is Hispanic. [thinking to himself about another woman] She's Boston-white. It's a mix. And I really feel that because we have acclimated so much to it, to the American system, I think they see us as equal. I really do.

Intermarriage

The meaningful interactions that Mexican Americans have with non-Mexicans often lead to romantic relationships and marriage. Social scientists consider intermarriage a significant yardstick of structural assimilation, because it signals a weakening of social barriers between groups. When many individuals from different groups marry one another, it indicates that the social distance between groups has diminished or even disappeared. Mexican-American intermarriage rates have always been considered relatively high (Grebler et al. 1970; Murguía 1982; Perlmann and Waters 2004; Rosenfeld 2002), especially considering that immigration continually restocks the pool of potential Mexican-origin marriage partners. Mexican-American respondents in both cities had married people not of Mexican origin (mostly whites) in large numbers, and even when respondents themselves had not intermarried, someone in their family (i.e., their children or their siblings) usually had.

Romantic relationships between Mexican Americans and whites during the time the oldest cohort came of age were virtually unthinkable. The social and economic gulf between Mexican Americans and whites in the past militated against such relationships, and social norms strongly discouraged them. Though some recalled romantic forays with whites during their youth, disapproving parents, most often the white ones, saw to it that any romance was short lived.

Upward mobility and more relaxed attitudes toward intermarriage have made ethnicity a relatively unimportant consideration in how the middle cohort of respondents chose their marriage partners. This was not always the case, however. Though the norms against intermarriage that prevented the oldest cohort of respondents from intermarrying faded with the passage of time, the middle cohort still ran up against these norms. Consider the case of Carl Mercado, a forty-three-year-old salesman in Garden City. Carl had been married twice, both times to white women. He married his first wife in the late 1970s and found that her parents shunned him because of his Mexican background: "The first two years it was basically me and her and my family. Her family pretty much had nothing to do with us. They did not even go to our wedding." Although the family eventually came to accept Carl, his marriage ended in divorce after nineteen years. Carl remarried, and the warm way his new in-laws treated him reflects more open attitudes toward interethnic marriage:

Her parents and her children—everybody accepted me, had no problem whatsoever. First time I met her parents, they both shook my hand. In fact her mother

hugged me. Her sisters hugged me and said, "Glad to meet you," and all that—
real warm. Her family is real, real friendly to me. [I] get along great with her
children and with her family.

If ethnic origin had become a decreasingly important factor in the choice of marriage partners for the middle cohort of respondents, it became virtually a nonfactor for the youngest cohort. Nearly all of the young respondents told me that race and ethnicity were unimportant in choosing a partner, and these beliefs did not stand on principle alone; many had in fact dated and in some cases married individuals not of Mexican origin .

The extent to which intermarriage is common among Mexican Americans and whites in Garden City and Santa Maria is not in any way peculiar. Survey research has shown intermarriage to increase with the more time Mexican-origin people have been in the United States (Landale, Oropesa, and Bradatan 2006; Rosenfeld 2002). Furthermore, Mexican-American intermarriage rates today are on par with those of other immigrant groups from the past (Perlmann and Waters 2004). Sociologist Thomas Macias's examination of intermarriage between people of Mexican and non-Mexican descent shows that it increases with each passing generation and that the factors explaining higher intermarriage rates for Mexican Americans are similar to those for other groups: longer residence in the United States and higher levels of education (2006: chapter 4). Macias also illustrates regional variation in intermarriage patterns, which differ according to the size of the Mexican-origin population from which the marriage partners are drawn. Sociologists Zhenchao Qian and Daniel Lichter (2007) show that intermarriage rates between whites and Latinos declined during the 1990s, because large-scale immigration from Latin America provided a larger pool of Latino marriage partners from which native- and foreign-born Latinos could choose. Indeed, intermarriage between native- and foreign-born Latinos rose during the 1990s. These findings point to the fact that intermarriage is a function of not only individual preferences and the level of discrimination but also potential opportunities to meet marriage partners who are not coethnics (Blau 1977). As the following chapter shows,

Mexican immigrants and second-generation Mexican Americans now constitute a significant part of the "marriage market" in Garden City and Santa Maria, and Mexican Americans do in fact date and even marry their immigrant coethnics. Still, as the interpersonal network data show, Mexican Americans are also embedded in a social structure that creates ample opportunities to date and marry across ethnic lines.

ASSIMILATION AND THE IMPORTANCE OF ETHNIC IDENTITY

The assimilation of European-origin groups points to an inverse relationship between structural assimilation and the importance of ethnic identity. Their structural assimilation contributed to the development of a symbolic form of ethnicity that is largely peripheral to their overall identity. Though white ethnics generally identify with an ethnic ancestry, their generational distance from the point of immigrant origin and the "thinness" of ethnicity in the larger social structure contribute to an ethnic identity that they invoke in largely superficial ways. Furthermore, ethnicity has little bearing on their life chances (Alba 1990; Gans 1979; Waters 1990).

Has structural assimilation led to a declining role of ethnicity in the lives of Mexican Americans? Ethnic identity for Mexican Americans in Garden City and Santa Maria is in some ways reminiscent of the form of ethnic identity witnessed among white ethnics. Each new generation born in the United States inherits fewer signals from the previous generation about the ethnically linked symbols and practices that their immigrant ancestors brought from Mexico: use of the Spanish language declines, observance of Mexican holidays and traditions decreases, knowledge of immigrant roots across generations diminishes, and so do familial and symbolic connections to Mexico. But, as this chapter begins to show (and the next chapter shows in great detail), the continual influx of Mexican immigrants provides an extrafamilial context that is "thick" with Mexican ethnicity, preventing the recession of ethnicity into a purely symbolic form.

Speaking Spanish, but Mostly English

A perennial concern among nativist commentators is that immigrants—
Mexican immigrants in particular—do not learn English and instead remain linguistically isolated from the rest of the U.S. population (Buchanan
2006; Huntington 2004b). While it may be true that the immigrant generation is often slow to pick up English, all evidence points to a Mexican-origin
population that is dramatically more proficient in English with each generation born in the United States, even if bilingualism endures (Rumbaut,
Massey, and Bean 2006; Telles and Ortiz 2008). Theories of language maintenance modeled from the experiences of European immigrants suggest
that use of the immigrant generation's mother tongue weakens with the
passage of each generation and nearly disappears by the third generation
(Fishman 1965, 1972).

These theories partly tell the story of a language shift among Mexican
Americans in Garden City and Santa Maria. In both places, the oldest cohort of respondents generally spoke fluent Spanish. Most of the
respondents explained that they had to speak Spanish in order to communicate with their immigrant parents. They primarily spoke Spanish at
home, and when they started school they had difficulty adjusting to an
environment that was unwelcoming and in some cases downright hostile to non-English speakers. Their lack of English fluency was a source
of ridicule and reprimand, and these painful experiences informed how
they raised their own children. Julie Ayala, a sixty-eight-year-old retired
clerical worker in Santa Maria, provided an explanation typical of many
respondents from the oldest cohort:

*I wish I would have spoken [Spanish] more to my kids. I'm so sorry that I didn't.
[. . .] I don't know why we didn't. I guess because we wanted to make sure that
they wouldn't have a hard time, probably, when they went to school. I remember
when I went to school how hard it was. My mom and dad spoke Spanish, so we
had a hard time.*

These oldest respondents believed eliminating Spanish from their children's linguistic repertoire would help their children gain the acceptance
in U.S. society that Spanish monolinguals lacked. The oldest Mexican

Americans' parenting practices were a response to pressures emanating from an ideology of Americanization, "a consciously articulated movement to strip the immigrant of his native culture and attachments and to make him over into an American along Anglo-Saxon lines" (Gordon 1964: 99).[10] Americanization manifested itself in the lives of Mexican Americans through severe punishment in school for speaking Spanish, an absence of services for a Spanish-speaking population, and a general disdain for the Spanish language.[11]

The middle cohort, at best, received reluctant Spanish-language training from their parents. Yet this reluctance did not yield uniform outcomes among middle-cohort Mexican Americans in the two cities. Tables 7 and 8 show that the Spanish-language abilities declined between the oldest and the middle cohorts in both Garden City and Santa Maria, but more middle-cohort Mexican Americans spoke Spanish well in Santa Maria than in Garden City.

Whereas slightly more than a fifth of middle-cohort Mexican Americans in Garden City reported speaking Spanish well, 68.4 percent of those in Santa Maria reported that they speak Spanish well. The parents of the middle cohort in both locales faced the pressure to Americanize, but in Garden City a hiatus in Mexican immigration after 1940 reduced the opportunities to speak Spanish outside the home. With few Mexican immigrants streaming into Garden City between the 1940s and the 1980s, no infusion of Spanish speakers kept alive what became a dying language during this period. Many respondents recalled believing that speaking Spanish was not only undesirable but also hardly necessary during this time period.[12] The relative utility of speaking Spanish today brings this point to light. As Ronnie Hinojosa, a forty-eight-year-old salesperson in Garden City, explained:

My mom and dad said they didn't know what the future holds for us, but they wanted to make sure we knew English a lot better, since we had to live here. My dad said, "If you want to learn Spanish, go back to Mexico and learn. But right here in the United States, you speak English." That's the way my folks grew us up. Now as times change, they want you to take Spanish, they want you to have three languages. [. . .] But boy, would I give anything to know Spanish real well like [Mexican immigrants] do.

Table 7.   Mexican-American Respondents in Garden City Who Speak Spanish Well,
by Cohort

(%)

	Speak Spanish Well	Speak Spanish Poorly or No Spanish
Oldest cohort (56 and older) ($n = 18$)	100.0 (18)	0.0 (0)
Middle cohort (36–55) ($n = 14$)	21.4 (3)	78.6 (11)
Youngest cohort (15–35) ($n = 28$)	10.7 (3)	89.3 (25)
All respondents ($n = 60$)	40.0 (24)	60.0 (36)

SOURCE: Data collected from Garden City.

Table 8.   Mexican-American Respondents in Santa Maria Who Speak Spanish Well,
by Cohort

(%)

	Speak Spanish Well	Speak Spanish Poorly or No Spanish
Oldest cohort (56 and older) ($n = 21$)	85.7 (18)	14.3 (3)
Middle cohort (36–55) ($n = 19$)	68.4 (13)	31.6 (6)
Youngest cohort (15–35) ($n = 23$)	13.0 (3)	87.0 (20)
All respondents ($n = 63$)	54.0 (34)	46.0 (29)

SOURCE: Data collected from Santa Maria.

The experiences of Mexican Americans in Garden City are roughly
similar to those of descendants of European origin groups after the
1930s. Much like Mexican immigration to Garden City in the first half
of the twentieth century, European immigration slowed to a trickle
after 1930, reducing the opportunities of the second and third generations to speak the language of the immigrant generation. Sociologist
Richard Alba explains: "The fall-off in immigration weakened the hold
of the mother tongues, even in the immigrant homes where the second-
generation was raised. This weakening hints at larger contextual effects
on language retention—changes in ethnic communities and institutions

resulting from the ending of the influx of immigrants fresh from the homeland" (1988: 223).

In contrast, Santa Maria has experienced a steady influx of Mexican immigrants, creating ample opportunities for respondents there to retain their use of Spanish. Even if Americanization bred reluctance among parents to pass on Spanish to their children, the constant influx of Mexican immigrants provided regular occasions to build on a rudimentary base of Spanish established inside the home. The case of Ana Fernández, a third-generation, forty-seven-year-old grammar school teacher in Santa Maria, illustrates the point. Ana spoke mostly English at home when she was growing up but spoke a small amount of Spanish in order to communicate with her grandfather: "Growing up, my grandfather spoke Spanish, and we were expected to speak Spanish to him. But our Spanish was pretty lousy." Despite learning little Spanish at home, her ability to speak the language markedly improved in college, where she took several Spanish-language classes. After college she took a job as the migrant education teacher in a grammar school in nearby Guadalupe, a town with a large Mexican-immigrant population. It was during that time that Ana's Spanish transitioned from a "classroom" variety to fluency.

Spanish-language maintenance patterns among Garden City's and Santa Maria's youngest respondents are similar, at around 11 and 13 percent, respectively. The youngest respondents in Garden City said that their inability to speak Spanish was rooted in the experiences of their parents and grandparents. Juan Serrano, a twenty-year-old Garden City college student, told me,

My great-grandma would tell my grandma, "This is America. You need to learn the ways of the Americans, and the Spanish language shouldn't be used here in America." So that's pretty much how my parents . . . my mom didn't learn Spanish, because my great-grandma told my grandma that. So that's pretty much how I don't speak Spanish now.

The cessation of Spanish speaking among earlier generations all but ensured that later generations would not learn the language from their parents or grandparents.

In Santa Maria, where most of the youngest respondents were third or fourth generation, the youngest cohorts of respondents tended not to speak Spanish despite the fluency of many of their parents. Their parents spoke primarily English at home and perhaps occasionally used the mother tongue of their immigrant ancestors. Interviews with the youngest respondents suggest that the assimilative inertia of generational progression within families was simply too great for their Spanish-language abilities to flourish, at least at a young age. It is important to note that many middle-cohort respondents in Santa Maria learned Spanish or improved on their existing ability to speak Spanish outside their parents' home in their early adult years, as was the case with Ana Fernández, the grammar school teacher in Santa Maria. Possibly the young respondents in both cities, like the middle cohort in Santa Maria, will learn much of their Spanish outside the home and eventually gain some degree of bilingualism (see Linton and Jiménez 2009). What is more certain, however, is that without a large immigrant population, the youngest Mexican-American respondents would likely have had an even weaker grasp of Spanish. Indeed, the large immigrant population in Garden City and especially in Santa Maria had allowed the youngest Mexican Americans to form friendships (both romantic and platonic) with Mexican immigrants and second-generation Mexican Americans, who imparted some Spanish. As I show in the next chapter, several of the youngest respondents said that their Spanish-speaking friends or a significant other had taught them some Spanish, helping to stave off its full disappearance.

Mexican Customs in Daily Life

Sociologists have firmly established that, for European-origin groups, the ethnically linked symbols and practices of the immigrant generation are thinned with each successive generation, eventually becoming merely a symbolic part of life for the later generations (Alba 1990; Waters 1990). Later-generation individuals may speak a few words of their immigrant ancestors' native tongue and invoke ethnicity through food and holidays, but these are largely token gestures. While ethnicity is not entirely optional for Mexican Americans in Garden City and Santa Maria (for reasons that I explain in chapter 5), most respondents had selectively incorporated Mexican ethnic customs into their everyday lives in ways similar to later-generation individuals from other ethnic groups (Tuan 1998; Waters 1990). Family gatherings, holiday celebrations, and food are primary ways that Mexican Americans maintain a connection to their ethnic roots.

Several respondents told me that having a large and relatively close-knit family was a way in which their Mexican ethnic background was manifested in their daily lives. Tracy Harris, a fifty-nine-year-old retired fashion consultant, believed that the closeness of Mexican families sets them apart from other families: "Well, our culture is different. Our families are really close knit. There's a lot of respect, at least among this family." Mexican Americans are not alone in identifying the importance of family as a distinctive trait of their ethnic identity. Pointing to the closeness of the family appears to be a fallback when other ethnically linked behaviors are lacking. Individuals from many groups explain the closeness of their family by invoking ethnicity, as Mary Waters's (1990) study of later-generation white ethnics shows.

Ethnic customs and practices can take on particular importance during holidays, with Americans celebrating them according to the traditions of their own ethnic origins. In some cases, however, Americans celebrate holidays that have been made popular by immigrants and their descendants but have no connection to the celebrants' own ethnic origins (Saint Patrick's Day, for example). Using survey data, Telles and Ortiz (2008) have found that at least 52 percent of Mexican Americans, regardless of generational status, celebrate at least one Mexican holiday but that, on average, they celebrate no more than one Mexican holiday. These findings suggest that, as far as holidays go, the practice of ethnicity is a part of the lives of Mexican Americans even in the later generations. Key to understanding the link between holidays and ethnic identity is analyzing *how* Mexican Americans celebrate Mexican holidays. Among the Mexican Americans I interviewed, some could not think of anything about the way they celebrated holidays that reflected their ethnic background, and many others mentioned only the presence of Mexican food. For example, a large number of respondents mentioned getting together with family to make tamales during Christmas and New Year's celebrations but said that they celebrated other "American" holidays in ways similar to non-Mexicans. Likewise, recognizably ethnic traditions made only minor appearances at family celebrations; birthdays and weddings, for example, only occasionally featured a piñata or Mexican food. A number of respondents said that they might hire mariachis to play at a wedding, anniversary party, or birthday celebration for an older member of the family, but these events were rare.

When it came to celebrating Mexican holidays, the people I interviewed did so sporadically and often in a form that scarcely resembled practices in Mexico. People of Mexican origin in the United States generally celebrate two major Mexican holidays, El Dieciséis de Septiembre (September 16), which honors Mexico's independence from Spain, and Cinco de Mayo (May 5), which marks the Mexican victory over the French army in the 1862 Battle of Puebla. While Cinco de Mayo is much more widely celebrated in the United States, Mexican Americans in Garden City have celebrated El Dieciséis, in what is known around town simply as "the Fiesta," since the 1920s. The celebration involves crowning a Fiesta queen, live music, a parade down Main Street, and a concert and dance during the evening. The Fiesta has come to represent the day when virtually all of Garden City's Mexican Americans (and many non-Mexicans) celebrate Mexican ethnicity, and for many it is the only public celebration of Mexican ethnicity in which they participate.[13]

Santa Maria, on the other hand, has no citywide celebration of El Dieciséis or Cinco de Mayo, and virtually none of the Santa Maria Mexican Americans I interviewed celebrated either of these holidays. I attended two Cinco de Mayo events in Santa Maria in order to get a sense of who celebrates and how. The first event was sponsored by a local Spanish-language radio station and took place at a nearby rodeo arena. The event featured Mexican-food booths and music performed by Mexican bands. Spanish was the dominant, if not the only, language heard at the event. Nearly all of the people in attendance were Spanish-speaking, and I presumed them to be Mexican immigrants on the basis of their style of dress and the fact that they spoke only Spanish. The second Cinco de Mayo celebration I attended took place at a local bar and grill. In contrast with the event at the rodeo arena, which seemed strongly connected to the original

Mexican holiday, this celebration seemed to be driven much more by corporate sponsorship. The bar and grill put on a commercialized celebration, displaying several Corona-brand beer posters and festive Mexican-style streamers that boasted, "Cinco de mayo Central!" The celebration featured a live band playing primarily American funk music from the 1970s and 1980s, discounted tequila-based drinks, and Mexican beer and food. The ethnically mixed crowd was entirely English-speaking. Aside from the food and drink, how this celebration of Cinco de Mayo related to the origins of the holiday was not clear. Several informants later told me that Mexican Americans are more apt to celebrate Cinco de Mayo by participating in events such as the one put on by the local bar and grill, if they celebrate it at all.

Severed Connections to Mexico and the Thinning of Historical Memory

In recent years social scientists have paid special attention to the enduring ties that immigrants have to their homeland. The increase in immigration to the United States since 1965 and the ease of travel and cross-national communication have facilitated the maintenance of ties between the United States and sending communities (Basch, Schiller, and Szanton Blanc 1994; Levitt 2001; Portes, Guarnizo, and Landolt 1999; Smith 2005a). These connections infuse immigrants in destination countries, and perhaps even the second generation there, with ways of life found in the countries of origin, and immigrants in destination communities use them to influence life in their homelands (Levitt 2001; Smith 2005a). Many, however, have questioned the durability of transnationalism beyond the immigrant generation. Evidence from studies of the second generation suggests that transnationalism is not a persistent phenomenon beyond the first generation (Kasinitz et al. 2002; Rumbaut 2002), though others argue that transnational ties change across generations but nonetheless endure (Levitt 2002).

Mexicans would seem to be the likeliest of immigrant groups to maintain such ties because of the close proximity of Mexico to the United States and also because of the long history of migration between these two countries. But evidence among Mexican Americans in Garden City and Santa Maria lends support to the notion that transnationalism attenuates over time. Nearly all of the Mexican Americans I interviewed had lost contact with family in Mexico, and any ties that still existed had become progressively weaker with the passage of time. The overwhelming majority of Garden City and Santa Maria respondents who had some contact with relatives in Mexico belonged to the oldest cohort. A number of these Mexican Americans, generally from the second generation, recalled visiting relatives in Mexico when they were younger but losing contact as time passed. Only a few said that they still had family in Mexico whom they knew or had visited. Communication and visits with family tend to be one-time events or at least sporadic. With few exceptions, most of the middle and youngest cohort of respondents had no communication with relatives in Mexico and did not know of any relatives there. Many had never visited Mexico, and those who had visited knew only the popular tourist destinations and towns along the border. Mike Fernández, a nineteen-year-old college student in Santa Maria, reflected on his travels to Mexico, which were confined to popular vacation destinations: "I've been to, like, Rosarito Beach and Ensenada and Tijuana, and I've been to Puerto Vallarta and seen those types of places [. . .] but those are the places tourists go." Respondents told me that visits to these locales failed to capture an authentic experience of Mexican life precisely because they are touristy and commercialized. Emily Strong, a seventeen-year-old high school senior in Garden City, spoke enthusiastically about her upcoming trip to Cancún, knowing full well that the tourist destination may offer only a superficial experience of her ethnic homeland: "Senior trip to Cancún—that's when I'm going to Mexico. Not really that it's a taste of Mexico, because that's just vacationers' paradise, but that's where I'm headed!" The loss of ties with family in Mexico does not mean that Mexican Americans' connection to their ethnic homeland is entirely severed, however. As the next chapter shows, immigrant spouses and friends occasionally help reconnect them to the country of their immigrant ancestors.

As generations progress and contact with Mexico wanes, so too does the respondents' knowledge of their immigrant ancestors. While Mexican Americans are aware that immigration is generally a part of

their own family history, the specifics of their family's immigrant narrative become fuzzier and in many cases completely fade over time.
The oldest cohort of Garden City and Santa Maria respondents were
the primary bearers of family-immigrant history. They were generally familiar with where their immigrant ancestors had come from
in Mexico, when their ancestors had come to the United States, and
why. Their extensive contact with the immigrant generation through
which family history was communicated had given them an expertise
that most later-generation Mexican Americans lacked. For the middle
cohort, knowledge of familial immigrant history had weakened among
Garden City Mexican Americans. In most cases, the middle cohort in
Garden City had only a vague idea about their families' immigrant
history while displaying much more familiarity with the experiences
that have defined Mexican Americans in the United States in general
and in Garden City in particular. Mexican-American respondents in
Garden City had built a distinctly Mexican *American* narrative revolv-
ing around the struggles of the oldest cohort to overcome poverty and
discrimination in order to create opportunities for Mexican Americans
today. Respondents in Garden City recited this narrative as if it were a
mantra of their history. The description that Kyle Gil, a thirty-five-year-
old auto body shop owner in Garden City, illustrates this narrative:

*My grandparents really fought hard here in the community, along with lots of
other people, for the Hispanic community. So I think that's always been in the
back of my mind. They worked hard to get where they're at.*

Yet they were almost entirely unfamiliar with the details of their immigrant origins or the experiences their immigrant ancestor may have had
in Mexico. What little historical knowledge they possessed was specula-
tive. The fuzziness expressed by one Garden City Mexican American in
response to my question about his family's immigrant history highlights
how most Garden City respondents recalled their immigrant origins:

*[sigh] You know, that would be years ago. It would have been my dad's family,
they came in . . . he had a bunch of brothers and, I think, one older sister that had
came in, [thinking to himself] oh God, back in the twenties and thirties. They
basically had come to work into the fieldwork, farmwork type scenarios—that
was all my dad's side.*

While the middle cohort in Garden City spoke in vague terms about their immigrant roots, the same cohort in Santa Maria invoked a Mexican-American narrative that is more steeped in the immigrant experience. They were far more familiar with the nitty-gritty details of their immigrant ancestors' migration and settlement. Their knowledge of family history had benefited from conversations with immigrant relatives (who were in many cases grandparents), and their parents had passed down the information from the immigrant generation during dinner-table conversations and family gatherings. While no definitive explanation for the differences between Garden City and Santa Maria respondents emerges from the interviews, the contrast may owe to the different historical patterns of immigration to Garden City and Santa Maria. In Santa Maria, where Mexican immigration remained steady throughout the twentieth century, the presence of Mexican immigrants has activated the immigrant experience as central to the Mexican-American narrative and as integral to Mexican-American identity. Not only was knowing that their family had come from Mexico important to the middle cohort, but so was knowing other details about that immigrant experience, such as how many generations one's family has been in the United States. This knowledge helped middle-cohort Santa Maria respondents situate themselves in the Santa Maria social milieu, which has always been a mix of whites, Mexican Americans, and Mexican immigrants. Middle-cohort respondents in Garden City, on the other hand, had developed a distinctly *American* understanding of the Mexican-American experience, because when they came of age no substantial Mexican-immigrant population existed to sensitize them to nativity-based distinctions among people of Mexican descent.

A look at the youngest respondents in Garden City lends support to this hypothesis. Not surprisingly, they knew little about their immigrant ancestors. However, some of these young respondents mentioned that they were curious to find out more, and this curiosity had been spurred by Mexican-immigrant and second-generation acquaintances. As Diana Bautista, an eighteen-year-old high school senior in Garden City, said, "I tend to want to know more about [my background] because of other people who have come from Mexico." The recent influx of Mexican immigrants had activated a curiosity about her immigrant roots that may not have existed for individuals who were her parents' age, because they had no similar immigrant reference group. Still, family history was primarily rooted in the United States for the youngest Garden City respondents, such as Kate Lebron, a twenty seven-year-old teacher, who told me, "I never heard any stories about how they came over. All I heard was what happened once they got here."

The youngest Santa Maria respondents had a slightly better grasp of their family's immigrant history, but it was still fairly vague. In most cases, the youngest Santa Marians knew where their immigrant ancestors had come from on at least one side of their family but were unsure of the details of their journey. Like the language divide, the generational chasm between these youngest respondents and their immigrant ancestors had led to the loss of much family history. However, the large Mexican-immigrant population had sensitized these youngest Mexican-American respondents in ways that may yet spur them to develop a keen interest in their immigrant roots, a point that becomes clearer in the next chapter.

Mexican Americans in Garden City and Santa Maria are by no means a group relegated to the economic, social, and political margins. Nor do they exhibit any sort of ethnic nationalism that keeps them from identifying with the United States. Far from it. They display significant structural assimilation as measured by socioeconomic status, residential location, participation in civic life and social cliques, and levels of intermarriage. The findings from Garden City and Santa Maria combined with survey research on Mexican Americans nationwide should help allay fears that Mexican Americans are not integrating themselves into U.S. society. It should also help put to rest concerns that Mexican Americans are experiencing insurmountable obstacles to mobility resulting in their status as members of a "rainbow underclass." Of course, as much of the survey research shows, Mexican Americans have not caught up to native-born whites among the structural measures of assimilation. Nonetheless, the degree to which they have experienced structural assimilation is quite remarkable considering the high degree of discrimination they faced for much of the twentieth century. The structural assimilation of Mexican Americans has also weakened the hold that ethnicity has on how parents raise their children. Over time, the use of the Spanish language diminishes, ethnic customs play a decreasingly important role in family life, and the ties that Mexican Americans have to their ethnic homeland diminish.

In many respects, these patterns of assimilation are reminiscent of those found among later-generation European-origin individuals. But the canonical view of assimilation that explained the European-origin experience does not fully capture what takes place with later-generation Mexican-Americans. These accounts of immigrant assimilation mostly take for granted that immigration wanes, leading each new generation born in the United States to diminished contact with immigrants fresh from the ethnic homeland. While the Mexican-American experience told from the canonical perspective may appear like a "classic" story of assimilation in many respects, the replenishment of a Mexican-immigrant population radically alters any further resemblance. Indeed, Mexican-American and European-origin assimilation patterns appear far less analogous when taking account of the ways in which Mexican-immigrant replenishment provides opportunities to engage in the practice of ethnicity.

FOUR Replenishing Mexican Ethnicity

Mexican Americans' structural assimilation and the intergenerational decline of ethnic traditions and customs within the family do not lead to a purely symbolic form of ethnic identity, as canonical theories of assimilation predict. Instead, immigrant replenishment provides a sun that staves off the twilight of ethnicity among later-generation Mexican Americans. The large Mexican-immigrant and second-generation populations have made Mexican ethnicity a prominent part of the social structure in these two cities, and ethnicity is a more accessible and salient aspect of Mexican Americans' social identity as a result.

The social "construction" of racial and ethnic categories and their corresponding identities is virtually taken for granted; these are not biological or "natural" aspects of social life. Rather, they result from human interaction and are shaped by social, political, and economic processes. Much of the recent theorizing of race and ethnicity has focused on the social construction of the boundaries that define groups and that enclose the "ethnic stuff" commonly referred to as culture. Scholars have illuminated the ways in which boundaries shift and are crossed and blurred (Alba 2005b; Alba and Nee 2003), the varying character and consequences of ethnic boundaries (Wimmer 2008b), as well as the ways in which individuals change ethnic boundaries (Wimmer 2008a). Boundaries are indeed important for understanding racial and ethnic change, but we cannot fully understand ethnic identity by focusing exclusively on boundaries. The expression of ethnic culture—art, music, food, language, style of dress, holidays, and so forth—is also central to the construction of ethnic identity. Ethnic boundaries and the culture they enclose are two sides of the ethnic coin; thus, considering both the cultural content of ethnicity and the ethnic boundaries that delineate groups is important. As sociologist Joane Nagel notes, culture "provides the content and meaning of ethnicity; it animates and authenticates ethnic boundaries by providing a history, ideology, symbolic universe and system of meaning. Culture answers the question: What are we?" (1997: 162). In this chapter I examine how ongoing Mexican immigration shapes Mexican Americans' answer to this question, by focusing on how Mexican Americans express their ethnic identity. In chapter 5 I turn to the other side of the ethnic coin by exploring how immigrant replenishment shapes ethnic boundaries.

If racial and ethnic identities are constructed (and I argue that they are), then the strength of attachment that people have to an identity rooted in ethnicity depends in large part on the availability of ethnically linked resources for their construction of that identity. As Richard Alba notes, "Groups that have a greater supply of cultural resources provide their members with more material to stimulate a sense of identity. Conversely, these groups also depend on that sense of identity; without it, the critical mass necessary to maintain the ethnic cultural supply would dissipate" (1990: 121). The cultural resources to which Alba refers can be thought of as "ethnic raw materials"—ethnically linked symbols and practices—that are necessary for the construction of a salient ethnic identity. If ethnic raw materials are lacking, then ethnic identity takes on a purely symbolic form and is not well integrated into an individual's overall identity. But if ethnic raw materials are in abundant supply, then the possibility of constructing an ethnic identity that is more central to an individual's identity increases. The experience of Mexican Americans shows that even if the ethnic raw materials are not passed down from the immigrant generation to the later generations within the family, Mexican immigration provides ample ethnic raw materials that help Mexican Americans construct an ethnic identity that is more central to their overall identity.

This chapter explains both the micro- and macroprocesses through which Mexican immigration provides Mexican Americans opportunities to engage in the practice of ethnicity. It shows how opportunities to access ethnic raw materials ultimately contributed to a more salient ethnic identity for the people I interviewed. Everyday interactions with Mexican immigrants and second-generation Mexican Americans allowed respondents abundant access to the symbols and practices associated with Mexican ethnicity. The presence of a large Mexican-immigrant population also provided more abundant and more frequent opportunities for them to feel connected to an ethnic identity through ethnicity's infusion into religion, civic organizations, mass media, and the cuisine that Mexican Americans access.

More than just demographic shifts act on Mexican Americans' ethnic identity. Larger ideological changes have made ethnicity a more desirable aspect of social identity. Long gone are the days when Americanization stood as the dominant ideology guiding nonwhites' forced homogenization. Instead, Americanization now stands alongside the formidable ideological contender of multiculturalism, which values, however superficially in some cases, a strong connection to one's ethnic origins. This multicultural ideology helps lift the stigma placed on Mexican ethnicity, making it a desirable and even a rewarding aspect of identity for Mexican Americans.

MEXICAN IMMIGRATION AND ETHNIC RAW MATERIALS IN THE SOCIAL STRUCTURE

The social structure in which Mexican Americans are embedded is replete with a Mexican-immigrant population that provides them with abundant opportunities to engage in the practice of ethnicity. Casual contact with Mexican immigrants in public spaces and in the workplace primarily strengthens Mexican Americans' ability to speak Spanish, and friendships and romantic relationships with immigrants and the second generation bring opportunities for Mexican Americans to engage in an array of ethnic practices closer to home. These relationships exposed the people I interviewed to holidays, cuisine, and other ties to Mexico that would not have existed had it not been for a large Mexican-immigrant population. Mexican Americans need not have direct interaction with immigrants to experience greater exposure to Mexican ethnicity. Immigration from their ethnic homeland injects heavy doses of ethnicity into the broader community, including churches, schools, restaurants, grocery stores, and mass media, providing Mexican Americans opportunities to partake in ethnically linked practices that make ethnicity more central to their identity.

Accessing Raw Materials through Casual Interactions

Unlike urban locales, where ethnic and racial segregation reaches into virtually every aspect of social life, the small size of Garden City means that Garden Citians from all backgrounds routinely mix. Even if Mexican immigrants live in neighborhoods separate from the town's middle- and upper-class populations, all residents interact at the one YMCA, the two major grocery stores, the one high school, and a handful of banks, restaurants, and retail stores. Santa Maria is larger than Garden City, and therefore Santa Maria's various populations can more easily exist in isolation from one another. Santa Maria has three high schools (two public and one private), several major recreational centers, many parks, grocery stores, and a multitude of banks and retail stores. Nonetheless, Santa Maria is a far cry from segregated urban centers like Los Angeles and Chicago, and so Mexican Americans and Mexican immigrants frequently mix.

Thus, in both Garden City and Santa Maria, Mexican Americans frequently interact with their immigrant coethnics during casual and unplanned encounters, which provide regular opportunities to participate in the practice of ethnicity, especially in the form of Spanish-language use. The failure of Mexican-American parents to pass on Spanish to the next generation, reported in the previous chapter, does not ensure that Spanish is altogether lost. Casual interactions with Mexican immigrants prevent it from receding into the distant background of Mexican Americans' ethnic identity. Mexican Americans who already speak Spanish often help immigrants negotiate English-dominant settings by providing driving directions, interpreting for a service clerk, or helping them read signs posted in English. Margie Solís, a sixty-year-old homemaker in Garden City, whose husband was born in the United States but raised in Mexico, said that such instances had been a routine part of her life:

If somebody speaks to me in Spanish, I speak to them back in Spanish. Or if we go to McDonald's or places of business, sometimes you need to. I've been asked to help somebody when they don't understand and translate for them. Like at [the grocery store], when I'm there at the grocery store or anywhere. If they ask me, I'll help.

Virtually all Mexican Americans conduct the daily business of their lives in English. For most it is their primary language at home and in public. This all changes when they interact with Mexican immigrants in public, however. A trip to the grocery store, a visit to the bank, or a trip to the local park can become a de facto Spanish-language immersion experience in which Mexican immigrants enable respondents to brush up on or even bolster their Spanish-language abilities.

Another arena that provides Mexican Americans with opportunities to use Spanish is workplaces where they have frequent contact with Mexican immigrants. Even those respondents who had only a limited foundation on which to build Spanish fluency found that their interactions with Mexican immigrants at work dramatically improved their ability to speak the language. Consider the case of Alexandra Pettite, a thirty-four-year-old office manager in Garden City. Alexandra did not speak Spanish at home while she was growing up, but as a child she was accustomed to hearing her parents speak the language. One of her first jobs was at the local beef-packing plant, where she worked alongside many Mexican-immigrant coworkers. Because of her job at the plant, her Spanish showed dramatic improvement: "I worked out at [the beef plant], and that really made me have to practice [Spanish] and use it and not be embarrassed that I was saying something wrong. And it just got better and better." At the time of my research, Alexandra was employed with the school district, where she prepared recently arrived immigrants to enter school. Her hiring for this job had had much to do with her ability to converse in both Spanish and English, and her frequent interactions with Mexican immigrants at work had only strengthened her near-perfect bilingualism.

At home, Spanish may form a symbolic aspect of linguistic life that includes a few occasionally used words or phrases. Even when Mexican Americans do not regularly speak Spanish at home, the presence of a large immigrant population prompts them to do so in their public lives. Elena Bradley, a forty-six-year-old second-grade teacher in Santa Maria, lived in Orcutt, a wealthy subsection to the south of Santa Maria, where very few Mexican immigrants reside. Opportunities for Elena to speak Spanish were few and far between at home. Her husband was also Mexican American but spoke virtually no Spanish, and Elena had heard Spanish when she was a child but only occasionaly spoke the language at home. Yet daily interactions with her immigrant students and their parents had provided ample opportunities for her to sharpen her Spanish-language skills. Prior to my interview with Elena, I looked on as she conducted a parent-teacher conference with the father of one of her students. The father was a dark-skinned Mexican immigrant who had been working in the fields all day. He wore a dusty, hooded sweatshirt and heavily soiled jeans that were stained with what appeared to be strawberry juice. He and Elena sat crunched into seats made for people half their size, and Elena spoke to the man with a Spanish that did not quite match his fluency but nonetheless showed her comfort in conversing in the langauge. She noted that his son had improved his math skills but was not doing so well in English. Elena later explained that although she was not allowed to conduct her lessons in Spanish because of state laws prohibiting bilingual education,[1] she routinely used Spanish to clarify a point to her students, and she almost exclusively spoke Spanish to the parents of her students.

In many cases, Mexican Americans learn Spanish during adult-hood only because they have a good deal of interaction with Mexican immigrants. Julie Ayala, a sixty-eight-year-old retired clerical worker, explained that her son was fluent even though she and her husband did not speak the language at home:

[He learns Spanish] from his workers, because he has a drywall business. So his workers, a lot of them speak Spanish. So in order to communicate, he picked up a lot from them. And still . . . he's come a long way, because now he can make himself understood and he can communicate with them, no problem.

The experiences that these Mexican Americans had in speaking Spanish at work typify those of other respondents. Mexican-American law-enforcement officials, teachers, coaches, retail clerks, pastors, secretaries, and nurses all reported that their use of Spanish at work helped them maintain and build on their Spanish-speaking abilities. As many respondents explained, they did not have to look for opportunities to speak Spanish. These opportunities often found them.

Certainly some Mexican Americans are selected for jobs because of their bilingual abilities. The large immigrant population creates a demand in the labor market for bilingual workers, particularly in jobs that require face-to-face interactions between customers and employees (Waldinger and Lichter 2003). This demand is reflected in the numerous job postings that specifically ask for applicants who possess some measure of Spanish-English bilingualism. Even if Mexican Americans enter these jobs with a small degree of Spanish fluency, their everyday use of the language prevents its atrophy and allows them to engage regularly in a practice widely recognized as central to Mexican ethnicity.

The influence that Mexican-immigrant replenishment had on language use among later-generation Mexican-American respondents in Garden City and Santa Maria appears to play out in large metro areas too. Analyzing metropolitan areas using U.S. Census data, April Linton and I (2009) show that an increase in the Latino foreign-born population between 1990 and 2000 positively influences the percentage of U.S.-born and 1.5.-generation Latinos who are bilingual, even when accounting for other factors. Clearly, bilingualism is not becoming the norm, and use of the Spanish language tends to decline with the passing of generations (Rumbaut, Massey, and Bean 2006). But ongoing immigration is also reducing some of that decline, making bilingualism a reality for some later-generation Mexican Americans.

Ethnic Raw Materials Passed through Friendships

More significant encounters make language and other ethnic symbols and practices increasingly accessible to Mexican Americans. They often form close friendships with immigrants and the children of immigrants, through which they engage in ethnically linked practices that have grown more difficult to find in their own families. Mexican Americans generally form friendships not with the most recently arrived Mexican immigrants but instead with Mexican immigrants who have been in the United States for long periods of time and have gained some socioeconomic advancement. Since later-generation Mexican Americans are, broadly speaking, middle class, Mexican immigrants and Mexican Americans are likely to establish friendships when they share a similar class status.

The youngest respondents (ages fifteen to thirty-five) were especially likely to form such friendships because the large Mexican-immigrant and second-generation populations are generally young. Schools in Garden City and Santa Maria are a mix of Mexican Americans, Mexican immigrants, and whites and places where friendships among members of all three groups form. The youngest Mexican Americans I interviewed often mentioned that these friendships sparked in them an interest in their ethnic ancestry that might not have existed if not for the large immigrant population. Annalisa Garza, a fifteen-year-old high school student in Garden City, noted,

[E]ven though I don't know what part of Mexico I'm from, I do know things about myself, things about my family. [. . .] And to be able to talk to somebody about that, I can relate to stories of their own. It's great. And if you didn't have [Mexican immigration], then you probably wouldn't be asking your parents questions: "Where? Why? What happened to so and so? So where is Uncle Whatever?" You wouldn't have any questions if you didn't have anybody [from Mexico] to talk to.

The presence of Mexican immigrants makes the immigrant experience a widely recognized aspect of a Mexican-American narrative and one that young later-generation respondents wanted to understand in order to weave it into their own ethnic identity. Friendships that extended across generational lines piqued young respondents' curiosity about their own immigrant past and their ethnic roots and spurred them to become more familiar with the Spanish language and the Mexican customs and tradi- tions that their families had lost long ago.

The network ties that Mexican Americans have to those closer to the immigrant generation give them a chance to do just this. Friendships with Mexican immigrants and their children had resurrected and in some cases given birth to Mexican traditions in the lives of Mexican- American respondents. Speaking in general terms about the influence his Mexican-immigrant and second-generation friends had on his ethnic identity, Eric Garza (no relation to Annalisa), a seventeen-year-old high school student in Garden City, commented,

[S]ome families that [immigrated] here just recently—they're a lot more in touch with their heritage, and they celebrate a lot more things that they probably would down in Mexico. And some of the things here,[. . .] families that have been here for generations kind of lost touch with those [aspects of our heritage]. I mean you see families like this, and I guess it kind of brings the heritage back into you sometimes. [. . .] Like in probably elementary school and middle school, most of the people I hung out with were all Caucasian. [I]t's not that I wasn't really in touch with my heritage; it's just that I really didn't know that much about it. And then when I started meeting a lot more friends [whose] families came up from Mexico recently, or they're really in touch with [their heritage], they start getting me interested in it. I am really starting to get in touch with my heritage, I guess you could say—basically like just celebrations of holidays and things like that.

The youngest respondents I interviewed recognized just how much various ethnic practices had faded within their own family, but they pointed out that their friendship ties to immigrants and second- generation Mexicans had reversed the evaporation of some of those practices. As Angel de Guzmán, a twenty-year-old operation intern in Santa Maria, noted,

Sometimes you get away from the old traditions, and some of them forget, but the elders never forget. But the newer generation do. [. . .] But [Mexican immigrants] come over here, it's like they're [. . .] bringing back the history, and it's like they're replenishing the next generation that almost forgets. So they kind of help us. They help the newer kids remember [our ethnic heritage].

Mexican Americans describe in more concrete terms how friendships with Mexican immigrants and second-generation Mexican Americans provide opportunities to engage the practice of ethnicity. Mexican Americans' ethnic identity is not merely an empty vessel that Mexican immigrants fill with ethnic stuff. In some ways, Mexican immigration redefines the content of Mexican ethnicity by introducing traditions that were never a part of Mexican Americans' repertoire of ethnic customs. Such is the case with the *quinceañera,* a coming-of-age event for Mexican-origin girls when they turn fifteen. *Quinceañeras* involve an elaborate celebration that includes a Catholic Mass, a large reception, and a court made up of friends and family that accompany the young woman for whom the *quinceañera* is celebrated. The growth of the Latino-immigrant and second-generation populations has brought about a boom in the number of *quinceañeras* and, with the boom, a growing recognition of the event in mainstream society.[2] The Mexican Americans I interviewed had never had *quinceañeras* in their own families, and their knowledge of this celebration and participation in it were entirely a product of its introduction by Mexican immigrants and second-generation Mexican Americans. Diana Bautista, in Garden City, noted that participating in her friend's *quinceañera* had led her to want to incorporate the celebration into her own life: "When I was a freshman, I did want a *quinceañera,* and I would have never wanted one unless I'd been around one or had been in one." Mexican Americans' participation in events like the *quinceañera* gives them the chance to connect with the cultural practices associated with her ethnic origins.

As with the oldest and middle cohort of respondents, immigrant and second-generation friends also helped the youngest cohort of my Mexican-American respondents resurrect a Spanish language that had been lost in their own family. While very few of the youngest respondents were fluent (recall from tables 7 and 8 that only about 11 and 13 percent of the youngest respondents in Garden City and Santa Maria, respectively, spoke Spanish well), their friendships helped them build a base of Spanish-language ability that would not have existed without these intergenerational ties. The youngest Mexican Americans I interviewed said that their friendship with Mexican-immigrant and second-generation individuals had provided opportunities to learn Spanish that they might otherwise have accessed only in a classroom setting. In some cases, Mexican-American and Mexican-immigrant friends helped cultivate Spanish-English bilingualism in one another. Kate Pacheco, an eighteen-year-old cosmetology student in Garden City, is a case in point. Her friendship with Mexican-born classmates helped refresh her Spanish-language skills and sometimes introduced her to new Spanish words and phrases:

We kind of teach each other what we don't know. So it's pretty fun, and I like it. They won't make fun of me or nothing because I don't know everything. But they try to teach me [Spanish]. If I don't know what they're saying, they'll just translate it for me.

Likewise, Faith Obregón, a sixteen-year-old high school student in Garden City, had Mexican-immigrant classmates who were eager to help her learn Spanish:

This girl in my algebra class, she was speaking it to me, and I was like, "I don't understand Spanish." She's just like, "You don't?!" So now every time I see her and we talk, she talks to me in Spanish, because she wants to help me learn. And she'll tell me what stuff means. And if I ask her a question about my Spanish homework, she'll help me.

Respondents' interactions with immigrants and second-generation Mexican Americans were not unequivocally positive or negative when it came to language. It is important to note that language often marks the boundaries of group identity, serving as a powerful indicator of who is an authentic member and who is not (see Menchaca 1995; Ochoa 2004). Mexican Americans who speak no Spanish find these same encounters to be painful reminders of the sharp boundaries between Mexican

Americans and Mexican immigrants, a topic I discuss in more detail in the next chapter.

The youngest Mexican-American respondents displayed a degree of comfort and familiarity with the presence of Mexican customs and Spanish language, because they were woven into a larger youth culture in Garden City and Santa Maria. The middle and oldest cohorts of respondents, however, did not uniformly experience this same comfort and familiarity. Garden City's Mexican-immigration hiatus during the middle of the twentieth century left the middle and oldest cohorts of Mexican Americans few opportunities to experience the same access to Mexican culture that the youngest cohort reported. Virtually no opportunities existed to speak Spanish outside the home, and certainly no Mexican-immigrant or second-generation friends were available to help them access a more salient form of Mexican ethnicity. As a result, they reported relationships with Mexican immigrants that were primarily relegated to informal interactions in public and in the workplace. But these contacts did not provide the same depth of opportunity to access ethnic raw materials. A few exceptions occurred, particularly among those in the middle and oldest cohorts of respondents who had married coethnic immigrants. Yet most Garden City respondents from the middle and oldest cohorts expressed a sense of awkwardness when interacting with what they saw as a distinctly Mexican-immigrant culture that was not so ubiquitous during their own formative years. Johnny Ocampo, a forty-four-year-old UPS driver in Garden City, conveyed some of the discomfort that many middle-cohort Mexican Americans in Garden City felt in the presence of their immigrant coethnics:

I'm walking up and down the aisles of the grocery store, and I'm looking just like everybody else, but I'm wearing Dockers, and I'm wearing Hush Puppies, and I'm wearing a shirt that doesn't have cowboy designs on it. It's not a T-shirt. And [Mexican immigrants are] looking at me like, "Oh my goodness. He's an uppity little thing, isn't he? He dresses like a white boy." And I know that I see that. I see that in people's eyes. And especially like this weekend. I didn't go [to the Fiesta Patria, but when I did go] [. . .] and I'm walking around there, and people look at you differently when they don't recognize you. And I don't go to the one o'clock Spanish Mass, and I don't really have strong ties to the Hispanic events. So when I go there and people see me, maybe I do stand out. I don't know. But they see me as being different than them. And I see them being different than me. I do. Together we are Hispanic. Together we are there to celebrate a culture or whatever. But there is a difference there. There is a strong difference. And especially when they come to me for a conversation in Spanish and I cannot answer them as correctly as I'd like.

For middle-cohort respondents in Garden City, Mexican immigrants represented a group with which later-generation Mexican Americans shared a common ethnic origin but from whom the middle cohort differed in how they expressed their ethnic identity. They believed that they had simply integrated too much into American society to feel comfortable around Mexican immigrants in ways that might yield the sorts of friendships the youngest cohort reported.

In contrast, Mexican Americans from all of the cohorts of respondents in Santa Maria reported having lasting friendships with people of Mexican origin from all generations, immigrants and the second generation included. The sort of generational mix within the Mexican-origin population present in both cities today has always been present in Santa Maria. Whereas friendships with Mexican immigrants revived Mexican ethnically linked practices among the youngest cohort in Garden City, a steady influx of Mexican immigrants to Santa Maria gave individuals from the middle and oldest cohorts nearly constant access to friends who passed on ethnic practices. The comments of Manuel Arnedo, a forty-three-year-old firefighter in Santa Maria, illustrate the taken-for-granted nature of the coexistence of Mexican Americans and Mexican immigrants in that locale:

[The Mexican-immigrant] presence in California—I've seen it all my life and have been in and out of it all my life, [so] I don't really think about [it] being, you know, like we've described [it] as being [a big deal] [. . .]. I don't think about it that way. To me they are just like the mountains and the sea and everything else.

While not all Mexican-American respondents in Santa Maria had formed close friendships with immigrants, they had a familiarity and experience with the immigrant population that made these friendships more likely to occur and more likely to add to Mexican Americans' access to things ethnic.

Intramarriage and Dating

As the last chapter showed, intermarriage is commonplace for Mexican Americans in both cities. Virtually none of the people I interviewed expressed opposition to marrying someone from another ethnic group, and a substantial number of respondents were in fact dating or married to people who were not of Mexican origin. Intermarriage patterns are partly determined by preferences that individuals have for marriage partners and the social norms that inform these preferences. But the opportunities that exist to meet individuals from a group are also critical (Blau 1977). Such opportunities are most often created by upward mobility. When individuals move up the socioeconomic ladder, they often find themselves in contact with fewer coethnics and more people from other ethnic groups, whom they may wind up marrying. Intermarriage often contributes to the thinning importance of a particular ethnic identity, because each spouse has less exposure to the people and practices associated with his or her ethnic origins. The thinning importance of ethnicity is also seen in the children of interethnic unions, who may have the option to choose ethnic identities from their varied ethnic strands and who most often treat their ethnicity as a symbolic aspect of identity (Jiménez 2004; Lee and Bean 2007).

But immigrant replenishment changes the marriage market in significant ways for Mexican Americans, providing expanded opportunities for them to marry those fresh from the ethnic homeland. U.S.-born Mexicans do not marry Mexican immigrants in large numbers, but as economists Brian Duncan and Stephen Trejo (2007) show, such unions do occur in an untrivial percentage of marriages involving at least one U.S.-born Mexican. Among all married U.S.-born Mexican men, 13.6 percent are married to a Mexican-immigrant woman, and 17.4 percent of U.S.-born Mexican women are married to a foreign-born Mexican man. Furthermore, immigration appears to be slowing the pace of interethnic marriages. Sociologists Zhenchao Qian and Daniel Lichter (2007) show that intermarriage rates among Latinos declined during the 1990s, and marriages between U.S.- and foreign-born Latinos showed an unprecedented increase. This increase was driven by heavy immigration from Latin America, which increased the stock of foreign-born Latino marriage partners available to U.S.-born Latinos.

Marriages between Mexican Americans and Mexican immigrants are significant for the ethnic identity formation of the people I interviewed. Just as ethnic intermarriage contributes to participants' thinning attachment to any one particular ethnic group, *intraethnic marriage* and dating across generational lines have the opposite effect, because they provide Mexican Americans greater exposure to Mexican ethnic symbols and practices. The case of Shannon Arrienta, a thirty-nine-year-old restaurant cook in Garden City, illustrates the myriad ways in which romantic partnerships inform the practice of ethnicity. Shannon's family had been in the United States for more than four generations; hers was a "founding" Mexican-American family in Garden City. The story of cultural assimilation that fits so many other Mexican Americans applies to Shannon: she did not grow up speaking Spanish, she never visited Mexico during her youth, and Mexican customs touched her childhood in only the most symbolic of ways. Much of that changed when Shannon married her husband, a Mexican immigrant who worked at the beef-packing plant. In the twenty-one years that she had been with him, her attachment to her ethnic identity became much stronger. To begin with, Shannon picked up a number of Mexican ethnic practices that had faded within her family. Although she spoke some Spanish while growing up, she learned a great deal more from her husband, with whom she spoke almost exclusively in Spanish. When her husband was at work, Shannon's bilingual children helped her as well. Describing her ability to speak Spanish, Shannon said, "I don't speak it all that great. I mean my kids can speak it better than me, but it don't bug me. They correct me, just like we correct them." The influence that her Mexican-born husband had on her ethnic identity extended into other aspects of her life. Shannon had only limited knowledge of her own family's origins south of the border, but she was keenly familiar with her ethnic homeland because of her husband's kinship ties to Mexico. Her husband helped her retie to a transnational community from which she had been severed a long time ago by the family in which she grew up. Shannon is unique relative to the other Mexican Americans I interviewed in that she had been to Mexico at all and even more so because she had visited nontouristy locales. She regularly visited her in-laws, who lived in a rural area in the state of Hidalgo. These visits helped her incorporate traditional Mexican cuisine into her renowned culinary repertoire. (Shannon proudly sent me away from our interview with a batch of tamales that she had made from a recipe that her mother-in-law taught her.) Although holidays bore almost no ethnic overtones when Shannon was growing up, she noted several ways in which her husband had injected Mexican customs into family celebrations. Tamales were a staple in her home during Christmas, Shannon rang in the New Year with the Mexican custom of eating twelve grapes (one for each month of the year) and making a wish for each, and traditional Mexican songs and piñatas were a mainstay at her children's birthday celebrations.

As with friendships, the oldest and middle cohorts of respondents in Garden City tended not to cross generational lines as frequently as their Santa Maria counterparts. There were exceptions, however, particularly among divorcees in Garden City. After divorcing, the "marriage market" for Mexican Americans from the middle and oldest cohorts in Garden City included a substantial number of Mexican immigrants. After divorcing his first wife, Joe Gil Jr., a fifty-six-year-old retired appliance salesman, married a woman born in Mexico, and his second wife provided him regular and abundant access to ethnic raw materials. Early in Joe's life, Mexican Americans occupied a low status in Garden City, and most Mexican Americans made efforts to shed any remnants of their ethnic origins in order to gain acceptance with whites. As Joe put it, he wanted to "assimilate into the society, into Garden City, so bad that you just wanted to be, I guess, English-speaking." But much changed in Garden City and in Joe's life, especially after he married his second wife. He began to speak Spanish in his home around 40 percent of the time, and he used Spanish to communicate with his in-laws:

[My wife's] dominant language is Spanish, so that's where I'm learning all of mine from. And her parents are from there too, so I speak to them in Spanish. I've gotten much better at it than I used to be. I'm just not totally fluent yet, but I'm getting there.

Because of the historically unceasing nature of Mexican immigration to Santa Maria, all cohorts of respondents had a fairly large supply of potential Mexican-immigrant marriage partners in their marriage market. Two of the respondents from the oldest cohorts were married to Mexican immigrants, and both noted how their marriage had facilitated the practice of ethnicity in daily life. Margarita Llanes, a sixty-year-old teacher's assistant in Santa Maria, was married to a man who came to the United States under the bracero program. Like Shannon Arrienta, from Garden City, Margarita had a good working knowledge of Mexican cuisine and customs, but interactions with her in-laws deepened that knowledge. When it came to holidays, Margarita explained,

We'd bring [my mother-in-law] over, and she would help and tell us how to do and prepare and stuff. [. . .] When I married [my husband], of course his [ethnic identity] was even stronger. And I started learning to fix a lot of things that his mother did too.

Mexican Americans' increased access to things ethnic need not be limited to marrying someone from the immigrant generation. Unions between later-generation and second-generation Mexican Americans produce a form of ethnic rejuvenation similar to that found in unions involving immigrants. Second-generation Mexican Americans are often a bridge between Mexican immigrants and Mexican Americans. The combination of their immigrant parents and birth in the United States lead to both their general familiarity with American society and their continued strong connections to Mexican culture (Smith 2005a). When Mexican Americans form romantic ties with second-generation Mexican Americans, they plug into a network of immigrants who provide ready access to ethnic raw materials. The experience of Hank Pacheco is illustrative. Hank was a twenty-seven-year-old corrections officer who spoke very little Spanish before dating his current girlfriend, a second-generation Mexican American. Hank's Spanish had improved because of his interaction with Spanish-speaking inmates but also because of his interaction with his girlfriend's parents. Not only did his girlfriend's parents encourage him to practice Spanish, but they also inculcated in him the value of passing Spanish on to his children, even though he did not speak Spanish in his own home while growing up:

Her mom speaks only Spanish, my girlfriend's mother. And I use Spanish a lot when I talk with her. [. . .] Actually that helps me a lot. [. . .] I go back to [my girlfriend's] family. They help remind you of things that you may have started to forget. For one, they help me realize the importance of speaking Spanish and passing that on.

Hank's use of Spanish would likely have faded if not for his relationship with a second-generation Mexican American. Hank's relationship with his girlfriend also illustrates the myriad ways that intergenerational relationships tie later-generation Mexican Americans into a larger network of individuals who are closer to the immigrant ethnic ground zero. Mexican Americans gain access to ethnic raw materials not just through their romantic partners but also through their partners' extended network of immigrant and second-generation kin.

It is important to note that marriages between immigrants and Mexican Americans are hardly the norm, partly because of class differences between Mexican immigrants and later-generation Mexican Americans. As Qian and Lichter (2007) point out, social class has a significant influence on the likelihood of these romantic unions. Working-class Mexican Americans, like Shannon Arrienta, are more likely to have regular contact with Mexican immigrants, since they generally share a similar class status. Mexican Americans with high levels of education are more likely to cross ethnic lines than working-class Mexican Americans when they choose marriage partners, although in some instances later-generation Mexican Americans find Mexican-born partners who are upwardly mobile.

Clearly, the availability of Mexican-immigrant marriage partners is a factor in the replenishment of Mexican-American ethnic identity. As the experiences of Shannon, Joe Jr., Margarita, and Hank show, marriages to immigrants allow Mexican Americans to experience a social space in which their significant other's family possesses a "thicker" form of ethnic identity than exists in the family in which they grew up. Their romantic ties to Mexican immigrants and second-generation individuals put them in contact with an entire web of extended family members who share the ethnic raw materials they possess in great abundance.

Institutional Contacts with Ethnicity

Even if Mexican Americans do not regularly interact with Mexican immigrants, they can easily access ethnically linked symbols and practices in the institutional setting in Garden City and Santa Maria. The large Mexican-immigrant population imbues institutions—churches, schools, cuisine, and mass media—with a strong Mexican flavor that further facilitates the breadth and depth of opportunities for Mexican Americans to engage in the practice of ethnicity.

Local firms and organizations are central mediators of these opportunities. Demographic shifts and civil rights legislation passed in the 1960s have forced organizations to demonstrate compliance with policies designed to create racial equality. The response of firms and organizations has created "an institutionalized consensus on the value of diversity" (Alba and Nee 2003: 57) that pervades, however superficially, contemporary American society. This value of diversity translates into more culturally sensitive and culturally relevant practices in the form of bilingual services, efforts to recruit a more diverse workforce, and campaigns to celebrate the various ethnic groups in American society. But firms and organizations also recognize that adopting such strategies is good for their bottom line.[3] Culturally sensitive and culturally relevant programs and policies help businesses increase profits, churches grow their membership, and political parties broaden their base. The strategies they invoke affirm Mexican ethnic identity but also facilitate the ability of Mexican Americans to access with regularity symbols and practices associated with their ethnic origins.

At the forefront of the organizational adjustments seen in Garden City and Santa Maria are churches. The church has always been an institutional core of immigrant communities and a place where immigrants and their children find simultaneously a connection to their homeland and a resource that helps them assimilate into U.S. society (Levitt 2007; Smith 2005a). In churches in Garden City and Santa Maria, several masses each Sunday are conducted entirely in Spanish.[4] They also host religious celebrations that are more typical of those celebrated in Mexico, such as feasts honoring various patron saints and masses honoring the

Virgin of Guadalupe. While these changes in local churches are meant to appeal to an immigrant congregation, they also prove to be a source of cultural rejuvenation for Mexican Americans. Most respondents said that they regularly attended English-language masses but occasionally went to the "Mexican" masses because those masses connected them to their ethnicity. For Lana Gutiérrez, a sixty-four-year-old retired educator in Garden City, the music at the Spanish-language masses provided her with a sense of comfort absent from other masses:

I go to the Spanish Mass every Sunday. And people say to me, "Why do you go to the Spanish Mass? You speak English." But this Spanish Mass fills a void in me that I have because of the Mexican music [. . .] it soothes me.

Religion is a key dimension of social life through which individuals experience their ethnicity, and the changes in religious celebrations meant to attract immigrants allow Mexican Americans to reconnect with aspects of their ethnic identity that begin to atrophy in their own families with the passage of time. Leon Peralta, a sixty-five-year-old retired teacher in Santa Maria, said that he enjoyed the Spanish-language masses because they allowed him to maintain greater contact with the Spanish language and, hence, his ethnicity:

I like to go to the Spanish mass even though I don't understand it as well as I do if I went to an English service. So it's one of my few connections to Spanish.

TRJ: What is it about the Spanish Mass that you like?

R: I guess I want to hang on to the fact that I am Mexican, and that's one way to do it. I want to keep the language, even though I'm not anywhere [near] fluent. That helps to maintain some of the Spanish. I guess that's the reason, just hang on to the little Spanish that I do have, the little Mexican that I do have.

Although older respondents were more likely to attend these masses, the younger Mexican-American respondents also found that the church provided rich opportunities to celebrate their ethnic origin. Melissa Santiago, a sixteen-year-old high school student in Santa Maria, ventured outside her middle-class neighborhood to attend Mass at a church in a Mexican-immigrant barrio because she liked the festive atmosphere of the Sunday Mass and parish-sponsored events:

TRJ: What do you prefer about [the church that you go to over others]?

M: Just the fact that at [the other church], I don't know, it's just the feeling that more Mexicans go to [the church I go to]. And it's cool, because they'll have like fiestas during the day. Like on a Sunday, they'll have this Mexican fiesta where a lot of people will come, and they'll have different foods. And that's what I like about it.

Even though Melissa lived in a predominantly white neighborhood and attended a private school where most of the students were white, going to a Mexican-immigrant church allowed her to engage in the institutionally based practices of ethnicity on a regular basis.

Mexican Americans need not be religious to find the ethnic raw materials that institutions provide. Like the churches, schools in Garden City and Santa Maria have adjusted their practices to accommodate the immigrant population. Schools regularly sponsor activities with Mexican cultural overtones. One of the high schools in Santa Maria has an award-winning *ballet folklórico,* or Mexican folk-dance group, and the high school in Garden City has a Latino dance group that performs various types of popular Latino and Mexican dance styles. Both of these groups include later-generation Mexican Americans. High schools in each city host clubs and organizations that celebrate Mexican and Latino culture. These organizations provide occasions for students to learn about Mexican and Latino culture and a school-sponsored space in which students can celebrate their ethnic origins. School curricula also provide opportunities for Mexican Americans to connect with their ethnic roots outside their homes. High schools in Santa Maria offer courses on Mexican-American history and culture, and schools host celebrations of Cinco de Mayo and El Dieciséis. Many of the youngest respondents said they had done reports on their ethnic background for history classes or read books by authors who shared their ethnicity. These assignments had piqued their interest in learning more about Mexican-American history and Mexican ethnicity. The infusion of ethnicity into school curricula and extracurricular activities has roots in the Chicano movement, during which Chicano students and teachers fought to force schools to reflect their ethnic origins more closely. But the recognition of Mexican ethnicity in schools today bears few overt connections to the activism of the Chicano movement. Instead, the continuing relevance of these curricular and extracurricular changes is a result of the large immigrant and second-generation Mexican-student population. These students create a demand for classes and on-campus clubs and organizations that further provide opportunities for later-generation Mexican Americans to be in touch with their ethnic origins.

Access to Mexican culture is also pervasive for Mexican Americans in the availability of Mexican cuisine. Individuals who exhibit a strong ethnic identity, as well as those who have only a thin ethnic attachment, experience and express their ethnic ancestry through food. But when immigration fades, ethnic cuisine takes on a distinctly American flavor that begins to lose its resemblance to cuisine from the ethnic homeland. What is more, when immigration wanes, food becomes a *primary* means through which individuals experience a purely symbolic form of ethnicity centered on sporadically invoked symbols (Alba 1990; Waters 1990).

For Mexican Americans, an abundance of ethnic cuisine constitutes but one of many ways in which they engage with a social structure rife with Mexican culture. The Mexican-immigrant population has increased the access to and stylistic range of Mexican cuisine in restaurants that dot the landscape in these cities. In contrast to the Mexican-*American* cuisine served in Mexican-American homes and restaurants, immigrant-owned establishments serve food more typical of Mexico: dishes featuring shredded beef, Mexican cream, corn tortillas, and *aguas frescas* (fresh fruit juices). Mexican Americans frequent restaurants owned by immigrants, enjoying the opportunity to sample a style of Mexican food that was lost in previous generations.

In addition to restaurants, immigrant-owned stores and commercial chain supermarkets in both cities carry food products from Mexico. These products are found not just in the "mom-and-pop" markets owned by Mexican immigrants; even the commercial supermarkets offer a far more extensive selection of Mexican food and ingredients than what is typically available in the "ethnic food" aisle of most chain grocery stores. These products include corn husks and *masa* (ground corn paste) for tamales, several kinds of peppers, *manteca* (lard), beans, and a large variety of tortillas. Although the immigrant-owned markets and commercial supermarkets stock these items primarily to meet the culinary demands of Mexican immigrants, Mexican Americans also purchase these products in order to make traditional Mexican dishes. Mexican food products were not widely available in the major markets prior to the resurgence of Mexican immigration to Garden City and would be difficult, if not impossible, for Mexican Americans to find otherwise. A similar situation exists in Santa Maria. Although Mexican food products and cuisine have long been available there, the number and variety have dramatically increased in recent years because of the spike in Mexican immigration. Margarita Llanes noted that her decision not to buy candy on a recent trip to Mexico was shaped by the near ubiquity of Mexican products in Santa Maria:

I might have been six years old, and there wasn't any place to buy any Mexican products. And now they're all over. [. . .] I told them [my husband's family] the other day when we went to Guadalajara . . . they said, "Are you going to take any candy back with you?" I said, "What for? It's all over there [in the United States]!"

Ana Fernández, of Santa Maria, reported frequenting major chain stores near a predominantly immigrant neighborhood in order to find products typical of those found in Mexico:

I shop at a [chain supermarket] down the way on that part of town because they cater to the Mexican population. So the meat is different; the staples that are stored in that store are more cultural. And I can find things I need, because I have a tendency when I'm making tamales that I want certain meat, and I need this or that.

Enjoying Mexican food is by no means an experience unique to people of Mexican origin. In fact non-Mexicans are fairly commonly found at various Mexican establishments in both towns, and Mexican food now holds a prominent place in the array of American "ethnic" cuisines that Americans frequently enjoy. But the enjoyment of ethnic cuisine need not be exclusive to Mexican Americans in order for it to constitute a practice that at the very least ties them more firmly to their ethnicity. Even if they consume Mexican food alongside non-Mexicans, they are connecting to an expression of their own ethnic origin.

Just as Mexican immigrants have brought about the availability of

Mexican food, so too has their presence increased the pervasiveness of a Mexican-inflected popular culture. The influence that Mexican immi- grants have on popular culture is a function of demographic shifts not just in Garden City and Santa Maria but in the United States as a whole. The mass media are ever more responsive to demographic shifts in their efforts to market to target audiences, including those based on ethnic- ity. Spanish-language television and radio stream in from Los Angeles, Florida, and Latin America to just about every home in the United States, including those of Mexican Americans in Garden City and Santa Maria. Mexican Americans' access to Spanish-language media links them to the language and popular culture associated with their ethnic origins. In regard to language, Mexican Americans who have some ability to speak Spanish watch television shows and listen to Spanish radio, improving their existing knowledge of the language and strengthening their attach- ment to the larger Mexican-origin community. Larry Morales, a sixty- one-year-old master mechanic in Garden City, recalled having virtually no access to Spanish-language media until the resurgence of Mexican immigration in the early 1980s. Since that time, he frequently tuned into Spanish-language radio:

See, I used to listen to white radio all the time. Now they've got a twenty-four- hour Mexican radio station that plays a lot of music. So I listen to it a lot. So I've lost the contact with American radio that I used to [have].

Likewise, Kate Lebron's grandmother largely replaced her favorite English-language daytime soap operas with Mexican *novelas*, which are abundant on Spanish-language television in Garden City:

Before immigration, before they started immigrating here so strongly, my grandma watched English soap operas. Now that the majority of our community is Hispanic and Spanish-speaking, they've got Univision, or whatever you call it, and we've got three to four Spanish channels.

Even the youngest respondents had developed a taste for Mexican and Latin American popular culture, now prevalent in Garden City and Santa Maria. Posters advertising the upcoming concerts given by well-known Mexican bands blanket the walls of local supermarkets and billboards. The event center in Garden City regularly features concerts with musical acts such as Los Tigres del Norte, Los Traficantes, and Lupillo Rivera. Sprinkled among the concertgoers are young Mexican Americans who normally attend with Mexican-immigrant and second-generation friends. The young people I interviewed had music collections that included Mexican and Latin American artists who have gained popularity in the United States. In lots of ways the youngest Mexican Americans I interviewed resembled virtually any other American youth in terms of their tastes in music and fashion. However, they were adding to their tastes a Mexican flavor that exists only because Mexican immigrants supply it.

Thomas Macias's (2006) study of third- and later-generation Mexican Americans in San Jose, California, and Phoenix, Arizona, also shows that the Spanish-language media are means through which later-generation Mexican Americans have contact with their ethnic origins. Macias argues that Spanish-language media allow for an experience of Mexican ethnicity that does not require interaction with Mexican immigrants but is mediated by mass media. In Macias's view, it nonetheless ties them to a larger "imagined" Mexican-origin community. Spanish-language media served a similar function for the Mexican Americans I interviewed. The small size of Garden City and Santa Maria compared with larger, metropolitan areas, such as San Jose and Phoenix, facilitated Mexican Americans' more frequent contact with Mexican immigrants. Spanish media thus worked in conjunction with the regular contact that respondents had with the immigrant community to strengthen their attachment to the Spanish language and to a larger sense of Mexican-origin "peoplehood."

MULTICULTURALISM: THE MORTAR FOR ETHNIC RAW MATERIALS

Clearly Mexican immigrants provide a multitude of opportunities for Mexican Americans to access ethnic raw materials. But the multitude does not explain the desire of later-generation Mexican Americans to take advantage of these opportunities. Scholars have noted that patterns of ethnic identity formation may have little to do with a migration-driven supply of ethnic symbols and practices. On the basis of his research in the United States and Europe, the late historian Marcus Lee Hansen observed that the second-generation children of immigrants, being insecure about their place in their parents' adoptive country, tried to distance themselves from their ethnic origins. The third generation, feeling more comfortable with their place in society, displayed a pride in their ethnic origins, even forming societies to document their ethnic history. Hansen's observations informed his formulation of the law of third-generation return, which he summed up in his oft-quoted assertion, "What the son wishes to forget the grandson wishes to remember" (1952: 494). Joane Nagel's (1995, 1997) research on Native Americans shows the power of politics and ideological shifts in reshaping ethnic identity. She demonstrates that "renewal" of Native American identity had nothing to do with demographic changes. Nagel explains the dramatic growth in the number of people identifying as Native American on the U.S. Census between 1970 and 1990 as a product of three developments: a federal Indian policy that urbanized Native Americans and created a group of intermarried, bicultural individuals who formed a network of ethnic organizations; a rise of ethnic politics that celebrated ethnic difference; and Native American political activism that promoted a pride in Native American ethnicity. While for some individuals this ethnic renewal involved reclaiming their Native American roots merely by checking boxes on census forms after having "passed" for white for much of their lives, for others it meant becoming actively engaged in Native American traditions and political causes.

Rather than coming from a nostalgic yearning for things ethnic brought on by temporal distance from the immigrant generation, Mexican Americans' desire to access the nearly ubiquitous Mexican ethnic raw materials comes in part from a post–civil rights thinking about race and ethnicity that Nagel identifies in her research on Native Americans. Multiculturalism now competes with Americanization as the dominant ideological view of race and ethnicity. As I pointed out in chapter 3, the oldest cohort of Mexican-American respondents came of age when Americanization guided views on immigrant assimilation. While Americanization still underwrites some opinions and policies related to immigration and ethnicity, the United States has seen an ideological shift. As anthropologist Marcelo Suárez-Orozco writes, "The cultural models and social practices that we have come to call multiculturalism shape the experiences, perceptions, and behavioral repertoires of immigrants in ways not seen in previous eras of large-scale immigration. A hundred years ago there certainly was no culture of multiculturalism celebrating—however superficial and ambivalently—ethnicity and communities of origin" (2000: 13). Multiculturalism provides a basis for more open attitudes about ethnic difference and holds up diversity as a value and a virtue. In practice, multiculturalism is most visible outside the policy arena and in the private sector.[5] Special months designated for the celebration of a particular racial or ethnic group, an emphasis on diversity in the workplace, and the growth and popularity of artistic expressions of ethnicity are among the various ways that multiculturalism manifests itself in U.S. society today.

For Mexican Americans, multiculturalism provides a "mortar" for the ethnic raw materials necessary for constructing a more robust ethnic identity. The role that multiculturalism plays in ethnic-identity construction becomes apparent when comparing differences among cohorts of respondents in my sample. Some of the respondents had lived through periods during which either Americanization or multiculturalism dominated. Recall that the oldest cohort of respondents (those fifty-six and older) was raised by their parents when Americanization reigned, and they in turn raised their own children according to its principles. As chapter 3 showed, the oldest cohort and even some middle-cohort Mexican Americans recalled that their parents were adamant that they speak only English and taught them to be "American" first. Indeed, before the days of multiculturalism, many Mexican Americans ran from opportunities to assert their ethnic identity and welcomed any chance to "pass" as non-Mexican.

Things are much different today, especially for Mexican Americans from the middle and youngest cohorts. The middle cohort came of age during and after the 1960s and 1970s—the height of the ethnic-pride movements that sowed the seeds of today's multiculturalism. Among these ethnic-pride movements was the decidedly anti-Americanization

Chicano movement, which advocated equal social, political, and economic rights for Mexican Americans and Mexican immigrants alike, as well as greater individual and institutional recognition of Mexican ethnicity (Muñoz 1989). Many Mexican Americans from Santa Maria who attended college at the time were influenced by the movement and clearly espoused its tenets during interviews. Manuel Esguerra, a fifty-one-year-old social worker in Santa Maria and the son of farmworkers, was involved in the Chicano movement during high school and college. In keeping with the principles of the movement, Manuel rejected Anglo conformity—what movement participants referred to as "assimilation"—and instead invoked multiculturalism:

I guess when I was going through college and learned the words called assimilation or acculturation, I didn't want that to happen to myself. I didn't want to become a college graduate and assimilate into materialistic things and suddenly not be able to enjoy my cultural music, my cultural foods, my values that I grew up with for my family. So I choose to still make that an important part of my life.

Manuel's choice to make Mexican ethnicity an important part of his life is shared by other Mexican Americans in Santa Maria. They seek out ways to participate in Mexican customs and celebrations by incorporating them into their lives. They look for opportunities to speak Spanish and to become involved in efforts to elevate the position of the Mexican-origin population, they join Mexican clubs and organizations, and they attend Mexican festivities. What is more, their desire to maintain a strong attachment is met with the wealth of opportunities that Mexican immigrants provide for doing this.

There is a tendency to think of multiculturalism as a cosmopolitan phenomenon that thrives in metropolitan centers like New York, San Francisco, and Chicago, but this limited sphere of involvement is not the case. While the Chicano movement did not have the impact on the lives of Mexican Americans in Garden City that it had on those in Santa Maria, a diffuse form of multiculturalism now prevalent throughout the United States informs the attitudes of Mexican Americans in Garden City as well. Special "diversity" days, civic committees on diversity and multiculturalism, and an annual multicultural conference are emblematic of this diffuse form of multiculturalism in Garden City. Mexican Americans there subscribe to the principle that feeling attached to an ethnic background, having a general sense of pride in that background, and being aware and tolerant of other ethnic groups are all positive. While no Garden City respondents were active in the Chicano movement, the views of many respondents reflect a multiculturalist stance that is an outgrowth of the ethnic activism of the 1960s and 1970s. As Dave Suárez, a thirty-two-year-old insurance salesman, put it, "It's not bad to be a little bit different than everybody else. It's kind of neat."

Multiculturalism's reach had extended furthest among the youngest Mexican Americans I interviewed. In contrast to the efforts made by Manuel and others in the middle cohort to espouse multiculturalism, respondents from the youngest cohort spoke of the virtues of diversity as a taken-for-granted part of their lives and the world around them. It perhaps became so much a part of their lives because of its pervasiveness in nearly all aspects of U.S. society today and because they knew no other way of thinking about racial and ethnic identity. Since the ethnic pride movements of the 1960s and 1970s, multiculturalism has informed some policies and institutional practices. As Nathan Glazer proclaims, "We are all multiculturalists now" (1997).

Multiculturalism provides tangible incentives that encouraged the youngest respondents to maintain an attachment to an ethnic identity. Most prominent among policies based on multiculturalism are affirmative action programs that aim to increase the number of racial and ethnic minorities in education and employment. In an age in which race and ethnic considerations are very much a part of decision-making processes about the distribution of scarce resources, the youngest respondents were well aware that most colleges and universities (public schools in California excluded)[6] give special consideration and scholarships to minority applicants, and they knew that employers take race into account in hiring. They believed that their ethnic identity is particularly important when dealing with school and job applications because of the advantages it may give them. The comments of Ramón Ramos, an eighteen-year-old high school student in Santa Maria, typify the awareness of many of the youngest respondents in both cities:

When I'm in school I notice that there's more of a chance to get scholarships and grants. That's one of the main things I see. And like for a job and stuff, they're gonna pick a Mexican over a white guy.

These policies communicate that respondents' ethnic identity is something of value. Even if the incentives to identify with their Mexican origins are material in these cases, policies based on race and ethnicity make up an important dimension of multiculturalism that positively recognizes ethnic differences.[7]

The institutional adjustments in response to Mexican immigration that I described in the previous section also communicate to Mexican Americans that their ethnic identity is a valuable resource. The demand for bilingual employees has radically changed the status of Spanish in each of the sample cities. Whereas speaking Spanish was once a liability, it is now an asset to Mexican Americans (and everyone else for that matter). Timothy Saenz, a thirty-nine-year-old theater manager in Garden City, attributed his inability to speak Spanish to its low status in the past. However, with the resurgence of Mexican immigrants to Garden City, he and others now viewed speaking the language as a plus:

You know it's really kind of strange for individuals, like, today to understand why someone like myself who is of Mexican ethnic background [does not] speak Spanish. But the best way I can explain that to you or anyone that would ask is that back when I was young, being bilingual was not the thing. If you wanted to be successful in life, as far as a career and so forth, it was English that you spoke. It wasn't just until recently that being bilingual was the big thing now. And I really can't blame my parents for not teaching me. I kind of wish that they would have so that I would know, but I can't blame them for that. Because you have to remember, they grew up in an era where if you were Mexican, that was a bad thing to be. If you spoke Spanish, that was a bad thing to be. So naturally, as parents, they're going to protect their children, because they want the very best for their children, so at the time when we were growing up, Spanish wasn't spoken. It wasn't even thought of. To be bilingual was like taboo almost. If you wanted to be successful, it was English that you knew and spoke. [. . .] I think the reason why [things have changed] is because, with people coming in from Mexico, it became more apparent that the Spanish language was going to have to be learned and taught [. . .] if you wanted to communicate with people. And also as far as with people from Mexico coming into the States, they're going to generate money or revenue as well, so you're going to cater to their needs as well as those of us who are Americans and speak English. So I think the overall picture is that it was needed, it was necessary. When I was young, it wasn't. But now it's a needed language.

The monetary rewards attached to bilingualism make concrete the benefits of an important aspect of ethnicity. Bilingualism is now treated as a "hard" skill that may give an individual an advantage in being hired and moving up in the workplace. City governments recognize bilingual employees as necessary for the provision of adequate services to its residents, and some respondents told me that they received additional pay for being designated as bilingual in their workplace. The police force in Santa Maria, for example, pays additional salary every month to bilingual officers who take "Spanish calls," and the school district in Garden City likewise pays bilingual employees a higher salary.[8] When bilingualism did not translate into direct monetary compensation, many nonetheless pointed out that their bilingual skills made them attractive job candidates. Even if Mexican Americans strive for bilingualism for purely "rational" purposes (i.e., higher pay, improved hiring opportunities, more job promotions, etc.), their ability to speak Spanish provides opportunities to form friendships and make acquaintances with Mexican immigrants and gives them access to other forms of Mexican culture through Spanish-language media, all of which help to "thicken" their ethnic identity. Perhaps equally important, policies and programs that positively reward bilingualism communicate that a core component of Mexican ethnicity—the ability to speak Spanish—is something that is of value in American society today.[9]

Multiculturalism also creates nonmaterial incentives for Mexican Americans to have a strong attachment to their ethnic identity. Mexican culture has become part of American popular culture in recent years. Evidence of its growing popularity can be seen in music, cinema, and print media. Earlier I discussed the influence of the Spanish-language media on the ethnic identity of Mexican Americans, but even the mainstream popular media is infused with Mexican culture, increasing its visibility and status. The popularity of Mexican-origin celebrities, such as Salma Hayek, Carlos Mencía, George López, Eva Longoria Parker, and Edward James Olmos; the success of television shows about Mexican-American families *(The American Family, The George Lopez Show, Resurrection Blvd., Ugly Betty)*; the proliferation of Mexican films *(Amores perros, Y tu mamá también)*; and films about people of Mexican descent in the United States *(My Family/ Mi familia, Real Women Have Curves, Tortilla Soup,* and *Quinceañera)* all contribute to the popularity of Mexican ethnicity in the mainstream.[10] This visibility reduces the stigma of being Mexican American and even gives it a certain cachet. Articulating the influence of popular culture on how the youngest respondents evaluated the desirability of their ethnicity, Marcela Muñoz, a nineteen-year-old junior-college student in Garden City, said:

There was a time where being Mexican American, Hispanic wasn't acceptable, that people purposely didn't speak Spanish. They purposely didn't teach their children about their culture because it was something to be ashamed of. Maybe it wasn't something that was accepted in society [. . .] it's becoming more socially acceptable. It's even becoming the "in" thing, where you see so many things cater to the Hispanic, Mexican, Latino population.

Popular culture is a signpost to which individuals look for information about what is acceptable and "hip." Young Mexican Americans are likely to see reflections of their ethnic origins in popular culture now more than ever, making them more open to the avenues that Mexican immigrants and second-generation Mexican Americans make so abundantly available for engaging in the practice of ethnicity.

It is important to note that multiculturalism has been met with staunch opposition. Many commentators and rank-and-file Americans rail against policies and programs informed by multiculturalism, asserting that they are threats to "American" identity (Buchanan 2006; Huntington 2004b). Nowhere have challenges to multiculturalism been more clearly displayed than in California in the 1990s. The state became the central front in a battle against multiculturalism. California's voter-passed propositions 209 and 227 respectively eliminated affirmative action in public institutions and ended bilingual education. More recently, a variety of measures have been introduced at the state and local levels that aim to stamp out the use of non-English languages, and individuals who emphasize a get-tough approach to immigration reform regularly associate unauthorized immigration with putative American cultural decay. These policies and critiques are no doubt powerful indicators of opposition to multiculturalism. Still, these challenges have not stamped out multiculturalism in U.S. society today. Indeed, as Nagel's (1995, 1997) research on Native American ethnic identity and the case of Mexican Americans in Garden City and Santa Maria show, ideological shifts matter in the degree to which people feel attached to an ethnic identity. However trite or superficial one might argue multiculturalism has become, it provides a heuristic for race and ethnicity that spurs Mexican Americans to seek opportunities to access ethnic raw materials.

THE GROWING IMPORTANCE OF ETHNIC IDENTITY

For Mexican Americans to have access to and a desire for the ethnically linked symbols and practices that immigrants provide is one thing. For this access to have a significant effect on the importance of ethnicity to their social identity is another. Interviews show that the ethnic raw materials that immigrants provide are not merely trappings of a symbolic ethnicity but powerful building blocks that are key to the construction of more salient ethnic identities. The abundance of these ethnic raw materials and multiculturalism make ethnicity a more central and deeply held part of respondents' identity. Respondents' comments show that Mexican immigration has indeed provided a sun that staves off the twilight of Mexican-American ethnic identity. Larry Morales summarized many of the ways in which Mexican immigration replenishes the importance of ethnic identity in the lives of Mexican Americans:

I think what [Mexican immigrants] do is bring pride; they bring a renewed heritage. I mean we're more aware of our cultural roots. We're discovering food we'd forgotten that was part of our staple. We've forgotten things we used to eat. And also they've brought new blood in. [. . .] So all that. And that's all brought new blood into the system. [. . .] We're creating a hybrid of the old and new. [. . .] So all that. And the church—the people that had lost the Lady of Guadalupe holiday, now it's celebrated. [. . .] They brought bread, where white bread was all I ever ate. And now you have the Mexican bread, Mexican cookies, Mexican desserts, and Mexican food that's different.

Others pointed out that if not for the large Mexican-immigrant population, the salience of their ethnic identity would be dramatically diminished. When reflecting on what his ethnic identity might be like were there no Mexican immigration, Rolando Fernández, a forty-eight-year-old physician, poignantly commented:

I would probably be "Roland" Fernández. Probably my name wouldn't be spelled with a Z. I'd speak no Spanish. I probably wouldn't make tamales at Christmas, and a lot of my cultural sensitivity and awareness is a direct result of the reality of the fact that I'm surrounded by culture. I'm surrounded by a culture that I understand, that I appreciate, that I love. And it continues to feed me. It's a source of nourishment. So if I had not become more acculturated by the presence of large numbers of immigrants here, it would have been completely opposite. I would be totally acculturated into mainstream culture. But now the mainstream happens to be predominantly Mexicano, and the Mexican culture tends to be . . . and if not Mexican, Mexican-American culture, and the combination of those two cultures. That's what's happening here.

Acculturation in Rolando's view now involves adapting not only to conventional notions of "mainstream" American society but to a mainstream that is increasingly defined by Mexican culture. Likewise, Frank Bustamante, a fifty-two-year-old high school teacher and administrator in Santa Maria, had regular contact with Mexican immigrants and second-generation Mexican-American students, who provided him the opportunity to engage in expressions of Mexican ethnicity that made him more attached to an ethnic identity:

I guess you could say after coming back and teaching, and I get involved with all these kids and doing that, I guess I could say I've become more Mexican.

TRJ: Tell me about that.

R: Well, just, I think being around a lot more kids of Mexican background and dealing with them, talking to their parents, and speaking a lot more Spanish than I used to, and those types of things. I think it kind of helped make me more aware of being Mexican and being in tune to my background and all that type of thing.

Mexican immigrants provide much more than superficial opportunities for Mexican Americans to engage in ethnic nostalgia or in attempts to rediscover ethnic roots that are largely absent in the social structures around them. The influx of Mexican immigrants provides access to a vibrant form of Mexican ethnicity that helps Mexican Americans construct a salient ethnic identity.

The ethnically linked symbols and practices that help define an ethnic group are important building blocks for ethnic identity construction but are by no means the only building blocks. The importance of ethnic identity is indicated by other forms of "ethnic behavior," including political action, economic relationships, social support, and the connection that individuals and groups have to their ethnic homeland. As I show in later chapters, immigrants play a vital role in Mexican Americans' ethnic identity in these other areas of social life too.

Mexican Americans in Garden City and Santa Maria bear a resemblance to the later-generation white ethnics among various measures of assimilation. But coethnic immigrant replenishment changes ethnic-identity construction for Mexican Americans as compared with white ethnics in profound ways. The continual influx of Mexican immigration provides ready access to the ethnic raw materials that prevent the recession of ethnicity into the distant background of social life. Mexican Americans are able to access ethnically linked symbols and practices through interactions with immigrants and second-generation Mexican Americans, ranging from serendipitous encounters to romantic partnerships. But Mexican Americans may not even need to have direct contact with immigrants. Churches, schools, restaurants, and grocery stores, as well as popular culture, also provide access to ethnic raw materials. Driving Mexican Americans' desire to access these ethnic raw materials is a multicultural ideology that makes a strong attachment to ethnic identity more desirable and even rewarding in American society today.

What bolsters the ethnic identity of Mexican Americans is a combination of two important factors—immigrant replenishment and multiculturalism. Could one of these factors alone account for the growing salience of ethnic identity for some respondents? Considering the case of European-origin groups provides more clues to the importance of each of these factors in shaping ethnic identity. In the late 1970s, a long line of research on the ethnic identity of later-generation white ethnics originated in scholarly debates about whether European-origin groups were experiencing a revival of ethnic identity. The revivalists argued that any thinning of ethnicity was temporary and that subsequent generations were returning to ethnicity as a central component of their identity (Novak 1973). With ethnic pride movements sweeping the nation, ethnicity could no longer be viewed as an aspect of identity that eventually melted into a larger part of American identity. As historian Matthew Frye Jacobson (2006) shows, multiculturalism profoundly influenced the expression of white ethnic identity too. Revivalists theorized that ethnicity was here to stay, even for later-generation white ethnics (Glazer and Moynihan 1970). In essence, revivalists argued that a shift in ideology from Americanization to multiculturalism would help ethnicity maintain its visibility and fervor.

Multiculturalism was not enough, however. Even as the popularity of multiculturalism grew in the 1980s and 1990s, white ethnics had *only* symbols of their ethnic roots to anchor their ethnic identity. Mass immigration from their ethnic homeland, unlike that of Mexican Americans, had ended decades ago, and the ethnic social structure contained only faint artifacts of ethnicity. Multiculturalism alone was not enough for these later-generation white ethnics to stave off the thinning of ethnicity, because there was no immigrant replenishment to support it.

Perhaps white ethnics were never caught up in the sort of ethnic politics that could provide a serious shot in the arm to ethnicity in the way that Native Americans, Mexican Americans, and other nonwhites were. Ethnic politics and a shifting ideological stance related to race and ethnicity explain a swell in Native American pride that contributed to an ethnic renewal (Nagel 1995, 1997). In fact, a combination of non-demographic factors accounted for the increased importance of Native American ethnic identity: policy, politics, and pride. These same factors help explain the strength of Mexican-American ethnic identity too. Race-based policies and the legacy of ethnic politics embodied in multiculturalism have helped shape the desire that Mexican Americans have to connect with their ethnic roots.

As my interviews show, multiculturalism is only part of what is behind the salience of Mexican-American ethnic identity. Mexican Americans may have attached greater importance to their ethnic identity even without immigrant replenishment. But the expression of Mexican-American ethnicity would surely have taken on a different form without the supply of ethnic raw materials that Mexican immigrants have provided. Ongoing immigration shapes the opportunities that Mexican Americans have to participate in the practice of ethnicity and the *way* that they engage in this practice. The abundant ethnic raw materials to which Mexican Americans have access only bolster the importance of ethnicity in their lives. Indeed, for them, the ongoing process of "becoming" American takes place in an environment that is increasingly Mexican in character. As Mexican Americans continue to move into the U.S. mainstream, they are bringing with them an ethnic identity that is more available because of immigration.

FIVE

The Ties That Bind and Divide

ETHNIC BOUNDARIES AND ETHNIC IDENTITY

The ways in which Mexican immigrants make ethnicity a salient aspect of Mexican Americans' identities manifest not only in the access they provide to the practice of ethnicity but also in the way their presence sharpens the boundaries that define Mexican-American ethnic identity. The hit movie *Selena* (1997) portrays a scene that suggests how these boundaries operate in the lives of Mexican Americans. *Selena* tells the story of the slain Mexican-American pop star who gains fame in both the United States and Mexico. At one point in the film, Selena learns that she will perform in Mexico for the first time and expresses enthusiasm to her father, Abraham Quintanilla. She assumes that her Mexican fans will share her excitement and accept her because of her Mexican heritage. But her father is quick to squelch her zeal, pointing out that she is not Mexican but Mexican American. In explaining the differences, Quintanilla says:

> Listen, being Mexican American is tough. Anglos jump all over you if you don't speak English perfectly. Mexicans jump all over you if you don't speak Spanish perfectly. We gotta be twice as perfect as anybody else. . . . Our family has been here for centuries and yet they treat us as if we just swam across the Rio Grande. I mean, we gótta know about John Wayne *and* Pedro Infante. We gotta know about Frank Sinatra *and* Agustín Lara. We gotta know about Oprah *and* Christina. Anglo food is too bland, and yet when we go to Mexico we get the runs! Now that, to me, is embarrassing! Japanese Americans, Italian Americans, German Americans, their homeland is on the other side of the ocean. Ours is right next door—right over there. And we gotta prove to the Mexicans how Mexican we are. And we gotta prove to the Americans how American we are. We gotta be more Mexican than the Mexicans and more American than the Americans both at the *same* time! It's exhausting! Damn! Nobody knows how tough it is to be a Mexican American!

The Mexican-American experience that Quintanilla describes in *Selena* mirrors that of respondents in Garden City and Santa Maria. They too described often feeling caught between two peoples and two identities. On one side is the large Mexican-immigrant population that defines Mexican ethnicity in these cities. On the other is the non-Mexican population that embraces some aspects of Mexican culture but does not accept Mexican immigrants. Because they were born and raised in the United States, Mexican Americans are accustomed to an American way of life; they speak primarily (if not only) English, they are culturally comfortable in negotiating American institutions, and they have acquired distinctly American tastes and lifestyle expectations. Yet they trace their ethnic roots to a country that sends more immigrants to the United States than any other country and shares a two-thousand-mile border with the United States. Mexican Americans share not just a common ethnic origin with these immigrants but also a social environment, in which large-scale Mexican immigration increasingly infuses a foreign flavor into Mexican ethnicity. Mexican Americans thus negotiate between their American nationality and way of life and their ethnic origin, which is heavily defined by foreign-born Mexicans.

The ethnic raw materials that Mexican immigrants supply and that Mexican Americans draw on are important to the formation of ethnic identity but are by no means the only ingredients. Also central are the boundaries that circumscribe groups. As anthropologist Fredrik Barth (1969) argued, ethnic groups are defined by the boundaries that distinguish them from one another. Sociologist Jimmy Sanders provides a useful definition of ethnic boundaries: "patterns of social interaction that give rise to, and subsequently reinforce, in-group members' self-definition and outsiders' confirmation of group distinctions" (2002: 327). Ethnic boundaries are made from categories that distinguish groups and the everyday behavior that the categories inform. At the individual level, ethnic categories and the behavior they inform divide "the social world into groups—into 'us' and 'them,'" and "offer scripts of action—how to relate to individuals classified as 'us' and 'them'—under a given set of circumstances" (Wimmer 2008b: 975).[1] The process that explains how boundaries fade and change is fundamentally the process of assimilation. My interviews with Mexican Americans and observations of them show that the factors that scholars generally invoke to explain the durability of ethnic boundaries—socioeconomic status, residential location, language abilities, and intermarriage (see Waters and Jiménez 2005)—do not provide a full explanation of how assimilation unfolds. As the everyday experiences of Mexican Americans show, the durability of ethnic boundaries is significantly affected by ongoing immigration.

Mexican Americans run up against the same ethnic boundaries that they have in many ways crossed. As Alba and Nee note, ethnic boundaries can function in several ways: they can become blurry, individuals can cross those boundaries that remain more or less intact, or ethnic boundaries can shift to include groups that were previously excluded. Boundary crossing may not necessarily alter the order of ethnic stratification (Alba and Nee 2003: 61). The Mexican Americans I interviewed are in many ways boundary crossers, because they have exhibited significant structural assimilation. Immigrant replenishment makes the boundaries they have crossed "brighter" (Alba 2005), and Mexican Americans become keenly aware of these boundaries in their daily lives.

Mexican Americans negotiate two sets of boundaries that immigrants make salient. The first are "intergroup boundaries," which are those between Mexican Americans and non-Mexicans. Mexican immigrants are frequent targets of nativism from non-Mexicans, who voice opposition to the social and economic changes resulting from Mexican newcomers. Although not aimed at Mexican Americans, nativist expressions had an indirect influence on the people I interviewed by making the boundaries between people of Mexican origin and non-Mexicans more rigid. Nativism is often couched in a racialized language that ties discontent about immigration to all people of Mexican descent, not just Mexican immigrants. This nativism activates immigration as a core event defining the Mexican-American experience, leading respondents to identify with the experiences of their immigrant coethnics. Race matters in how Mexican Americans experience boundaries, particularly when they are mistaken for immigrants. In a context of heavy Mexican immigration, skin color and sometimes surname become markers of ethnic origin, nativity, and even legal status in such a way that Mexican Americans become the direct targets of nativism.

Mexican Americans also encounter "intragroup boundaries" that divide them from their immigrant coethnics, further locking them in an in-between status. Immigrants define what it means to be a "real" person of Mexican descent, and respondents described facing high expectations about their ethnic authenticity from Mexican immigrants, second-generation Mexican Americans, and even non-Mexicans. The people I interviewed were often treated as inauthentic when they were unable to live up to the criteria for group membership that others imposed, and they managed these boundaries with a combination of strategies, ranging from active resistance to passive retreat.

Understanding how Mexican Americans experience and respond to these two types of boundaries helps to explain where the Mexican-origin population is situated in America's racial and ethnic landscape. As this chapter shows, discrimination still marks the Mexican-American experience well into the later generations. But racism pure and simple does not account for this discrimination. Race combines with continued Mexican immigration in such a way that Mexican immigrants become a prism that refracts nativism into the lives of Mexican Americans. The

findings from this chapter begin to reveal a Mexican-origin population that cannot neatly be described as an aggrieved minority or an
assimilating ethnic group but one that is instead more like a permanent
immigrant group that perpetually struggles with the turbulent process
of assimilation.

NATIVISM'S INDIRECT INFLUENCE
ON INTERGROUP BOUNDARIES

The overarching perception among non-Mexicans is that the Mexican-
origin population is largely foreign. In both Garden City and Santa Maria,
Mexican immigrants are the most visible among people of Mexican
descent and among immigrants in general. Although a sizable foreign-
born population from other countries lives in these cities, Mexicans have
come to represent all immigrants there, primarily because the number of
foreign-born Mexicans dwarfs that of any other immigrant population
in either city. According to the 2000 U.S. Census, Mexicans make up
84 percent of all foreign-born individuals in Santa Maria and 76 percent
of the foreign-born population in Garden City.[2] Adding to the visibility
of Mexican immigrants and the high degree to which Mexicanness is
equated with foreignness is the politicization of Mexican immigration
and the U.S.-Mexico border. Indeed, Mexican immigrants are the focal
point of political debates regarding immigration at the local, state, and
national levels.

Because of their predominance, poverty, and cultural differences,
Mexican immigrants are the primary targets of anti-immigrant fears.
Non-Mexicans express their anxiety about immigration, Mexican
immigration in particular, in both public and more interpersonal ways.
At the core of these expressions are anxiety, fear, and intolerance in
regard to the ways that Mexican immigrants are changing these cities.
In John Higham's classic historical account of European immigration,
he uses the term *nativism* to describe anti-immigrant fears. According
to Higham, nativism is "an intense opposition to an internal minority
on the ground of its foreign (i.e., 'un-American') connections" (1963: 4).

Both academic and popular discourses often use *racism* to describe anti-immigrant sentiment. Invoking this term to describe aggression directed at Mexican immigrants is tempting, given that the history of the West and the Southwest is fraught with animosity toward people of Mexican descent (Griswold del Castillo and de León 1997; Gutiérrez 1995; Meier and Ribera 1993). Yet *racism* does not fully capture the anti-immigrant, and indeed the anti-Mexican-immigrant, sentiment in Garden City and Santa Maria; *nativism* does.[3] Racism—a system of domination, including a set of collective beliefs based on essentialist notions of race (see Omi and Winant 1994)—is tied up with nativism. Nativism can be informed by racism, as has been the case historically with Mexican immigrants. But nativism can be motivated by many other factors, including legal status, job competition, and sociocultural change, even if these factors are bundled with race. Racism, then, is a central factor accounting for anti-immigrant sentiment but certainly not the only factor.

Mexican Americans are never the intended targets of nativist expressions. Their immigrant coethnics are. These expressions nonetheless have a profound influence on the Mexican-American experience, because they reinforce the intergroup boundaries between them and non-Mexicans. These boundaries become more vivid not through social distance from non-Mexicans but through interactions with them. As Barth notes, "Ethnic distinctions do not depend on an absence of social interaction and acceptance, but are quite to the contrary often the very foundations on which embracing social systems are built" (1969: 10). As I showed in chapter 3, some of these interactions result in Mexican Americans and non-Mexicans crossing ethnic boundaries, most notably in the form of interethnic dating and marriage. But this very contact also brings into focus the ways in which boundaries endure. The extent to which the Mexican Americans I interviewed were well-integrated into the core social, political, and economic structures in each city—the extent to which they had crossed boundaries—had provided ample opportunity for them to interact with non-Mexicans. These interactions had often allowed respondents to witness the pernicious nativism directed at their immigrant coethnics.

Interviews from Garden City and Santa Maria reveal three ways in which Mexican Americans become aware of intragroup boundaries: nativist public expressions, nativism communicated in interpersonal expressions, and most vividly when Mexican Americans are treated as foreigners.

Shouting It Out: Public Expressions of Nativism

The heavy influx of Mexican immigrants to Garden City and Santa Maria has spurred sociocultural change, much to the displeasure of many among the established population. Spanish-language media, the proliferation of interpreters and bilingual services, the presence of Mexican specialty-food stores and restaurants, and public celebrations of Mexican holidays are vivid cultural imprints. Long-time citizens, especially non-Mexicans, do not necessarily welcome these changes, and they sometimes make it publicly known. The disdain they express most often centers on the increasing use of non-English languages, on a perception that immigrants take advantage of misguided policies that are tilted in their favor, and on a belief that immigrants are a drain on public resources, especially where welfare, education, and health services are concerned (see Sánchez 1997).[4]

Nativist expressions are particularly visible when delivered by public figures. Most notorious among the public denouncements of immigrants in Santa Maria were statements made in 1990 by its mayor at the time, George Hobbs. A leader with a reputation for being brash and outspoken, Hobbs pointed to Mexican immigrants as the source of what he perceived to be a growing blight on the city. Speaking to a local civic organization, he proclaimed,

> At this time in Santa Maria, we have a Mexican problem. We have a difficulty with scads of illegal aliens that have come across the border, and they've made our neighborhoods look not like Santa Maria neighborhoods. In certain streets people (are) gathered around drinking beer, smoking cigarettes. It's a formidable experience for a lot of the older people who have been here for a long time. . . . That's not speaking, of course, of our Santa Maria Mexicans that have been here forever. Those people came here with the idea of becoming Americans. (Sparks 1990)

The mayor's comments gained infamy in Santa Maria when they made headlines in the *Santa Maria Times,* a local newspaper with wide distribution in the city, and remained in the news for days. Despite Hobbs's qualifier that he was not speaking about long-time Santa Maria residents of Mexican descent (i.e., later-generation Mexican Americans), his proclamation that Santa Maria has "a Mexican problem" etched a lasting memory in the minds of Santa Maria's Mexican-American population. Following his statements, scores of residents, including some Mexican Americans, protested and called for his resignation. I was not in Santa Maria to observe directly the impact of his comments, but their reverberations were still evident years later. Several Santa Maria respondents recalled the comments during interviews. Gigi Bartolome, a sixty-one-year-old retired retail clerk, reflected, "It kind of made me mad because he was talking about Mexicans. What he actually was talking about was illegals. But he said 'Mexicans,' so every Mexican in town took it as them." Hobbs's statement ignited such a strong reaction among Mexican Americans, like Gigi, partly because he racialized his nativist worries. Using the term *Mexican problem,* he tied poverty, crime, and overcrowding to Mexicans; thus, the statements reflected not just concerns about these issues but also a general animosity toward all people of Mexican descent.

The opinion section in the local newspaper is a popular pulpit for nativists, especially when issues surrounding immigration turn up in the local or national news. I conducted my research in Santa Maria shortly after the attacks of September 11. Residents of this community, like those of the United States as a whole, displayed a heightened sensitivity to issues of national identity and perceived foreign threats. The events of 9/11 prompted a spate of letters to the editor of the *Santa Maria Times* regarding Mexican immigration, including the following:

I have witnessed the alarmingly accelerating disappearance of my WASP culture. . . . My quandary has been exacerbated by the events of Sept. 11, causing me to re-examine the value of my own culture and that of others, especially my Hispanic neighbors. Please justify (you don't have to "explain" it—I'm living with it): 1) Why Mexicans, especially, feel they have no duty to acculturate to the customs, laws and language of the United States (I already know about Guadalupe-Hidalgo); 2) The Mexican/Latino lack of ability to acculturate, vis-à-vis other foreign immigrants; 3) How Mexicans/Latinos expect my respect when their presence in my country is, for the majority, the result of the criminal act of illegal immigration traceable back however many generations (in spite of any artificial subsequent "legalization"). (*Santa Maria Times*, 1/30/02)

The sentiments of this author speak to the persistence of nativism resulting from the unabated presence of Mexican immigrants. The author recognizes the long history of Mexican immigration to the United States and therefore casts his nativist ire not just at Mexican immigrants of today but also at the descendants of earlier waves of Mexican immigration whose presence he perceives to be "the result of the criminal act of illegal immigration traceable back however many generations." Like Mayor Hobbs, the author presented his fears about a putatively slow assimilation of immigrants not as a problem having to do with immigrants in general but as a problem tied to "Mexicans" in particular.

The Internet has given nativists the ability to reach large numbers of people, furthering the visibility of their anti-Mexican immigrant stance. During the 2002 campaign for the Kansas State Board of Education, won by a candidate who ran on an anti-immigrant platform, the local newspaper sponsored an online chat room where individuals could share their views on education and unauthorized immigration. The chat room quickly filled with opinions about immigration, Mexicans, and related issues. Several people posted messages supporting the winning candidate's platform, including the following:

I agree with the person that stated it's not fair for our children to have to learn the Mexican language just so the Mexicans can survive in this community, whether it be an adult or a child. If they want to live in OUR country . . . LEARN THE LANGUAGE FIRST!!! You wouldn't catch me going to a foreign country without knowing their language. Mexicans can at least learn our language before they come over here, well enough [so that] you don't have to keep asking them what they are saying. I don't feel that illegal or legal Mexicans should go to any of our schools, like the other person said, it puts a damper on OUR society! And further more [*sic*], no one, and I mean no one, is going to tell me that this community belongs to the Mexicans now and that America belongs to them, as did one gentleman in a college course I was taking did [sic]. It's like we're being taken over by aliens! (posted 9/9/02)

Much like the writer of the letter printed in the Santa Maria newspaper, the author directs his anger about the proliferation of non-English language, specifically Spanish, toward "Mexicans," not just foreign-born Mexicans.

I conducted interviews during a time period when immigration was not such a prominent part of political discourse and prior to a time when the national media began paying a good deal of attention to immigration in the midst of the 2006 and 2007 congressional debates about immigration reform. Thus, public expressions of nativism in Garden City and Santa Maria during my time there tended to be episodic. Nativists now voice their ire for immigrants on a much bigger national stage, and some of the most outspoken anti-immigrant commentators have become household names. Their nearly daily rants against immigration on national television and radio likely add salience to the more local public expressions of nativism that I report here. The power of these comments to harden boundaries comes from their high visibility. Even if it occurred infrequently while I was in Garden City and Santa Maria, publicly voiced nativism weighs heavily on the minds of Mexican Americans there, as evidenced by the number of respondents who brought up such expressions during interviews.

Up Close and Personal:
Encountering Interpersonal Expressions of Nativism

Regular encounters with interpersonal expressions of nativism only bolster these intergroup boundaries. Mexican Americans in Garden City and Santa Maria frequently hear nativist comments directed at immigrants during their interaction with friends, peers, coworkers, and strangers.

Many of the people I interviewed experienced their ethnic identity primarily through the ethnic boundaries that these encounters highlight. Even respondents for whom ethnicity was minimally important in most realms of life reported feeling especially tied to their ethnic background when they bumped up against nativism. The experiences of Ryan Bradley are typical of many of the people I interviewed. Ryan, a sixteen-year-old high school student in Santa Maria, lived in a large house in an upper-middle-class subsection south of the city. Ryan was like many teenagers in Santa Maria. He spoke with an informal but energetic California patois, wore clothes right out of the latest fashion magazines, sported spiky hair with bleached-blond tips, and dreamed of a career in acting. He was also proud of his Mexican heritage and asserted it as a mild form of rebellion against his mostly white, upper-middle-class suburban surroundings. But Ryan's ethnicity became most important to him when he perceived an attack on people of Mexican descent:

If there's a threat that's apparent on somebody else who is of the same descent that I am, and the other person is being totally racist about it and it's all just hate of color, that's when my background comes to be more important to me. Even if the person who is doing it, who is of any other descent, is my friend, and he's ragging on this other guy because he's the same descent as me, I would stand up for the guy the same descent as me, because I don't like people to hate. I don't think that's cool at all. That's when [my ethnic background] steps up to me. [. . .] I have a friend—when we were in junior high we were just the same. And then when we hit high school he got all into the confederate flags and all the weird stuff, and him and a bunch of the guys would always be drawing Nazi signs or whatnot and saying "KKK rocks" and stuff like that. And he was picking on this guy that I didn't know. And he was Mexican, and they were bagging on him because he was Mexican, and I'm just sitting there going, "Hey. I'm Mexican too." [He said,] "No, no, no, this doesn't concern you. You're cool. This guy is not." And I'm just like, "Hey, back up." And I just totally got in his face, because I was getting mad. [. . .] They were calling him a wetback and just totally dissing on him because he was Mexican. I don't know if they had a problem with him because of who he was, but that's not what I heard coming out of their mouths. And I didn't think that was cool at all.

As Ryan's comments show, when Mexican Americans encounter nativism, they often assert a "reactive" form of ethnic identity. According to sociologists Alejandro Portes and Rubén Rumbaut, this type of ethnicity develops "in reaction to the situation, views, and discrimination . . . that turn the circumstances of national origin into the primary basis of group solidarity, overwhelming other competing identifications such as those based on class" (1990: 96). In their study of the second generation, Portes and Rumbaut (2001) argue that the Mexican-American second generation displayed a form of reactive ethnicity in the aftermath of Proposition 187, the 1994 voter-approved California ballot initiative that would have barred unauthorized immigrants from accessing a range of public resources had it not been found unconstitutional. As my interviews demonstrate, reactive ethnicity emerges even in later-generation Mexican Americans, whether or not they are the direct targets of nativism. Interpersonal expressions of nativism of the sort Ryan witnessed evoke a heightened ethnic identity, making it important to Mexican Americans in precisely those situations in which their Mexican-born coethnics, and indeed their entire ethnic group, appear to be threatened.

Respondents in each city reported incidents similar to Ryan's, but important differences in the persistence of nativism exist between Garden City and Santa Maria. While the steady influx of Mexican immigration to Santa Maria has helped maintain ethnic boundaries, the interrupted pattern of immigration to Garden City has made reemerging ethnic boundaries important. The Jim Crow–like discrimination that defined relations between Mexican Americans and whites in Garden City during the first half of the twentieth century broke down, enabling Mexican Americans to move into neighborhoods outside the barrio, gain upward mobility, form friendships with non-Mexicans, and even intermarry. However, in the eyes of some Mexican Americans, the influx of Mexican immigrants into Garden City in the last twenty years has rebuilt some of the division with which Mexican Americans in an earlier era were all too familiar. As Timothy Saenz observed,

I've heard people talk, and they don't say very nice things about the Mexican people from Mexico. [. . .] The main thing I hear is, "They're coming into our country, learn our language, learn our ways." It's almost like it's taking a reversal, like it's coming back around again. What my grandparents suffered, I mean when they suffered, everything they went through with each generation has gotten better for each generation. But now it seems like it's going back around again. And basically what the people from Mexico are hearing and what they say about them is what basically my grandparents dealt with.

The reintroduction of these boundaries can be seen in the daily lives of Garden City respondents. Marcela Muñoz, a nineteen-year-old junior-college student, worked at a local retail store as a customer-service agent in Garden City. Early in our interview, Marcela acknowledged the nativism that her ancestors had faced upon coming to the United States and said she had witnessed similar forms of nativism in her job. She relayed the following instance in which a white customer expressed anger because of the Spanish phone menu on the customer-service line:

We have a Spanish recording. And a guest called and she was asking about American flags. [I said] like, "No, Ma'am. We're not scheduled to get any more until July. We're sorry for the inconvenience." [. . .] But she just opened her mouth, and she was like, "Oh and by the way, what is up with that Mexican crap?" Like that. So I of course was like, "Ma'am, over half of our community understands Spanish." And she started going off on me. I was like, "Ma'am, I'm Mexican American." And she didn't know what to say! She just hung up.

Because Marcela spoke without an accent, the caller assumed that she was white and therefore felt sufficiently comfortable to express her discontent. The caller expressed anger about the Spanish menu, targeting Mexicans with her generalized nativist fears about the proliferation of non-English languages. Like Ryan, Marcela responded with a form of reactive identity, firmly asserting her own identity as a person of Mexican descent.

These small events are part and parcel of Mexican Americans' daily lives. Virtually every Mexican American I interviewed recounted a similar story, indicating that nativism figured prominently in how they experience their ethnic ancestry. Combined with the public expressions of nativism, these interpersonal experiences remind Mexican Americans of the foreign status that their ethnic group occupies, and Mexican immigration produces a nativist response that, both directly and indirectly, affects all people of Mexican descent.

HOW INTERGROUP BOUNDARIES
BECOME MORE RIGID

How do nativist expressions affect Mexican Americans' ethnic identity? Past research on Mexican Americans suggests several possibilities. Mexican Americans could decide to become the purveyors of nativism, crossing the boundary entirely and adopting the nativist views of those on the other side (Newton 2000; Ochoa 2004). Some do in fact do just this, but as I show in the next chapter, such a response tends to be part of an ambivalent reaction to Mexican immigration. Mexican Americans may also decide that the best strategy for dealing with nativism is to disregard it and do nothing, since Mexican immigrants are the intended targets (García Bedolla 2005).

But Mexican Americans in Garden City and Santa Maria do not simply shrug off encounters with nativism that brightens ethnic boundaries. Instead, they adopt these boundaries in constructing their own ethnic identities. Though the previous chapter shows that respondents exercised some choice in how they accessed and utilized ethnic raw materials in constructing their ethnic identities, the imposition and adoption of boundaries make ethnic identity anything but optional or inconsequential. Nativist expressions become an important feature in how Mexican Americans describe a larger Mexican ethnic narrative.

Mike Fernández's comments illustrate this point. Mike, a nineteen-year-old junior-college student in Santa Maria, lived in an upper-middle-class neighborhood and attended a private high school. He described his family as "a white family who is Mexican," because his ethnic background played only a small role in his family's life. But his ethnic background became important to him when he heard nativist comments about Mexican immigrants:

When somebody will say something about Mexicans or, something like that, and it's not said towards me, it's not directed towards me, but at that point, I'll feel myself discriminated against. I'll put the discrimination on myself, feeling that even though they're not directing it toward me, I can't help but feel that it's degrading towards me in some way, when in fact I know it's not meant directly towards me; it's a general comment. But it just kind of makes me uncomfortable.

The reasoning that Mike offered for feeling uncomfortable reflects his attachment to a larger ethnic narrative centered on the immigrant experience:

[T]hey're speaking about a Mexican family or a Mexican person, and I know that; though my family is not in that position, somewhere along down before me, somebody in my family, I'm sure, has been in that position. And although I'm not in it, and probably never will be in that position, I just think that back when my ancestors were in that position and people were the same way towards them.

Although Mike may have had only a vague idea about his family's immigrant history, Mexican immigrants are a real-life representation of his family's historical experience. My exchange with Lucia Pacheco, a nineteen-year old-college student in Santa Maria, reveals similar sentiments:

[T]here's total discrimination against Hispanic people. And then they may not be sending it directly towards me, but I feel it too, because [of] the negativity, because of who I am and who my family is. [. . .] There's times when you'll be in the mall or something, and [Hispanic] people will walk by, and people make really rude comments about who they are. And I just try to shut it off, but it gets to me.

TRJ: What about it gets to you?

R: The fact that people can be so mean and negative towards somebody. They can't help who they are or what they are. [. . .] It's usually people that are from Mexico that you know that they're from Mexico because they don't speak English or something. Or they make fun of people because of the way they dress. And they're Mexican and they call them like gangster or vato or something like that.[5]

TRJ: You said that bothers you because that's who you are and who your family is. What do you mean by that?

R: It's who I am. It's what I am actually. I am Hispanic. My family is Hispanic. I shouldn't feel bad about being Hispanic, and people shouldn't really talk bad about us, because we're just as human as they are. We have feelings and emotions.

Similarly, Diana Bautista told me,

I tend to feel kind of when they talk about [Mexican immigrants], that kind of hurts me too. Because somewhere along the line we . . . my great grandparents *have come to the U.S., so I tend to feel a link between people from Mexico that just come here, to American people. I mean in the sense that I know somewhere along the line my family went through the same thing that they're going through now, learning the language and learning a totally different way of life than what they're accustomed to.*

Mexican Americans, like Mike, Lucia, and Diana, feel a connection to Mexican immigrants vis-à-vis their own immigrant ancestors, a connection that leads them to internalize the nativism so fervently hurled in the direction of their immigrant coethnics. In identifying with the Mexican-immigrant experience, respondents took nativist attacks on immigrants as an affront to all people of Mexican descent, including themselves.

Why would Mexican Americans adopt such a stance instead of creating distance or showing benign indifference? Virtually everyone in my sample was, broadly speaking, middle class and had gained their class status through a combination of blue-collar, semiprofessional, and professional occupations. Though Mexican Americans are in some ways vulnerable to the sort of discrimination aimed at Mexican immigrants (as I show later in the chapter), their class status allows them to deflect some of this discrimination, and they can voluntarily internalize the boundaries that nativism makes apparent without it posing a significant threat.

Mexican Americans actively internalize these boundaries partly because letting go of ethnic attachments is not so easy. Ethnicity is not part of human hard wiring (it is a product of social construction), but it has proven to be a enduring way that people categorize themselves and others (Cornell and Hartmann 1998). Even white ethnics, for whom ethnicity plays a relatively weak role in the construction of social identity, claim an ethnic identity, however symbolic (Waters 1990). Shedding an ethnic identity in the face of nativism is thus not so simple as changing a piece of clothing that has gone out of fashion. Ethnic identity is far too fundamental to how individuals think of themselves in contemporary U.S. society.

For Mexican Americans, the indirect effects of nativism make ethnicity anything but a consequence-free option. The large influx of immigrants from Mexico spurs a nativist reaction aimed squarely at Mexican immigrants and, in some cases, at an entire history of Mexican immigration. But nativists do not always hit their intended targets. Whether nativists voice their opinions in public forums or in interpersonal encounters, Mexican Americans are the victims of collateral damage resulting from the imprecise use of ethnicity to describe more general fears about immigration.

"GUILT BY ASSOCIATION": DIRECT ENCOUNTERS WITH NATIVISM

Nativism is a real feature of Mexican immigrants' everyday lives, but Mexican Americans are also the direct recipients of nativism when they are mistaken for Mexican immigrants. These instances reveal the importance of race in how Mexican Americans confront intergroup boundaries. Past research firmly asserts that Mexican Americans have suffered significant racial discrimination, adversely affecting their social, political, and economic trajectories (Acuña 1972; Almaguer 1975, 1994; Murguía and Telles 1996; Ngai 2004; Telles and Murguía 1990). As I pointed out in the introduction, scholarship routinely invokes theories of racial conflict suggesting that the Mexican-origin population is best characterized by colonialism, discrimination, and racism at the hands of a white majority.

Race matters in the lives of Mexican Americans, but their experience shows that the role it plays is more complex than theories of racial conflict suggest. The formation of race and the meaning attached to it are highly contextual and must therefore be understood in the context in which they operate. The central factor shaping how race operates in Garden City and Santa Maria is demographic. The contentious historical relationship between Mexicans and non-Mexicans in the Midwest (see García 1996) and West (see Almaguer 1994; Camarillo 1996; Griswold del Castillo and de León 1997; and Meier and Ribera 1993) lurks in the background of the Mexican-American experience today, but in Garden City and Santa Maria the massive presence of poor and largely unauthorized Mexican immigrants structures how race affects the Mexican-American experience. In a context of heavy immigrant replenishment, ancestry, nativity, and even legal status become highly racialized.

Respondents reported that race most directly affected them when their skin color led others to assume that they were foreigners. Consider the case of Ronnie Hinojosa, a forty-eight-year-old salesman at a prominent department store in Garden City. He lived in a middle-class neighborhood with his wife, who was white, and their two small children. Ronnie had dark skin and spoke with the midwestern twang typical of Kansas natives. He answered my questions with a polite and jovial demeanor that I came to expect from Garden City residents. However, Ronnie became much more serious when he discussed how his skin color had led others to assume that he was foreign-born:

I was at work, and this lady called in. She wanted to know about a [stereo] or [CD player] or something and I told her all about it, and I said, "Who am I speaking to?" And she told me her name was [Dana]. And she said, "What's yours?" I said, "My name is Ronnie. I work in [electronics]." "OK, I'll come and see you, Ronnie." She came in and the other sales people came and she said, "Is Ronnie here? I didn't get his last name." I came up and said, "What can I do? My name is Ronnie. What's yours?" She said, "[Dana]." I said, "Nice to meet you [Dana]." [She said,]"So you're the one I talked to. You're Spanish! I didn't know that. The way you spoke I didn't even realize you were Spanish." See what I mean? It's just my background and raising and English—that if I didn't have any accent she just assumed I was just another salesman. That's what I get a lot too. But I mean she was fine. She was just shocked that I was a Mexican. And then the way I talked to her [on the phone], she thought I was just another educated, college white kid that worked in a nice department. That's who she wanted to speak [with]. But she still bought something from me. But she thanked me for being knowledgeable of my products and [for speaking] English real well. I didn't question her, but I didn't know what she meant by it. I kind of felt like maybe she felt like I just crossed the border and just got this job, and I speak real good English.

Without a substantial Mexican-immigrant population, the customer might have assumed that Ronnie was a Mexican American whose family, like so many others in Garden City, had been in the United States for several generations. But with a large immigrant population, Ronnie's skin color became a convenient cue to nativity, and he came to be seen and treated as a foreigner who spoke English surprisingly well.

Erin Santiago, an eighteen-year-old college student in Santa Maria, believed that her dark skin had left her vulnerable to overly vigilant retail clerks who followed her around when she shopped:

I guess I feel like when I'm walking through a store, the sales lady is white and she sees me and she probably thinks, I don't know, "This Mexican girl, how does she have any money to afford this?" So they follow you around the store. Asking you, "Do you need any help?" You know in reality that they're not thinking that. They just want to see what you're gonna steal or something. And then I guess they also speak to you very slow, probably thinking that you don't speak English.

Research and media accounts are replete with reports of this sort of treatment experienced by African Americans and Latinos. Audit studies that compare how people from different groups are treated in various situations show that blacks, Latinos, and whites who apply for loans, seek to rent apartments, and look for employment receive differential treatment that falls along racial lines (see, for example, Massey and Lundy 2001; Pager 2003; and Yinger 1986). The results of this sort of discrimination are pernicious for both Mexican Americans and African Americans. But race does not operate in the same way for all groups that are categorized as "minorities." For Mexican Americans, unlike African Americans, immigration plays a significant role in how race shapes their experience. In the case of Mexican Americans, the interplay of immigration and race—stereotypes that flow from assumptions about dark-skinned Mexicans as foreigners—is what leads to discriminatory treatment.[6]

Even if respondents did not have dark skin, they were not entirely insulated from such treatment. Non-Mexicans often tagged respondents who had a Spanish names as foreigners. Surnames often serve as markers of ethnic origin for many groups. Certain surnames signal when someone has, for example, Italian, Polish, or Irish ancestry. But when immigration continues, surnames mark not only ancestry but also nativity, as shown in the experiences of Rolando Fernández Jr., a twenty-one-year-old college student in Santa Maria. Rolando recalled,

Actually, freshman year in college, living in the dorms . . . I guess with a name like mine, I'd go over and say, "Hi! I'm [Rolando Fernández]." And [they would say,]"Oh really? Are you a foreign-exchange student?" And I'd just kind of chuckle like, "No, actually I grew up about half an hour from here." Like, "Oh really? Where did you guys get . . . when did you come to the country?"

Other respondents reported frequently being asked, "Where are you from?" upon revealing their first and last names. Although once a clear sign of ethnic ancestry, surnames from European countries have become indistinguishably woven into the fabric of American names. Surnames that start with *O'* or end in *-ski* are not automatically associated with immigrants, as they once were. Not so for people with Spanish surnames. The large Mexican-immigrant population has made Spanish surnames more firmly associated with an immigrant population. In both Garden City and Santa Maria, the sections of the phone book with names like "García," "Fernández," and "Hernández" have grown exponentially in recent years, making Spanish surnames bright threads in the local social fabric.

The assumption that Mexican Americans are foreigners can have more serious repercussions, especially when law enforcement is involved. The small size of Garden City allows Mexican Americans to interact frequently with non-Mexicans. As some people in Garden City say, "Everyone knows everyone." This means that Mexican Americans' identity as a member of the Garden City community writ large can often trump their ethnic identity in the eyes of non-Mexicans, who often know which families have a long history there. But when Mexican Americans leave Garden City, their group affiliation becomes more open to interpretation by others who, in the absence of information about Mexican Americans' familial history in the United States, rely on skin color and assumptions about Mexicans as foreigners to identify them. Consider an instance that Carl Mercado recounted. Carl was well known to most people in Garden City, having been born and raised there. Yet his experience during a business trip with the predominantly Mexican-immigrant crew he managed shows how things change when Mexican Americans leave Garden City:

About five years ago, me and my crew were going to Pennsylvania to work. And me and two of my guys were in one of the company vehicles, just going down the interstate. Highway patrolman pulls us over, checked my license out. I was driving. He asked me where I was going. I told him I was on our way to Pennsylvania for work. He says, "You're going clear from Kansas to Pennsylvania to work?" I said, "Yeah." We had all the luggage for six guys in our vehicle because we were in a [Chevy] Suburban; wasn't doing nothing wrong. I wasn't speeding. He told me that he pulled me over because I was going . . . the speed limit was sixty-five and I was going sixty-nine. He pulled us over. And after I told him we were going to Pennsylvania, he seen all that luggage in there, he became suspicious. He goes, "Just wait a minute here. I'll be right back." And he went to his car, and he called for backup. He called for a drug-sniffing dog. And the next thing you know, there's three more highway patrolmen. And they ordered us away from our vehicle, and he wanted to check our vehicle for drugs. Didn't give me any reason for him to do that. I got nervous. I knew none of my guys had any of that stuff, because I knew the workers I took didn't do that. And they searched our vehicle. They made us feel like criminals. It had to do with our race. I know it did. Took out all our luggage. Opened all of our luggage, checked everything. He just didn't feel comfortable believing me that we were going to Pennsylvania to do a job and we had all this luggage. He thought we had stolen it. Car wasn't registered to me, because it was a company vehicle. That was another thing against me. But that more than anything, that made me mad. And then they took all of our stuff out of the vehicle. They inspected it, and then they just left it there on the side of the highway. Said we could go. One of the guys that I was with, his wife makes up burritos. The drug-sniffing dog smelled the burritos and started going crazy. Right away they put their hands on their guns and told us to step way back. I just felt violated that day.

The anger and sense of violation that Carl expressed came not just from the hassle incurred when he was pulled over but also from the police officers' perceived use of race as a cue to his and his passengers' legal status and criminal intent. The frequency with which police pull over African Americans without just cause has spawned the phrase "driving while black." The example that Carl recounted might be described as a case of "driving while Mexican." But it was not just Carl's or his passengers' "Mexicanness" that led the police officer to pull him over. It was also the association that the officer drew between Mexican immigrants and the U.S.-Mexico drug trade that led him to pull over Carl and then call in backup to search the vehicle.

In contrast to Garden City, Santa Maria has a considerably larger population and therefore a looser social network, which leaves Mexican Americans more open to the effects of confusion about their nativity. Although respondents in Santa Maria had become well integrated into nearly every aspect of social, political, and economic life there, others still assigned them a foreign identity on the basis of the assumption that Mexicans are not just foreigners but *unauthorized* foreigners. The experiences of Pedro Ramírez, a fifty-two-year-old Mexican-American educator, are illustrative. Pedro, a middle-class Mexican American with a master's degree, lived in an upper-middle-class area north of Santa Maria and was quite proud of his middle-class status. During our interview he showed me photos of the three-thousand-square-foot house he owned and shared with his white girlfriend. Despite being middle class, Pedro's appearance left him open to stereotypes about his ethnicity, nativity, and legal status. He recounted an especially troubling experience of being pulled over by an INS official after doing yard work at a rental property he owned:

I've got my pickup loaded with equipment in the back, and I see a light flashing in my rear window. I look at it, and it's right behind me. So I pull over. I start to get out, and I look at the car, and I start laughing because it's not law enforcement. It's this guy with a Smokey the Bear hat and wraparound glasses. It's la migra. It's the INS, the Border Patrol! So I get out, and the guy says, "¡Vete aquí!" I go, oh no, and I'm laughing. I come over and say, "May I help you?" He says, "Do you speak English?" I said, "What the hell do you think I just said?" He says, "Do you have some ID?" I go, "What the hell do you want to know if I have ID for? I wasn't going past the speed limit. Besides you're not a cop. You're the Border Patrol. All right, I'll play your game." He said, "Do you have some ID?" So I pull out my driver's license and show him my wallet. "Do you have anything else?" I said, "Yeah." And I showed him my social security card. He wanted to reach for it, and I go, "You ain't getting this. Forget that." He goes, "You have anything else?" I go, "Sure I do." So I pull out my American Express card. And it's green. I said, "Don't leave home without it. This is harassment." Guilt by association: Mexican needing a haircut and a shave on a Friday afternoon with bandanna around his neck, with an old pickup truck loaded with mowers and edgers and stuff like that. So I wrote down the license plate number and got his badge number and sent a formal letter. Sent several. And I got several responses in return: "Oops, sorry"—guilt by association.

The large number of Mexican immigrants in the Santa Maria Valley, many of whom are farmworkers, creates the perception that to be of Mexican descent is to be an unauthorized immigrant farmworker. The INS official who pulled over Pedro clearly did not consider that Pedro could be a middle-class, third-generation Mexican American who was simply doing yard work on the weekend. Rather, the official used a combination of Pedro's skin color, style of dress, and the equipment in his truck to gauge Pedro's ethnic origin, nativity, and legal status. As Pedro might put it, the officer deemed him "guilty by association."

This assumption of foreignness is not unique to Mexican Americans in Garden City and Santa Maria, and the ways that Mexican Americans in general experience ethnic boundaries may depend on whether they live in a rural or urban locale. Sociologist Cynthia Duarte's (2008) research on later-generation Mexican Americans in the Los Angeles area shows that Mexican Americans who have moved out of ethnically concentrated neighborhoods have little access to opportunities to engage in the practice of ethnicity, but nonetheless their frequent contact with non-Mexicans leads them to be regularly confronted with expectations of their presumed foreignness. Likewise, Gilda Ochoa's research (2000, 2004) in La Puente, California, a Los Angeles suburb, shows that Mexican Americans who have dark skin also report cases of mistaken identity similar to those I report here. Like my respondents, Mexican Americans in La Puente face instances in which non-Mexicans believe they are foreigners or believe that Mexican Americans possess the same cultural traits that immigrants possess (e.g., the ability to speak Spanish).

Similarly, Japanese and Chinese Americans are also lumped with foreign-born Asians on the basis of race. Mia Tuan's (1998) later-generation Japanese and Chinese respondents had experienced instances in which whites relied on perceptions of Asians as foreigners and expected them to exhibit characteristics associated with foreign-born Asians. Together, these studies show how immigration informs the meaning assigned to race. In the absence of immigrant replenishment, later-generation members of an ethnic group become part of a large corps of American ethnics. But when immigration continues, race and foreignness are linked, and members of the later generation remain in many ways foreigners in the eyes of the mainstream.

"GOOD" AND "BAD" MEXICANS

The Mexican-American experience is not entirely defined by encounters with nativism. Even though respondents often witnessed nativism from non-Mexicans and were occasionally mistaken for foreigners, non-Mexicans sometimes set Mexican Americans apart from their immigrant coethnics. Interactions with friends and acquaintances sometimes led non-Mexicans to very different conclusions about respondents' ethnic identity. Non-Mexicans often reminded respondents that the people of Mexican origin about whom they expressed antipathy were Mexican immigrants ("bad" Mexicans), *not* Mexican Americans ("good" Mexicans).

The interviews I conducted abound with instances in which Mexican Americans are told by acquaintances that they are somehow different from immigrants or that they are more similar to non-Mexicans than to immigrants. In Garden City, the distinctions drawn between Mexican Americans and Mexican immigrants are markedly more pronounced than in Santa Maria. Because of a gap between waves of Mexican immigrants, non-Mexicans are aware of distinctions between the established Mexican-immigrant population and the more recently arrived Mexican immigrants. A "commonsense" understanding of the difference sometimes operates in Garden City. Those descended from the first wave are considered "good" Mexicans, because they have become integrated members of the city. Those from the new wave are "bad" Mexicans because of their foreign status and cultural distinctiveness. Kyle Gil, the thirty-five-year-old auto body shop owner who was married to a white woman and lived in a middle-class section of Garden City, was frequently told by non-Mexicans that he was a "good Mexican":

I've had a lot of people that tell me, "You know, [Kyle,] we don't think of you as a Mexican. We think of you as one of us." [. . .] But in the past I've never had the strength to ask them, "What does 'one of us' mean?" [. . .] But I've had several people tell me that they never have thought of me as being Mexican, just being one of them.

The inclusiveness that comes with being "one of us" is to be considered in relation to the exclusion of those who are not like one of us, namely, Mexican immigrants. Even so, this inclusiveness has its limits. Although Mexican Americans have ample contact with non-Mexicans, their full belonging as "one of us" is limited to the extent that non-Mexicans lump Mexican Americans and immigrants together and to the extent that Mexican Americans draw linkages between their own narrative and that of immigrants.

Non-Mexicans in Santa Maria also draw distinctions between Mexican Americans and immigrants. However, such distinctions are not as easy to make there, since Mexican immigration to Santa Maria has been continuous, creating a vast mixture of people from different immigrant generations and cohorts. Nonetheless, respondents reported instances in which they had achieved inclusive status on the basis of how different they were from Mexican immigrants with respect to nativity and class. These distinctions often came into play when non-Mexicans qualified their nativist comments. As John Rojas, an eighteen-year-old Santa Maria junior-college student, relayed:

I have a Mustang. It's a '98, so it's pretty new. And I was with one of my friends from work, and we were driving, and what happened? She goes, "I hate it when Mexicans drive nice cars." And she's white. [. . .] And I was like, "Really? Why? Do you think it would be bad if Mexicans would drive Mustangs?" And she was like, "Oh, when have Mexicans ever driven Mustangs?" —something like that. And I looked at her and said, "You're riding with one!" And she was like, "What?" And I'm like, "Yeah, I'm a Mexican. I'm driving a Mustang. What does that make me?" She goes, "I don't mean like you."

John's friend implied an image of Mexicans that did not include middle- or upper-class American-born people of Mexican descent who might have the financial means to drive a nice car. Rather, his friend implied a conception of Mexican identity that emphasizes poverty and foreignness. This dichotomous notion of Mexican identity communicates a certain sense of belonging but one that comes at a price. To "belong" requires that Mexican Americans not invoke an ethnic identity like the one that Ryan and Marcela displayed earlier. Doing so would make them appear less like "one of us" and more like one of them.

The implied dichotomy of good and bad Mexicans also leads respondents to feel as though they have to prove continually that they are full members of American society. They feel compelled to combat stereotypes that they are poor immigrants, which might lead others to consider them bad Mexicans. The task of proving that one is a good Mexican is especially apparent when respondents compare the Mexican-American experience with the experiences of white ethnics. The following exchange with Lydia Gutiérrez, a forty-nine-year-old Santa Maria resident who worked in real estate, illustrates the distinction between Mexican Americans and the descendants of early waves of immigrants from Portugal and northern Italy that settled in Santa Maria:

If you think about "X" family, I don't think they have that problem of, "Oh, they've been around; they're good Mexicans. They're good Swiss-Italians, or they're good Portuguese." I don't think those groups have that, whereas the Mexicans that have been here for a while or those of us that aren't like those ones that just came recently [do]. There's a distinction there, although I guess you don't find a lot of Swiss-Italian or Portuguese coming. [. . .]

TRJ: So why do you think there's a difference between Swiss-Italian and Portuguese versus Mexicans with respect to this problem you're talking about?

R: I think it's just because [pauses] I don't know. I just think people have this thing about being Mexican. And I think too because we have people coming on a constant basis. It's a reminder of who we are. But I don't see them having that distinction of being good or bad. The Portuguese never get in trouble.

As Lydia pointed out, Mexican immigrants are a reference group to which non-Mexicans compare Mexican Americans. They evaluate Mexican Americans' place in society in comparison to both their immigrant ancestors and those who continue to cross the border today. In contrast, Swiss-Italians and Portuguese, two groups with a long history in Santa Maria but no present-day immigration, rarely, if ever, navigate these dichotomous categories.[7] They, like other European groups for whom immigration is a thing of the past, are free to be as ethnic or nonethnic as they like without being compared with foreign-born brethren.

ETHNIC EXPECTATIONS AND INTRAGROUP BOUNDARIES

The heavy influx of immigrants to Garden City and Santa Maria not only makes the boundaries that circumscribe Mexican Americans more rigid; it also introduces intragroup boundaries among people of Mexican descent.[8] As chapter 4 demonstrated, Mexican immigrants contribute to Mexican Americans' access to the practice of ethnicity. So far, this chapter has shown how the presence of a large Mexican-immigrant population brightens intergroup boundaries. There is a tendency to think of ethnic raw materials and the boundaries that distinguish groups as occupying opposite sides of the same ethnic-identity coin (see Barth 1969). But the two are quite intimately related. Indeed, contestation over what counts as an authentic display of ethnicity (the use of ethnic raw materials) can become the very basis for both intra- and intergroup boundary formation. Such is the case for Mexican Americans who fail to live up to expectations about group authenticity informed and often imposed by Mexican immigrants and second-generation Mexican Americans.

In Mary Waters's (1990) study of later-generation white ethnics, she astutely notes that her respondents have ethnic options: they have the freedom to choose their ethnic identity, and these choices carry few, if any, consequences. Their license to choose identities, Waters argues, is a result of the freedoms granted in part by those outside their ethnic group. Since they have light skin, white ethnics are not easily identified with the particular group or groups to which they trace their roots. The ethnic and racial distinctiveness of these groups has faded to such an extent that few strong notions remain about what traits individuals from one of these groups ought to exhibit. Put another way, the freedom to choose identities that white ethnics have is partly granted by the lack of imposition placed on them by people outside their ethnic group. But surely such imposition is absent within their ethnic group as well. Ethnicity has thinned to such a degree for white ethnics that group members require nothing more from one another than a mere claim that their ancestors came from a particular homeland. Seldom would anyone be surprised or disappointed if fellow Italian Americans, Czech Americans, or Polish Americans failed to speak the tongue of their immigrant ancestors or did not have tastes that somehow display their ethnic origin. Without any subsequent immigration to refresh ideas about what it means to be a member of these ethnic groups, ethnic group authenticity carries few expectations.

Things are different for Mexican Americans. They face a stringent authentication process that requires them to display characteristics that were much more likely to be present among their immigrant ancestors, who, in many cases, came to the United States a hundred years ago. Mexican Americans are not fully free to choose their identity, partly because Mexican immigrants, second-generation individuals, and occasionally non-Mexicans bolster a notion of Mexican ethnicity that is informed by the large immigrant population. Because they are more distant from their own immigrant generation, some Mexican Americans are unable to live up to these expectations. Mexican immigrants and the young second generation set the criteria for ethnic authenticity, rebuffing Mexican Americans' claims as "real" Mexicans. Likewise, non-Mexicans expect Mexican Americans to carry the traits of their immigrant ancestors despite their later-generation status.

Language as a Gatekeeper

The boundaries between Mexican Americans and Mexican immigrants are particularly apparent when it comes to the use of Spanish. Although many people of Mexican descent in the United States, including many in my sample, do not speak Spanish, immigrants from Mexico and other Latin American countries maintain Spanish as a central component of group identity. The ability to speak Spanish has become a near requirement to prove authenticity. Interviews with the youngest respondents abound with experiences in which immigrants or young second-generation individuals called into question respondents' authenticity because of their inability to speak Spanish.

The school setting could be a particularly contentious place for young respondents, because their Spanish-speaking peers used language as the litmus test for ethnic authenticity. Recall from chapter 4 the cases in which immigrants or second-generation Mexican American friends had assisted respondents in learning Spanish in schools. These encounters could also lead to tension over language. I noted in chapter 4 that Faith Obregón, the sixteen-year-old high school student in Garden City, cited instances in which Mexican-immigrant and second-generation friends had been enthusiastic to help her learn Spanish. But Faith also described encounters in which other immigrant and second-generation peers had shamed her for her inability to converse in Spanish:

They ask me, they say, "Are you white?" And [I'm] like, "No." Because I don't speak Spanish, and this school is like, if you speak Spanish, then you're a Mexican, and if you don't, then you're white [. . .] because, I don't know, they're just like, "What are you?" Like, "Are you half white?" Like if I told them, "Yeah, I'm half white," they'd believe me. It's like, "No." And when I do tell them that I'm full Mexican, they're like, "Na uh!" They're like, "You're lying!" And then they ask, "Do you know Spanish?" It's like, "No." And then they think it's like so wrong that I don't know Spanish. But I'm trying.

TRJ: Why do you think they think it's wrong that you don't know Spanish?

R: Because I'm Mexican, and I'm supposed to.

Generational progression and an ideology of Americanization have combined to weaken Spanish-language use among later-generation Mexican Americans, leaving young respondents ill-equipped to live up to expectations about what it means to be a "real" Mexican.

The use of language as a gatekeeper is hardly confined to adolescents. Adult respondents had also run into boundaries in their interactions with immigrants. Mexican Americans from the middle cohort reported that immigrant coethnics had questioned how they could be of Mexican descent and not speak Spanish. This boundary maintenance was especially upsetting to Manuel Arnedo, a forty-three-year-old firefighter in Santa Maria. Manuel was raised by his grandfather, who taught Manuel to think of himself not in ethnic terms but as an "American." This meant shedding use of the Spanish language. As a result, Manuel's Spanish-speaking colleagues had often ribbed him about his English monolingualism:

I get angry at people that make fun of the fact that I'm not fluent in Spanish like other Spanish-speakers, other people that come from a Mexican background, and [they] tease me about it.

My observation of an encounter between Donald Mercado and a Mexican-immigrant youth at a restaurant in Garden City further illustrates how language authenticates individuals as "real" Mexicans. Donald and I met for a beer and a bite to eat at a local Salvadoran restaurant. When we arrived, the restaurant was largely empty, except for the owner, the owner's younger sister, and a young Mexican immigrant named Andrés. Donald and I struck up a conversation with Andrés and invited him to sit with us. Since Donald spoke only English and Andrés only Spanish, I translated for the two. The conversation progressed in a mostly cordial fashion, until Andrés wondered aloud in an indicting tone how it could be that Mexican Americans, like Donald, could be Mexican and not speak Spanish. Andrés went on to assert that Mexican Americans choose not to speak Spanish because they are ashamed of their ethnic roots. In response, Donald explained that discrimination cast Spanish-language use in a negative light and made learning it undesirable. In an effort to communicate to Andrés his embarrassment for not learning Spanish, Donald hung his head in shame. The regret that many Mexican Americans express for not speaking Spanish is often self-imposed, as Donald expressed in the restaurant. This regret comes not only from a sense of having lost out on the social and economic opportunities that come with bilingualism but also from the sense that their English monolingualism leaves them unable to prove their ethnic worth to those who impose strict criteria for authenticity.[9]

"You Don't Act Mexican": Style and Tastes as Authenticators

Language is not the only authenticator of Mexican ethnicity. The choices that individuals make about cultural consumption can also determine the extent to which others regard them as "authentic" members of an ethnic group (Warikoo 2007). Immigrants and the young second generation often challenge Mexican Americans about their style of dress, tastes, and the company they keep. Mexican Americans are well familiar with the styles and tastes popular in the United States (although as I pointed out in chapter 4, American popular culture increasingly includes a Mexican flavor). Some Mexican-American respondents said that the popular, preppy style of their dress left them open to criticism, because these styles are closer to Anglo-American fashions. Ramón Ramos, in Santa Maria, is a case in point. Rolando described himself as a patriot who aspired to a career in the military. He believed that such a career would make him a role model to other students of Mexican descent. However, some of his acquaintances at school equated his career aspirations, style of dress, and inability to speak Spanish with "white" orientations, charging that he was not fully Mexican as a result:

There's people at school say that I'm white. I mean, [I'm] stereotyped by it. The brand I wear, which is Quicksilver and Anchor Blue in jeans. And I'm just trying to do something positive. Like I said, I want to be in the military, be a police officer. I want to be a positive role model for Mexican Americans and [show] that there's a place for us in law enforcement and the military.

TRJ: You have to back up and tell me about this. Why do people think that you're white? What do you mean by that?

R: Because of just the way I dress and type of music I like sometimes and because I don't know Spanish.

In the eyes of those who impose boundaries, Mexican ethnicity and mainstream American culture are at odds. Having tastes and styles that lack obvious Mexican overtones leaves Mexican Americans vulnerable to criticism about their ethnic authenticity.

Although fellow students never accused Lori Rojas, a forty-year-old financial records coordinator, of acting white when she was in school, she recalled being teased because her involvement in school activities put her in contact with many non-Mexican students. Some of the Mexican immigrants and second-generation students had perceived Lori's high level of participation to be a slight to her ethnic background:

In junior high I did have a lot of trouble, because some girls didn't believe me that I was Mexican when I would say I was Mexican. Or they would say that I didn't act like I was Mexican. So I had problems in junior high.

TRJ: What did they mean when they said you didn't act like you were Mexican?

L: I don't know. They wanted me to maybe dress like they did and act like they did, and I didn't. I wasn't trying not to be or [to] act like it. I didn't feel I had to act a certain way because of my background. But I was a cheerleader, sports, outgoing, so I guess they felt I shouldn't have done that. [. . .] In junior high one time I walked into the bathroom, and they were all standing by the door and they wouldn't let me go in, because they said that I thought I was too good. I couldn't go in; it was their bathroom and they wanted me not to go in. And [they said] I didn't think I was Mexican and acted like I was too good to be their friends.

The notions of Mexican ethnicity that Lori described are informed by the large presence of Mexican immigrants and the second generation, who carry a form of Mexican ethnicity that is closer to that of their ethnic homeland. Their large numbers have helped to define what it popularly means to be Mexican. At the heart of this definition are the ability to speak Spanish, dark skin, a taste for Mexican culture (including food and music), the donning of clothing commonly found among Mexican youth (some respondents suggested that these styles include baggy pants for men and tighter-fitting clothes for women), and speaking with an accent that does not resemble a "white" accent. Mexican Americans who cannot authenticate themselves in relation to these criteria are often cast aside by those who police the boundaries of ethnic legitimacy.

Confrontations with rigid constructions of ethnic authenticity are not

unique to Mexican Americans. Among African Americans, school success can be grounds for contesting authenticity. High-achieving African-
American students are sometimes regarded by lower-achieving peers as
betraying their African-American roots if their school success appears
to come at the expense of their allegiance to black youth culture (Carter
2005). Though charges of inauthenticity do not account for poor school
achievement among blacks (Cook and Ludwig 1998; Tyson, Darity, and
Castellino 2005), high-achieving students who do not display the cultural trappings associated with black youth culture are accused of "acting white" (Fordham 1996; Fordham and Ogbu 1986). The bounds of
authenticity may become blurred, particularly in a multiracial setting in
which young people see clearly demarcated lines between authentic and
inauthentic cultural consumption. Sociologist Natasha Kumar Warikoo
(2007) shows that Indian-origin second-generation high school students
carve out a cultural space that combines hip-hop, which is regarded as
high-status in urban schools, and traditional Punjabi *bhangra* music. This
cultural hybridity allows students to be seen as culturally authentic but
also "cool." Tests of authenticity that involve "harder" criteria may not
allow for hybrid forms of authenticity. As sociologist Joane Nagel (1997)
points out, claims to Native American ancestry have very real consequences for everything from qualification for federal programs to child
custody rights. Nagel notes that, with the paucity of objective criteria for
deciding who is Native American, some organizations require proof of
enrollment in a federally recognized nation or tribe.

Mexican Americans cannot pass the authenticity tests they face with
similar sorts of proof. They must depend on their ability to meet a set
of cultural criteria that the large presence of immigrants helps to determine and that are enforced by Mexican immigrants, second-generation
Mexican Americans, and even non-Mexicans.

Notions about Authenticity from Non-Mexicans

Mexican immigrants are not the only ones who impose notions of ethnic
authenticity. In many instances, non-Mexicans assert strong ideas about
ethnic authenticity informed by recent immigration and the perception

of Mexicans as a foreign group. As with the expectations that Mexican immigrants and the second generation impose, the use of the Spanish language is a central component of the expectations that come from non-Mexicans. They often assume that Mexican Americans speak Spanish, an ability much more likely to be found among immigrants and the second generation (Rumbaut, Massey, and Bean 2006). Take the example that Ryan Bradley provided from his experience at school:

I had a teacher freshman year, and the first day they met me, they thought it would be nice if they talked to me in Spanish, just straight Spanish. And I was just like, we don't even speak that much Spanish, you know? And they thought that was my native language. They thought it would be more comfortable for me. They even said that if it would be more comfortable to speak in Spanish, and I think they just thought that right off the bat.

Mexican Americans' experiences at work also highlight how non-Mexicans assert these expectations. Several respondents reported instances in which non-Mexicans had asked them to serve as interpreters at work. These non-Mexicans were surprised when they discovered that the Mexican-American respondents were unable to do so. Take the case of Lucia Pacheco, the nineteen-year-old college student in Santa Maria who worked at a local pizza restaurant:

[T]here is this one girl who I work with; she stereotyped me as a Mexican because of my name, just my name. Before she even knew me, she assumed that I spoke Spanish. And she would always send [Spanish-speaking] people to me to talk to me. And I'd have to send them away, because I didn't know what to say to them or help them. [. . .] It was my name. [. . .] [I]n one instance, she's like, "This is Lucia Pacheco. She doesn't speak Spanish and doesn't like hot food!" And I thought that was kind of inappropriate of her to say. But she was my manager, and I couldn't really say anything.

Later-generation white ethnics are rarely, if ever, expected to speak the language of their immigrant ancestors, but immigrant replenishment ensures that Mexican Americans regularly face these expectations. Because Mexican-immigrant replenishment makes the criteria for ethnic authenticity clear, Mexican Americans lack the option to assert an ethnic identity that departs from the notion that Mexicans are necessarily a foreign group. Such assertions rarely go without challenge from non-Mexicans, Mexican immigrants, or the second generation, who impose strict notions of Mexican ethnic authenticity.

MANAGING BOUNDARIES

Ethnic boundaries are not fixed, and Mexican Americans are certainly not passive bystanders who are hopelessly squeezed between inter- and intragroup boundaries. They manage these boundaries by employing a combination of strategies that are a delicate balancing act between signaling affiliation to their ethnic ancestry and also firmly asserting that they are Americans. The strategies they employ depend on the type of boundary that they encounter—inter- or intragroup. These strategies fall within the typology of boundary-making strategies that sociologist Andreas Wimmer (2008a) lays out.

When Mexican Americans encounter nativism directed at their immigrant coethnics, they engage in what Wimmer calls transvaluation, whereby actors "reinterpret or change the normative principles of ethnic stratification" (Wimmer 2008a: 13) by trying to equalize the status of their own group with that of others. Mexican Americans offer a corrective to those who express nativist sentiments in interpersonal encounters. They accomplish transvaluation by first pointing out that they "are Mexican too" as a way to communicate that nativist comments are unwelcome. Invoking a sense of common identity with Mexican immigrants communicates the gross inaccuracies of the stereotypes embedded in nativist expressions. By citing themselves as "Mexicans too," they point out that attaching ethnicity to discontent about immigration includes Mexican Americans, who, as they attempt to indicate, share many similarities with people who are not of Mexican origin. Chapter 7 includes a more extensive discussion of how and why Mexican Americans stand up for their immigrant coethnics. Suffice it to say here that taking a stand against nativism is just one of the ways that Mexican Americans respond to the boundaries that nativism makes apparent.

Mexican Americans' response to the more pernicious forms of nativism most often involves a different strategy. They engage in what Wimmer calls boundary "contraction," wherein actors draw "narrower boundaries and thus [disidentify] with the category one is assigned to by outsiders" (Wimmer 2008a: 12). While respondents did not deny their Mexican ancestry, the threat of being mistaken for an immigrant led them to signal in not-so-subtle ways that they were in fact part of the U.S.-born population and not part of the Mexican-immigrant population. In interpersonal interactions, Mexican Americans preempt stereotypes from people whom they fear may confuse them for a non-English-speaking immigrant. Take the case of Donald Mercado. Recall from earlier in this chapter that Donald did not speak Spanish at all and that this was sometimes a source of shame when Mexican immigrants confronted him about it. Donald's dark skin may have led some to believe he was an immigrant, and his readiness to speak first in interactions with non-Mexicans was a defense mechanism against such a perception:

I think sometimes people will look at me and kind of be ready to say something to me because they are fearful that I'm going to say something in Spanish to them. That would catch them off guard. But what I do when I go to, let's say out of town or out of town area, I usually will speak first, and I'll always ask, "How are you doing? How are you doing? What's going on today?"

Bob Fernández, the fifty-two-year-old graphic designer in Santa Maria, invoked similar strategies in interactions with his neighbors:

I think when I see the stuff in the newspaper, whether it's Hispanics or Mexicans or whoever that's doing it, it just brings a stigma onto all of us. Because I think there's a lot of the public out there that on first view, their initial thought is, "Oh, here's another Mexican." [. . .] You always wonder moving [into a new neighborhood], "Are the neighbors across the street saying, 'Oh, here comes another Mexican family"? And I guess I'm the type of person that never lets people's attitude affect me. Like the neighbors across the street were rather cool for a long time, and it could possibly have been because they didn't like Mexicans. I really don't know. [. . .] But I'm the type that if I see them out there, I'm gonna holler across the street, "Hello! How are you?" Just force them to say hello, force them to be nice.

These mechanisms for signaling their American nationality are part of a larger strategy for Mexican Americans to fend off potential experiences with nativism. Middle-class Mexican Americans often use symbols of their class status (recall that Pedro showed the INS official his American Express credit card) to send the message that they are in fact U.S.-born people of Mexican descent. Among the symbols that Mexican Americans deploy are homeownership, certain consumer items, vacation destinations, and occupation. By invoking markers of their class status, Mexican Americans send a clear signal that they are not the poor unauthorized immigrants that many people imagine when they think of Mexican-descent individuals. They attempt to communicate that they are, rather, integrated members of U.S. society.

Mexican Americans adopt a different set of strategies when it comes to managing the intragroup boundaries that become apparent when they encounter ethnic expectations from Mexican immigrants, second-generation Mexican Americans, and even non-Mexicans. They display a combination of frustration, polite opposition, and retreat. Many contest those who question their authenticity by challenging any implied assumptions about what it means to be a "real" Mexican. By claiming their own inclusion as authentic Mexicans, respondents attempted to expand the bounds of inclusion—what Wimmer calls "boundary expansion"—from which immigrant and second-generation Mexican American had sometimes excluded them. Rafael Solís, a thirty-year-old pastor in Garden City, had faced many such situations while growing up. When I asked how he used to respond to challenges to his ethnic authenticity, he said,

I would just ask them why? "Prove it, or what makes you more than me? Both my parents are Mexican. My parents are Mexican. You tell me how I'm not . . . how you're more [Mexican] than I am or I'm not a Mexican." I would want them to explain to me why.

Rafael, like many respondents, effectively "pushed back" when questioned about his ethnic authenticity. In so doing, they asserted that their identity as people of Mexican descent was dependent not on their ability to live up to commonly imposed expectations, like speaking Spanish, but more generally on ancestry from Mexico.

Other Mexican Americans take a "softer" approach in making the case for their inclusion inside the Mexican ethnic boundary. They attempt to educate those who impose exclusionary boundaries by explaining the factors that have contributed to their inability to prove their ethnic worth in the face of intragroup boundaries. These explanations often include moments in which Mexican Americans act as "armchair sociologists." They explain that their family has been in the United States for multiple generations and that negative attitudes about Spanish-language use during their childhood led to significant social sanctions for using the language. The conversation between Donald Mercado and Andrés that I recounted earlier illustrates the use of just such a strategy. Donald was quick to show his shame for not speaking Spanish, but he was also intent on helping Andrés understand that structural factors account for why Spanish-language use had faded within his family: generational progression and negative attitudes about Spanish earlier in his life.

Other Mexican Americans choose not to manage these boundaries at all and instead retreat. By avoiding situations where boundaries may become salient, they engage in a subtle form of boundary contraction. They deemphasize their Mexican ethnic ancestry by avoiding situations in which their ethnic identity is likely to become a focus of interpersonal encounters. They sometimes avoid Mexican restaurants that immigrants frequent, stay way from Mexican-immigrant and second-generation peer groups at school, and avoid public spaces in which Spanish is the dominant language. Faith Obregón's retreat from such situations can be seen in the uneasiness she felt about spending time in front of the school auditorium, a popular haunt for Spanish-speaking Mexican students passing their free time:

I'd feel really uncomfortable hanging out by [the auditorium], where all the Mexicans are. I'd feel like they look at me like, "You shouldn't be here, because you don't know Spanish, and you're not like us." I'd feel really uncomfortable there.

Such settings remind Mexican Americans that they do not possess the key criterion for Mexican ethnic authenticity: the ability to speak Spanish. When Mexican Americans are in the presence of large numbers of Spanish speakers, they feel as though they are constantly being judged by those who are more "authentic." Faith and others have sometimes concluded that it's better just to avoid such judgment altogether. Avoiding such situations does not involve retreating from Mexican identity entirely. Mexican Americans who employ this strategy still describe themselves as being proud of their Mexican ancestry. Retreating does, however, mean that Mexican Americans occasionally avoid settings in which particular expressions of ethnic identity are central to social acceptance.

In addition to bolstering the salience of Mexican Americans' ethnic identity through the provision of ethnic raw materials, the large Mexican-immigrant population bolsters the boundaries that shape the Mexican-American experience. Though Mexican Americans' structural assimilation suggests that they have crossed ethnic boundaries to some degree, boundaries remain intact, thus making ethnicity less symbolic, less optional, and a more consequential aspect of their identity. The "foreignness" of Mexican ethnicity created by the recent and heavy influx of Mexican immigrants into Garden City and Santa Maria reinforces intergroup boundaries between Mexican Americans and non-Mexicans, as well as intragroup boundaries among people of Mexican descent. Intergroup boundaries become more rigid when non-Mexicans make nativist comments in public forums or in interpersonal settings, attributing their nativist fears to all Mexicans. Non-Mexicans also mistake Mexican Americans for immigrants, further sharpening the divide between "us" and "them." Respondents expressed feeling the indirect effect of this nativism when it had led them to invoke their own immigrant history, drawing parallels between their ancestors' experiences and those of today's Mexican immigrants. In so doing, respondents came to identify with the immigrants' plight, as the experience of immigration and assimilation becomes ever more central to the Mexican-American narrative.

The legacy of conquest and racial discrimination visited upon people of Mexican descent for more than 150 years underpins how Mexican Americans experience race, but the findings from this chapter suggest that current Mexican immigration more powerfully structures how race shapes the Mexican-American experience. Because heavy Mexican immigration has cast the entire Mexican population as a foreign group, their dark skin becomes a cue not only to ethnicity but also to nativity and even legal status. In the absence of other information, non-Mexicans rely on skin color and sometimes surname to gauge Mexican identity, often treating all as foreigners.

The "foreignness" of Mexican identity also sharpens intragroup boundaries among people of Mexican descent. Mexican immigrants and second-generation individuals have come to define what it means to be authentically Mexican, and this definition entails, at the very least, speaking Spanish. But more than just defining the criteria, Mexican immigrants, young second-generation individuals, and occasionally non-Mexicans police the boundaries of ethnic group membership, calling into question Mexican Americans' legitimacy when they are not able to openly display characteristics that would "prove" their authenticity.

It is important to consider the consequences of these boundaries for Mexican Americans, especially whether they impede their incorporation as full members of American society. Mia Tuan (1998) frames the question by asking if later-generation Chinese Americans and Japanese Americans are "forever foreigners." It seems appropriate to ask a similar question about Mexican Americans. My interviews and observations show that ethnicity is not a symbolic, optional, and inconsequential aspect of identity for Mexican Americans as it is for white ethnics. Furthermore, continuing Mexican immigration has much to do with the nonsymbolic nature of Mexican ethnicity. As chapter 3 illustrates, Mexican Americans are in many ways centrally located in the mainstream of Garden City and Santa Maria, which might lead to the conclusion that they are not forever foreigners. Clearly they are not. Such a classification would belie Mexican Americans' display of significant structural assimilation. Yet the foreignness of Mexican ethnicity reinforces the sense among non-Mexicans that all people of Mexican descent are poor and perhaps even unauthorized foreigners. The large immigrant population makes Mexican Americans' ethnicity more of a nocuous part of their daily experience and one that is at times central to their interactions with non-Mexicans. While Mexican Americans are not forever foreigners, the foreignness of their ethnic ancestry, constantly reinforced by immigrant replenishment, limits the extent to which they feel comfortably situated in the American mainstream.

This chapter also speaks to the larger puzzle of the place of the Mexican-origin population in America's racial and ethnic landscape, whether Mexican Americans experience U.S. society as an aggrieved racial group or as an assimilating immigrant ethnic group. While Mexican Americans have assimilated into U.S. society to a large extent, continuing Mexican immigration bolsters both the intra- and intergroup boundaries that distinguish later-generation Mexican Americans. Race shapes Mexican Americans' experiences, but it interacts with immigration. The meaning assigned to race in Garden City and Santa Maria comes from a context of mass Mexican immigration. In an American society that sees race before anything, race influences the experiences of many Mexican Americans by limiting their ability to be seen as American ethnics. The findings in this chapter suggest, then, that people of Mexican origin are more like a permanent immigrant group, and the replenishment of an immigrant population ensures that this group must continually struggle for integration into U.S. society.

Mexican Americans' position between inter- and intragroup boundaries leaves them in a difficult spot. The foreign flavor of Mexican ethnicity increases the costs associated with Mexican-American identity. Respondents were able to associate comfortably with non-Mexicans, but boundaries became apparent when non-Mexicans made nativist remarks about Mexican immigrants and when they mistook respondents for immigrants. Yet their association with Mexican immigrants also raised the costs of being Mexican American, since respondents had to "work at" being Mexican in order to prove their authenticity. As Abraham Quintanilla quipped in the quote near the opening of this chapter, "Being Mexican American is tough." Occupying the space between these boundaries oftentimes requires Mexican Americans "to be more Mexican than the Mexicans, and more American than the Americans."

SIX

Assessing Mexican Immigration

THE MEXICAN-AMERICAN PERSPECTIVE

As the last two chapters have shown, not only do foreign-born Mexicans provide abundant access to ethnic raw materials, but also they influence the boundaries of ethnic identity. The large Mexican-immigrant presence places Mexican Americans in an in-between position that makes them seem at times not completely American and at other times not fully Mexican. This in-between position shapes how Mexican Americans view immigration from their ethnic homeland. As U.S.-born people of Mexican descent, the people I interviewed are part of the larger "host" population that evaluates whether Mexican immigration is positive or negative for the United States, whether immigration should be limited, kept at current levels, or increased. But my respondents also trace their ethnic origins to the country that sends more immigrant "guests" to the

United States than any other in the world. They thus evaluated Mexican immigration from their perspective as both U.S.-born citizens and ethnic Mexicans. What, then, do Mexican Americans think about Mexican immigration?

Public opinion research suggests that Mexican Americans' views may differ from those of other Americans. Because of cultural similarities and network ties to foreign-born coethnics, they may have an affinity for Mexican immigrants that leads them to more accommodating opinions. This "cultural affinity" hypothesis finds some support in survey research in particular locales, such as Southern California (Espenshade and Calhoun 1993), but it does not explain the opinions that Latinos have expressed in nationally representative surveys (Espenshade and Hempstead 1996). Others have argued that Mexican Americans' structural integration—time spent in the United States, English-speaking ability, and socioeconomic status—is a more powerful determinant of their stance on immigration. This "structural position" hypothesis posits that the more generations Mexican Americans have been in the United States, the less attached they become to an ethnic identity, and their opinions about immigration come to resemble the more restrictionist stance of other U.S.-born citizens (de la Garza and DeSipio 1998; de la Garza et al. 1992; Newton 2000). Even if Mexican Americans' opinions become more restrictionist over the course of several generations, the majority of later-generation individuals still appear to hold largely accommodating views (Telles and Ortiz 2008: 255–60).

This chapter brings the focus down from the aerial perspective provided by survey research and shows not just what Mexican Americans think about immigration but also how they form their opinions. The in-depth interviews that I conducted with later-generation Mexican Americans help explain the complexity of their opinions in ways that survey research hints at but does not fully capture. The first part of the chapter looks at Mexican Americans' opinions about levels of Mexican immigration and unauthorized Mexican immigration. Much like recent survey research, my interviews demonstrate that Mexican Americans are largely accommodating in their views, arguing that immigration should not be restricted. The reasons that they hold these accommodating opinions cannot be explained merely by their class position or level of socioeconomic integration, however. Their views are partly explained by their internalization of core American ideals combined with their identification with the Mexican-immigrant experience as part of a larger Mexican-American narrative. The few who carry ambivalent and more restrictive views see Mexican immigration as a financial burden that produces lost opportunities for U.S. citizens. They see today's Mexican immigrants as undeserving recipients of public benefits that were unavailable to their own immigrant ancestors.

The second half of the chapter examines another important dimension of Mexican Americans' opinions about immigration from their ethnic homeland: its influence on the social standing of Mexican Americans. The findings I presented in the last two chapters suggest that Mexican immigration affects Mexican-American ethnic identity in ways that might be regarded as both beneficial and deleterious to their social standing. Survey research also suggests that Mexican Americans may hold ambivalent opinions about immigration (Binder, Polinard, and Wrinkle 1997; Espenshade and Calhoun 1993; Espenshade and Hempstead 1996). In fact, my interviews show that respondents in Garden City and Santa Maria had even more ambivalent opinions than the survey research suggests. The larger ambivalent response with which American society greets Mexican immigrants structures how Mexican Americans view the impact of immigration from their ethnic homeland. On one hand, American society shuns Mexican immigrants, seeing them as contributors to social and economic ills. Accordingly, respondents expressed the belief that the immigrant population dampens the status of the entire Mexican-origin population. On the other hand, Mexican ethnicity carries value in a multicultural United States that prizes ethnic diversity as a core component of democracy and as an avenue for industries to appeal to new market niches. This more positive response leads Mexican Americans to see immigration from their ethnic homeland as a benefit that increases the demand for ethnic Mexicans' representation in firms, organizations, and politics while also giving the entire Mexican-origin population cachet in popular culture.

CONSIDERING MEXICAN IMMIGRATION

As debates about immigration rage in the United States, media accounts reinforce the perception of primarily two competing factions: native-born whites (and some blacks) on one side and Latinos on the other. Whereas native-born whites argue that Mexican immigration leads to cultural ruin, higher crime rates, job displacement, and strained public services, Latinos are said to believe that immigrants fulfill a demand for labor, contribute to the U.S. economy, do not commit crimes, and are simply trying to make a better life for themselves.[1] Public protests and cable-TV news broadcasts give life to these caricatures by providing a stage for shouting matches between white opponents of immigration and their Latino adversaries. This presentation of the immigration debate glosses over the vast internal differences among people of Mexican origin (and among Latinos more generally) in relation to legal status, socioeconomic status, language, and generational status. Interviews from Garden City and Santa Maria show that Mexican Americans' opinions and attitudes about immigration are much more complicated than these caricature presentations indicate. Though Mexican Americans are largely accommodating in their opinions and attitudes, their views are not rooted in ethnic nationalism or a desire for "open borders." Instead, they come from their connection to the immigrant experience in combination with an internalization of core American ideals related to freedom and opportunity.

"This Is a Nation of Immigrants": Accommodating Views on Mexican Immigration

Population growth in Garden City and Santa Maria over the last twenty years owes primarily to Mexican immigration. As I showed in chapter 5, non-Mexicans frequently express their vitriolic opposition to Mexican immigration and the ways that it has changed these cities. Like their non-Mexican counterparts, Mexican Americans articulate strong opinions about whether the United States should work to limit Mexican immigration or maintain a relatively open border. Most respondents, however, held accommodating views. When asked about immigration, both authorized and unauthorized, they expressed the general belief that the border should remain open and had virtually no opposition to current levels of immigration. They premised their views on a combination of core American ideals and psychological and emotional linkages to immigrants vis-à-vis their own immigrant ancestors, immigrant friends, and spouses.

One of the most strongly stated rationales that respondents provided for not restricting immigration is that the immigrant experience is a core feature of Mexican-American identity and indeed American national identity. They frequently invoked the historical experience of immigrants, both Mexican and non-Mexican, as a source of economic and social invigoration, and respondents who were close to that immigrant experience tended to hold the most unequivocally accommodating views. Rolando Fernández is a case in point. During his youth, Rolando worked with his father, a former farm laborer from Mexico, to organize farmworkers with César Chávez and the United Farm Workers.[2] Even though his status as a physician distances him socioeconomically from his immigrant-laborer roots, the immigrant experience has an emotional resonance with him and informs his views:

This country would not be what it is today without immigrants—not only Mexican immigrants, but immigrants of all types. Ours is an immigrant nation. So I would firmly, strongly believe we should continue to allow open borders for immigration.

Likewise, Margarita Llanes was close to the immigrant experience because her parents were born in Mexico and also because her husband was a foreign-born Mexican who came to the United States as a *bracero* in the 1950s. She too premised her accommodating views on the idea that immigration is fundamental to the American national identity:

I wouldn't stop it, because the U.S. is made up of lots of nationalities. [. . .] [W]hy should we say who should be allowed to come or not? Had it not been for somebody, our parents wouldn't be here; our parents wouldn't have come. I mean we were immigrants at one time or another.

For many Mexican Americans, restricting immigration would violate the now popular notion that the United States is a "nation of immigrants." This was far from a trite slogan for the people I interviewed. It had deep resonance, partly because of their own families' biographies, which show the Mexican-origin population to be a people of immigrants, both now and in the past. But they also saw shutting the door on Mexican immigrants as antithetical to the importance of immigration as a defining event in a large national narrative.

Even more contentious than Mexican immigration in general is the issue of unauthorized Mexican immigration. Debates about immigration today most often center on Mexico, which sends the largest share of unauthorized immigrants, at around 59 percent (Passel 2008). Yet the issue of legality did little to change respondents' largely accommodating opinions. They invoked similar rationales related to their identification with the immigrant experience and core American ideals. They saw a close connection between today's unauthorized immigrants and their own immigrant ancestors, leading them to stake out a more sympathetic position. According to Johnny Ocampo, the forty-four-year-old UPS driver in Garden City,

Everybody that ever came to this country came on a risk, not on a piece of paper. They are changing the way Garden City is? I don't think so. My grandfather was undocumented too. So was my grandfather on my mom's side. I think it's only important to present these papers to somebody else. I think anybody that's ever come across that border illegally is coming across to do better. And so you don't need that documentation for yourself; you need it for somebody else. And I know I'd be willing to go to the risk to make my child's life better.

For Mexican Americans, certain aspects of the immigrant experience resonate, and being unauthorized is a particularly salient one. Their accommodating views are born not just of their identification with the immigrant experience writ large but especially of their identification with the particularities of the *unauthorized* immigrant experience. They invoke notions of belonging in U.S. society predicated more on hard work and ambition than on legal documents.

Personal relationships with unauthorized immigrants exerted an even more powerful influence on the views of the people I interviewed. Recall from chapter 4 that some Mexican Americans date and even marry Mexican immigrants, some of whom were unauthorized at one time. These romantic bonds tend to soften opinions about unauthorized immigration. Dave Suárez, the thirty-two-year-old insurance salesman in Garden City, was married to a woman from Mexico who originally entered the United States without authorization but was now a U.S. citizen. His insider's view of her experiences had made him more sympathetic to the plight of other unauthorized immigrants:

See, I'm a little different because my wife at one point was undocumented. I mean, her family was. And once you get past that, you realize [that they are] people, and they're going through those struggles and like everybody else's family did, either now or in the past, or whatever.

Johnny's and Dave's comments speak to the recognition on the part of many Mexican Americans that unauthorized entry and the struggles that go with it have become central to the large Mexican ethnic narrative in the United States.

Views about immigration were not guided by connections to the immigrant experience alone but also by respondents' internalization of core American ideals, particularly as they relate to the American dream. Historian Camille Guerín-Gonzáles describes the American dream in the following way: "The American dream promised economic opportunity and security—which would free people to realize their intellectual, physical, and spiritual potential—as the foundation for basic rights of individual citizens" (1994: 2). The principles embedded in the American dream are deeply resonant among Mexican Americans, because they believe they are that dream's beneficiaries. They point out that their own immigrant ancestors endured the struggles stemming from immigration and assimilation so that future generations could fully realize opportunities in the United States. Today's Mexican immigrants, they argue, ought to have a chance to access the American dream in much the same way that their immigrant ancestors did. As Kyle Gil commented,

I think if you stop the Mexican immigration that you change everything that the country has ever stood for. It's always been open to everybody. I don't think

it would be fair for all of us that are here and have made our lives better and we got that chance and we got that opportunity. [. . .] There's too much open space out in this world, in this country. There's plenty of room for other people. And I think it would be unfair to not let them have the opportunity to live their life's dreams. I don't think that would be a good idea to put a wall across the border.

Inez Fernández, a sixteen-year-old high school student in Santa Maria, echoed Kyle's sentiments:

They just want to be able to make a better life for themselves compared to what they had in Mexico. I know it's not the best down there, but America has always had good standards and stuff. And if they want to make something of themselves, they should be allowed to.

A number of the people I interviewed, like Inez, believed that Mexican immigrants have sincere intentions of improving their lives, and they boasted of the United States as a place where the possibility for immigrants to do so is real. They implicitly extolled an individual's right to pursue his or her ambitions, and they believed this right is not reserved for U.S. citizens. In their eyes, "closing the gates" after so many other previous waves of immigrants have reaped the benefits of being in the United States would be unfair.

The issue of legality does little to change Mexican Americans' steadfast belief that the American dream should be accessible to all. They invoke many of the same core American ideals in explaining their view of unauthorized immigration that they use in discussing the authorized sort. Carlos Morales, a twenty-year-old junior-college student in Santa Maria, commented,

I mean I don't see anybody coming to the U.S. as being illegal. It's like if you come here, do your work and do what you gotta do to make a living. I don't see anything different about illegal immigrants. If work's there, take it.

TRJ: When you say you don't see anyone being illegal, what do you mean by that?

R: I mean I've always grown up [believing] that this is a free country. And if you want to come here, so be it. I'm not gonna stand there kicking you out or trying to stop you from coming.

In contrast to what survey research suggests, the greater the degree to which Mexican Americans have assimilated, perhaps the more accommodating their views. The people I interviewed saw their own upward mobility as a testament to an American dream that should be available to all who seek it. They subscribed to the notion that entitlement to opportunities in the United States is determined not by legal status but by a willingness to work hard and to play by the rules once north of the border.

"Softer" explanations of the benefits of population change also guided the respondents' accommodating views. As I discussed in chapter 4, many Mexican Americans wholeheartedly subscribe to a multiculturalism, which extols the virtues of racial and ethnic diversity. Some see Mexican immigration as a positive addition to the United States, precisely because immigrants contribute to the country's diversity. They note that Mexican immigration invigorates a population that might otherwise become socially and culturally stagnant. Drawing on his own pluralist version of the melting-pot metaphor, Ron Terán, a fifty-nine-year-old school administrator in Santa Maria asserted,

They add contributions to society whether they're from Mexico or anywhere else. The melting pot—you don't come out as one, but you have a lot of different cultural experiences. And I've always thought that more is better. You all shouldn't look like one. Everybody brings something special to wherever they settle at.

The reasoning that Mexican Americans provide for their more accommodating views speaks to survey research on Latinos' opinions and attitudes about immigration. Both of the competing hypotheses that social scientists have used to explain Latinos' opinions about immigration—"cultural affinity" (Espenshade and Calhoun 1993) and "structural position" (de la Garza and DeSipio 1998; de la Garza et al. 1993)—have a kernel of truth, but neither fully explains how Mexican Americans form their opinions. My interviews suggest that in some ways, Mexican Americans' opinions have very little to do with their ethnic identity. The grounds on which they premise their views are partly rooted in ideals to which many Americans subscribe, irrespective of their ethnic origins: freedom, opportunity, and diversity. Where ethnic identity does play a role in shaping Mexican Americans' accommodating views, it has less to do with "affinity" for a people who share their culture and more to do with an identification with the immigrant experience—one that is characterized by unauthorized entry, low-wage labor, discrimination, and the struggle for a better life. What they latch on to are not abstract cultural connections but an immigrant experience that is tightly woven into virtually every aspect of the Mexican narrative in the United States.

"It's Good and in Another Way It's Not": Mexican-American Ambivalence about Mexican Immigration

Mexican Americans are not immune to holding restrictionist opinions, however. A much smaller group of respondents was ambivalent about Mexican immigration. They held contradictory opinions rooted in their simultaneous belief in the American dream *and* their concerns about population change and adherence to the law. They recognized the virtues of immigration that other respondents mentioned, but their concerns about population growth, crime, and fiscal prudence tempered their enthusiasm for these virtues.

Rita Morales, a sixty-three-year-old office manager in Garden City, was especially ambivalent in her opinions. During the interview she frequently wavered between what she saw as positive about Mexican immigration—that it creates opportunities for people to better their lives—and what she saw as a drawback—that Mexican immigrants may have a negative influence on the community. The following comments highlight her ambivalence:

It's good, and in another way it's not. I think it's good that they can come over here and make a better life, and they don't have to live in the poverty that they were living in before. What I don't like is that a lot of times they don't adapt to the ways of America. They want to come over here, and they want to live just like they lived in Mexico. But that's not all of them. That's just some. And then I think that a lot of times maybe it's not good for all of them to come over. Because there's a mixture of people, and a lot of times there are people that are dealing drugs or people that maybe have committed serious crimes, and they're coming to our communities, and we don't know anything about them. But I think it's great that they can come over here and make a better life than what they had before, because I've seen how some of them lived in Mexico. And so I think it's great that they can come over here. And those that come over here and want to continue their education and stuff, I think that's great that they have that opportunity. On the other hand, like I said, we're getting all kinds of drug dealers and people that might have a background of crime or something. And I don't like that at all.

Other respondents voiced admiration for Mexican immigrants even as they expressed dissatisfaction with policies they perceived to be too permissive of immigration from Mexico. Samantha Salcedo, a middle-aged (she declined to give exact age), junior-college administrator in Santa Maria, is a case in point. Although she believed immigration needs to be limited, she carried favorable views about immigrants themselves:

I don't feel that they can open the door and just let everybody in, because we don't have the resources. We don't have enough water, we don't have enough housing. [. . .] I have a lot of sympathy for them, and I think they're very courageous to want to come over here and work. But you asked me earlier about immigration. I think immigration itself, it all has to be planned.

Among respondents with ambivalent opinions, the issue of immigration pulled at their heartstrings while pushing up against their sense of what is best for their community and country.

The issue of unauthorized immigration only heightened the ambivalence that some respondents expressed. Their more accepting beliefs about Mexican immigration in general were conflicted with their support of the American rule of law. While respondents were sympathetic to the plight of unauthorized Mexican immigrants, the idea that so many immigrants come without authorization sat uncomfortably with them. Consider the comments of Lauren Fernández, a seventeen-year-old high school student in Santa Maria:

I don't think it's cool. I think that they should make . . . I don't know. I guess illegally probably isn't the greatest thing, but I'm sure that also they're trying just to have a better life for themselves and for their family and just trying to get education for their kids and stuff. So I think that they're not really trying to have, like, a negative [impact] on our community and stuff. But I also think they should be here legally, be citizens to live here.

TRJ: Why do you think some people come here illegally?

R: Probably so they don't have to pay for all the stuff to be citizens and go through all the paperwork and everything. But I don't really have a reason. I don't understand why they can't go through that to be a citizen, because I don't think it takes very long. I don't think that they would enjoy a bunch of people from the U.S. coming in and invading their country. So I don't think they should ours.

As with other ambivalent Mexican Americans, Lauren struggled to reconcile the compelling human story of the unauthorized immigrants who desire a better life with her belief that individuals ought to obey the law. If respondents who carried ambivalent views about Mexican immigration believed that the United States is being "invaded," they also believed that those who "invade" have a very compelling reason for doing so.

"Close the Gates!" Restrictionist Views of Mexican Immigration

A small group of Mexican-American respondents came to very different conclusions about immigration from their ethnic homeland when they invoked connections to their immigrant ancestors in combination with their American national identity. Instead of believing that the United States ought to remain accessible to Mexican immigrants, they concluded that the U.S.-Mexico border needs to be sealed. These respondents tended to come from the lower middle class. They saw today's Mexican immigrants as having a deleterious fiscal impact on U.S. society as a whole, but especially on themselves and their loved ones. In their view, today's Mexican immigrants are spoiled compared with their own immigrant ancestors, who made their way in U.S. society without any assistance.

Gigi Bartolome, the sixty-one-year-old retired retail clerk in Santa Maria, expressed some of the most staunchly restrictionist opinions about Mexican immigration I heard. Gigi lived in a Santa Maria neighborhood that had changed from ethnically mixed and working-class in character to one in which Mexican immigrants predominated. Upset by what she perceived as the decline in the quality of life in her neighborhood, Gigi was adamant that the border should be sealed:

I think it should stop now, because we've got too many. And yeah, maybe it is good for our country, because they're the ones that do the fieldwork. But it has gotten out of hand now, I think, because they're abusing the system now.

Similarly, Martha Garza, a sixty-two-year-old retail salesperson in Garden City, was decidedly restrictionist in her opinions about Mexican immigration. Her cousin, Dolores, a fifty-nine-year-old office manager, supported Martha's comments, chiming in throughout the interview:

M: Don't let any more Mexicans in!

D: Yes. Don't let any more Mexicans in!

M: Put a stop there at the border. Don't let any more people in. Let us take care of our own people here and then . . .

D: But yet the beef plants, who else is going to do that work? They will—the Southeast Asians, the Vietnamese; they'll go out there and work. Good pay, but they take that work, and they'll work out there. But it's got its advantages and disadvantages. It's got its good and bad. They come in here and the crime rate . . . The police are always . . . The police briefs or whatever in the newspaper . . . Mexicans most wanted in the back page of the newspaper. And it is domestic violence has gone up and stuff. It ain't nothing for them to shoot and kill their wives if they think that's the right thing to do. And the dances—the police are always going there and breaking up fights and all this stuff and the loud music that they play. There's always people complaining about that. Like I said, there's good and there's bad. It's good for the economy, because if they really felt it here when [one of the beef-packing plants] burnt down, they felt it. Wal-Mart was always packed.

Martha and Dolores saw Mexican immigrants as having an overall negative influence on the local community, citing frequent reports of crime and a high-profile murder-suicide case involving a Mexican-immigrant couple. Among virtually all respondents there was a recognition that Mexican immigrants play an important role in the economy by pouring money into it and by filling jobs that most American workers regard as undesirable. The extent of the economic importance of immigration became especially clear in Garden City when one of the local beef plants burned down in the winter of 2000. Many immigrants moved away, and retail shops suffered without their usual customer base. Even after considering the economic benefits, the few who held restrictionist beliefs were adamant that Mexican immigrants produce a net social and economic loss.

Not surprisingly, the few respondents who held restrictionist views about Mexican immigration were even more steadfast in their restrictionist stance when it came to unauthorized immigration. Their opposition came from a perception that unauthorized immigrants are unworthy recipients of public resources and a drain on public coffers.[3] Most Mexican Americans have experienced some mobility, but for others mobility has been limited; thus, Mexican immigration presents a perceived threat. None of the people I interviewed mentioned job competition as a reason for wanting to limit Mexican immigration. But their class status and personal experience led them to see immigrants as a threat to their economic well-being. They opined that a lack of authorization allows immigrants to take advantage of the benefits that come with living in the United States without having to be responsible contributing members of the national community. For example, Lori Rojas believed that unauthorized immigrants are able to avoid paying taxes and other costs of life in the United States, such as car insurance:

I think they shouldn't be illegal, because they can come over here and work and don't have to pay taxes and go back to Mexico. And we work here, and they take a lot of money out for our taxes. I think that's unfair. But I think if they're gonna be here that they should be legal and have to do everything that we have to do: have to pay taxes, have to have car insurance. I don't understand how someone could . . . If it was me, I have to have my car registered. I have to have car insurance. There's been two occasions where there's been accidents in our family, and the other people weren't even here legally. They had no insurance, and nothing happens to them. If I was to go hit somebody, I'd be in trouble if I didn't have it. So they don't have to have the same things that we do. But they just go back to Mexico, and they don't have to worry about anything.

Lori believed that unauthorized immigrants get a free ride because they have no legal responsibility to participate in U.S. society. Like Lauren Fernández, she adhered to the notion that immigrants can make a simple choice to be in the United States legally, even though Mexicans have limited access to legal migration (see Chavez 1998; Massey, Durand, and Malone 2002).

Perceptions about Mexican immigrants as an economic drain became especially apparent when respondents recalled instances in which they believed that unauthorized immigrants had benefited from public resources at their expense or that of a loved one. Some respondents submitted that the United States should attend to its citizens before immigrants, especially before unauthorized immigrants. But they said this assistance is not what is taking place. They shared accounts in which they or someone they knew was denied various forms of public assistance, while people whom they believed to be unauthorized were beneficiaries of an all-too-generous welfare system. Such anecdotal evidence led them to conclude that unauthorized immigrants are taking a piece of the pie that rightfully belongs not just to U.S. citizens in general but to people they know personally. Gigi Bartolome provided the following story about her son and daughter-in-law to explain her views:

He got hurt on his job, and he wasn't working. And they had no money coming in. They applied for food stamps. They got turned down. They had three little ones at home to feed, but they got turned down because he had had a good job. Well, he had a good job, but he wasn't making any money anymore. And my daughter-in-law went off. When they turned him down, she said, "Yeah, if we were druggies or illegals, we'd have everything. You would have given us everything!" And the lady told her to calm down, and she goes, "No! All I'm asking you is for food stamps to feed my kids with, and you have to turn us down. But these illegals get everything." My son was telling her to be quiet, because there were some sitting there, you know? But I mean she was so angry at the way they turned her down. And if it hadn't been for me buying their groceries, they would have starved.

Mexican-American respondents who carried restrictionist opinions, unlike those who held more accommodating views, invoked a form of American identity that sees immigration as a zero-sum game in which Americans like themselves are being cheated by unauthorized Mexicans. The perception among these respondents was that unauthorized immigration has helped throw the American welfare state out of whack, such that those who are least entitled to government assistance—unauthorized Mexican immigrants—receive more assistance than those who are most deserving—American citizens. Although respondents who expressed this opinion supported their arguments primarily with anecdotal evidence, their perception was their reality, and they saw a United States in which "out-of-hand" unauthorized immigration is robbing them of prosperity.

Even though the commonalities between the experiences of today's Mexican immigrants and those of their ancestors created sympathy among some respondents, those with more restrictionist views cited differences between those experiences to support their views. Some noted that today's Mexican immigrants are qualitatively different from their own immigrant ancestors. They opined that an all-too-generous welfare state has imbued today's Mexican newcomers with an inflated sense of entitlement. They extolled "rugged individualism" in explaining the experiences of their immigrant ancestors, who integrated into American society without an extensive web of social services and without what they saw as coddling informed by multiculturalism. Some Mexican Americans espoused their immigrant ancestors' individual efforts as a way to illustrate their belief that today's immigrants should make it on their own laurels. Julie Mercado, a forty-five-year-old secretary in Garden City, invoked her grandmother's experiences in concluding that Mexican immigrants today should have to do the same:

Just to know the history, background. I guess like I said, I got to know how my grandmother struggled. I guess I take that back [in time] almost, because, you know, I think I look at the Mexican population now, and I say, "Well, you know, nobody helped my grandparents back then." They didn't know the language. Everything is bilingual now. We have a lot of help out there. I think, "Well, nobody helped my grandmother to learn [English] [. . .]," and I guess I do think, "You need to work for your money. I mean you need to work hard and earn for yourself."

The absence of assistance for their immigrant ancestors as well as their own mobility, however nominal, led many to believe that such assistance is unnecessary in order to make it in U.S. society. What some perceived to be an abundance of aid supports the conclusion that today's Mexican immigrants are "spoiled." Johnny Rincón, a sixty-three-year-old liquor store owner in Santa Maria, stated,

They give them too much. And that's why they're all coming over here. They get all the freebies, and half of the taxpayer is supporting the other half. And I don't think that's right. Let them work like we all did!

When held up in comparison to their immigrant ancestors, today's wave of Mexican immigrants comes to be seen as undeserving, partly because of their unauthorized status, but more so because some respondents see them as not having "earned their keep."

Mexican Americans' responses to questions about Mexican immigration, both authorized and unauthorized, reveal more than just what they thought about immigration. Their responses also strongly suggest the importance of historical and contemporary immigration to the Mexican-American experience. Whether they believed that the gates of American immigration ought to be left open, as most did, or slammed shut, the experiences of their own immigrant ancestors served as a lens through which they viewed Mexican immigration today.

Their responses also show that Mexican Americans possess a national identity firmly rooted north of the border. Most respondents expressed a belief in the American dream as a reason for their accommodating opinions. Others relied on a version of American national identity that led them to call for closed borders in order to protect Americans like themselves. Regardless of what they concluded, the grounds on which they explained their opinions do not suggest that they carried separatist tendencies, deep-seated ethnic nationalism, or a desire for Mexican-origin social and political domination, as some have feared (Buchanan 2006; Huntington 2004b). Instead, they internalized core American ideals. Some respondents who held accommodating beliefs cited the United States as having provided their immigrant ancestors with access to social and economic opportunity and security and opined that this same opportunity and security should exist for today's Mexican immigrants, which suggests their internalization of ideals that most Americans hold dear. Political scientist Rodolfo de la Garza and his colleagues conclude much the same in their survey-based study of Mexican-American and white beliefs in core American political values: "Ethnicity does not systematically affect patriotism, but when it does, its impact is positive rather than negative. . . . Mexican Americans at all levels of acculturation who are United States citizens express patriotism at levels equal to or higher than do Anglos" (de la Garza, Falcon, and García 1996: 346). Indeed, Mexican Americans' opinions about immigrants tend to reveal that an attachment to their ethnic group and their American national identity are quite compatible.

Although Mexican Americans express largely accommodating opinions about immigration, they do not all share the same view. No crystal-clear explanation for the variation in opinions among Mexican-American respondents emerges from the interviews, but the interviews suggest possible explanations. What is clear is that their views have little to do with direct job competition with immigrants. Newly arrived Mexican immigrants and Mexican Americans are in entirely different labor markets and therefore do not see each other as competitors for jobs. Any sense of economic competition comes from the belief that Mexican immigrants are a drain on public coffers or that immigrants take benefits away from less-well-off Mexican Americans.

That said, social class may account for some of the differences in opinions among Mexican Americans. The most accommodating views about immigration tended to be held by respondents who were firmly planted in the middle and upper classes. They were much less vulnerable, though not completely immune, to the sort of mistaken identity I reported in the previous chapter, since their class status inoculated them against the direct effects of anti-Mexican nativism. Furthermore, middle- and upper-class Mexican Americans, like other Americans in the same class statuses, may stand to gain from the presence of low-wage Mexican laborers, who provide cheap services to the economically well heeled. Respondents from these classes may therefore have been more inclined to see Mexican immigration as generally a good thing. Those respondents who held the more restrictionist views tended to be lower-middle-class individuals, who had gained entrance into middle-class status through blue-collar work. Their class status did not provide the same buffer from anti-Mexican nativism that middle- and upper-class Mexican Americans enjoy, and their less accommodating views may have been motivated by a sense of threat to their status. Moreover, they may have been less well positioned to afford and benefit from the cheap services—gardening, day care, construction, and so forth—that Mexican immigrants provide. They were thus less apt to see economic benefits accruing from Mexican immigration, which may in turn have colored their views about Mexican immigration more generally. The second half of this chapter lends some credence to these explanations.

It is also quite possible that Mexican Americans' opinions are rooted in larger liberal or conservative political ideologies. I did not ask respondents about which side of the political spectrum they most identified with, and drawing any inference about the effect of political identification on the basis of my interviews is nearly impossible for me. Had I asked respondents about their political affiliation, nothing indicates that this line of questioning would have yielded more clarity, since opinions about immigration cut generally across the political spectrum like few other issues.

"THEY AFFECT US ALL": BELIEFS ABOUT THE IMPACT OF IMMIGRATION ON MEXICAN AMERICANS' SOCIAL STANDING

Mexican immigration carries special resonance for Mexican Americans, because they share an ethnic origin with the largest immigrant group in the United States.[4] Because of this shared ethnic origin, Mexican immigration has the potential to impact Mexican Americans' social standing. How do Mexican Americans view this impact? My interview respondents expressed much more ambivalence regarding the impact of Mexican immigration on their own lives than they did in their views of the levels of Mexican immigration and unauthorized immigration. They saw the influence as both a curse and a blessing, as having both costs and benefits. Their ambivalence was shaped by the more general ambivalence with which American society greets Mexican immigrants. The costs derive from a widespread nativist response to Mexican immigration, which in turn induced fear among respondents that Mexican immigration dampens the status of all people of Mexican origin. But respondents also cited clear benefits accruing from a more welcoming response that derives from a combination of multiculturalism and market forces that aim to attract immigrant labor and spending. Multiculturalism and this market-led response produces a demand for Mexican-American political and professional representation and gives Mexican culture greater visibility in American popular culture, both of which Mexican Americans see as a benefit of immigration.

"They Give Us All a Bad Name": The Cost of Mexican Immigration

Virtually all Mexican Americans see Mexican immigration as a cost to their social standing, but those who hold the most restrictionist views of it tend to see immigration from their ethnic homeland as having almost no benefits. Most, however, express a greater degree of ambivalence, seeing benefits to Mexican Americans' social standing that counterweigh the price of Mexican immigration.

The costs they perceive emanate from a single source: the effect on the overall image of the Mexican-origin population. They believe that what happens among their immigrant coethnics reflects on all people of Mexican descent, including Mexican Americans. Many note that Mexican immigrants have a largely negative influence on the overall image of Mexican-origin individuals and that this negative image comes from local and national media, which continually tie crime and unauthorized immigration to the Mexican-origin population. Garden City's cable-access television station and local newspaper frequently displayed the names and photos of the most wanted criminals in the county, which included Latinos whom Garden City residents presumed to be Mexican immigrants, because the names and faces were unfamiliar to long-time residents. Garden City respondents believed that these reports cast the entire Mexican-origin population in a negative light. Ellen Iturbe, a forty-four-year-old secretary in Garden City, explained:

Sometimes I used to feel angry, because I think maybe that's when there were more people from Mexico coming in. And I used to tell [my husband], "God!"

You started reading things in the paper, and it would upset me, because I'm thinking it makes us look bad. And we're the local[s], from here. And yeah, I would get mad at things that you read in the paper. Because we're not all like that. I mean you know . . . I felt sometimes I would think that, "Then everybody thinks that we're all like that. And we're not."

Negative representations of Mexican immigration in the media only stoked local residents' ire toward the immigrants. The highly charged, negative reception that often greets Mexican immigrants influenced respondents' perception that immigrants hurt the image of the entire Mexican-origin population. Local residents often loudly voiced complaints about the lifestyle characteristics of Mexican immigrants, which they believed contribute to degradation of local life. They saw the housing strategies that immigrants employ (multiple people living in a single dwelling), their overall cleanliness, and their behavior in public as evidence of a lack of acculturation. Well aware of these complaints from local non-Mexican residents, some Mexican Americans feared that these lifestyle characteristics contribute to negative stereotypes that other local residents applied to Mexican-American residents. Among the respondents voicing their concerns, Johnny Rincón, who held restrictionist views of Mexican immigration in general, echoed the ire of non-Mexicans.

[Other people] probably say, "Look at those guys. They're all the same." Because the way these guys are living, it kind of hurts us in some ways. [. . .] The housing, how they live, leaving their cars, what they're driving, the way they dress, their overall rudeness too. A lot of people complain [that] they're real rude people, the ones that come from over there. You know, [if] something happens I say, "Excuse me," or something like that. A lot of times these people don't say, "Excuse me." We get a lot of that, especially in stores. They let their little kids run in the aisles, eating all the food and opening packages. And todos mocosos [with mucus on their noses], with the diapers. They should keep those kids a little cleaner.

The small group of respondents who held entirely restrictionist views regarding Mexican immigration were also those who were most unsympathetic about the immigrants' plight and believed that the difficulties associated with their poverty and adjustment to U.S. society cast all people of Mexican descent in a bad light.

The overwhelming majority of Mexican-American respondents, however, were more measured in how they discussed their concern about the costs of Mexican immigration. They expressed sympathy toward immigrants' struggle even as they voiced disappointment about the ways in which this struggle may reflect poorly on all people of Mexican descent. Lupe Bustamante, a fifty-eight-year-old office manager in Santa Maria, was sympathetic toward Mexican immigrants and expressed unequivocally accommodating views about them. Yet when I asked her about the influence that the presence of Mexican immigrants had on her life, she expressed disappointment that the housing strategies that immigrants employ may affect how people see Mexican Americans like her:

Well, I think one of the ways [it influences Mexican Americans] is I hear more negative things about Mexicans now. I mean, you hear more negative things because of that.

TRJ: Does that influence your life in any way?

R: Makes me angry, that's about it. And sometimes they make me angry because I think a lot of them, if they tried, they could do a little better. But I think mostly it just makes me angry. I wish that it wasn't that so many of them had to live together like that, because if you live two to three families in a house or in one place, it's bound to get rundown. So it's just an impact on the city, so therefore people will start saying things. And you hear it, and it does make you mad, or it does me anyway.

Respondents often "heard things" through personal interactions or read opinion letters in the newspaper, like those cited in chapter 5. More than being upset by the immigrants themselves, Lupe and others expressed a general disappointment regarding the existence of a situation in which high housing prices forced immigrants to employ strategies that precipitated a backlash from long-time residents.

The feeling that Mexican immigrants threaten the image of all people of Mexican descent also related to respondents' sense that they have to defend themselves against negative stereotypes related to the foreignness of the Mexican-origin population. Some told me they felt they had to prove to non-Mexicans that they were indeed *U.S.*-born Mexicans.

Mexican-American respondents of all class statuses expressed this concern. Recall from chapter 5 that Donald Mercado and Bob Fernández, both professionals, invoked preemptive greeting strategies with whites in order to head off any perception of them as foreign-born Mexicans.

Age also affects how Mexican Americans see the potential threat that Mexican immigration creates for their social standing. The youngest respondents voiced concerns about their image, but they worried much less about being mistaken for immigrants than they did about being taken for "gangsters." The likelihood that the youngest respondents would be confused for immigrants is less than for older respondents. Younger Mexican Americans display styles of dress, patterns of speech, and tastes that reflect a strong familiarity with American popular culture and signal their native-born status. Yet young respondents said they had to guard against being stereotyped as "gangbangers" or "gangsters," an identity that is most often associated with the second generation (Vigil 1988). The large number of immigrants in Garden City and Santa Maria has also produced a large and growing second generation. Scholars of the immigrant second generation have shown that assimilation is particularly precarious for these Mexican Americans. They negotiate between their parents' expectations, which are informed by an immigrant experience, and their identity as a U.S.-born minority, which can leave them open to discrimination and blocked mobility (Waters 1999). The experiences of the adolescent second generation are made more difficult by a lack of parental control resulting from the children's greater familiarity with U.S. society compared with that of their parents, who often do not speak English and spend the bulk of their time working. The second generation can fall prey to harmful influences in U.S. society that threaten the well-being of all adolescents (regardless of generation), but the second generation is especially vulnerable to these influences because their parents, who work long hours, struggle to keep an eye on them and because discrimination can depress their hopes and aspirations.[5]

The struggles of today's second generation instill concerns among young Mexican Americans that they will be painted by others with the same brush. Eric Garza, of Garden City, worried that other people thought he was a gangbanger. Eric was a high-achieving student who was active in extracurricular activities on his high school campus. His closest friends were whites, immigrants, and second- and later-generation Mexican Americans. However, Eric was still concerned that people would apply gangster stereotypes to him:

[L]ike at our school there's lots of people that I guess they could be considered in gangs and things like that. And lots of people look at those as being Hispanic. And then like me, I've had straight A's ever since I was little. I've always been real well behaved, never really gotten in any trouble. And they kind of see me and they're kind of like, "Well what are you?" They think maybe I should be a thug and causing trouble all the time and everything. [. . .] I bet you some do. Like some of them, there's people at school that think, "Yeah, Hispanics are troublemakers. They're all the ones in gangs and everything like that." But then there's some other ones that just think of it as a whole and think everybody like that is Hispanic.

The large second generation helps define what it means to be a young Mexican American in the eyes of non-Mexican residents in each city. While a substantial number of second-generation Mexican Americans steer clear of any sort of gangster life and do exceptionally well in school,[6] those who do not fare so well often stand out. The difficulties that characterize adaptation by second-generation Mexican Americans are similar to the struggles that defined the second generation among earlier immigrant groups (Child 1943; Foote Whyte 1943; Perlmann and Waldinger 1997). But as immigration ceased for these groups, later-generation adolescents negotiated their place in U.S. society without having to contend with stereotypes largely informed by the precarious circumstances of the second generation. The durability of these stereotypes for Mexican Americans is directly tied to the perpetual presence of a second generation, which must cope with precarious adjustment processes. As anthropologist Diego Vigil notes in his research on Chicano gangs, "It is a second-generation urban American experience that, in the Chicano case, is a continually renewed phenomenon because of continued immigration" (1988: 6).

While Mexican-American respondents in both Garden City and Santa

Maria expressed similar sentiments, perceptions of immigrants' negative influence on the image of Mexican Americans were more pronounced in Garden City, where respondents had developed a narrative that is in some ways distinctive from that of their immigrant coethnics. Because a break occurred in immigration to Garden City, respondents there tended to compare their image in the community during the Mexican-immigration hiatus to their image since its resurgence. The comparison led some to believe that Mexican immigrants have cast a bad light on the positive image that later-generation Mexican Americans have worked so hard to cultivate. This belief was especially prevalent among respondents from the middle and oldest cohorts, who had lived through both the recession and resurgence of immigration from Mexico. They recalled a time when Mexican Americans fought to become part of the mainstream in Garden City, and they expressed pride in having gained acceptance as full-fledged members of the community. But some in Garden City had a sense that the increased presence of Mexican immigrants threatens to return Mexican Americans to their status as second-class citizens. As Timothy Saenz, the thirty-nine-year-old theater director, explained,

My parents, my grandparents worked hard so that I could be where I am today. And I feel like the Mexicans coming in from Mexico are going to . . . if they don't Americanize themselves, if they don't learn to be an American, then they're going to bring those of us that our grandparents and parents worked so hard to get us to this point, they're going to bring it down again.

Although respondents in both cities believed their image was vulnerable, the comparison between the time when no Mexican immigrants were coming to Garden City and today exacerbated respondents' fears about how Mexican immigration may have contributed to the fragility of their image.

The Benefits of Mexican Immigration: Raising Our Stature

If respondents saw the effect of Mexican immigration on the image of the entire Mexican-origin population as a cost, they also perceived significant benefits resulting from immigration from their ethnic homeland. Just as a nativist reaction directed at immigrants led the people I interviewed to conclude that immigrants hurt the image of Mexican Americans, multiculturalism and the accompanying value of diversity created a more welcoming context of reception for foreign-born Mexicans. Mexican-American respondents believed that their ethnic origin has yielded some advantages in an age of multiculturalism. They opined that the political, social, and economic ascendancy of Mexican Americans in Garden City, Santa Maria, and nationwide would be impossible if not for ongoing immigration. They said that the large immigrant population in their community has created a demand for people of Mexican descent in important political positions and occupations, thereby "pushing" Mexican Americans up a metaphorical socioeconomic ladder.

The benefits accruing from Mexican immigration are particularly evident in local politics. Both Garden City and Santa Maria have a number of Mexican-origin elected officials. During the time of my fieldwork, three of the five members of the city commission (in Garden City) and three of the five city council members (in Santa Maria), including the mayor, were of Mexican descent. Citing the political benefits of Mexican immigration, Hank Pacheco, of Santa Maria, noted:

Actually now we're starting to take a lot larger role. Like, you know, our former mayor now is in the state legislature. I think our current mayor—is he Mexican too? But, like, our city council has a lot more Hispanics or Mexicans now. [. . .] I have a couple friends whose dads—it's sort of related I guess—he's part of the Kiwanis and all these other different organizations. And he's VP of a bank, and they do all of these things. And there's a lot more Mexican-American people that are being involved in all these organizations now too, that are influential on the public, a lot more.

TRJ: What do you think has changed to make that happen?

R: For the public to be more accepting? I think part of it is the increase in Mexican population. That's definitely one of them. As far as politics, a lot of your support is gonna come from your own type of group, your own ethnic group. A lot of it. But I think it's just the fact that the city government is representative of your area, and so it's someone that has taken the initiative to say, "You know what? I need to speak up for this group." And actually knowing what they're talking about and getting enough people to listen and then by doing that, it makes other groups of people in the area kind of open their eyes and take notice a little bit. I think it's been a really positive thing.

In an age in which racial and ethnic representation are seen as core components of American democracy, the immigrant-driven growth of the Mexican-origin population creates a demand for people of Mexican origin in key positions. Public and private firms and institutions thus often turn to Mexican Americans to fill this demand. Well aware of this, Mexican Americans like Hank see immigration as having a positive influence on their political ascendancy.

Mexican Americans express similar views about the positive effect of Mexican immigrants on their position in the labor market. The financial penalties that anti-discrimination laws impose motivate many businesses to hire a diverse workforce and promote the principles of multiculturalism in order to demonstrate compliance with civil rights laws (Alba and Nee 2003). But the cost of discriminating against Mexican immigrants in Garden City and Santa Maria comes from the potential loss of revenue as much as it does from the fear of legal sanction. Since Mexican immigrants make up such a large proportion of the population in each city, businesses that discriminate against them or exclude them stand to lose substantial revenue. As a result, businesses have worked to accommodate and attract immigrant clientele, most notably through the presence of bilingual employees found in banks, grocery stores, restaurants, gas stations, and retail stores. Mexican Americans, especially those who speak Spanish, believe that they are the primary beneficiaries of strategies that firms employ to attract and accommodate immigrants. They are in demand because employers believe that they have a keen familiarity with American institutions and culture *and* have the ability to communicate effectively with Spanish-speaking clientele. Aaron Briseño, a seventeen-year-old high school student in Garden City, whose grandfather taught him to speak Spanish, worked at the local grocery store. He believed his ability to communicate with Spanish-speaking customers made him an attractive employee:

[Speaking Spanish is] one of the reasons I got a job at [the grocery store]. A lot of Hispanic people live on that side of town, and they tend to shop at that store. And I put on my application that I was a good translator, and sometimes people

back in pharmacy or [the] grocery department need me to translate for them, and I do that.

Several other respondents noted that their employer provided additional pay to workers who spoke Spanish, a reward for bilingualism that exists only because of the large Mexican-immigrant population. "Bilingual pay" is especially prevalent in public sector jobs that require employers to interact with Spanish-monolingual immigrants. The use of financial incentives to attract and retain bilingual workers is not unique to Garden City and Santa Maria. April Linton and I (2009) found that roughly 46 percent of the municipal governments in the U.S. metro areas we surveyed offer additional pay to bilingual employees. Mexican Americans are not the only potential beneficiaries of bilingual pay, since one need not be of Mexican (or Latino) origin to speak Spanish. But for those Mexican Americans who grew up speaking Spanish, the skill is seen as a part of their ethnic ancestry that carries a reward in the labor market precisely because of the large Mexican immigrant population.

Mexican Americans perceive the rewards of immigration not just as the presence of direct monetary benefits but also as a more positive valuation of Mexican ethnicity in the labor market. At the low end of the labor market, employers use ethnicity and nativity as proxies for work ethic and to build a workforce that is likely to get along (Waldinger and Lichter 2003). But at the top of the labor market, employers often use ethnicity for what John Skrentny (2007) calls "racial symbolism," or benefits that organizations perceive from having a diverse workforce. The immigrant-driven growth of the Mexican-origin population raises the value that organizations see in having "Mexican" representation in their workforce. The young and high-achieving Mexican Americans I interviewed are especially apt to perceive the rewards of racial symbolism that is informed by Mexican immigration. As Rolando Fernández Jr., of Santa Maria, remarked,

I see [Mexican immigration] a much bigger plus than any minus, especially in California. Like I said, not to be exploitative, but I'm going to definitely at some point use my name and use my background to advance myself. Not just . . . obviously for partially selfish goals, but at the same time because I feel that the higher status I can reach, like I was saying earlier, I can bring somebody along with me.

Professional Mexican Americans' class position allows them to fend off the perceived negative effects that respondents pointed out as being a cost of immigration, and their professional status enables them to benefit from the need for racial and ethnic representation in professional occupations. Some respondents, like Rolando, had partly altruistic motives to use their occupational and class status to "give back" to the Mexican-immigrant community. But they also recognized their ethnic background to be an increasingly valued individual asset that owes to the immigrant-driven growth of the Mexican-origin population.

Some scholars have identified Mexican immigration as a source of negative racialization of Mexican Americans (Telles and Ortiz 2008), but Mexican-American respondents also saw an element of opportunity in the way that immigration affects the social standing of all people of Mexican descent. Because racial and ethnic representation is seen as crucial for the vitality of many firms and organizations, the demand for Mexican representation is at a premium. As many respondents saw it, the singularity of Mexican identity that is perceived by non-Mexicans becomes an asset, because Mexican Americans are the most likely to "get the call" when firms and organizations want Mexican or Hispanic representation. To be sure, at the bottom of the occupational hierarchy, employers prefer Mexican immigrants over Mexican Americans (Waldinger and Lichter 2003). But Mexican Americans' origins in the same ethnic category, in addition to the practical benefits of their English proficiency, U.S. citizenship, and familiarity with U.S. society, make them better positioned to reap the advantages that come with the demand for racial and ethnic representation.

The Benefits of Mexican Immigration

OCCUPATIONAL AND SOCIAL QUEUING

In addition to the specific political, economic, and social influences that Mexican Americans mention, they also believe that the presence of Mexican immigrants has effectively pushed them upward in the occupational and social queue. Mexican Americans told me that life would be much worse for Mexican Americans without the presence of immigrants, because they might be stuck at the bottom of an occupational hierarchy in which workers are sorted into jobs that are coded by ethnicity. When I asked Erin Santiago, of Santa Maria, if things would be better for Mexican Americans if there were no immigrants, she replied,

It would be different, because maybe we would get stuck with the jobs picking the strawberries and all of that kind of stuff, I guess. God, it would be different! That's the first thing that comes to my mind.

Erin, like other respondents, believed immigrants have taken the spots previously occupied by Mexican Americans who have moved up and out of low-wage work, such as fruit and vegetable harvesting. Ethnic succession in low-wage jobs has long been a feature of assimilation in urban centers (Waldinger 1996). When an immigrant group gains an economic foothold, it often moves out of occupational niches only to be replaced by another immigrant group. In Garden City, but especially in Santa Maria, succession is marked not by ethnic change but by generational progression. Low-wage jobs have long been done by Mexicans in these cities, and the constant supply of Mexican immigrants continually fills these positions as the U.S.-born second and third generations move on to other occupations. Mexican immigration thus continually reinforces the coding of these jobs as "Mexican work." Respondents believed that low-wage work is still characterized as "Mexican" and that, without Mexican immigrants, growers would still turn to what would consequently be the only source of "Mexican" labor: Mexican Americans.[7]

Others believed that Mexican immigrants have helped Mexican Americans advance socially by providing a comparison group that helps non-Mexicans distinguish between native- and foreign-born Mexicans. Such distinctions lead non-Mexicans to perceive Mexican Americans as integrated members of the community. Carlos Morales, a 20-year-old college student in Santa Maria, stated,

I mean, OK, we've been here since day one, or whenever my parents were born. But people see them growing up, and the people there know how they are, but then you get constantly all these immigrants coming in, and people might know my dad's Mexican, but they know he's not from Mexico. They know he doesn't work in the fields. Just they wouldn't have that to compare, like, they wouldn't have him to compare to an immigrant.

Respondents like Carlos believed that when non-Mexicans express negative sentiments about people of Mexican descent, they are able to distinguish Mexican Americans from their immigrant coethnics. As I pointed out in chapter 5, non-Mexicans often make such distinctions by asserting in interpersonal interactions that there are "good" Mexicans and "bad" Mexicans. In some ways, Mexican immigrants serve the same purpose for Mexican Americans that African Americans did for the Irish, who emphasized their differences from blacks in order to make their case for their whiteness (Ignatiev 1995; Roediger 1991). Mexican Americans do not employ the racist strategies that the Irish did in vying for acceptance in U.S. society, but my respondents believed that the mere presence of Mexican immigrants sets up a comparison that may, in fact, be advantageous to the economic and social position of Mexican Americans.[8]

From the perspective of the people I interviewed, immigrants serve as a point of reference that allows Mexican Americans to be recognized as ethnic Americans distinctive from their immigrant coethnics. Although individual Mexican Americans are often lumped together with immigrants, respondents believed that immigrants may help to elevate the position of Mexican Americans in each city by showing just how far they have come from their poor immigrant origins.

THE GROWING CACHET OF MEXICAN CULTURE

Mexican-immigrant replenishment and the resulting increase in the Mexican-origin population carry less tangible, but still significant, benefits in the minds of many Mexican Americans, particularly those from the youngest cohort. They assert that the growing Mexican population means that there is a majority Mexican-origin youth population to which they can claim membership. My exchange with Melissa Santiago, of Santa Maria, illustrates this belief:

TRJ: Does the fact that more [immigrants] have come, does that influence your life in any way?

R: Well yeah, just the fact that there are people living in Santa Maria that are like me and that are Mexican on both sides. And they're just like me.

TRJ: What if there were no Mexican immigrants in Santa Maria at all? What would things be like for people like yourself, whose families have been here for a long time?

R: Be kind of weird, because maybe you'd be like . . . or only a certain amount of people would be the only Mexicans here, to where if there was a lot of white people, you'd feel out of place maybe.

To be a Mexican-American youth in Santa Maria is to be a part of a growing majority, and one that is, in many ways, defining the mainstream. For young Mexican Americans, this sense of belonging makes them part of an "in group," perhaps not in terms of their political and economic power, but certainly in terms of their ability to define what is hip. As one high school respondent put it, "The white kids gotta blend in with the Mexicans." The sentiments that Melissa expressed are not unique to Santa Maria, where people of Mexican descent make up the numerical majority. Even in Garden City, the youngest respondents believed there are social benefits to the growth of the Mexican-immigrant population. According to Emily Strong, a seventeen-year-old high school senior,

It's cool because there's more people like you. I mean you're common now, and sometimes it's really nice to stick out, and sometimes it's not because people watch your every move. So when [you have a lot in] common, you have a lot of people that are like me and when they all care about each other.

The immigrant-driven growth of the Mexican-origin population (and the general Latino population, for that matter) has also facilitated the infusion of Mexican culture into American popular culture, further eliciting positive feelings among respondents about the effects of Mexican immigration. As corporate America recognizes the immense profit to be made by appealing to Latino identity, it has launched targeted marketing campaigns in order to attract this population's spending (Dávila 2001). This "market-driven multiculturalism" (Zolberg and Long 1999: 26) gives the Mexican-origin population growing prominence in popular culture as television, film, print media, and music increasingly reflect and celebrate Mexicanness. In view of these shifts in popular culture, respondents believed that being a person of Mexican origin carries a social benefit. Articulating these sentiments, Mark Santos, a twenty-nine-year-old social worker in Garden City, told me,

I see a lot of positives. Our culture has a lot of great things to offer. Of course our music is now mainstream; it's big time. Our festivities are growing in every city. Everyone is picking it up and doing those things and celebrating what we celebrate and what we stand for. I think it's great.

Older Mexican Americans in Garden City are aware of how demographic and ideological shifts have converged to change the mix of costs and benefits related to Mexican immigration. They note the difference in the status of their ethnicity in Garden City today as compared with the time prior to the resurgence of immigration and see a much more positive outlook. The differences are apparent not only in the visibility of Mexican ethnicity in mainstream culture but also in the esteem that respondents attach to being persons of Mexican descent. Joe Gil Jr., of Garden City, reflected on how the resurgence of immigration, combined with the efforts of local businesses to cater to Mexican immigrants, had warmed his feelings about his ethnic identity:

The first half of my life, it was rough. I didn't feel too good about [being Mexican American]. But as things began to improve, as the population of the city changed the mix and we got more Hispanic people in town, the language began to change; yeah, I felt a lot better about it. You bet I do now. You bet! [. . .] Not until the influx of the beef plants, and then people started coming in—then things began to change. Then they were catering to them, you bet. Power of the buck makes a big difference.

The effort to profit from the growing number of Mexican immigrants has, in the eyes of Mexican Americans, given some power to the Mexican-origin population to define popular culture and, indeed, the American mainstream. Being a person of Mexican origin in the United States today is more in vogue than ever, and Mexican Americans believe that the large immigrant population has given all people of Mexican descent the critical mass necessary for Mexican ethnicity to be a force in defining what is cool.

Whether Mexican Americans hold accommodating views of Mexican immigration, more restrictionist views, or are ambivalent, the immigrant experience in their own family serves as an important point of reference for how they understand present-day Mexican immigration. When Mexican Americans see similarities between today's Mexican immigrants and their own immigrant ancestors, as most do, they express much more accommodating opinions. They believe that the United States should remain open to Mexican immigrants and that today's immigrants are entitled to the American dream that their own immigrant ancestors accessed. Their understanding of the present-day experience vis-à-vis that of their own immigrant ancestors does not preclude their invoking core American values in explaining their accommodating views of present-day immigration. They argue that closing the border grinds against the American ideals of equality and opportunity and the American dream. But when Mexican Americans emphasize differences between their immigrant ancestors and today's Mexican immigrants, they tend to hold restrictive opinions about immigration. A small minority of respondents noted that today's immigrants benefit from services that were unavailable to their own immigrant ancestors, who had to make their way in American society without public assistance. The abundance of services, they argued, makes today's Mexican immigrants spoiled relative to the immigrants of yesteryear. Furthermore, Mexican Americans who hold restrictive attitudes premise their beliefs on an American identity that sees success in the United States as a zero-sum game. They opine that tax-paying citizens like themselves should not have to foot the bill for the costs of unauthorized immigrants, who they believe take much more than they contribute to public coffers.

Mexican Americans' beliefs about how Mexican immigration affects their social standing further point to the importance of immigration to the Mexican-American experience. Mexican Americans see both costs and benefits associated with Mexican immigration. On one hand, respondents believed that immigration threatens the image of all people of Mexican descent. Though they generally held sympathetic views of immigrants themselves, they lamented the structural conditions that make Mexican immigrants a lightning rod for public debates about social and economic conditions in the United States in general and in Garden City and Santa Maria in particular. On the other hand, respondents saw Mexican immigration as a benefit that increases the demand for "Mexican" representation in the public and private sectors, provides a point of comparison showing just how much Mexican Americans have advanced, and gives the Mexican-origin population cachet in American popular culture.

As with previous research (Binder, Polinard, and Wrinkle 1997; de la Garza and DeSipio 1998; de la Garza et al. 1993; de la Garza et al. 1991; Newton 2000), this chapter shows that Mexican Americans' level of integration matters in how they see the costs and benefits of Mexican immigration. The interviews show that Mexican Americans' structural integration is a source of ambivalence, however. The large degree to which they have integrated into U.S. society precipitates a fear that the influx of a large, poor, and mostly unauthorized coethnic immigrant population will threaten their own status as integrated Americans. Yet the extent of their structural integration positions them to realize the benefits of membership in a massive ethnic group in an age of multiculturalism. Precisely because of their elevated levels of educational attainment and occupational status, the most upwardly mobile believe they benefit from policies and programs that positively recognize racial and ethnic origins.

It is important to note that changing sentiment in U.S. society, either positive or negative, likely alters how Mexican Americans see the costs and benefits of Mexican immigration. I interviewed Mexican Americans during a period when Mexican immigration was not front and center in national policy debates. But in 2006 and 2007, Mexican immigration became a central focus of policy makers and pundits as the U.S. Congress considered immigration reform legislation. At no point in recent history has the ambivalent balance that characterizes the American response tilted more negatively. When this largely negative response becomes vocal, as it has in recent years, Mexican Americans' fears about the harmful effect of Mexican immigration on the social standing of Mexican Americans may deepen and overshadow the benefits they recognize. Nonetheless, Mexican Americans still likely weigh these fears against the potentially positive effects of immigration they see emanating from market forces and popular culture, which tend to work independently of policy decisions.

And so Mexican immigration, as Mexican Americans see it, is a double-edged sword that yields both costs and benefits. Both edges of this sword are made sharp by a larger context of reception that simultaneously stigmatizes the entire Mexican-origin population and makes Mexican ethnicity a more accessible and more desirable feature of everyday life for Mexican Americans.

SEVEN

Ethnic Drawbridges

On a warm evening in the spring of 2002, the Santa Maria City Council chamber was bursting at the seams. Over a hundred people, mostly Mexican immigrants, crowded into the narrow chamber, and those who could not find a seat stood in the hallway just outside. Many carried signs with slogans such as "Santa Maria is our community," "I love Santa Maria," "Future teacher in Santa Maria," and "I want to learn English." Also among the people in the chamber were long-time residents of the city, mostly older whites, who sat stoically as the immigrants displayed their placards. The unusually large crowd at the meeting showed up to voice their opinions about a proposed community center in the predominantly Mexican-immigrant area known as Newlove, named for the street that runs through the neighborhood. The name of the neighborhood belied conditions there. Newlove was at one time a blighted area characterized by overcrowding, crime, and dilapidated properties. City officials made strident efforts to improve conditions with increased policing and strict enforcement of the housing code. Capping their efforts was a proposed federally funded community center that would offer resources, such as classes and clinics, aimed at helping immigrant families.

Dozens of individuals approached the podium to voice their opinions to the five-member council. The white speakers, who lived in a neighborhood adjacent to Newlove, strongly opposed the community center. They argued that it would cause increased traffic, crowding of streets with parked vehicles, and blight in Newlove that would spill into the nearby neighborhood, thereby driving down property values. Speakers who supported the center—most were Latino, but some were white—appealed to the need to serve an immigrant population that is eager to integrate into Santa Maria. They cited the potentially positive influences of the center on the neighborhood and on Santa Maria as a whole, noting that the immigrants and their children represent Santa Maria's future.

Among those who spoke in favor of the center was Renaldo Salcedo. He approached the podium with a confidence and poise that made him stand out from the speakers that had gone before him. He articulately told the council that the community center would be an asset for all of Santa Maria. The center, Salcedo claimed, would be a place for people to come together to voice concerns and to better the community as a whole. He then quietly returned to his seat. In many ways, Salcedo seems among the least likely of individuals to have voiced an opinion in favor of a center that would aid poor immigrants. His socioeconomic standing could not be more different from the vast majority of immigrant residents in the council chambers that evening. He is a successful businessman who has built a car-alarm business that has made him one of the more well-to-do residents of Santa Maria. Salcedo is also a later-generation Mexican American whose immigrant roots are in his distant past.

The scene in the city council chambers suggests that we can learn a lot about the effect of Mexican-immigrant replenishment on Mexican-American ethnic identity, not just from Mexican Americans' opinions and attitudes regarding their foreign-born coethnics, but also from how Mexican Americans react to those coethnics. Mr. Salcedo's short speech in the chamber of the Santa Maria City Council suggests a guiding metaphor for this chapter. His class position indicates that he has crossed the metaphorical river of assimilation, and by speaking in favor of the community center, he lowered a drawbridge to Mexican immigrants, aiding them in crossing that same river. Conversely, Mexican Americans may raise this same drawbridge to preserve the distance between themselves and Mexican immigrants. If what Mexican Americans *say* about effects of immigration on their ethnic identity suggests a degree of ambivalence, then what do their *actions* indicate about how they see themselves situated in U.S. society vis-à-vis Mexican immigrants? Do they lower a drawbridge to Mexican immigrants, treating them as part of a unified group consisting of all people of Mexican origin? Or do they raise the drawbridge, suggesting that generational, class, and sociocultural differences overwhelm any sense of ethnic solidarity?

Ethnic identity is expressed not merely in symbols and practices that people attach to an ethnic origin. It also manifests though purposive action aimed at achieving a particular end.[1] Scholars have shown ethnicity to be a particularly important force behind political and economic action. Early research on political participation and racial and ethnic identity shows that the strength of an individual's ethnic consciousness has positive and significant effects on their propensity to be politically active (Verba and Nie 1972; also see García Bedolla 2005). But as racial and ethnic groups have become more heterogeneous in their class profile, political scientists have examined whether class distinctions within a group undercut the power of race and ethnicity to guide political behavior. As political scientist Michael Dawson (1995) points out, the growth of the black middle class has the potential to undo the political homogeneity of blacks, since class interests among middle-class blacks may trump racially defined political interests.[2] Dawson shows, however, that middle-class blacks still see their individual fate linked to that of all blacks, and race thus remains the lens through which middle-class blacks view their group interest. Likewise, political scientist Jennifer Hochschild (1995) argues that middle-class blacks feel a sense of responsibility for all members of their race group. This sense of responsibility may come from the kinship ties that often connect middle-class blacks to poorer blacks or because they tend to live in relatively close proximity to poor blacks (Pattillo-McCoy 1999; Stack 1997).

For Mexican Americans, not just class status may drive a wedge though group politics but also differences in generation-since-immigration status. Research on Latino political behavior suggests that generational, class, and sociocultural differences among ethnic Mexicans may lead more assimilated Mexican Americans to turn their backs on their immigrant coethnics. On the basis of her ethnographic work in two Los Angeles Latino communities, political scientist Lisa García Bedolla (2005) argues that effective political mobilization takes place when individuals feel positively attached to their ethnic origins and have a sense of ethnic self-worth. García Bedolla finds that Latinos who are closer to the immigrant generation and who live in the predominantly Latino-immigrant East Los Angeles tend to be more politically mobilized. In contrast, middle-class and later-generation Latinos internalize the social stigma attached to Latino identity and thus lack a sense of ethnic self-worth. Their efforts to distance themselves from Mexican immigrants highlight their internalization of this stigma, which in turn makes them less likely to become politically active.

Class differences within an ethnic group may be even more relevant to economic purposive action, since the high socioeconomic status of some individuals puts them in a position to effectively assist coethnics who have a more tenuous economic foothold in U.S. society. The degree to which the cross-class flow of resources within an ethnic group takes place depends in large part on a sense of ethnic solidarity among group members. The preeminent example of how ethnic solidarity promotes cohesion that facilitates the flow of economic resources and social capital within an ethnic group is the Cuban enclave in Miami. Portes and Bach's (1985) study of the role of the coethnic community in the economic integration of Mexican and Cuban immigrants shows that the Cuban enclave provides an advantage to Cuban immigrants over and above their Mexican counterparts. Entrepreneurial Cuban exiles that came to Miami in the wake of the Cuban Revolution provide an economic foundation in the enclave. Later-arriving Cuban immigrants, who are often poor and have little education, enter Miami and have access to networks, jobs, and capital that flow through a resource-rich enclave held together by shared identification.[3]

Individuals may draw on more than just a sense of shared ethnicity to guide economic behavior. Their purposive economic action can also be motivated by particular events that they associate with a larger ethnic narrative. Sociologists Jody Agius and Jennifer Lee (2009) show that the propensity of middle-class 1.5- and second-generation Mexican Americans to provide financial support to poor kin is not driven by a sense of linked fate rooted in a history of discrimination and oppression. Rather, they provide economic assistance to poor kin because of their identification with particularities of the Mexican-immigrant experience—what Agius and Lee call the "immigrant narrative"—which is fraught the struggles associated with poverty and a lack of familiarity with life in a new land.

Similar to Dawson in the conclusion that he draws about a sense of linked fate among middle-class African Americans, I showed in the previous chapter that Mexican Americans believe their fate is, in some ways, tied to that of Mexican immigrants. They see poor, unauthorized immigrants contributing to sour perceptions of all ethnic Mexicans, but they also believe that immigrant-driven growth gives political, economic, and cultural clout to the group. A sense of linked fate, however, does not lead them to become politically involved. Like García Bedolla's middle-class, later-generation respondents, the Mexican Americans I interviewed were not active in "Mexican-American" causes. They tended not to be at the forefront of immigrant-rights movements or highly visible campaigns like the one in which Mr. Salcedo participated. Nor were they the anchors of an ethnic enclave through which they aided coethnic immigrants. Their *everyday* actions nonetheless suggest a great deal about how Mexican immigration factored into their ethnic identity. My analysis of what Mexican Americans do includes examining their political mobilization and economic relationships but also their everyday interactions with Mexican immigrants. Looking at these everyday acts of solidarity and division, as well as commitment-intensive acts, provides a fuller picture of Mexican Americans' response to Mexican immigrants.

Mexican Americans' everyday interactions with other immigrant coethnics reveal that class and sociocultural differences between Mexican Americans and foreign-born Mexicans did not lead my respondents to turn their backs on immigrants, to cross the ethnic boundary entirely. Mexican Americans in Garden City and Santa Maria frequently lower drawbridges to assist foreign-born coethnics. Yet they generally reach out to immigrants in ways that are not likely to garner a lot of attention. For most, instances of reaching out are episodic and usually take place in everyday encounters in public settings. For others, their job requires them to aid immigrant coethnics, but a sense of ethnic solidarity leads them to these jobs to begin with. Some more upwardly mobile respondents had actively sought out opportunities to assist immigrants, drawing on their class status and influence to come to the aid of Mexican greenhorns. If Mexican Americans reach out to Mexican immigrants using collectivist strategies, they do so in response to institutional confrontations with anti-Mexican nativism. As with the 1.5- and second-generation Mexican Americans that Agius and Lee (2009) studied, the motivation of later-generation Mexican Americans to reach out to immigrant coethnics is driven by their connection to immigration as a defining event in a larger Mexican-American ethnic narrative.

Unity is certainly not the order of the day among all Mexican Americans. Those who want to restrict Mexican immigration and see immigration from their ethnic homeland exclusively in terms of its costs seek to raise drawbridges. They work to achieve distance through everyday encounters, particularly in their use of public space and in the choices they make about where to live and where to send their children to school. Social class differences between these respondents and Mexican immigrants were narrower; thus, they worked to raise drawbridges for fear that their class made them vulnerable to status degradation. But their efforts to create distance did not lead them to disown Mexican immigrants. Even when Mexican Americans raise drawbridges, they believe that they violate certain norms of ethnic unity by drawing distinctions between themselves and on "their own kind."

LOWERING DRAWBRIDGES: EXPRESSIONS OF UNITY

The largely accommodating views that Mexican Americans expressed in the previous chapter translate into everyday actions in which they lower ethnic drawbridges to Mexican immigrants. In most cases, their aid to immigrants entails little or no sustained interaction but instead takes place in the course of daily life. In other instances, Mexican Americans reach out to immigrants through the duties of their job. Only in response to a perceived external threat do Mexican Americans take up more collectivist approaches to aiding or defending immigrants.

Everyday Instances of Lowering Drawbridges

Mexican Americans display a form of unity with immigrants that is unlikely to make headlines. Most of the Mexican Americans I interviewed did not actively seek out opportunities to express unity with Mexican immigrants. They tended to be occupied with the quotidian matters that structure most people's lives: family, work, the household, health, and leisure. Nor were they activists reminiscent of those in the Chicano movement. But the absence of their participation in less "showy" forms of unity does not mean that they did not reach out to Mexican immigrants at all.

The respondents regularly came to the aid of immigrants through the course of their daily lives, particularly where language was involved. Recall from chapter 4 that they occasionally translated for Mexican immigrants in serendipitous encounters that provided opportunities to use Spanish, whereas it might otherwise have atrophied. These encounters were also instances in which they displayed unity with immigrant coethnics. They used their bilingual abilities to help immigrants negotiate everyday situations that can be confusing and frustrating for Spanish monolinguals. Since members of the oldest cohort were most likely to be bilingual, they were regularly in a position to assist Mexican immigrants with translation at banks, the post office, restaurants, and grocery stores. Although bilingual employees are common in Garden City and Santa Maria, they are not always available to assist Spanish-monolingual

Mexican immigrants, and so Mexican Americans often lend a hand. Lydia Arroyo, a forty-four-year-old nonprofit manager in Santa Maria, provided a description of such instances, which were typical of those mentioned by many other bilingual respondents as well:

If there's a person in the market that's having trouble conversing with someone and I just happen to be standing nearby, I'll walk in and just interrupt and excuse myself and [say], "Did you need some help with something?" I mean that's what I'll do. Or if somebody is just trying to communicate, somebody who is monolingual and is trying to speak to somebody who only speaks English, and [is] trying to get this message across, I'll just step in.

For older Mexican Americans who live in neighborhoods with large immigrant populations, these encounters are even more common. Although most respondents from the middle and youngest cohorts lived in middle-class areas with few Mexican immigrants, many of the older people I interviewed remained in working-class neighborhoods with large numbers of immigrants. These neighborhoods were once solidly working-class and multiethnic. Much like what has happened in neighborhoods with large Mexican populations in Los Angeles (Duarte 2008; Telles and Ortiz 2008), over time, whites had moved out, and Mexican immigrants had begun to move in. Older Mexican Americans have not had the means to move out, and they have eventually become surrounded by foreign-born Mexican neighbors. Because these older, lower-middle-class Mexican Americans live in close proximity to Mexican immigrants, opportunities to lend a hand to immigrants can quite literally land on their doorstep. Hazel Washington is a case in point. Hazel, an elderly woman, founded a prominent Mexican-American organization in Santa Maria. As I interviewed her about the history of her organization, we were interrupted by a knock at the front door. Hazel's husband, who is white, answered and soon after called for her to come to the door. The visitor was a neighbor, a Mexican-immigrant woman who was holding her young son's hand with one hand and had a pile of mail in the other. The woman explained to Hazel in Spanish that she did not quite understand a letter she received from the power company, and she asked Hazel to translate. As Hazel helped her neighbor, her husband explained to me that these requests are almost a daily occurrence, and Hazel has gained a reputation among their immigrant neighbors as someone who is willing to help out with such matters.

The aid that some Mexican Americans provide is motivated by more than just the general values of neighborliness and courtesy that people in small towns generally hold. They reach out to Mexican immigrants in everyday life out of a sense of ethnic solidarity. In particular, they are spurred to help immigrant coethnics because of the importance they place on the immigrant experience as a central part of a larger Mexican ethnic narrative. Indeed, the immigrant experience led respondents to draw a connection between their own immigrant ancestors and today's Mexican newcomers. Ronnie Hinojosa provided just such an explanation for why he helped an elderly Mexican-immigrant couple whose car ran out of gas near his home in a middle-class neighborhood of Garden City. The couple remained stranded for a long period of time, and no one in Ronnie's neighborhood was willing to assist them. Ronnie speculated that his white neighbors were reluctant to help because the couple spoke only Spanish and perhaps because of stereotypes linking Mexican immigrants to crime. When Ronnie arrived home, he immediately rushed to their aid. As he explained:

Nobody would help them. They went to my neighbor here, and [he's a] nice guy. But he said, "Naw, I can't help you." That kind of bothered me, because he'd do anything for me. [. . .] But then my neighbor over here, great lady [. . .] she wouldn't help them either. [. . .] I went over there and they speak a little English. I said, "What can I do for you?" She told me. I asked her if she needed gas. She said, "Yeah." I said, "Just a minute." I pulled up, got them hooked up. Told them to pump the gas. I bet we spent thirty minutes. I got them started. [They] said, "Thank you." I said, "No problem." I just feel like, to me, I love to take care of older people, because they have so much knowledge. But some people judge people because they're just drifters or somebody. I don't look at it that way. I think everybody is equal. That little lady there reminded me of my grandma in a way. And that's why I wanted to help her.

Helping a stranded motorist is hardly remarkable in a place with lots of social capital, like Garden City. But in this case the people who needed

a hand were immigrants, who some in Garden City regard as "drifters."
Drawing on the experiences of his own immigrant grandmother, Ronnie
saw the couple not as strangers but as coethnics linked to him through
his own grandparents' immigrant experience.

This same reasoning compelled other people I interviewed to reach out
to Mexican immigrants, even if they did so only in small ways. Ricardo
de Guzmán, a seventy-seven-year-old retired custodian in Santa Maria,
often provided friendly advice to his immigrant neighbors. Ricardo's parents had been born in Mexico, and he had spent much of his childhood
working alongside them in fruit orchards and vegetable fields throughout California. He and his Mexican-born wife still lived in the same
house in which they had raised their children, who were now successful
professionals in Santa Maria. The neighborhood had changed dramatically over the years and now had a large immigrant presence. The time
he spent working with his parents while growing up informed his eager-
ness to offer advice to his Mexican-born neighbors regarding everything
from education to their rights as laborers. As Ricardo explained, he was
especially keen to advise women:

*I tell them about the laws, what they should do. Not because I'm a saint or
anything. I'm just human like anybody else. [. . .] I don't like to see a woman
work out there [in the fields]. I have unpleasant memories. They work hard.
Maybe they need it and everything, but none of the young women of our race
should be working out there. I can't see that. [. . .] That's the reason that I help
them. I don't like to see just the ones of my race working there. That's . . . I can't
do anything about it. But inside, I don't like it.*

It is virtually commonsense knowledge that Mexican immigrants do
the fieldwork in Santa Maria, and most Santa Maria residents recognize
this work to be excruciatingly mundane and physically taxing. Many residents are also aware of the exploitation that some fieldworkers endure.
Unpaid wages, insufficient housing, and inhumane working conditions
are all too common for fieldworkers. Ricardo felt a special sympathy
for Mexican immigrants, particularly women, who do the same type
of backbreaking work that his parents once did. Ricardo displayed an
encompassing ethnic solidarity when he identified Mexican immigrants

as people of his "own race." This shared sense of identity, combined with sympathy that came from his parents' experience in the fields, informed his belief that women who share his "race" should not have to labor in the fields. Ricardo invoked a somewhat antiquated notion of gender and work, which holds that manual labor is reserved for men. However old-fashioned Ricardo's beliefs may be, seeing Mexican-immigrant women doing such work spurred him to lend them advice in hopes that they would not become victims of exploitation.

A sense of shared ethnic origin also leads many Mexican Americans to come to the defense of their immigrant coethnics in encounters with non-Mexicans. Recall from chapter 5 that respondents frequently encountered nativism during interactions with non-Mexicans. Mexican-American respondents relayed numerous instances of such run-ins and spoke about their efforts to take a stand in opposition to nativism directed at immigrant coethnics. Consider how Eric Garza, of Garden City, reacted when he confronted a substitute teacher about the teacher's treatment of a Mexican-immigrant student:

We had a substitute teacher—I think it was last year—that was really picking on this kid all hour long. And he was Hispanic, and she was white. And I mean, everything she said just went directly towards him. I mean he'd do one little thing wrong, and she'd just start jumping on him for it. And I was really starting to get upset about it. And I stood up [to] her, and I told her, "Like, what's your problem? He's not doing anything wrong. Just leave him alone!" And I mean she almost sent me to the office for it. And it really made me mad, because he was kind of sitting back . . . I mean, me and him in that class we had together, we kind of formed a pretty good friendship. And his parents are actually from Mexico. He could speak Spanish real fluently, and his English was real rough and everything. But I mean he'd just be sitting back, drawing a picture of something, and [she'd] start jumping on him for not doing his work when he already had it done. And it was really just upsetting me about it. Because, I was like, "He's already got it done. Why are you jumping on him for [not] doing it when half the other class is not doing their work?"

Eric had a reputation for being an outstanding student, and he was popular with his peers. His status on campus made him an unlikely recipient of the type of prejudice that his Mexican-immigrant friend experienced, but it also positioned him well to be an effective advocate for Mexican immigrants. As Eric illustrated, ethnicity took on added importance for respondents in these situations; having a shared ethnic origin with immigrants compelled him to take their side in troubling situations.

The nativist comments that respondents frequently heard also positioned them to correct inaccuracies embedded in stereotypes about people of Mexican origin. As I discussed in chapter 5, many close friendships between Mexican Americans and non-Mexicans led the people I interviewed to be tagged sometimes as "good" Mexicans who have integrated into U.S. society. Because Mexican Americans are perceived as somehow different from the immigrant population, non-Mexicans often feel comfortable sharing nativist sentiments with them. Christie Mendiola, a forty-nine-year-old health club supervisor, often heard nativist comments from a good friend who is white. But Christie was rarely silent in such instances. She recounted the following story to illustrate how she responded when confronted with anti-Mexican nativism:

We were in the store and, yes, [some people in front of us] were rude. They kind of got in line and stayed there. They were gonna get a candy bar, and they just stayed there. And [my friend] goes, "Tsk." And I said, "I'll tell them." I said, "Men, we were here." And they didn't do nothing. And she goes, "You know we were here first, and you all need to get to the back of the line." And they just kind of [looked at us] like, "I don't understand." So I kind of interpreted a little how we were here first. And they got mad. But they were very rude. So after it was over, [my friend] said, "These Mexicans, they think just because they're not from our country they can do whatever they want, say whatever they want." And I just said, "That's the color of my skin too. I'm Hispanic." [She said,] "But you're not a Mexican." [I said,] "Yeah, I am a Mexican. I'm Hispanic." [. . .] I get mad sometimes at the Hispanic people for being rude. But that doesn't mean that I'm condemning them because of the color of their skin. I'm mad because of the way they're being rude. And that's all. But I do have to correct [my friend] sometimes. [. . .] I say, "You guys talk about the Mexicans and everything, but boy you sure go down to our restaurants, don't you?" And she'll start laughing. But I make it a point to tell her about where she can go so far. But once she starts throwing it all out, then I'll stop her.

Christie clearly agreed with her friend's assessment of the way the men conducted themselves. And she could have just as easily ignored her friend's comments and even joined her in voicing complaints about the men who cut in line. After all, Christie was born and raised in the United States and was better off economically than most immigrants. However, her shared ethnic origin led her to proclaim that she is "Mexican too" in order to communicate the inaccuracy of stereotypes about people of Mexican descent.

These serendipitous opportunities to assist immigrants are the most common form of drawbridge lowering for good reason. They generally involve no sustained commitment on the part of Mexican Americans and are thus neither time nor effort intensive. Furthermore, this sort of aid to Mexican immigrants is the least risky expression of unity. Assisting Mexican immigrants in everyday encounters makes Mexican Americans unlikely to run into the nativist rebuke that comes with highly visible displays of unity, such as protest. Nonetheless, the everyday ways that Mexican Americans reach out to immigrants should not be dismissed, since Mexican Americans are more apt to reach out than to walk away when presented with an opportunity to lend a hand.

Lowering Drawbridges at Work

The success of immigrants in American society often depends on the help they receive from their coethnics. Immigrants find jobs, housing, child care, and other forms of support embedded in the network ties they have to coethnics. This social capital—resources accessed through network ties—often flows from more established immigrants with a strong foothold in the new society to newly arrived immigrants who are looking to get a leg up, as with the Cuban enclave in Miami (Portes and Bach 1985). The Mexican-origin population does not have a Miami equivalent. People of Mexican origin are spread throughout the United States, the population is more generationally diverse, and they are not unified by disdain for the leadership in their ethnic homeland, as are Cubans.

These factors may combine to explain the absence of a similar enclave economy among Mexican immigrants. But despite this absence, established Mexican Americans can be a source of social capital for Mexican immigrants. The social capital they provide takes on a more mediated form than that found in ethnic enclaves, however. When social capital flows from Mexican Americans to their immigrant coethnics, the network ties are often facilitated by job duties. But these duties are not the only thing that compels Mexican Americans to lend a hand; many select these jobs in part precisely because they allow them to "give back."

The growth of the Mexican-immigrant population has necessitated a host of services that have led to job creation in education, law enforcement, and social work. Mexican Americans have stepped into these jobs in large numbers. Consider Mark Santos, something of a hometown hero in Garden City. He was born and raised there and left town for only a couple of years, during which time he completed his bachelor's degree while twice earning all-American honors in track and field. After graduation, Mark returned to Garden City to become a coach at the local high school and a social worker. His popularity was evident when he ran errands in town, and dozens of people stopped to speak with him. Mark's popularity also made him an effective social worker. His work involved helping immigrant families get settled with funds from a federal grant for housing and for school supplies and lunches for children. During a day I spent with Mark, we visited a home that he had helped secure for a family that recently arrived in Garden City from Mexico. As we entered the small home with construction debris strewn about the floor, Mark greeted the landlord with a firm handshake and a familiar hello that rang out in his midwestern twang. Mark spoke earnestly with the owner, telling him how nicely the home was coming along and how happy the family was to be moving in. He told the owner how hard-working the family was and how they had to spend a stint at the temporary shelter across the street before they could secure housing with Mark's help. Landlords might be reluctant to rent a home to such a family. Their low income may make it more difficult for them to cover the rent. Also, stories of illegal subleasing and overcrowding are widespread, and landlords thus fear that their properties will become dilapidated. Nonetheless, the landlord seemed pleased to rent the house to the immigrant family, and it was Mark's personal connection to him that had provided him the assurance he needed to rent the house to the

immigrant family. Mark's status as an established member of the community and a person of Mexican descent made him a bridge between the
Mexican-immigrant family and the white landlord.

Like Mark, a number of teachers, school administrators, and school
staff make efforts, through their jobs, to improve the lives of immigrants.
Schools are one of the most important points of contact between immigrants and American society, and in schools many Mexican Americans
provide assistance and guidance for their immigrant coethnics. Consider
the case of Ron Terán, of Santa Maria. Ron's ascendancy into Santa
Maria's middle class is quite remarkable. He grew up in labor camps,
and his second-generation parents worked in the fields surrounding
Santa Maria. By the time of my interview with him, Ron had a master's
degree and was a respected administrator in the school district. Despite
his successes, he displayed a strong commitment to making his school a
more welcoming place for students and their immigrant parents:

*I think the main thing if you respect [immigrant parents] and welcome them to
a school, they always feel part of it. I never try to make them feel embarrassed.
If they come to conferences, they're always apologetic if they're coming straight
from work. They have their red hands from strawberries, or their pants smell
because of strawberries and stuff. I don't really care. They have that interest to
come in after they get off, they come. And I appreciate that. Same thing when
they go home. Our meetings are at 6:30 so they can get home, because they get
up early. And they go home, take a shower, and come back and come to open
house. We have back-to-school-night; they come for school-site counseling. But
you have to ask. The last meeting we had school-site counseling, one of the first
ones, it was all in Spanish, because I had no Anglo parents that came. We had
like forty-five parents, and it was great for me because I conducted the meeting in
Spanish. I didn't have to go back and forth. The only ones that have complained
here are the Anglo parents, because [it] took so long to go from Spanish to
English. And I confronted the dad of one of the kids. I asked him if he wanted me
to run the meeting only in English to cut it shorter. But I had an obligation to
my Spanish parents, because the Anglo parents weren't the only ones that come
to school. And he wanted to know if I could run separate meetings on separate
nights, and I said no. It's just as important that you hear the same things that
they're hearing.*

Having grown up in a family of farmworkers, Ron had an intimate understanding of the life that his students and their parents lived. As Agius and Lee's (2009) research suggests, being one generation removed from poverty, as in Ron's case, makes some Mexican Americans empathic with the plight of today's poor immigrants and spurs in them a desire to give back. What is more, Ron's job as a principal put him in a position to do just that on a daily basis. Although the nature of the support he provided was subtle, Ron nonetheless was instrumental in helping to integrate immigrants into the Santa Maria schools.

Mexican Americans like Mark and Ron are bound by the duties of their job to work with immigrants, but ending up in such jobs is often a deliberate choice of theirs. Consider the case of Manuel Esguerra, a fifty-one-year-old social worker in Santa Maria. Manuel's parents were immigrant farmworkers in Santa Maria, but he leaped up the socioeconomic ladder. He had a bachelor's degree from a nearby university. Manuel had been active in the Chicano movement while in college, and his activism had led him to seek a job that allowed him to work with people of the same ethnic origin. Manuel worked in Guadalupe, a small town west of Santa Maria, where residents are overwhelmingly poor, Mexican-immigrant farmworkers.[4] Virtually all of Manuel's cases involved immigrant families from Mexico. As Manuel explained, it was no coincidence that he worked with these particular families:

Professionally, the majority of my kids and their parents are Latino. That's not just the way it happened. I chose to work out in Guadalupe, knowing that they were an unidentified group out there. People were not supervising them correctly. And [the social workers] were being spread out, maybe thirty kids spread out between twenty [case workers], where there was actually no supervision going on there but a lot of crime. Knowing that I was bilingual and I thought maybe I could make a difference if I took on that challenge. And I do have a great relationship with the kids. They know that I can speak Spanish to the parents and understand what's going on in the home. [. . .] And they know that I've been there, that I myself went through hard times as a child. I quit school, went out to work in the fields, and got involved with a lot of drinking. And then I turned my life around. [. . .] So I preach to them that life doesn't have to be a dead end because you're Hispanic. And they are coming from the same type of families that my parents grew up with me. Most of these parents are new from Mexico. They're raising their kids who are teenagers. [They are] hardworking families, good kids, strong kids, kids who are very athletic. But fifteen or sixteen, they've already been doing drugs for two to three years. Their grades have gone pshhhhhhw [downward slide whistle]. I get in there with being bilingual, bicultural, and I try to get them back on their feet.

Two things underpinned Manuel's desire to work with poor immigrant and second-generation Mexican Americans. The first was his participation in the Chicano movement, which had instilled in him a positive attachment to his ethnic roots and a sense of ethnic self-worth, which García Bedolla (2005) argues are necessary for political participation among Latinos. Manuel's positive attachment had not led him to become politically involved, but the duties of his job nonetheless provided a means of giving back. The second underpinning was his biography. Manuel was only one generation removed from poverty, and his own delinquent behavior as an adolescent provided him with a sense of empathy for those with whom he worked.

A shared ethnic origin, along with common experiences of immigration and the hardships of assimilation, lead Mexican Americans to go beyond the required duties of their jobs when they work with Mexican immigrants. Ron's and Manuel's cases show that some Mexican Americans are especially attentive to the immigrant and second-generation coethnics whom they serve. They are imbued with the belief that one's work should involve giving back to the community from which they came, and the large influx of Mexican immigrants into Garden City and Santa Maria ensures that many jobs are available through which Mexican Americans can do just that.

Isabel Hinojosa is another example of someone who used her job to aid Mexican immigrants, but she did not feel compelled to do so in the same way that Mark, Ron, and Manuel did. Isabel, a 57-year-old owner of a small grocery store, had been a long-time resident of Garden City at the time of my interview with her. She and her husband had sold Mexican-food products since they opened the store in the 1970s.

The recent boom of Mexican immigration to Garden City had made the store popular with immigrants, and it remained popular with Mexican Americans and even non-Mexicans. Isabel had made her store more than just a place where immigrants could find Mexican food; it was also a place where they could find emotional comfort and material support. As I interviewed Isabel in the front of her store, several immigrants entered and greeted her in Spanish with a sense of familiarity. *"Hola, mija"* (hello, my daughter), Isabel replied with a warm smile. She explained why she was so friendly to her Mexican-immigrant clientele:

I like to make these people from Mexico, make them feel at home and not to forget about where they came from. [. . .] In my store I just make them feel welcome. I don't know. Every time I talk to some gentleman, young man, I always call them my son, "mijo." [. . .] And some of them really crack up, and they call me "mother"! [laughs] "Mom, how are you?" And they make me feel good. Even the young ladies, I call them "mijas," like they were my daughters.

Isabel also provided Mexican immigrants with free child care for short periods while they attended a doctor's appointment or a job interview. On several occasions I visited the store and found her child-sitting. It may very well be the case that Isabel's kindness and free child-care services came from mostly economically rational motives. As a business owner it may have made sense for her to put a welcoming face on her store and offer child care to encourage her customers to shop there. After all, with the growth of similar immigrant-owned grocery stores, child care would give her store a competitive edge among immigrants. Isabel gave no hint that she was motivated purely by economic gain, however. She said that she liked to make immigrants comfortable in her store out of empathy for their situation. She recalled battling bouts of homesickness when she moved to the West Coast after she had married and now wanted to provide the comfort to Mexican immigrants that she had lacked:

Because when I got married, I moved to California, and it was kind of hard. You're away from home. And it is kind of lonely. You wish you were home. You miss those cookouts on weekends with your family. You miss that. And I believe these customers of mine that are from Mexico feel they could do a lot of [those] things if they were home.

Isabel's store had become a place where food, emotional support, and the practical benefits of child care easily mixed.

Organized Efforts to Lower Drawbridges

For the overwhelming majority of people in my sample, efforts to assist immigrants were confined to everyday encounters and the workplace. Still, some took a more active approach to lowering drawbridges to their immigrant coethnics, spearheading organized efforts to lend a hand. These respondents were not activists who engaged in tactics reminiscent of the Chicano movement, nor did they engage in protest politics similar to those of some Mexican Americans in other settings (Ochoa 2004). They were, instead, upwardly mobile individuals who worked through more conventional means, such as ethnically based organizations, volunteer organizations, and social entrepreneurship.

Mexican Americans explain their efforts to come to the aid of immigrants as originating in a desire to see them become more integrated members of U.S. society. This effort is not motivated by a drive to minimize the potential "damage" that Mexican immigrants might do to the image of Mexican Americans.[5] Rather, it is motivated by a desire to help immigrants enjoy the benefits of full participation in U.S. society, thereby advancing the entire Mexican-origin population. Consider the case of George Ortega, a forty-one-year-old UPS office worker in Garden City. George was a fast-talking man who spoke with a great deal of passion about the problems facing the Mexican-origin population. He did not speak Spanish, even though his wife, a Mexican immigrant, and children did. He believed that one of the biggest, yet most neglected, problems in Garden City is the inadequate dissemination of information to the Spanish-speaking population. According to George, there is no public arena through which immigrants can receive information pertinent to Garden City and southwestern Kansas. He relayed the following story in explaining why the lack of information is such a problem:

We talk about issues, and what was so sad about this is that when we were attacked in New York on [September 11], we talked [only] about twenty minutes [on] Spanish talk radio and everything [else] was music, all day long. So the question is, are we educating people? No. Are we giving information to the Hispanic people in western Kansas? [. . .] Maybe seven years ago, seven or eight years ago [. . .] there was a couple that drived [sic] from Dodge City to Garden City, and it was bad weather. They didn't speak no English. No one told them [about road conditions]. They didn't speak no English. [. . .] They were telling people not to go out. It was the worst road by Ingalls, Kansas. I call it "dead-man curve" when it comes to winter. They were hit by a semitruck. They died instantly. They left one girl behind. When I pass it [on my way home], the whole car was in flames. And I said to myself, this is tragedy. This is tragedy because there was no information given to them.

This experience had motivated George to create a weekly Spanish-language talk show that highlighted important local and national issues, including immigration law, local civic events, and parental involvement in school. George produced the show, while his business partner—a Mexican immigrant and local businesswoman—hosted it.

Like the motivations of many Mexican Americans committed to serving the immigrant population, George's devotion came partly from his own understanding of the immigrant experience. Though he did not grow up in an immigrant family, he had acquired an insider's view from his wife, who came from Mexico in the early 1980s. His wife's experiences helped George see the importance of having an informed and civically engaged immigrant population, motivating him to better the lives of those who share experiences similar to those of his wife. He believed that his talk show was part of a larger project that created opportunities for new leaders of Mexican descent to emerge. Speaking about two Mexican-immigrant women who helped him with the show, George told me,

They can relate with [the immigrants]. They can communicate with them; they can talk to them about it. They have a standard. They don't have to stop and think about [speaking Spanish]. It's like [the Mexican-American leaders]; I told them, "You guys are out. We're all out. Step aside. Let them play the role now. It's their turn. All you need, you and I and [other Mexican-American leaders], we need to step aside. It's their turn now. You need to support them. Because why? Because you don't know how to communicate. I don't either. [. . .] You have a big heart. You want to help them, but you can't help them. You need

people in position that can relate with them and support them. That's all you
can do." Myself? I don't speak Spanish. Therefore, my wife, I need some help,
she'll help me out. I always tell her, "Be part of it. You're next. It is your turn to
be part of this. Not me. You have my support."

Since George, like many of his contemporaries, did not speak Spanish,
he believed they could not possibly be leaders of the next generation
of Mexican Americans but could only help to create a forum for such
leaders to come forward.

Like George, Naomi Gómez, a sixty-eight-year-old retired teacher
and social worker, was heavily involved in efforts to help Mexican
immigrants integrate into U.S. society, and her motivation came from a
belief in the centrality of the immigrant experience to the identity of the
Mexican-origin population. Naomi was originally from New Mexico,
not descended from any immigrants at all. Her family lived in New
Mexico when it became part of the United States under the 1848 Treaty
of Guadalupe Hidalgo. (After our interview she showed me the original
Spanish land grant that her family had obtained in the early 1800s.)
Naomi was one of the few Mexican Americans to graduate from UCLA
in the 1950s, after which she spent several years as a teacher and school
librarian before becoming a social worker. Even though she was retired
at the time of our interviews, she was hardly idle. She spent her evenings
teaching adult classes in English as a second language, and she also
taught community college courses to immigrants about how to apply and
interview for jobs. As Naomi explained, "If they're going to go out and
compete with the [mainstream], they need to know what they're going to
get into. And I wanted to be there to help." Naomi's own family history
provided little insight into the immigrant experience; nonetheless, her
ethnic identity gave meaning to her volunteer work:

I guess you might say [my ethnic background is] important, because I wouldn't
be teaching where I am if it weren't important, if I didn't believe in my ethnic
background and what I've seen people go through.

Ethnic Mexicans who are in need of a helping hand are overwhelmingly
immigrants, and any expressions of ethnic identity related to volunteer

work will almost inevitably entail serving immigrants or their children. Even if Naomi's family had no immigrant origins in the United States, the importance of the immigrant experience to her ethnic identity is clear in the connection she drew between her volunteer work with Mexican immigrants and the importance of ethnic identity as a motivating force behind this work.

The aid that respondents provided to Mexican immigrants occasionally came in the form of a collective effort. Many respondents were members of ethnically based clubs and organizations whose activities included efforts to improve the lot of the immigrant population. Many small groups dot the ethnic organizational landscape in Santa Maria and Garden City, but local chapters of two national organizations predominate: the League of United Latin American Citizens, and the American G.I. Forum (AGIF), a Latino veterans association. LULAC began in the late 1920s as a Mexican-American civil rights organization that advocated for equal treatment of Mexican Americans and for their full participation in American society.[6] The AGIF was formed by Mexican-American World War II veterans, who saw little improvement in their status in the United States upon returning from war. Headed by later-generation Mexican Americans, these organizations still have a civil rights component, but LULAC in Garden City and the AGIF in Garden City and Santa Maria now serve mostly as social clubs and scholarship-granting organizations.

The role of immigration in Mexican-American politics is so prominent in the current time period that it is virtually impossible for organizations like LULAC and the AGIF to ignore issues related to immigrants. An informal meeting of leaders of the Garden City chapter of the AGIF that I attended illustrates just how important immigrant issues have become to these organizations. The group of Mexican-American veterans and their spouses sat around a large kitchen table at the home of an AGIF member, strategizing how to respond to nativist comments made in the monthly newsletter of Garden City's American Legion Post, another veterans' organization to which most AGIF members belong. Published in the newsletter was an anonymous chain e-mail that espoused a staunch English-only stance. At the bottom of the chain e-mail, the commander of the Garden City Post attached his own commentary: "My feelings exactly!! Why should English be the 2nd language like it is in Garden City. *This is America*" (emphasis in original). The members of the AGIF were appalled by the comments, seeing them as an affront to all people of Mexican descent who have served in the armed forces. The group composed a response on AGIF letterhead, condemning the commander's comments. Their response heralded the record of Mexican-origin servicemen and women and provided specific examples of Mexican immigrants who had won the Medal of Honor. The authors wrote, "We find the content of this article particularly offensive to veterans and citizens of Mexican-American descent. . . . Those of us who can speak both English and Spanish are an asset to this community and to this country as well. Since when is speaking fluent English a sign of patriotism? Our fore-fathers, grandfathers, and fathers proudly served in the United States Armed forces when some of them did not speak fluent English. They answered the call when their country called upon them."

Their response does not draw distinctions between today's Mexican immigrants and themselves. Instead, the authors engaged in what Wimmer (2008a) calls "transvaluation"; that is, they responded to ethnic boundaries by attempting to equalize the position of Mexican Americans and white Americans in the ethnic hierarchy. These Mexican-American veterans claimed their immigrant coethnics as part of a legacy of Mexican-origin military service extending from the present to the distant past. The AGIF in Garden City has a long history of advocacy, but what is different about its advocacy today is that it responds to prejudice aimed at immigrant newcomers, not second- and third-generation Mexican Americans. The success of the previous AGIF leadership in creating opportunities for Mexican Americans has in many ways allowed today's leadership to take a stand in response to nativism. The class standing of today's leaders is not as fragile as it was for previous Mexican-American leaders, so their status is less likely to take a hit if they stand up for their immigrant coethnics. Furthermore, their military service gives them a degree of credibility in responding to nativist attacks. As political scientist Ronald Krebs (2006) shows, African-American World War II veterans in the United States and the Druze minority in Israel have used their military service as an effective rhetorical tool in demanding full citizenship rights in their respective countries. Mexican Americans and other Latinos have drawn on their military service for similar ends, particularly through their participation in organizations like the AGIF (Ramos 1998). The response of the Mexican-American veterans in Garden City demonstrates that military service continues to be a powerful rhetorical tool. It allows them to effectively demand full belonging for all people of Mexican descent—both U.S.-born and foreign-born—while also using their patriotic credentials to short-circuit retorts about their ethnic loyalties corrupting their allegiance to the stars and stripes.

Respondents were not engaged in highly visible political efforts aimed at advocating for immigrants, nor did they live in ethnic enclaves in which they provided their immigrant coethnics with various forms of support. Nevertheless, assisting Mexican immigrants was part of their everyday lives. Whether they reached out in chance encounters, through their jobs, or through organized efforts, the Mexican Americans I interviewed were motivated in part by their identification with the immigrant experience as a central part of a larger Mexican ethnic narrative. Their lowering of drawbridges to Mexican immigrants suggests that, despite differences in class, nativity, and sociocultural characteristics, ethnic identity exerted substantial influence on how the people I interviewed responded to Mexican immigrants in their everyday lives. Instead of turning their backs on the poorer, less-assimilated coethnics, they generally lent a hand when opportunities presented themselves.

Still, a select group of respondents went out of its way to assist Mexican greenhorns, and these tended to be those who had the firmest economic and social foothold in American society. Why would those most socioeconomically distant from Mexican immigrants be some of the most active in reaching out to them? To begin with, Mexican immigrants are in no way an economic threat to middle- and upper-class Mexican Americans. Economists would say that in the labor market Mexican immigrants are "complements" of Mexican Americans, not "replacements" of them. Furthermore, upwardly mobile Mexican Americans are the least vulnerable to the consequences associated with being lumped with immigrants. Their class status and good reputation better position them to reach out to immigrants, because they have access to resources and are much less vulnerable to the discrimination that many poor Mexicans and Mexican Americans face. What is more, these upwardly mobile Mexican Americans grew up in lower-middle-class and poor families; thus, they have an intimate understanding of the hardships that today's Mexican immigrants face—and understanding of an "immigrant narrative" (Agius and Lee 2009)—that leads them to give back.

Upwardly mobile Mexican Americans are also most likely to gain from efforts to elevate the status of Mexican immigrants. Recall from chapter 6 that upwardly mobile respondents were particularly apt to see the immigrant-driven growth of the Mexican-origin population as a benefit, because this growth creates a demand for "Mexican" representation in the public and private sectors. The status of all people of Mexican descent depends to a large degree on sheer numbers, but the adage that "there is strength in numbers" does not tell the full story. The status of ethnic Mexicans can ascend only as quickly as those with low status can "run the race." By reaching out, upwardly mobile Mexican Americans— the "fastest runners"—help bring their immigrant coethnics up to speed, elevating the status of all ethnic Mexicans. Combining large numbers with elevated status only adds to the benefits that upwardly mobile Mexican Americans reap from Mexican immigration.

What accounts for why Mexican Americans reach out to Mexican newcomers, however, is not just jockeying in a race for status. An ethic of giving back also emanates from a legacy of political activism. Many of the upwardly mobile Mexican Americans I interviewed were politically socialized during the Chicano movement of the 1960s and 1970s. A primary goal of the movement was to improve the civil rights and social standing of all people of Mexican descent in the United States, including immigrants (Muñoz 1989). These Mexican Americans carried the philosophy of this movement with them and employed its values, even if they no longer utilized the protest tactics popular during the movement. Noting a similar trend among later-generation Mexican Americans in San Jose, California, and Phoenix, Arizona, sociologist Thomas Macias observes, "Even if the confrontational Chicano activism of the 1960s and 1970s has waned in recent decades, the spirit of that era persists in the willingness of Mexican Americans to volunteer in organizations that acknowledge their debt to the past through work done in the predominantly working-class community" (2006: 131).

The spirit of the movement lives in Garden City as well, even though its smaller Mexican-American professional class had little or no direct involvement with the original movement. Yet the major tenets of this and other ethnic pride movements, many of which are embodied in multiculturalism, have entered the mainstream, and Mexican-American professionals have adopted them as a motivating force behind their efforts. For upwardly mobile Mexican Americans, giving back has become a central tenet of ethnic expression and one that leads them to direct their efforts toward elevating the position of those among the Mexican-origin population who are most in need: Mexican immigrants.

RAISING DRAWBRIDGES:
CREATING DISTANCE FROM MEXICAN IMMIGRANTS

Not every encounter between Mexican immigrants and Mexican Americans led respondents to display ethnic unity. Some engaged in boundary contraction, in which actors shift emphasis to lower levels of group differentiation, such as nativity and class, in order to create new boundaries (Wimmer 2008a). Social class and sociocultural divisions between the Mexican-American respondents and immigrants overrode the unity that most respondents displayed, leading them to seek distance from coethnic immigrants by highlighting the distinctions between the two groups. Those who distanced themselves from immigrants came from the same minority that wanted to restrict Mexican immigration and saw immigration purely in terms of its costs. Much like the respondents who lowered drawbridges, those who raised them did not do so through activism or any sort of strident political efforts. None of the people I interviewed were, for example, part of an organized effort to promote English only or closed borders. They instead displayed distance from Mexican immigrants through the course of their quotidian activities, particularly as they related to their neighborhood affairs, the use of public space, and decisions about where to send their children to school. But respondents did not see their efforts to create distance from immigrants as unfettered by ethnicity. They articulated an uncomfortable irony in trying to distance themselves from people with whom they shared an ethnic origin.

A primary way that Mexican Americans aim to create social distance is through their residential location. The size of each sample city is small enough that any geographical distinctions between poor, immigrant neighborhoods and middle- and upper-class neighborhoods are a matter of just a few blocks. Still, distinctions are evident. In Santa Maria, the northwestern areas of the city are characterized by poor immigrants, and the southeastern portions tend to be more white and wealthier. In Garden City, poor Mexican immigrants predominate in southern neighborhoods, while northern areas contain larger concentrations of middle-class whites and Mexican Americans. When Mexican Americans do move, they are usually motivated by aspirations that have little to do with distancing themselves from poor Mexican immigrants. As Richard Alba and Victor Nee explain, "Individuals striving for success in American society often do not see themselves assimilating. Yet the unintended consequences of practical strategies and action undertaken in pursuit of familiar goals—a good education, a good job, a nice place to live, interesting friends, a good education, economic security—often result in specific forms of assimilation" (2003: 41).

For the few older respondents who remained in neighborhoods in which large immigrant populations now reside, following economic aspirations was not a realistic option. Like many of their counterparts in urban areas (Duarte 2008; Telles and Ortiz 2008), they lacked the resources to leave, and their close proximity to Mexican immigrants had led to confrontations with immigrant coethnics and ultimately to withdrawal from neighborly interactions. Such was the case with cousins Dolores and Martha Garza. The two women lived in a lower-middle-class neighborhood in Garden City, where an increasing number of Mexican immigrants reside. The Mexican immigrants who have moved in tend to be those who have been settled in Garden City for several years and have gained enough of an economic foothold to rent or own a home. Still, the

sociocultural differences between Mexican Americans and their coethnic immigrant neighbors can create a wedge. Recall from chapter 6 that
the cousins generally expressed restrictive views of immigration, calling
for closed borders. The feelings they expressed about their neighborhood are consistent with their views on Mexican immigration. Consider
their reaction when the home next door went up for sale:

M: [W]e were kind of worried who we were going to get as neighbors when they
bought the house. So when we see that [white] couple, I said, "Phew! We won't
be hearing that loud music!"

D: I even told the realtor, "I hope it isn't any Mexicans that are moving in here."
Those were my words! [laughs]

M: We don't want any wetbacks living here, do you?

D: No thank you. I said, "Please don't sell to any Mexicans here!" They'll start
with their loud music and having their pickups.

M: And being with your own kind, what can you say? You can't go out there
and say, "Turn the music down," in their pickups. [. . .] They'd say, "Why
not? Don't you like our music?" And then they think you're prejudiced against
them, your own people. So there you are: I thought, "Thank God we got the
neighbors we got."

Martha and Dolores believed that Mexican immigrants were a drag on
the quality of life in the neighborhood. Their financial situation gave them
less freedom to change neighborhoods, so Martha and Dolores managed
their discontent with their immigrant neighbors by avoiding contact with
them as much as possible. At first glance, the distance between the two
women and their neighbors may seem hardly remarkable. After all, in
many parts of the country, neighborhoods are increasingly composed
of people who live near one another but have very little meaningful
contact (Putnam 2000). Garden City is different in this respect, however.
Residents pride themselves on their sense of hospitality and courteous-
ness. The casual waves, friendly conversations from one side of the street
to the other, and general familiarity that commonly exist among neighbors in Garden City were absent from relations between Martha and
Dolores and their immigrant neighbors. In view of this norm in Garden

City, Martha and Dolores's withdrawal is a significant sign of distance making.

However adamant Martha and Dolores were about their wishes that no more Mexican immigrants move into their neighborhood, and despite their avoidance of their immigrant neighbors, the cousins' comments suggest that they still saw a linkage between themselves and immigrants. Even as they explained their frustration, they noted that it was difficult to levy complaints about Mexican immigrants because they regarded them as their "own kind." While they sought distance from these people because of their differences, when it came to sociocultural characteristics and, to a lesser extent, social class, they saw irony in such efforts, because they recognized Mexican immigrants as part of a common ethnic group that cannot be completely divided by generation, class, and culture.

The fear that respondents expressed about being lumped with Mexican immigrants led some to be quite active in their efforts to create distance. Social class plays a significant role in why Mexican Americans actively seek distance as opposed to unity. Mexican Americans in the lower end of the middle class cannot so easily deploy class status as a trait that differentiates them from immigrants. Their lack of significant upward mobility leaves them feeling much more vulnerable to the threat of status degradation that may come from being lumped with poor coethnic immigrants. Unlike respondents firmly in the middle and upper classes, these lower-middle-class Mexican Americans look for other means to signal that they are not poor immigrants.

The way in which they negotiate public spaces reveals the everyday maneuvering they do to create this distance. Unlike larger cities, where residential segregation separates people by race and class in most dimensions of life,[7] Mexican Americans and Mexican immigrants in smaller cities are not isolated from each other, and any distance that exists is a result of a concerted effort. In the eyes of many Garden City and Santa Maria residents—Mexican Americans and whites alike—Mexican immigrants have established some social spaces as distinctly "Mexican." These spaces include local parks, retail stores, shopping malls, and some restaurants that are popular with immigrants. Large numbers of Mexican immigrants routinely gather in these spaces on Sundays, when many have the day off from working in the packing plant or in the fields. Knowledge of the popularity of these spaces among Mexican immigrants spurred some respondents to avoid them.

These respondents feared that non-Mexicans would be unable to draw distinctions between U.S.- and foreign-born Mexicans, resulting in the sort of direct experiences with nativism that I discussed in chapter 5. Some Mexican-American respondents said that immigrants exhibit behavior that is all too indicative of a lack of assimilation, and they believed it would be highly undesirable for non-Mexicans to see them, the respondents, in a similar light. Lina Totten, a forty-three-year-old legal records coordinator in Garden City, articulated such fears. Lina lived in a lower-middle-class area where she had only a few Mexican-immigrant neighbors. She held largely negative views of Mexican immigrants and lamented the sociocultural changes resulting from their increasing numbers. Lina tried to avoid public spaces where immigrants concentrate because she didn't not like the crowds and feared that others would mistake her for a foreigner:

We avoid Wal-Mart if at all possible on weekends, because that's when they're all there. That sounds bad. Do you think that sounds bad? I mean, I'm sitting here saying, "They separate themselves." We're all the same! [laughs] And then I'm turning around and saying I try to avoid them. It doesn't make sense. You're one way or the other. You can't be both. I don't like feeling like that, though. I really don't. But they live here like they lived in Mexico. And they don't have to.

TRJ: Tell me more about Wal-Mart. Why would you avoid going?

R: Because they're in there, and they take over. You cannot get out of their way. I mean, if you're coming down the aisle, they'll just cross right in front of you. They don't care if your cart hits them. And then they'll turn around and give you this dirty look like, "What are you doing?" If they even do that. And they just walk around like I'm in their country. And I don't like that feeling. I really don't. And then sometimes I can feel from the Anglos that they're avoiding me, because they put me in that [category]. I'm a Mexican. I'm not from Mexico, but I'm a Mexican. They can tell. Some of them can. Or maybe they think they can tell. But we're not the same.

By avoiding spaces where Mexican immigrants gather in large numbers, Lina believed that she could avoid the perception from others that she too was a poor immigrant. Still, her comments were fraught with ambivalence. She wavered between the assertion that she was different from Mexican immigrants and the belief that ethnicity tied her to them. Even as Lina discussed her avoidance of immigrants, she expressed internal conflict that came from the recognition that, despite differences in social class (however marginal) and national origin, ethnicity did not permit her to create distance without self-rebuke.

Local parks and shopping malls are popular haunts for Mexican immigrants on weekends, and that popularity among immigrants makes these places unpopular for some Mexican Americans (and other city residents). The large presence of immigrants in the parks leads some Mexican Americans to adopt a language popular among nativists. They note that some public spaces have been "invaded" or "taken over" by immigrants, particularly on Sundays. Take the comments of Ernie Garza, a fifty-four-year-old dental assistant in Garden City:

Just like I told you. We've got the zoo now. Summer, they take over the zoo. I'm saying "they" [says to himself in effect]. Sometimes my wife and I will go through there, and it used to be all mixed. Now it's just . . . how do I want to say it? It's not our group, you know, that lived here a long time. But something new that they took over the zoo, and on weekends, you can't go through there.

Like Lina, Ernie observed that the large numbers of immigrants at the local zoo make it undesirable for established residents. Mexican immigrants in Garden City and Santa Maria have claimed "cultural citizenship," "developing specifically Latino cultural forms of expression" (Flores and Benmayor 1997: 2) in some public spaces. But it is a citizenship that some Mexican Americans do not believe they share. As many respondents explained, simply too many sociocultural differences exist among Mexican Americans for cultural citizenship in these spaces to include all people of Mexican descent. Even if Ernie chose to distance himself from Mexican immigrants by staying away from "Mexican immigrants spaces," his comments, like Lina's, suggest that the distance did not overwhelm the power of his ethnic identity to color how he understood his own efforts to create distance. This recognition tinges Ernie's comments with an ambivalence that comes from his sense that he violated certain norms of ethnic solidarity. Ernie's self-critical aside—*I'm saying "they"*—indicates his belief that a certain irony resides in distancing himself from people who, because of their ethnic origin, may in many ways share a sense of "we-ness" more than a sense of "they-ness" with Mexican Americans.

The selection of schools is another means through which some Mexican Americans create distance from foreign-born Mexicans. School segregation is alive and well in the United States (Boger and Orfield 2005; Fischer and Tienda 2006), and the racial and ethnic backgrounds of children in schools often serve as a proxy for school quality in the minds of Americans. In Garden City and Santa Maria, ethnicity combines with nativity to cue residents about the desirability of a particular school. Parents in Garden City have no choice about where their children attend high school, because there is only one. Parents in Santa Maria, on the other hand, can choose from three high schools, two public and one private. Some Mexican Americans send their children to the two high schools in Orcutt, a wealthy subsection south of Santa Maria, where the schools have good academic reputation. These two schools also happen to have a much smaller Mexican-origin population (and many fewer Mexican immigrants and second-generation Mexican Americans).[8] As a result of its demographic makeup, the main high school in Santa Maria has gained an inferior reputation in the city, and some of the teens I interviewed said that they would prefer to attend schools in Orcutt because of their academic reputation but also because they fear that they may become targets of violence or ridicule in a predominantly "Mexican" environment.

A conversation I had with Lori Rojas, who had just recently moved to an upper-middle-class part of town, shows how some Mexican Americans think about school choice in Santa Maria. Lori reported that the public school in Santa Maria was "scary" because the kids "just looked different" from the ones with whom her sons attended school. Her worry stemmed not just from a fear of crime but also from her perception of the academic quality of the school. She claimed that the main high school in Santa Maria had to lower its standards and have low expectations of its students. Lori voiced a widely held perception that a large number of Mexican-origin students (especially poor immigrant students) signals a low-quality school. Although she focused on academic reasons for her opinion, she attributed the perceived lower academic quality in Santa Maria to the students, most of whom are of Mexican origin. The high school in Santa Maria has an academic reputation much like that of other high schools in which the majority of the student body is made up of poor minorities. Although test scores suggest that the validity of this reputation has some merit,[9] some Mexican Americans decide not to send their children to those schools not only because of the academic reputation but also because of the ethnic and class composition of the student body.

Much like the other respondents, Lori saw irony embedded in her attempts to keep her children out of "Mexican" schools. She told me that she felt "bad" about "being prejudiced against her own people," indicating that an ethnic consciousness troubled her in regard to her efforts to distance her family from Mexican immigrants.

The fears and opinions that respondents expressed in chapter 5 about the ill effect of immigrants on the social standing of Mexican Americans translate into attempts to create distance between themselves and Mexican immigrants. In fact, Mexican Americans who carry the most restrictionist opinions and perceive the greatest costs associated with Mexican immigration are the most avid drawbridge raisers. Lower-middle-class Mexican Americans are more likely than others to try to create distance, partly because they are less able to deploy their class standing as a defense against being lumped in with poor Mexican immigrants. What is clear from the interviews, however, is that even as Mexican Americans distance themselves from their immigrant coethnics, a certain degree of ethnic consciousness influences how they rationalize their efforts. They regularly interrupt themselves with expressions of self-rebuke when they describe their distancing behavior. Their way of explaining this behavior blurs what their distancing efforts say about their ethnic identity. Whether or not respondents noted that they felt guilty for distancing themselves from "their own people," or noted that Mexican Americans and Mexican immigrants are "all the same," or that using the term *they* to refer to immigrants is not entirely accurate, they implied that class and sociocultural differences do not completely overwhelm the power of ethnic ancestry to bind them to Mexican immigrants.

Later-generation Mexican Americans are not likely to spearhead a demonstration or a social movement advocating for immigrant rights. If we look at Mexican Americans' engagement only in the most visible forms of "ethnic action"—protest politics, organizational involvement, and participation in an ethnic enclave—we miss the important ways that they create unity with and division from Mexican immigrants in daily life. Instances of drawbridge lowering appear in chance encounters with immigrants in Mexican Americans' jobs, in their organizational involvement, and in social entrepreneurship. Their motivation for reaching out to Mexican immigrants cannot be explained by a strong ethnic consciousness or a sense of linked fate. Instead, it comes from their belief in a shared ethnic origin that requires them to use their class position to give back to those struggling to make their way in American society. But Mexican Americans draw on more than a generalized sense of ethnic solidarity; they also draw on their identification with the immigrant experience vis-à-vis their own immigrant ancestors in explaining why they lower drawbridges to immigrants. Some, though relatively few, Mexican Americans work to distance themselves from immigrants. Even when they do, however, they express discomfort with raising drawbridges on foreign-born Mexicans, whom they see as "their own kind."

The expressions of ethnic identity that show up in what individuals do (or do not do) for the sake of their ethnic group suggest that Mexican immigration has a profound impact on the Mexican-American ethnic identity. For later-generation white ethnic groups, expressions of ethnic identity are relegated almost exclusively to the use of symbols and ethnically linked practices, partly because their ethnic origins are not in any way defined by a group of poor, struggling immigrants who are targets of nativism. Rarely do white ethnics engage in purposive action underpinned by a strong sense of ethnic identity. In contrast, expressions of ethnic identity among Mexican Americans include much more than symbols and practices; they also include displays of solidarity with, as well as distance from, Mexican immigrants struggling to make their way in U.S. society. The fact that Mexican Americans have to make choices in their daily lives about whether to reach out to immigrant coethnics shows just how strongly their identity as ethnic Americans is tethered to the immigrant experience, both past and present.

EIGHT Conclusion

No other group in the United States provokes more concern about the country's future than ethnic Mexicans. Fears about their assimilation come from scholars, pundits, and policy makers of all political stripes. Some claim that people of Mexican origin are reluctant to adapt to a putative American way of life and thus choose to live outside the U.S. mainstream. Others argue that ethnic Mexicans are not assimilating because their opportunity to do so is stymied by historical and present-day discrimination. Often lost in these debates are Mexican Americans whose ancestral roots extend deeply into U.S. history. Analysis of these later-generation Mexican Americans is often overshadowed by the enormous amount of attention paid to immigrants and the second generation. The experiences of the roughly 30 percent of ethnic Mexicans whose families have been in the United States for three generations or more provide a better picture of the assimilation of this group, since the process of assimilation has had ample time to unfold.

This book has shown that with respect to later-generation Mexican Americans, these fears about assimilation are unfounded. Mexican Americans are not ethnic nationalists, nor are they relegated to the margins of U.S. society. Though they have not experienced socioeconomic assimilation to a degree equal to that of white ethnics, they have nonetheless seen significant intergenerational structural assimilation, especially in view of the harsh forms of discrimination they confronted for much of the nineteenth and twentieth centuries. Furthermore, the hold that ethnicity has on how Mexican-American parents raise their children has weakened with each passing generation. Despite what appears to be a classic story of assimilation in some respects, however, the replenishment of a Mexican-immigrant population alters the relationship between structural and cultural forms of assimilation that scholars have taken for granted. Immigrants provide Mexican Americans with abundant access to the ethnic raw materials—ethnically linked symbols and practices—that make for a more salient experience of ethnicity. Because of the presence of their immigrant coethnics, Mexican Americans are never far from the language, food, and traditions that come from their ethnic homeland. Access to these ethnic raw materials is facilitated not just by the growing immigrant population but also by multiculturalism, which makes ethnicity a more acceptable and more desirable aspect of identity.

Ethnicity is constructed with more than just cultural practices. It is also made up of boundaries—both intergroup and intragroup—that distinguish groups from one another. For Mexican Americans, these ethnic boundaries remain brightly drawn because of the presence of a large immigrant population. The people I interviewed regularly encountered the sharp edges of these boundaries when they ran into nativism directed at immigrants. Whether witnessed in interpersonal interactions or in highly visible public displays, Mexican Americans run into a racialized form of nativism that attributes discontent about immigration to all people of Mexican descent, not just immigrants. Nativism struck a chord with respondents, because it highlights the immigrant experience as a central event defining what it means to be a person of Mexican descent in the United States. They thus saw nativist attacks against immigrant coethnics as an affront to all people of Mexican descent, regardless of generation. Nativism can touch the lives of Mexican Americans more directly when their skin color and surname lead others to tag them as foreigners. If nativism makes Mexican Americans feel too Mexican at times, the high expectations they face about what it means to be an "authentic" person of Mexican descent make them feel not Mexican enough. Intragroup boundaries emerge when later-generation Mexican Americans fail to live up to strict notions of ethnic authenticity imposed by immigrants, the second generation, and even non-Mexicans.

Mexican Americans' opinions about immigration from their ethnic homeland further reveal the complex ways in which continued immigration shapes their experience. The immigrant experience and the internalization of core American ideals lead most to opine that the United States should remain open to new immigrants. A small minority draws a different conclusion, stating that the southern border should be sealed to immigrants, whom they see as inferior in character relative to their own immigrant ancestors. But Mexican immigration had a special resonance with the people I interviewed. The ethnic origin that they shared with the largest group of contemporary immigrants could make their own social standing vulnerable to profound shaping by immigration. Respondents expressed ambivalent views about how Mexican immigration affects the social standing of Mexican Americans. As they saw it, Mexican immigration yields both costs and benefits. The costs come from a fear that the low status of coethnic immigrants is a drag on the status of all people of Mexican descent, both Mexican- and U.S.-born. But in an age in which ethnic identity can come with a positive recognition in politics, the labor market, and popular culture, Mexican-American respondents also saw immigration from their ethnic homeland as a benefit that gives all people of Mexican origin political and economic clout and cultural cachet.

The good degree of structural assimilation that most later-generation Mexican Americans have experienced puts them in a position to assist poorer, coethnic immigrants. The Mexican Americans I spoke to were hardly political activists who displayed highly visible forms of advocacy on behalf of immigrants. But they did not disown their immigrant coethnics. Most Mexican Americans, particularly those who hold accommodating views of Mexican immigration, come to the aid of immigrant coethnics in everyday encounters, suggesting that class and sociocultural differences do not entirely divide them from Mexican immigrants. Instead, a shared ethnic narrative rooted in the immigrant experience binds them. Even the few respondents who worked to distance themselves from immigrants rebuked themselves for pulling up the ethnic drawbridge on "their own kind." For these distance makers, class and sociocultural differences were sources of division, but they did not entirely overwhelm their recognition of a shared ethnic origin.

These findings have important implications for how to understand the place of the Mexican-origin population in America's racial and ethnic landscape and for theories of assimilation. The experiences of Mexican Americans in Garden City and Santa Maria suggest that people of Mexican origin are not an aggrieved minority that has confronted insurmountable obstacles to mobility. Nor are they an ethnic group that is gradually assimilating into U.S. society in same way that European-origin groups did. The continual influx of Mexican immigration makes the Mexican-origin population something of a permanent immigrant group that perpetually struggles with assimilation. Furthermore, their experiences show that the duration of an immigration wave is a central factor shaping how processes of assimilation and ethnic identity formation unfold.

LOCATING THE MEXICAN-ORIGIN POPULATION IN AMERICA'S RACIAL AND ETHNIC LANDSCAPE

Two general views have framed how scholars understand the Mexican-origin population. On one hand, scholars have painted this population as an aggrieved minority that has experienced persistent discrimination and blocked entrance into the American mainstream (Acuña 1972; Almaguer 1975; Ochoa 2004; Telles and Ortiz 2008). From this perspective, ethnic Mexicans are regarded as a people whose prospects for upward mobility are dragged down by a history of colonization and persistent racial discrimination. To the extent that they do experience assimilation, it is mostly of a negative sort. Indeed, some scholars contend that poverty and racism place the Mexican-American second generation on a downward path of assimilation into a "rainbow underclass" (Portes and Rumbaut 2001). On the other hand, others paint a brighter picture, arguing that people of Mexican origin are an assimilating ethnic group that is experiencing steady, if slow-paced, assimilation. They note that Mexican Americans' significant intergenerational socioeconomic progress and intermarriage patterns suggest that the barriers to mobility break down over time. This second perspectives sees their assimilation as more similar to than different from that of white ethnics (Alba 2006; Alba and Nee 2003; Skerry 1993; Smith 2003, 2006).

The findings I presented in the preceding chapters suggest that both these theoretical platforms contribute to our understanding of the Mexican-origin experience but that neither captures the lived experiences of Mexican Americans. Ongoing Mexican immigration is a central factor shaping Mexican-American assimilation and ethnic identity formation. Without taking immigrant replenishment into account, we find a poor fit between Mexican-origin experience on the ground and the existing theoretical perspectives that explain it. Simply too much evidence of assimilation exists for us to regard ethnic Mexicans as an aggrieved minority. Yet ethnicity remains far too important in their lives to regard them as an assimilating ethnic group.

Underpinning the view of ethnic Mexicans as an aggrieved minority is an emphasis on the history of colonization and the ensuing racialization of the Mexican-origin population (Acuña 1996, 2000; Almaguer 1975; Omi and Winant 1994). The first Mexican Americans who lived in what is now the southwestern United States experienced second-class citizenship because that land was forcefully taken from Mexico in 1848. Not long after annexation, whites came to dominate social, political, and economic life in the new U.S. territory, relegating Mexicans there to a marginal status. Little doubt exists that colonization set the tone for relations between people of Mexican origin and whites through most of the twentieth century. In many places in the Southwest, they lived in segregated neighborhoods, attended segregated schools, and were locked out of higher education and good jobs.

While history shapes collective destinations, it is not destiny. To begin with, very few of today's Mexican Americans trace their roots to the estimated maximum of fifty thousand Mexicans who were in the American Southwest during its annexation (Jaffe, Cullen, and Boswell 1980, cited in Massey, Durand, and Malone 2002). Therefore, few Mexican Americans are the direct heirs of the discrimination visited upon those original southwesterners. Furthermore, people of Mexican origin currently live under conditions quite different from those of their colonized predecessors. Civil rights laws have made illegal the forms of discrimination visited upon the colonized Mexicans of the nineteenth century, and twenty-first-century norms confer great stigma on such treatment. The level of assimilation seen among Mexican Americans in education, income, and housing also belies notions of a colonized group (Alba 2006; Brown 2007; Macias 2006; Smith 2003, 2006; Telles and Ortiz 2008; Tienda and Mitchell 2006). To be sure, people of Mexican origin, particularly poor immigrants, still suffer discrimination, and later-generation Mexican Americans can be victims of collateral damage from nativism carelessly hurled at Mexican immigrants. But the discrimination they experience is largely a function of contemporary immigration more than a legacy of colonization.

Scholars of the Mexican-origin population also cite race as a significant factor shaping their experiences today. Though people of Mexican descent are phenotypically diverse, most have dark skin that makes them identifiably different from the white majority. The importance of race has had much to do with their historical and present-day treatment. After the annexation of the Southwest and during the first part of the twentieth century, race determined the status of the Mexican-origin population. Whites regarded Mexicans as a separate race, particularly because of their "Indian blood," even if they reasoned that their European origins made them a cut above Native Americans (Almaguer 1994). In parts of the Southwest and Midwest, Mexicans lived under a system of Jim Crow–like segregation resulting from a system that saw them as racially inferior. They were often barred from public swimming pools, refused service at restaurants, and restricted to certain neighborhoods (García 1996; Meier and Ribera 1993). In the current era, some evidence suggests that race matters for people of Mexican descent. Sociologists Edward Telles and Edward Murguía have shown that phenotype accounts for differences in income and schooling within the Mexican-origin population (Murguía and Telles 1996; Telles and Murguía 1990). Analyses of the second generation also rely on race as a key variable explaining why today's young second generation has a more difficult time making it in U.S. society than the lighter-skinned European second generation of yesteryear did (Portes and Rumbaut 2001; Portes and Zhou 1993).

The findings presented in this book show that race matters in the Mexican-American experience but not for the reasons that others have asserted. In the present context, immigration informs the meaning attached to race. As I showed in chapter 5, instances in which race matters in the lives of Mexican Americans are virtually always linked to notions of Mexicans as foreigners, as seen in situations in which respondents were mistaken for immigrants. In less injurious but still significant instances, non-Mexicans sometimes assumed that the people I interviewed possessed the cultural repertoire of their immigrant coethnics because of the way they looked or their surnames.

The importance of immigration in how Mexican Americans experience race becomes clearer when considering a hypothetical that I posed to my respondents during each interview: What would things be like for later-generation Mexican Americans had there been no Mexican immigration after 1940? Ideally, differences between Mexican Americans in Garden City and Santa Maria would reveal in explicit terms how immigration patterns factor into the racial and ethnic identity formation. I did not, however, find differences between these two groups. Nonetheless, a relevant comparison case does exist: the southern and eastern European groups whose immigrant ancestors came in large numbers at the turn of the last century. We can have little doubt that early Mexican immigrants and their descendants had it worse than these European-origin individuals. Colonization set the stage for a hostile context of reception that greeted the first wave of Mexican immigrants. The fact that ethnic Mexicans were more phenotypically different from the white majority than European groups were also contributed to a sharper racialization. Parallels between Mexican and European immigrants also exist, however. Much like Mexican immigrants, southern and eastern European immigrants were legally "white on arrival" (Guglielmo 2003) but in practice were regarded as nonwhite. Nativists of the day fretted that "swarthy" immigrants might contaminate the American gene pool, creating a mongrel race (Higham 1963). Even though they could leverage their nonblack identity in their effort to belong in U.S. society, which eventually came to see them as white (Ignatiev 1995; Jacobson 1998; Roediger 1991, 2005), the white majority nonetheless generally considered them inferior because of perceived racial differences.

The racialization of European-origin groups had much to do with their foreign status. A number of things set them apart from the white majority: they looked different from U.S. whites, they did not speak English, they held low-wage, low-status jobs, and they concentrated in poor immigrant ghettos. Immigration, or a lack thereof, also significantly affected their ability to be seen as white. Restrictive immigration laws passed in 1921 and 1924, along with two world wars and an economic depression, severely curtailed immigration from southern and eastern Europe. As historian David Roediger (2005) points out, immigration restriction assuaged nativist fears about the ability of these immigrants and their descendants to assimilate: "The new demographics of immigration [after 1924] dramatically undercut political mobilizations based on fear of an 'invasion' insofar as there was every indication that the invasion of 'hunkies' and 'guineas' had been decisively turned back. Subsequently, experts reasserted the progressive views of Theodore Roosevelt and others that in the right proportions new immigrants could, properly digested, even invigorate U.S. 'stock'" (149).

As immigration subsided, a substantial second and third generation came of age in a U.S. society decidedly less characterized by their coethnic immigrants. As a result, the social, economic, and political distance between people once considered "hunkies" and "guineas" and the white majority shrank, changing their status from distinctive race groups to "white ethnics." Indeed, with the end of immigration from southern and eastern Europe, "immigrant communities . . . lost many of the cultural attributes that marked them as unfit to enter the white house of U.S. nationalism as full equals" (Roediger 2005: 151). Because mass immigration from Europe never reemerged, their status as members of a white mainstream would only become firmer over the course of the twentieth century.

What, then, does the experience of white ethnics suggest about the link between immigration and race among people of Mexican origin? What it does not suggest is that race is irrelevant; rather, it points to what makes race relevant: immigration. The history of white ethnics shows that demographic shifts related to immigration shape how a group's racial status is constructed and how the end of immigration allows for a group's racial status to be reconstructed. The constant influx of Mexican immigration provides persistent fodder for racializing people of Mexican origin as foreigners. Mexican-immigrant replenishment makes it impossible for ethnic Mexicans, even if they are several generations removed from their immigrant origins, to change their racial status as European-origin groups did. Indeed, immigration continuously buttresses the association between Mexicanness and foreignness.

If colonization and race—the two primary variables invoked by those who see Mexicans as an aggrieved minority—do not fully explain the Mexican-origin experience, neither does treating people of Mexican origin as an immigrant ethnic group whose assimilation parallels that of white ethnics. This perspective is more likely to invoke human capital—the bundle of skills and work experience—as a central mechanism explaining assimilation. Mexican immigrants have always come to the United States with some of the lowest levels of education of any immigrant group and, thus, have a tougher climb up the ladder of mobility. Furthermore, the majority of Mexican immigrants come to the United States without authorization, adding a severe handicap to their assimilation (Bean et al. 2007; Bean and Stevens 2003).

Seeing people of Mexican origin as an assimilating immigrant ethnic group also has its shortcomings. This view implies that with enough time in the United States, people of Mexican origin will ultimately assimilate, that the ethnic boundaries for people of Mexican origin will eventually disintegrate so long as upward mobility continues. As the findings from the preceding chapters show, this is far from a safe assumption. Immigrant replenishment provides even upwardly mobile, later-generation Mexican Americans with regular access to the ethnic raw materials around which ethnic identity coalesces. The continual influx of immigrants also ensures that later-generation Mexican Americans run into the sharp ethnic boundaries—both intergroup and intragroup—that distinguish groups. Indeed, immigrant replenishment is a shot in the arm to ethnicity, adding to its salience even among those whose human capital suggests that they are quite assimilated.

The findings presented in this book suggest that the Mexican-origin population in America's racial and ethnic landscape is not best described as an aggrieved minority or as an assimilating ethnic group. The Mexican-origin population is more like a permanent immigrant group. The persistent influx of Mexican immigrants during the last century has introduced a consistently large group of Mexican newcomers who reinfuse ethnic raw materials into the Mexican-origin population but who also renew the link between "Mexicanness" and the struggles associated with assimilation. What distinguishes the Mexican-origin population from other former immigrant groups is not that they face these struggles at all but that these struggles never quite go away. Each new generation born in the United States does not march ever more distantly away from an immigrant generation until people of Mexican origin become just another American ethnic group. Instead, later-generation Mexican Americans continue to be surrounded by an immigrant population that rejuvenates both ethnic practices and ethnic difference.[1]

The status of the Mexican-origin population as a permanent immigrant group becomes clearer when viewing collective identities as narratives that tell the story of what it means to be a member of a particular group. As Stephen Cornell (2000) points out, the formation of narratives involves the selection, plotting, and interpretation of key events that define the experiences of an ethnic group. Narratives are anything but static. As events change, so do the narratives that are developed to make sense of them. Events central to the narrative at one point may recede into the background at another, while new events and the way in which they are imbued with meaning give rise to new narratives about "who we are" and "who they are."

If the American national identity is a patchwork of many smaller narratives coming from different ethnic groups, then immigration is certainly a defining event in both the constituent ethnic narratives and the larger American one. John F. Kennedy long ago proclaimed in the title of his book that the United States is "a nation of immigrants" (1964), and many since then have also invoked the term to describe the nation. The idea of the United States as a nation of immigrants can be deceiving, for only some groups are fully included in this national narrative. Ethnic groups whose narratives are completely sewn into the fabric of American identity are those for whom the immigrant experience is a past event that can be looked upon with a certain degree of nostalgia. Instead of being defined by the rupture associated with immigration and the turbulence linked to assimilation, ethnic groups that have a firm place in the larger national narrative are defined by having completed the bumpy process of assimilation; they are distinguished by having "made it" in U.S. society. The term that Kennedy made popular might be more accurate if it were amended: "a nation of descendants of immigrants who overcame the hardships of immigration and assimilation." On the basis of his study of ethnic identity among white ethnics, Richard Alba similarly describes a lore among them that befits this amended term: "From every group, one hears essentially the same story of people who came poor, suffered from discrimination and other early burdens, but worked hard and eventually made their way in the new land" (1990: 313–14). The historical distance from the immigrant experience, significant upward socioeconomic mobility, and intermarriage have muted smaller differences that once demarcated the group narratives of those who journeyed from Europe. Today, as Alba points out, white ethnics recognize a larger shared narrative centered on having risen above the struggles of the immigrant generation, such that the groups to which they trace their ethnic roots are no longer defined by their foreignness.

We are constantly reminded that belonging in the larger American national narrative is reserved for groups whose immigrant experience is behind them. Take, for example, a television commercial for an investing company that aired during the stock-market downturn of the early 2000s. The commercial begins with old, grainy, black-and-white movie clips of thousands of immigrants coming to the United States through Ellis Island, as they enthusiastically wave American flags and shoot grins at the Statue of Liberty. The people are clearly poor and tired, but their faces gleam with hope and the promise of the American dream. Spurring viewers to be inspired by the immigrants' willingness to risk it all for a better life, the commercial concludes by proclaiming, "The biggest risk is not taking one at all." The ad aims to instill bravery in investors facing a bear market, but it also appeals to a nostalgia that underlies the European-immigrant experience. The commercial could just as easily have shown Mexicans immigrants coming to the United States on trains in order to escape the Mexican Revolution. These immigrants surely took as much of a risk as their European contemporaries. Including Mexican immigrants in such a commercial just would not resonate, however. No similar feeling of nostalgia is associated with Mexican immigration because it is ongoing. Much as they have throughout the last century, Mexican migrants continue to arrive in large numbers to meet the U.S. demand for low-wage labor while facing a nativist reaction that paints them as a source of social, political, and economic ills. Indeed, the U.S.-Mexico border is seen as a problem that needs solving rather than as a source of hope that was once symbolized by the Statue of Liberty and Ellis Island.

The Mexican ethnic narrative is not indistinguishably woven into the larger American narrative because of the prominent and present-day role of immigration. Other events figure into this narrative. Colonization, the struggle for civil rights, the Chicano movement, and the ascendancy of Mexican Americans in politics are all events that respondents in Garden City and Santa Maria mentioned as important to what it means to be Mexican American. But nothing defines this narrative today more than immigration. Because Mexican immigration is an ongoing event, people of Mexican descent living in the United States cannot be nostalgic about the immigrant experience, even if their ancestors came to the United States near the time of mass European migration. Such nostalgia requires a psychological and historical distance from the immigrant experience that later-generation Mexican Americans lack. The absence of nostalgia comes from more than just their personal contact with Mexican immigrants. The public nature of debates about Mexican immigration elevates the importance of immigration as a defining event in the Mexican-American narrative, preventing the *Mexican*-immigrant experience from becoming part of a nostalgic understanding of immigration central to membership in the larger national narrative.

Mexican Americans assert a narrative that departs from the one that predominates in U.S. society, pushing back against the dominant image of the Mexican-origin population as a foreign group. They may claim themselves to be "hyphenated Americans," just like other later-generation descendants of immigrants. But immigration elongates the hyphen between "Mexican" and "American" in the eyes of many non-Mexicans. Even if others "exit" the group by not identifying at all as a person of Mexican origin (Alba et al., forthcoming; Duncan and Trejo 2005), a pattern that intermarriage precipitates, immigration lends credence to the dominant narrative of the Mexican-origin population as an unmeltable foreign group.

MEXICAN IMMIGRATION: A DOUBLE-EDGED SWORD

Though recent scholarship on later-generation Mexican Americans cites immigrant replenishment as a source of their racialization (Telles and Ortiz 2008), the effect of Mexican immigration on the Mexican-American experience is far from unequivocally negative or positive. Indeed, Mexican immigrants represent something of a double-edged sword for Mexican Americans. On one edge of this sword are the tight coupling of foreignness and Mexicanness that immigrant replenishment reinforces and the accompanying nativism that primarily confronts Mexican immigrants but also affects Mexican Americans. As the experiences of interview respondents in Garden City and Santa Maria show, the large number of Mexican immigrants bolsters the ethnic boundaries that Mexican Americans confront, and respondents themselves feared that newcomers negatively color how people perceive the entire Mexican-origin population.

Mexican Americans are not drawn to an ethnic identity like moths to a flame, however. Advantages rest on the other edge of this sword, the most significant of which are shaped by multiculturalism, which pervades U.S. society today. Multiculturalism certainly does not negate the widespread backlash against Mexican immigrants. Discrimination against them remains fervent, and a strong and vocal segment of U.S. society still advocates an ethnically chauvinist, Americanizationist form of assimilation. But multiculturalism does, nonetheless, create a context that is welcoming of ethnic differences and translates into policies and practices that provide incentives for people of Mexican descent to remain attached to an ethnic identity. The presence of a large Mexican-immigrant population allows Mexican Americans to do just that more easily than the fully assimilated descendants of other immigrant groups. Instead of having a merely symbolic attachment to their ethnic roots, Mexican Americans have abundant access to the ethnically linked symbols and practices that allow for a richer experience of ethnicity. While many Americans lament being ethnically plain in a U.S. society with vibrant ethnic flavors, immigration permits Mexican Americans to have an ethnic identity firmly anchored in an ethnic origin that maintains its fervor.

The benefits that Mexican Americans enjoy as a result of continued immigration go beyond their access to the practice of ethnicity that flavors their social identity. Multiculturalism has made diversity a value that guides decision making about the distribution of valuable resources, translating into concrete rewards associated with Mexican ethnicity. Immigration restocks the Mexican-origin population with individuals whose language and socioeconomic status make the entire population a "visible minority." This high visibility in an age of multiculturalism renders the Mexican-origin population a group that requires representation in politics, employment, and education. As Mexican-American respondents noted, they were often the first to get the call when there was a need for "Mexican" representation, and they benefited from affirmative action policies that colleges and universities employ in admissions and in divvying up scholarships.

The deployment of race and ethnicity in employment, politics, and education is often problematic, however. There is no shortage of ill-reasoned complaints that unqualified minorities gain access to opportunities solely on the basis of their ethnic origins, and politicians of all ideological stripes unscrupulously manipulate racial and ethnic identity for political gain. Furthermore, either edge of the sword can be sharpened by the prevailing view of Mexican immigrants. If, for example, the debate about unauthorized Mexican immigration is running hot (as it was in 2006 and 2007), then the advantages attached to Mexican ethnicity likely decline relative to the disadvantages. Yet the people I interviewed clearly acknowledged both. The recognition of the Mexican-origin population as a political and economic constituency deserving of attention leads to the immigrant-driven growth of this population yielding very recognizable benefits for Mexican Americans that exist alongside the costs of their image as a perpetual foreign group.

LESSONS FOR THE STUDY OF ASSIMILATION

I have argued that the Mexican-origin population is exceptional in many respects, particularly in regard to the duration and extent of immigration. Some scholars consider Mexican immigrants so exceptional that they present data for immigrant assimilation with and without the Mexican-origin population so as not to skew results for other groups (see, for example, Smith and Edmonston 1997). Even if it stands out from other groups, the Mexican-origin case has much to teach us about the study of immigration and assimilation.

Assimilation Over Time: Generations and Cohorts

In formulating theories of assimilation, scholars have generally taken for granted the cessation of immigration, and they have thus made little mention of the duration of immigration as a variable that shapes how groups assimilate. But as the case of later-generation Mexican Americans suggests, this omission produces an incomplete understanding of the factors shaping assimilation. Canonical accounts of assimilation were formulated on the experiences of European-origin groups, whose immigration to the United States took place during a discrete period, with a definitive beginning (roughly 1880) and end (roughly 1920). Because mass European immigration had about a forty-year life span, never more than three generations of a particular group were alive at the same time, and each new generation born in the United States thus had less and less contact with the immigrant generation (see Massey 1995).

Generational progression still captures assimilation in most of its dimensions, particularly those related to socioeconomic status, residential location, and marriage. Milton Gordon (1964) placed these subprocesses under the umbrella of "structural assimilation" and posited that this kind of assimilation leads to "identificational assimilation," or a sense of "peoplehood" as taken from the host society. The findings from Garden City and Santa Maria suggest that immigrant replenishment loosens the connection between structural assimilation and identificational assimilation. When the duration of immigration is prolonged, a large number of individuals may experience a great deal of structural assimilation, but identificational assimilation does not necessarily follow as closely as it does for other groups. Indeed, continued immigration provides access to the ethnically linked symbols and practices central to ethnic identity that even the most structurally assimilated individuals access, while it also animates the boundaries that distinguish groups.

Central to assimilation is the concept of ethnic boundaries, which are animated by the everyday ways that groups are distinguished from one another. Assimilation takes place when ethnic boundaries fade, when an "ethnic distinction and its corollary cultural and social differences" (Alba and Nee 2003: 11) have declined. Even though structural assimilation may allow individuals to cross boundaries made "brighter" (Alba 2005a) by continued immigration, these boundaries remain a prominent force in everyday life. Indeed, when immigration is ongoing, crossing these boundaries in work, marriage, and residential location does not lead to the kind of inconsequential, optional form of ethnic identity experienced by those whose ethnic origins are no longer replenished by immigration (Alba 1990; Waters 1990). Immigrant replenishment staves off the twilight of ethnicity, even if it does not stymie structural assimilation.

Paying attention to immigrant replenishment in the study of assimilation has implications for how scholars measure assimilation. From very early on, scholars posited that generation is the key temporal marker of assimilation. Those who studied the assimilation of European groups assumed that learning the generation of an individual was a reasonable way to determine that individual's level of assimilation. Generally one could assume that the first generation experienced the greatest struggle to fit into the new society, that the U.S.-born second generation became more integrated, even if their integration was still turbulent, and that the third generation, having been U.S.-born to U.S.-born parents, was almost entirely assimilated (Fishman 1965; Gordon 1964; Warner and Srole 1945). This three-generation model takes for granted that each new generation born in the United States has less contact with immigrants from their ethnic homeland. This was largely a safe assumption in the study of European groups because of the tight correlation between immigrant generation (birth distance from the immigrant point of origin) and cohort (people born in the same time period). European immigration took place during a relatively discrete span of time, so the successive generations were born during predictable periods: the first generation was born during the late 1800s and early 1900s; the second generation, in the 1910s and 1920s; and the third generation, in the 1930s, 1940s, and early 1950s. In addition, this strong correlation between generation and cohort reliably ensures that individuals who experienced ethnic change internal to any particular ethnic group (as measured by generation) also experienced the same historical circumstances in which this change took place (as measured by birth cohort) (see Alba 1988).

The Mexican-American experience shows that immigrant replenishment weakens the correlation between generation and cohort. When immigration is replenished, each birth cohort is composed of a mix of generations. For example, in addition to the post-1965 second-generation Mexican Americans, who are mostly in their teens and twenties, a significant second generation exists in virtually every other birth cohort as well. Each generation of Mexican-origin individuals is made of people from a mix of birth cohorts, and each birth cohort contains individuals from many immigrant generations. The historical circumstances associated with the birth cohort into which individuals are born shape their assimilation in ways that are perhaps as important as their generational status. For example, the children of Mexican immigrants who escaped the Mexican Revolution from 1910 to 1920 and the children of Mexican migrants who arrived in the 1980s are all "second generation," but they have come of age in rather different historical periods. Life for the older second generation was shaped by major historical events such as the Great Depression, Jim Crow–like racism in many parts of the Southwest, and World War II. The early years for the newer second generation have been characterized by rising income inequality, deindustrialization, multiculturalism, the war on terror, and an increasingly globalized economy. The use of a straightforward generational analysis to assess the socioeconomic status or ethnic identity of second-generation Mexican American misses important historical factors shaping their assimilation.

The case of the Mexican-origin population suggests that generation may not mean what it has in other cases. If immigration from a particular country takes place over a protracted period of time, resulting in a detachment of birth cohort and generation, then using only generation to gauge temporal change may not be enough. As recent studies of Mexican-origin socioeconomic mobility have shown (Smith 2003, 2006; Telles and Ortiz 2008), a more complete way to measure assimilation is to use generation, which captures processes of ethnic change internal to the group, *and* birth cohort, which captures historical fluctuations in opportunities and constraints external to the group. As this book has shown, using both generation and cohort as temporal gauges of assimilation sheds light on ethnic change (see also Jiménez and Fitzgerald 2007).

Immigrant Replenishment beyond the Mexican-origin Case

The utility of considering how immigrant replenishment shapes assimilation and ethnic identity construction can be seen through a brief application of the insights from this book to the cases of other ethnic groups that have experienced immigrant replenishment. Though the Mexican-origin population has experienced a heavier and more sustained immigrant replenishment than any other group, it is not the only group whose population has been restocked by immigrant newcomers. On the West

Coast, later-generation Punjabis, Filipinos, Japanese, and Chinese have been replenished by coethnic immigrants. Poles in Chicago and the Irish in Boston have also seen newer waves of immigrants follow much older ones. Sociological research focusing on the experiences of later-generation Chinese Americans, Japanese Americans, and Polish Americans shows how the effects of immigrant replenishment on ethnic identity differ depending on the timing, source, and scale of immigration.

Asian groups have a long history of immigration to the United States. Predating the first large waves of Mexican immigrants were Chinese and Japanese migrants, who came primarily to the West Coast in the late 1800s and early 1900s. The Chinese Exclusion Act ended legal Chinese immigration in 1882, and twenty-five years later, in 1907–8, the United States and Japan signed the Gentlemen's Agreement, ending migration from Japan to the United States. The Immigration Act of 1924 virtually sealed the United States from legal Chinese and Japanese immigration by barring the entry of those deemed ineligible for citizenship, which included all Asian immigrants. Chinese and Japanese immigrants suffered from some of the harshest discrimination visited upon any immigrant group. The naturalization ineligibility of immigrants from these groups until 1952 and the internment of thousands of Japanese Americans during World Ward II evince their marginal position in U.S. society. Today, the descendants of these Chinese and Japanese immigrants are well into the fourth and fifth generations, and despite the hardships their ancestors faced, they have experienced significant assimilation (see Alba and Nee 2003: chapter 3).

Later-generation Chinese and Japanese Americans also experience immigrant replenishment, but its effects on them are different from its effects on Mexican Americans. The surge in immigration from Asia since 1965 has produced dramatic demographic changes, to which Chinese and Japanese immigrants have made a relatively small contribution. In 2006, Chinese immigrants constituted 5.1 percent of the total foreign-born U.S. population, or 1,906,341 individuals, and Japanese immigrants made up only 0.9 percent, or 353,576 of all foreign-born individuals (Migration Policy Institute 2008). The small scale of immigrant replenishment from Japan and China, these immigrants' distribution throughout the United

States, and the long absence of immigration from these countries guar-
antee that today's Chinese and Japanese immigrants provide too few
ethnic raw materials to support a salient form of ethnic identity among
later-generation coethnics. Sociologist Mia Tuan shows that they draw
on traditions from their ethnic roots only sporadically and symbolically:
"Asian ethnics exercise a great deal of flexibility regarding the cultural
elements they wish to keep or discard from their personal lives. What
they have retained by way of cultural traditions is largely symbolic and
a novelty" (1998: 155).

Even if Chinese and Japanese Americans are not being replenished
with the ethnic raw materials that ongoing coethnic immigration provides, the recent large influx of immigrants from East and Southeast Asia
has sharpened the intergroup boundaries they experience between themselves and other Americans. These boundaries are hardened not by the
immigration of coethnics but rather by the immigration of "coracials"—
Asians who may differ in their ethnic origin but who share a common
racial identity in the U.S. context. Whereas Chinese and Japanese immigrants constitute but a small proportion of today's foreign-born population, immigrants from all Asian countries (excluding India) make up
roughly 20 percent of the total foreign-born U.S. population, with Korea,
Vietnam, and the Philippines, in addition to China, contributing the
largest numbers. Furthermore, among Asians in the United States, the
large majority (64 percent) is foreign born (Zhou 2004: 33). Much like
the Mexican-origin population, foreign-born Asians significantly define
what it means to be Asian in the United States today. In U.S. society, which
does a poor job of recognizing the significant generational and national-
origin differences among Asians, later-generation Chinese and Japanese
Americans experience the intergroup boundaries that Asian-immigrant
replenishment reinforces. Tuan (1998) shows that Chinese and Japanese
Americans, like Mexican Americans, face non-Asians' assumptions about
their foreignness. (For example, "Where are you from?" is an all too
common question.) They also encounter ethnic expectations regarding
their knowledge of language and culture, disappointing non-Asians
when they fail to display a form of ethnicity more likely to be found
among the immigrant generation. Tuan shows that these expectations

emanate much more from non-Asians than they do from Chinese and Japanese coethnics, in contrast to the experience of Mexican Americans: "A major reason underlying the assumption of foreignness stems from contemporary Asian immigration. The influx of unprecedented numbers of immigrants has complicated the lives of native-born Asian ethnics because most non-Asians are unable or unwilling to recognize generational differences" (1998: 158). Immigrant replenishment from Asia has led to Chinese and Japanese Americans living under what sociologists Min Zhou and Jennifer Lee call the "immigrant shadow" (2004: 13). Chinese and Japanese Americans experience this shadow because of the intergroup boundaries it makes salient.

In the case of Polish Americans, immigrant replenishment may reinforce intragroup boundaries, while intergroup boundaries remain largely unaffected. Though immigration from Poland is most often thought of as part of the great European migration from the turn of the last century, Polish immigration to Chicago continued well after the spigot of migration from southern and eastern Europe was closed in 1924. Sociologist Mary Patrice Erdmans (1998) shows that Polish immigration to Chicago occurred in three large waves, spanning much of the twentieth century and consisting of economic migrants who arrived around the turn of the century, World War II émigrés exiled by war and the rise of a communist regime, and those who left their homeland in the late 1970s and 1980s for political and economic reasons. Erdmans's study of "Chicago Polonia" (i.e., immigrant Poles and Polish Americans in Chicago) in the 1970s and 1980s demonstrates that later-generation Polish Americans, the World War II émigrés, and the new Polish immigrants shared a common ethnic origin, social space, and a desire to see Poland break its communist chains. But the collective attempts to push for change in their ethnic homeland revealed significant intragroup boundaries among Poles in the United States. While Polish-immigrant replenishment did little to sharpen the intergroup boundaries, it created obvious intragroup boundaries regarding ethnic authenticity and appropriate strategies for collective action. Later-generation Polish Americans exhibited the trappings of white-ethnic symbolic ethnicity, including sparse use of the Polish language and the episodic use of ethnic symbols as a primary means to "be ethnic." But their expression of ethnic identity did not go without challenge from Polish immigrants, who believed their own direct linkages with the ethnic homeland gave them greater clout in defining Polishness in the United States. As Erdmans notes, "The 'us-them' divide [in Chicago Polonia in the 1980s], along which identity was constructed, was an in-house border. They believed they ought to cooperate because they had the same goal; but differences among generations and migrations led to internecine conflict. . . . Other identities, however—in particular, the ethnic and immigrant identities—were on opposite poles in a community struggling to define the meaning of Polishness in America" (1998: 232).

As the experiences of later-generation Mexican Americans, Chinese Americans, Japanese Americans, and Polish Americans show, paying attention to the duration of immigration provides a fuller understanding of processes central to assimilation: the creation, maintenance, and fading of ethnic boundaries, as well as the use of ethnically linked symbols and practices around which ethnicity coalesces.

As global economic integration, cheap and rapid transportation, and durable social networks that span national boundaries drive migration, these and other groups will likely experience replenishment. Immigrant replenishment most certainly shapes assimilation, but its effects may differ depending on a number of factors. As this book and the case of Chinese, Japanese, and Polish Americans show, how this replenishment affects assimilation depends a great deal on the timing, source, and scale of immigration. Other factors are also likely to matter, such as the character of the immigrants involved in the replenishing. In the Mexican-origin case, the status of Mexican immigrants as unauthorized and poor certainly shapes how immigrant replenishment affects later-generation Mexican Americans. Thus, the study of assimilation would greatly benefit from understanding not just how immigrant replenishment affects assimilation but also how other factors interact with replenishment to shape assimilation outcomes.

This book brings into focus the question that Samuel Huntington poses in the title of his book, *Who Are We?* We are, in fact, a nation of immigrants. But we are also a nation that is much more comfortable with the immigration that is behind us than with the one that is currently taking place. Our comfort comes from our having grown accustomed to the manners in which past waves of immigrants have changed American identity. Today's immigration may seem threatening by comparison, because U.S. society is changing before our eyes.

And so the experience of Mexican Americans encapsulates the experience of a U.S. society grappling with how immigration fits into its national identity. Historian Matthew Frye Jacobson has observed that the United States' acceptance of European immigration as part of its national narrative culminated with "the displacement of Plymouth Rock by Ellis Island in our national myth of origins" (2006: 9). One day perhaps the border crossing between San Diego and Tijuana will stand with Ellis Island in our national mythology. The question that remains is whether that can happen even as the Mexican-origin population is replenished by immigrant newcomers.

APPENDIX A Methodological Issues

Doing ethnographic research is not exactly like making sausage, but it is not altogether different either. Behind what I hope readers will find to be a well-organized, data-driven argument in this book is a pretty messy process of collecting and making sense of mounds of interview transcripts and field notes. The next few pages provide a behind-the-scenes look at this process. My aim in this section is twofold. First, I hope to be as transparent as possible about how I did this research so that readers can judge for themselves the validity of my analysis and conclusions. Second, I hope to impart some lessons from my own experience in doing fieldwork that may prove useful to other researchers as they go about grinding the meat that is their data and putting it into casings so that their findings are more meaningfully ingested by readers.

SELECTING A SAMPLE AND COLLECTING THE DATA

Since this study does not employ a random sample of respondents, exactly how I chose them and the logic I used to select them are important to outline. I began with three sample-selection criteria. First, I looked for Mexican Americans whose families had arrived in the United States prior to 1940. I wanted a sample of individuals whose time in the United States roughly paralleled that of later-generation descendants of European immigrants, who have been studied extensively in other research on ethnic identity (Alba 1990; Waters 1990). The year 1940 is nearly twenty years after mass European immigration came to an end, and the first wave of Mexican immigration generally continued until the early 1930s. But during the 1930s, many Mexican immigrants (and some of their U.S.-born children) returned to Mexico (many by force), and the number of Mexican immigrants in the United States in that decade experienced a net decline. Thus, virtually all of the people I interviewed placed their family's immigrant origins in the United States in the 1910s and 1920s. Only 4 of the 123 individuals with whom I conducted in-depth interviews traced their roots to the estimated 50,000 people who were in the southwestern territory when it became part of the United States under the 1848 Treaty of Guadalupe Hidalgo.

I also selected a sample of people who had lived in Garden City or Santa Maria for most of their lives, including the period during which I interviewed them. Since I began this research intending to discover whether historical patterns of Mexican immigration make a difference in ethnic identity, I wanted to interview people who had lived through fluctuations in Mexican immigration.

Finally, I interviewed only Mexican Americans who considered themselves to be "entirely" of Mexican origin. I did not interview multiethnic individuals for whom Mexican ancestry is one of many ethnic strands. Since being of mixed ethnic origins complicates identity formation in unique ways (Harris and Sim 2002; Jiménez 2004; Lee and Bean 2007; Salgado de Snyder, López, and Padilla 1982), I did not include multiethnics and multiracials in the sample so as not to conflate the unique identity processes of people of multiple racial and ethnic backgrounds with the identity processes of Mexican Americans, who consider themselves to be "unmixed" in America's racial and ethnic schema. To be sure, intermarriage is a key feature of assimilation. As some scholars have noted, intermarriage is *the* yardstick of assimilation (Waters and Jiménez 2005). Mexican-descent individuals exhibit high rates of intermarriage across generations (Macias 2006; Perlmann and Waters 2004; Rosenfeld 2002). By excluding the offspring of these unions, I may underestimate Mexican-American assimilation and overestimate the effect of immigrant replenishment on Mexican-American ethnic identity, since unmixed Mexican Americans may feel more attached to a single ethnic origin. Yet, my own previous research (Jiménez 2004) shows that the multiethnic offspring of these unions gravitate toward their Mexican ancestry despite their mixed status (also see Duncan and Trejo 2007). They also encounter many of the same negative and positive aspects of the inter- and intragroup boundaries of Mexican ethnicity that "pure" Mexican Americans describe. Keeping in mind that some people of mixed origins may stop identifying as people of Mexican descent is also important. As economists Brian Duncan and Stephen Trejo (2007) show, some censused "attrition" has occurred among people of Mexican origin, likely the result of mixed Mexican Americans exercising the option not to claim a Mexican identity when filling out census forms. Likewise, Alba and Islam (forthcoming) show a great deal of change in identification among Mexican Americans between the 1980, 1990, and 2000 U.S. Censuses. Of course, their everyday ethnic identity (as opposed to how they identify when they are forced to check boxes on census forms) is another matter. But these findings and my own interview-based research suggest that mixed Mexican Americans may have latitude in how they claim and assert their ethnic identity.

Once I found individuals who fit the sample selection criteria, I gathered a "snowball" sample of respondents. I began with a few key individuals who referred me to others to interview. Since birds of a feather tend to flock together, compiling a snowball risks the selection of a group of individuals who have similar characteristics and beliefs, thus biasing my findings. Therefore, I made efforts not to rely on one "flock." I used several different networks to recruit respondents in order to avoid interviewing a homogeneous sample. When I recruited the youngest respondents, for example, I did not rely on schools alone. Doing so would have led me to leave out potential high school dropouts or young respondents enrolled in some form of alternative school. Instead, I relied on multiple networks of individuals to find respondents.

Recruiting respondents usually involved making phone calls and asking individuals if they would be willing to allow me to interview them for a PhD dissertation I was writing on Mexican Americans. I always told these individuals that I had been referred to them and provided the name of the individual who referred me. In other cases, potential new respondents were family members of established respondents, and I was able to recruit them by requesting an interview when I finished interviewing another family member, usually a parent or sibling. In a few cases, I met respondents during the course of my daily routine. I often started conversations with individuals while at the gym, during trips to the grocery store, or while purchasing office supplies. The respondents I met through happenstance revealed, with some gentle probing, that they fit the criteria I was looking for. Combined, these techniques were very effective in compiling a sample. Of the 127 individuals I contacted for interviews, 123 accepted my request. I did not offer respondents any compensation for interviews. I found that people generally regarded the interviews as having some intrinsic value. They often told me that they enjoyed the process or at least found it interesting.

I conducted virtually all interviews in respondents' homes, since they were the places in which most said they felt comfortable, and they were generally the most convenient location for respondents. Conducting the interviews in their homes was also advantageous for the sort of data gathering that takes place outside the formal interview process. Being in respondents' homes offered me the opportunity to see how ethnicity permeated their life in multiple ways. I was able to see how they decorated their living space, what types of foods they ate, how they interacted with their neighbors, how family members interacted with one another, and what sort of leisure activities occupied their free time.

I tape-recorded each interview. Knowing that some people can be intimidated by recording equipment, I tried to place the recorder in a position that was close the respondent but out of sight. After a few minutes, most respondents seemed to forget about the presence of the recorder altogether. I also took copious notes during each interview. These notes served two purposes. First, they were a backup in the event that my recorder malfunctioned, which, thankfully, happened only once. Second, the notes helped me follow the twists and turns of the interview. I often jotted down statements that respondents made in passing and returned to these comments later in the interview to see if they proved to be windows into topics central to my overall research questions. I conducted all of the interviews in English, except for one, which was a mix of Spanish and English. As I report in chapter 3, English was the dominant and often the only language my respondents spoke. They therefore felt quite comfortable doing interviews in English. Interviews ranged in time from one to four hours but normally took about ninety minutes to complete.

I also conducted interviews with key informants in each city to gain a better understanding of the contextual factors that might shape the Mexican-American experience in each place. These interviewees included local law enforcement personnel, city officials, beef plant employees, a labor contractor, teachers, school administrators, business owners, and political activists. I did not tape-record these interviews but did take detailed notes. These interviews were helpful for understanding local history, institutions, the economy, and politics, all of which play a role in Mexican-American ethnic identity formation.

I also took hundreds of pages of fieldnotes during my time in each city. These fieldnotes came from three types of observations. The first type was observations I made as I "shadowed" three respondents in each city during a typical day of work. My objective was to gain a better understanding of how ethnicity operated in their everyday life. I began by selecting respondents whose jobs required a good deal of interpersonal interaction. I then asked respondents with whom I had developed a good rapport if they would allow me to accompany them during a single workday. Since I already had a good relationship with these respondents, they happily agreed. During my day of "shadowing," I did my best to be an unobtrusive observer. I positioned myself so as to see and hear all of the interactions in which subjects engaged, but I also remained at enough distance to give them a sense of privacy. The individual whom I shadowed often introduced me to coworkers and clients, explaining to them that I was writing a dissertation about Mexican Americans. This generally satisfied the curiosity and possible concern of those who were not initially aware of why I was there.

A second source of fieldnotes came from observations I conducted in a major high school in each city. In Garden City, my connections to an administrator and coach enabled me to gain virtually unfettered access to the local high school. The principal gave me a laminated pass that allowed me to come to the campus and leave at my own discretion. I merely had to sign in at the front desk before entering the school. In Santa Maria, I also had connections to a teacher and coach who allowed me to observe his classroom and accompany him during the time between class periods. In both places I sat in on several classes, observed students hanging out in the hall, and attended school-sponsored extracurricular events. When I observed in classes, I generally sat in the back of the class and jotted down notes. I paid close attention to where students sat in the classroom, how they interacted with one another before and after class, how they participated in class discussions, and how they interacted with the teacher. During the time between classes and at extracurricular events, I took notes on how students arrayed spatially, how they interacted with one another, and who participated in school events.

Finally, I took copious notes about unplanned observations that I made during my daily life in each city. I made it a point to try to carry my notebook with me wherever I went. If my notebook was not with me, it was nearby, usually in the car. A trip to the grocery store, the gym, the local mall, or a restaurant often provided key insights into the Mexican-American experience. When I did see something relevant to my research, I quickly jotted down a few notes, usually just enough to remind me of what I had seen so that I could fill in the details when I got home later. If, for some reason, I did not have my notebook with me, I would find a relatively quiet place and leave a voice note on my cell phone, explaining what I had observed. I later retrieved these voice notes and wrote a more detailed description of my observations when time permitted.

With the 123 in-depth interviews, roughly 20 informational interviews, and notes from participant observation, I had what seemed like a mound of data to sort through. I began by hiring a professional transcriber to transcribe my interviews. I was fortunate enough to have a grant from the National Science Foundation that covered the costs of these transcriptions. I decided, however, to transcribe a few of my initial interviews myself in order to see what kinds of adjustments I needed to make to my interview protocol and my interview technique. Nonetheless, a professional transcriber did the bulk of the transcriptions, and this ultimately saved me countless hours of work.

Once all of the interviews were transcribed and the fieldnotes were moved from paper to computer files, I used ATLASti, a software package designed for analyzing qualitative data. ATLASti allows users to attach coding categories to blocks of text and then to compare similarly coded blocks of text across interviews. I began by creating a few key coding categories and attached them to relevant portions of text across all interviews. I then went through all text that I had coded in a particular way and applied more detailed coding categories to these portions of text. I used both the general and the more detailed coding categories to write an analysis of my findings.

DOING PLACE-BASED RESEARCH

When I talk about this research, many people ask, "Why Garden City, Kansas, and Santa Maria, California?" Their question makes a lot of sense, especially because neither of these cities is likely to come to mind when most people think of Mexican Americans. As I explain in the introduction, I chose these two cities for theoretical reasons. I wanted to see if the interrupted historical pattern of Mexican immigration to Garden City might make the experience of ethnicity different for Mexican Americans there as compared with Mexican Americans in Santa Maria, where immigration from Mexico has been virtually constant for the last hundred years. I found that these historical patterns did not yield significant differences in ethnic identity but that continuing Mexican immigration is nonetheless central to the formation of Mexican Americans' ethnic identity. Even though the cases I chose did not provide the outcomes I expected, a comparison can nonetheless be made to the European-origin groups that have not experienced immigrant replenishment, and I draw on the extensive research done on this population throughout the book. While not a perfect comparison, it does provide a contrast to the Mexican-origin case, which allows me to make more general claims about the effects of immigrant replenishment.

I use my interviews with Mexican Americans from these two cities in order to make larger claims about what it means to be Mexican American today and to assess the place of the Mexican-origin population in the larger U.S. racial and ethnic landscape. Given the nature of my data, my claims beg the question, What can we reasonably conclude on the basis of a limited number of interviews in two relatively small towns? The findings from this research are not statistically representative. How Mexican Americans experience U.S. society depends a great deal on the historical and contemporary particularities of the various regions of the country in which they reside. But the people I interviewed shared much in common with Mexican Americans in other settings. Findings from qualitative studies of Mexican Americans in San Jose, California, and Phoenix,

Arizona (Macias 2006); La Puente, California (Ochoa 2004); and Santa Paula, California (Menchaca 1995) are quite similar to the findings in this study and, I would argue, support my claim that continuing Mexican immigration plays a central role in how Mexican Americans experience their ethnic identity. These other qualitative studies also suggest that Mexican Americans in Garden City and Santa Maria are not anomalistic compared with Mexican Americans in other parts of the country.

Another key issue in studying a particular place or multiple places relates to who is *not* studied. Because I interviewed only people who lived in these two locales at the time of my research, I did not interview Mexican Americans who may have either grown up there or lived there for a significant period of time but moved away prior to my research. This is not an insignificant point, given that the reasons why people move may be directly related to processes of assimilation. Many Mexican Americans have moved out of Garden City and Santa Maria in order to pursue school and better economic opportunities. It was fairly common for respondents to speak of family and friends who had enjoyed a great deal of occupational success. Some told me about a cousin who was a lawyer in Denver, a brother who was a journalist in San Jose, or a sister who worked in corporate sales in New Jersey. Certainly these people are part of the two research cities' larger story of assimilation that I was unable to access because of fiscal and time constraints. I nonetheless factor accounts of their successes and failures into the larger portrait I paint of Mexican American assimilation in chapter 3.

GAINING ACCESS AS AN INSIDER AND AN OUTSIDER

The status of a researcher as an insider or an outsider (someone who does or does not share a set of relevant characteristics with the population of interest) constitutes a primary challenge in trying to gain access to respondents. In my case, I was both an insider and an outsider to Mexican Americans in Garden City and Santa Maria. My outsider status came from never having lived in either of the two cities I studied. In the case of Garden City, I had never visited the city before I became interested in studying it. My foray into Garden City began by consulting with Donald Stull, an anthropologist at the University of Kansas who has done extensive research on the beef-packing industry in the city. Once I convinced Professor Stull that I had honest intentions, he put me in touch with several key individuals in Garden City. These people turned out to be valuable "gatekeepers" to many people there. I quickly learned that invoking the names of these gatekeepers gave me instant credibility with Garden Citians from all walks of life. Having key gatekeepers willing to vouch for me, along with the palpable midwestern hospitality of Garden City, made gaining access to respondents relatively easy.

I was somewhat more of an insider in Santa Maria, but only by association. My father spent his high school years there, and my grandmother and several aunts, uncles, and cousins still reside there. I was thus able to use their contacts to get in touch with respondents. Invoking the names of my family members generally made potential respondents quite willing to speak with me.

My racial and ethnic identity also determined my status as an insider and an outsider. As the son of a Mexican immigrant (my father came from Mexico as a young child) and a fourth-generation Italian American (all of my mother's grandparents were Italian immigrants), my ethnic identity generally made me an insider to multiple populations in each city. My Mexican-American respondents accepted me as a person of Mexican descent because of my Spanish name but also as someone who, like them, is culturally comfortable negotiating U.S. society. In some cases, older respondents were curious about my identity—probably because of the combination of my Spanish name and very light skin—and they sometimes spoke a few words in Spanish to me to be sure I was of Mexican descent. My ability to converse with them in either language generally made me an insider in their view.

I was also able to interact quite smoothly with the Mexican immigrants I encountered, though they were not part of my interview sample. My ability to speak Spanish and my familiarity with Mexico facilitated my friendship with several Mexican immigrants through which I gained greater familiarity with life in both cities. My identity as an American and my light skin also helped me to make connections with non-Mexicans (most of whom were white). During many casual encounters, non-Mexicans often felt comfortable revealing their opinions and attitudes (both positive and negative) about Mexican Americans and Mexican immigrants. I believe that my light skin led them to assume that I would agree with their opinions or at least be sympathetic to their views.

In short, I easily overcame my status as an outsider to both cities, and my ethnic and racial identities made me an insider with virtually all of the people I interviewed. In general, I believe that researchers, particularly those in the early stages of their career, make too much of the insider-outsider issue. Plenty of examples exist of "outsiders" who have done a superb job of studying populations that differ from their own racial and ethnic origins (Bloemraad 2006; Foote Whyte 1943; Gans 1962; Levitt 2001; Liebow 1967; Smith 2005a; Venkatesh 2000; Wacquant 2003, 2008; Waters 1999). While a researcher may never completely gain insider status, what is most important is establishing a rapport with the people under study, and this does not necessarily require sharing the same racial or ethnic origin.

In addition to those I have cited above, several other factors helped me gain access to and the trust of respondents. First and foremost, I did my best to be polite but was also persistent. I often had to call respondents several times to set up an interview, and inevitably some respondents canceled at the last minute or failed to show up. I followed up with these individuals and was generally able to conduct the interviews eventually. I sent respondents a handwritten thank-you note after I interviewed them. Not only did I think it was a matter of common courtesy to thank people who had donated their time to my research, but also doing so made these people more inclined to refer me to others. I also found it useful to have various "badges of legitimacy" in order to earn the trust of potential interviewees. I carried business cards with my name, institutional affiliation and logo, and contact information at all times. I also maintained my Web page on my departmental Web site. Several people I interviewed told me that they had done an Internet search on my name and that they knew I was "legit" when they saw my Web page.

I also gained the trust of respondents by promising them anonymity and confidentiality in the write-up and eventual publication of my research. Given that most institutional review boards insist that researchers give their subjects such assurances, this may seem like a banal point. I found it quite important, however, to promise anonymity and confidentiality. People in Garden City and Santa Maria, places where "everyone knows everyone," were well aware that what they told me in interviews had the potential to hurt their reputation if word got out about what they had said. I often had to put my promise of confidentiality to the test when other respondents would try to coax out of me information that others had provided during interviews, and I regularly had to tell them that I could not talk about other interviews.

In many ways, doing research in small cities made access easy. With a few key gatekeepers in my corner, the "access doors" to respondents swung wide open. The difficulties of access to organizations, firms, and individuals that others report in their research in big cities (see Waters 1999, for example) did not apply in Garden City and Santa Maria. A certain small-town and, in the case of Garden City, midwestern hospitality made gaining access downright easy in some cases. The response I got from a high school principal when I asked if my presence on campus would trouble parents is emblematic of my experience: "This is a small town. No one cares about that stuff."

APPENDIX B List of Respondents

Garden City Respondents

NAME	GENDER	AGE	OCCUPATION	EDUCATION LEVEL	GENERATION IN UNITED STATES
Donald Mercado	Male	47	Nonprofit manager	Some college	3
Lana Gutiérrez	Female	64	Retired educator	Bachelor's	2.5
Hank Arenas	Male	79	Crossing guard	10th grade	2
Naomi Mercado	Female	70	Retired nurse	GED	2
Vilma Garza	Female	81	Homemaker	GED	2
Bob Ocampo	Male	43	Maintenance worker	Some college	2
Mark Santos	Male	29	Social worker	Bachelor's	4 and 2
Johnny Ocampo	Male	44	UPS driver	High school	2.5
Al Hinojosa	Male	55	Shop owner	Some college	2.5
Lina Totten	Female	43	Legal records coordinator	High school	3
Marcela Muñoz	Female	19	Student	College student	3 and 4
Carl Mercado	Male	43	Data operation salesman	Some college	3
Alexandra Pettite	Female	34	Office manager	Some college	3 and 2
Ernie Garza	Male	54	Dental assistant	GED	3
Paul Bautista	Male	20	Sales manager	Some college	4
George Ortega	Male	41	UPS employee	Some college	3
Ronnie Hinojosa	Male	48	Electronics salesperson	Some college	3
Gus Gouveia	Male	35	Bank officer	Associate's	2 and 3
Janelle Fernández	Female	22	Shipping clerk	Some college	3 and 4
Matthew Hinojosa	Male	31	Electronics salesperson	Some college	4

(continued)

Garden City Respondents (continued)

NAME	GENDER	AGE	OCCUPATION	EDUCATION LEVEL	GENERATION IN UNITED STATES
Rafael Solís	Male	30	Pastor	Bachelor's	3 and 2
Mary Solís	Female	21	Day care supervisor	High school	3 and 2
Juan Serrano	Male	20	Student	College student	3 and 4
Teresa Mercado	Female	19	Student	College student	4
Margie Solís	Female	60	Homemaker	Some college	2
Isabel Hinojosa	Female	57	Shop owner	Some college	3
Rick Ocampo	Male	25	Plumber	Some college	4
Lydia Campos	Female	71	Retired nurse	Nursing degree	2.5
Julie Mercado	Female	45	Secretary	Some college	3.5
Martha Garza	Female	62	Retail salesperson	Some college	2
Dolores Garza	Female	59	Office manager	High school	2
Joe Gil Jr.	Male	56	Retired appliance salesperson	Some college	3
Dave Suárez	Male	32	Insurance salesman	Bachelor's	4
Joe Gil	Male	82	Retired railroad worker	8th grade	2
Shannon Arrienta	Female	39	Restaurant cook	High school	4
Raymond de la Garza	Male	28	Juvenile probation officer	Some college	3
Larry Morales	Male	61	Master mechanic	Some college	3
Kyle Gil	Male	35	Auto body shop owner	High school	4
Ramona Gil	Female	80	Homemaker	GED	2

Name	Sex	Age	Occupation	Education	
Gilbert Mariano	Male	70	Retired salesperson	Some college	2
John Iturbe	Male	15	Student	High school student	3
Ellen Iturbe	Female	44	Secretary	High school	2.5 and 3
Kent Iturbe	Male	15	Student	Some high school	4
Faith Obregón	Female	16	Student	High school student	4
Christina Iturbe	Female	18	Student	College student	3
Annalisa Garza	Female	15	Student	High school student	4
Christie Mendiola	Female	49	Health club supervisor	Some college	3
Diana Bautista	Female	18	Student	High school student	4
Vanessa Toledo	Female	15	Student	High school student	4
Emily Strong	Female	17	Student	High school student	4
Bobby Hinojosa	Male	15	Student	High school student	4
Eric Garza	Male	17	Student	High school student	4
Paul Sánchez	Male	77	Retired dairy worker	5th grade	2
Neil Ocampo	Male	81	Retired restaurant owner	High school	2
Sara Gutiérrez	Female	87	Retired dry cleaning manager	11th grade	2
Aaron Briseño	Male	17	Student	High school student	3 and 2
Rita Morales	Female	63	Office manager	11th grade	2
Kate Lebron	Female	27	Teacher	Bachelor's	4
Timothy Saenz	Male	39	Theater manager	Design school	4 and 3
Kate Pacheco	Female	18	Student	Cosmetology school student	4
Timothy Saenz	Male	39	Theater manager	Design school	4 and 3

(continued)

Santa Maria Respondents

(IN THE ORDER IN WHICH THEY WERE INTERVIEWED)

NAME	GENDER	AGE	OCCUPATION	EDUCATION LEVEL	GENERATION IN UNITED STATES
Leon Peralta	Male	65	Retired teacher	Master's	Unknown
Rolando Fernández	Male	48	Physician	Medical school	2.5
Wendy Garavilla	Female	59	Teacher	Master's	3
Sam de Guzmán	Male	52	Education administrator	Master's	2 and 3
Rolando Fernández Jr.	Male	21	Student	College student	3 and 5
Margarita Llanes	Female	60	Teacher's aide	Some college	2
Ana Fernández	Female	47	Teacher	Bachelor's	3
Samantha Salcedo	Female	refused	Education administrator	Master's	2.5
Marcos Cabrera	Male	74	Retired heavy-equipment operator	3rd grade	3
Lydia Gutiérrez	Female	49	State real estate manager	Bachelor's	3
Hope Fernández	Female	49	Teacher	Master's	3
Catherine Gómez	Female	32	Lawyer	JD	3
Robert Garavilla	Male	19	Student	College student	3 and 4
Micky Garavilla	Male	16	Student	High school student	3 and 4
Lydia Arroyo	Female	44	Nonprofit manager	Some college	Native Californian
Christina Ronquillo	Female	64	Homemaker	Some college	2.5
Lupe Bustamante	Female	58	Office manager	Some college	2
Eric Bustamante	Male	60	Retired delivery truck driver	Some college	3
Manny Alvarado	Male	81	Retired liquor store owner	Trade school	2
Manuel Esguerra	Male	51	Social worker	Bachelor's	2 and 3

Name	Sex	Age	Occupation	Education	Generation
Maria Alvarado	Female	73	Homemaker	High school	2
Dana Alfonso	Female	50	Office manager	Some college	2 and native Californian
John Piñeda	Male	67	Plant manager	High school	2
Roberta Piñeda	Female	65	Homemaker	High school	2
Naomi Gómez	Female	68	Retired teacher and social worker	Bachelor's	Native southwesterner
Manuel Arnedo	Male	43	Firefighter	High school	2 and 3
Angel de Guzmán	Male	20	Operation intern	High school	3 and 4
David Calderon	Male	52	Police officer	Some college	2 and 4
Ricardo de Guzmán	Male	77	Retired custodian	11th grade	2
Vicki Ramos	Female	80	Retired nurse	Vocational school	3
Ron Terán	Male	59	School principal	Master's	3
Carmine Gutiérrez	Male	17	Student	High school student	4
Lori Rojas	Female	40	Financial records coordinator	Some college	4
Bob Fernández	Male	52	Graphic designer	Bachelor's	4
Mike Morales	Male	51	Maintenance worker	High school	3
Hank Pacheco	Male	27	Correctional officer	Associate's	4
Erin Santiago	Female	18	Student	College student	4 and 5
Elena Bradley	Female	46	Teacher	Master's	2 and 3
Pedro Ramírez	Male	52	Teacher	Master's	3
Lucia Pacheco	Female	19	Student	College student	4
Gigi Bartolome	Female	61	Retired retail clerk	10th grade	3
Frank Bustamante	Male	52	Teacher and administrator	Master's	3
Johnny Rincón	Male	63	Liquor store owner	High school	2 and 3
John Rojas	Male	18	Student	College student	5
Mike Fernández	Male	19	Student	College student	3 and 4

(continued)

Santa Maria Respondents (continued)

NAME	GENDER	AGE	OCCUPATION	EDUCATION LEVEL	GENERATION IN UNITED STATES
Mark Rojas	Male	16	Student	High school student	5
Lauren Fernández	Female	17	Student	High school student	3 and 4
Carlos Morales	Male	20	Student	College student	3 and 4
Inez Fernández	Female	16	Student	High school student	3 and 4
Melissa Santiago	Female	16	Student	High school student	3 and 4
Joaquina Guevarra	Female	83	Homemaker	9th grade	Native southwesterner
Bill Montoya	Male	58	Retired police officer/small business owner	Associate's	2
Tracy Harris	Female	59	Retired fashion consultant	High school	2
Jorge Guevarra	Male	83	Retired delivery truck driver	High school	2
Ryan Bradley	Male	16	Student	High school student	3 and 4
Julie Ayala	Female	68	Retired clerical worker	High school	2
Timmy Campos	Male	18	Student	College student	4 or greater
Maria Bañuelos	Female	24	Office assistant	Some college	4 or greater
Diana Ariola	Female	24	Bank teller	High school	3
Elisa Ramos	Female	16	Student	High school student	4
Ramón Ramos	Male	18	Student	High school student	4
Mateo Gutiérrez	Male	98	Retired railroad worker	Less than 1 year	1.5
Bridget Sánchez	Female	15	Student	High school student	4

APPENDIX C Interview Questions

I. INDIVIDUAL IDENTITY FORMATION

Race and Hispanic Categories

1. Show respondent the race and Hispanic questions for the 2000 Census and instructions if necessary. Ask how he or she would respond to that question. Then ask how he or she came to that response.

2. How do you think your siblings would respond?

3. How would your parents respond?

4. How would your children respond?

5. How would you respond for your children?

6. What box do you check when filling out forms for a job or school? How did you come to that answer?

Family History/Background

1. Do people in your family ever discuss family background or family history? [If yes] What kind of things do they talk about?

2. [If respondent descends from immigrants] Tell me about how your family came to the United States from Mexico.

    — Where did they come from? [Probe for state in Mexico.]

    — Why did they leave?

    — How did they come here?

    — Where did they first settle?

    — How did you learn about this?

Child Rearing

1. How would you characterize the way that you were raised?

    — Tell me about anything specific to your ethnicity.

    — What role did your parents want your ethnic background to play in your life?

2. Do Mexican Americans have a particular way of raising their children? [If yes] How would you characterize it?

    — What about Mexican immigrants?

3. Tell me about how you [will] raise your children.

    — What would you do differently from your parents?

    — What would you do the same?

Schools

1. Starting with grammar school and continuing to the highest level of schooling that you completed, tell me about the schools that you went to.

    — [Probe for friends' race and ethnicity]

    — [Probe for race and ethnicity of other students (Mexican American/Mexican immigrants).]

2. Tell me about the activities that you were involved in outside school while growing up.

   — Was there anything specific to your ethnic background?

   — What was the ethnic background of most of the people in these activities?

Neighborhood

1. Tell me about the neighborhood or neighborhoods that you grew up in.

   — Was it characterized by a certain ethnic group? [If yes] Which?

   — What about the neighborhood that you live in now?

2. How would you compare the neighborhood that you live in now to the one that you lived in when you were a child?

   — [Probe for immigrant population.]

   — Is it better or worse?

Language Use

1. Do you speak any other languages besides English?

   [If yes]

2. Which languages?

3. How did you learn these languages?

4. When do you speak these languages?

   — workplace?

   — social settings?

   — family gatherings?

5. Whom do you speak with?

   — grandparents?

   — parents?

   — children?

   — coworkers?

6. Do you read or write these languages?

   — Where did you learn?

   — When do you read or write these languages?

7. Do your parents speak Spanish?

— Do they read or write?

— [Probe for instances of translating for parents.]

8. Do you ever listen to music or watch TV that is in Spanish? [If yes] What do you watch or listen to? When do you listen to or watch Spanish programming?

Peer Group/Social Networks

1. What ethnic group are your closest friends from?

2. Do you have any friends who were born in Mexico? [If yes] How did you meet them?

3. How often do you spend time with American-born Mexican people? In what context?

4. How often do you spend time with Mexican immigrants? In what context?

Dating Habits/Marriage

1. Are you married?
[If yes]

2. What is your spouse's ethnic background?

— parents' reaction?

3. Was ethnicity a factor in whom you married?

4. Did you ever date someone who is not of Mexican descent?

— parents' reaction?

5. Did you ever date an immigrant?

6. What are your expectations for whom your children marry?
[If not married]

7. Are you in a dating relationship right now? What is that person's ethnic background?

8. Is ethnic background a factor in any way in whom you date? How so?

9. What are your parents views on dating?

— Do they prefer that you date certain people rather than others? Which groups?

— Would you date an immigrant? Why/why not?

— Is skin tone a factor in whom you date?

Church Participation

1. What is your religious background?

2. Do you attend church services regularly?

   [If yes]

3. Tell me about the church you attend.

   — language of services?

   — racial and ethnic background of other churchgoers?

Holidays/Celebrations/Ethnic Customs

1. Starting in January, which holidays do you celebrate?

2. Is there anything special about how you celebrate these holidays?

   — ethnic-specific customs?

   — traditions?

   — family gatherings?

3. Did you celebrate these holidays when you were growing up?
   [If yes] What did you do to celebrate them?

4. Do you celebrate specific nonethnic holidays with any ethnic activities or customs?
   [If yes] What do you do? What about when you were growing up?

5. Are any Mexican customs or practices part of your routine life? Which? Have you always done these things? What about when you were a child? Will/did you teach your children these customs and/ or practices?

Travel Experience

1. Have you ever been to Mexico?

   [If yes]

2. Tell me about that.

   — Why did you go?

   — When did you go?

   — Who did you visit?

— Who did you go with?

— How long were you there?

— What did you do?

— What places did you visit?

3. How many times have you been?

4. How did you feel about your ethnic background after coming back?

5. Do you have any relatives in Mexico?

[If yes]

6. Where do they live?

7. Have you ever visited them? When?

Work Experience

1. Do you have a job?

[If yes]

2. What do you do?

3. Is your workplace characterized by any particular ethnic group? [If yes] Which?

4. How are people generally hired there?

— [Probe for networks.]

5. How did you get your job there?

— [Probe for who helped respondent find the job.]

6. What is the ethnic background of

— supervisor?

— coworkers?

— people who work under you?

7. How would you characterize the relations between you and the other employees?

— [Probe for relationship between Mexican immigrants and Mexican Americans.]

8. Does your ethnic identity matter very much at work? [If yes] How so?

9. Some people feel that that their ethnic identity is a help at work, and some people feel that it's a hindrance. What does it mean to you at work?

Organizational Involvement

1. Are you involved in any organizations?

   [If yes]

2. Tell me about these organizations.

   — ethnic specific?

3. How long have you been a member? Why did you join these/this organization?

   — [Probe for involvement with immigrants.]

4. Tell me about any organizations that your children are involved in.

   — Do/did you participate in these organizations with your children?

Informal Interactions and Ethnic Identity Issues

1. Is being of Mexican descent generally important to you? Explain.

2. How important is it to you that people recognize you are of Mexican descent?

3. How important was your ethnic identity to you when you were

   — in grammar school?

   — in high school?

   — after high school?

   — now?

   — [Follow up with "Why?" for all.]

4. Tell me about any contexts or situations when your ethnic background might be especially important to you.

   — family?

   — at school?

   — at work?

   — during recreation?

   — during holidays or celebrations?

   — when you vote?

   — at church?

5. Are there times when you feel particularly proud of your Mexican ancestry? [If yes] When? Why?

    — Are there times when you feel particularly ashamed of your Mexican ancestry? [If yes] When? Why?

6. How often are you asked about your ethnic background?

    — Why do you think someone would ask?

7. Do people ever think that you are from Mexico (i.e., phone marketers, advertisers who send direct mailings in Spanish, strangers in encounters with you)?

    — Tell me about how you responded.

Costs/Benefits

1. Do you think there is anything negative associated with being of Mexican descent? [If yes] What makes this negative? Have you always thought this way? [If no] How did you come to change your ideas?

2. Do you think there is anything positive associated with being of Mexican descent? [If yes] What? What makes this positive? Have you always thought this way? [If no] How did you come to change your ideas?

3. Have you ever benefited from being of Mexican descent? When? How?

4. Have you ever experienced discrimination because you are of Mexican descent? What happened?

II.   ETHNIC SOLIDARITY

Now I'd like to ask you a few questions about your experience with Mexican immigrants.

Perceptions of Commonality

1. How would you compare Mexican immigrants with people like yourself whose families have been in the U.S. for several generations?

    — similarities?

    — differences?

2. How would you compare documented and undocumented Mexican immigrants?

3. Do you think the presence of Mexican immigrants affects the lives of people who have lived here for many generations?

— How about your own life?

4. Can people in Garden City/Santa Maria usually tell the difference between Mexican Americans and Mexican immigrants? [If yes] How?

5. Can people in Garden City/Santa Maria tell the difference between kids who were born in the U.S. but whose parents were born in Mexico and those kids whose families have been in the U.S. for several generations? [If yes] What are the differences?

III. ATTITUDES TOWARD MEXICAN IMMIGRANTS

Perceptions of Others' Opinions of Mexican Immigrants

1. What do you think is most other people's opinion about Mexican immigrants? Why do you think they feel this way?

— What about Mexican Americans' opinions?

2. How do your opinions about Mexican immigrants compare with those of most other people in Garden City/Santa Maria?

3. How would you characterize the way in which immigrants are generally treated in Garden City/Santa Maria?

General Opinions

1. Have Mexican immigrants had any effect on the image of Mexican Americans such as yourself in Garden City/Santa Maria? [If yes] How so?

— What about undocumented Mexican immigrants?

2. Some people have said that Mexican immigration is good for our country, while others believe immigration from Mexico is bad for our country. What is your opinion on this issue?

— What about undocumented Mexican immigrants?

3. Some people argue that Mexican immigrants are generally good for our economy, while others believe that they are bad for our economy. What do you think about this idea?

— What about undocumented Mexican immigrants?

4. What do you think things will be like for the descendants of today's Mexican immigrants in Garden City/Santa Maria in fifty years?

Opinions about Services for Mexican Immigrants

1. Some people argue that Mexican immigrants receive too much help, while others think they deserve more help. What do you think about these ideas?

    — What about services for undocumented immigrants?

2. Some people say that Mexican-immigrant children slow the progress of other students because they do not speak English, while other people believe they do not harm the progress of other students. What do you think about this idea?

Stereotypes and Social Perspectives

1. How would you compare today's Mexican immigrants in Garden City/Santa Maria with those of your immigrant ancestors?

    — work ethic?

    — crime?

    — use of public services?

    — openness of society to them?

    — English-language acquisition?

2. A wide array of explanations has been given for why many people of Mexican origin are poor. Why do you think this is the case? How did you come to form this opinion?

3. Some people have said that American society is generally open and that Mexican immigrants can make it as long as they work hard. Others would argue that discrimination and poverty block Mexican immigrants from making it. What do you think about these ideas?

    — How do you think things were for your immigrant ancestors?

    — Is there any difference between their experience and the experience of today's Mexican immigrants?

    — What about for undocumented Mexican immigrants?

4. Some people believe that Mexican immigrants are generally lazy, while others believe that they are generally hard working. What is your opinion?

— What is your perception of the Mexican immigrants who came to the U.S. when your ancestors did?

5. There is a wide array of beliefs about the influence that Mexican immigrants have on crime. Some think they cause crime, while others think they are law-abiding people. What is your perception?

— What is your perception of the Mexican immigrants who came to the U.S. when your ancestors did?

— What about for undocumented immigrants?

6. There is also a wide array of opinions about recent Mexican immigrants' use of the welfare system. Some people think that Mexican immigrants do not use welfare very much, while others believe that they depend too much on welfare. What do you think?

— What is your perception of the Mexican immigrants who came to the U.S. when your ancestors did?

— [Probe for distinctions related to undocumented Mexican immigrants.]

7. Do you notice a difference is skin color between recent Mexican immigrants and Mexican Americans?
Explain.

ADDITIONAL QUESTIONS ASKED OF HIGH SCHOOL STUDENTS

1. Are there different groups of students who hang out together at school?

[If yes]

2. How are these groups characterized?

3. Are you a member of one of these groups? [If yes] Which one?

4. What ethnic group are your closest friends from?

— [Probe for differences in generations.]

5. Do teachers treat people from these groups differently from one another? [If yes] What is the difference in the way they are treated?

6. Are certain students more successful in school than other students? [If yes] What makes these students so successful?

7. Are certain students more popular than other students?
   [If yes] What makes them so popular?

Club and Organizational Involvement

1. Are you involved in any activities outside the classroom?
   [If yes]

2. Tell me about these activities. What do you do in them?
   — ethnic specific? [Probe for involvement with immigrants.]

3. How long have you been a member? Why did you join this organization/these organizations?

Peer Group/Social Networks

1. Do you ever talk about race, ethnicity, or ethnic identity with other students at school?
   [If yes] What do you talk about?

2. How often do you spend time with American-born Mexican people? In what context?

3. Do people ever ask you about your ethnic background?
   [If yes] What do you think prompts them to ask you?

Dating Habits

1. Are you in a dating relationship right now?
   [If yes] What is that person's ethnic background?

2. Is ethnic background in any way a factor in whom you are attracted to?
   [If yes] How so?

3. What are your parents views on dating?
   — Do they prefer that you date certain people rather than others?
     [If yes] Which groups?
   — Would you date an immigrant?
     [If yes] Why/why not?
   — Is skin tone a factor in whom you date?

Recreation

1. What do you do for fun outside school?

2. Are there any particular places, like clubs or restaurants, where you like to hang out? [If yes] Tell me about these places.

   — [Probe for ethnic background and nativity of clientele.]

3. What do you think most other people at school think about the students from Mexico? Why do you think they feel this way? What about Mexican Americans' opinions?

Notes

1. INTRODUCTION

1. The term *American* can be used to refer to North, Central, and South America, and the use of this term to refer to the United States alone is indicative of the hegemonic relationship between the United States and other nations in the Americas. However, I occasionally use *American* in regard to the United States and its citizens because there is no other widely recognized, parsimonious adjective or noun to refer to them.

2. Alexandra Minna Stern (2005) shows that the crossing the border was not so easy for everyone. In Laredo, Texas, for example, Mexican migrants were inspected for disease and stamped with indelible ink to show that they had passed inspection.

3. People of Mexican origin hardly agree on what to call themselves, and

the various labels that they use (*Mexican, Mexican American, Chicano, Latino, Hispanic*, etc.) often convey personal and political identities. I have tried to select labels that I believe most people would find respectful. *Mexican American* refers to individuals whose ancestry is Mexican and whose family has been in the United States since before 1940. I use *Mexican immigrant* to refer to individuals who were born in Mexico and now reside in the United States. *Mexican origin, ethnic Mexicans,* and occasionally *Mexicans* refer to all people, foreign or native born, who are of Mexican descent. I also very occasionally use the term *Chicano* when referring to Mexican Americans during the Chicano movement of the 1960s and 1970s. I use the terms *Latino* and *Hispanic* interchangeably, but tend use *Hispanic* when making reference to survey categories and *Latino* when referring to an individual or group of people who trace their ancestry to Latin America or Spain. I refer to people who have no Mexican ancestry as *non-Mexicans*. I also use *white* to refer to people who are white but not Hispanic.

4. I use the term *unauthorized* instead of *illegal* or *undocumented* to describe this category of migrants because it best captures their legal and social situation in the United States. Although these migrants have crossed the border "illegally," the overwhelming majority live law-abiding lives once inside the United States (Sampson, Morenoff, and Raudenbush 2005). Thus, *illegal* does not accurately describe their situation. Nor does *undocumented* capture their situation, for many migrants purchase false documents or use documents issued by the Mexican consulate.

5. Estimates vary, but Massey, Durand, and Malone (2002) place the number at fifty thousand.

6. Mexicans are not the only group to experience a protracted period of immigration, however. German and Irish immigration lasted through much of the nineteenth and early twentieth centuries. Likewise, Polish immigration to Chicago has taken place over a rather protracted period of time (Erdmans 1998).

7. Mexicans were often significantly undercounted in early censuses, which almost certainly underestimated the number of foreign-born Mexicans in the United States at the times they were conducted.

8. Although sociologists Manuel Gamio (1930, 1931) and Emory Bogardus (1970), economist Paul Taylor (1932, 1934), and, later, Leo Grebler and his associates (1970) produced in-depth analyses of the Mexican experience, these accounts never made it into the canonical understanding of assimilation.

9. As Haney-López (1996) shows, the legal construction of whiteness had significant consequences for who was allowed citizenship during the late nineteenth and early twentieth centuries. Court decisions about a group's race relied on both biological and commonsense understandings of whiteness.

10. Borjas (1999), in contrast, argues that it is not so much the economy that has changed as it is the skill level of the immigrants. He uses data on immi-

grants' years of schooling to show that the skills gap between today's immigrants and the native born is larger than in the past.

11. The theory of segmented assimilation has its detractors. Many have argued that segmented assimilation presents an overly pessimistic view, noting that the Mexican-American second generation does not exhibit characteristics that conform to predictions about their prospects of ending up in a rainbow underclass. See Waldinger and Feliciano 2004; and Waldinger, Lim, and Cort 2007.

12. Waldinger and Feliciano (2004) find no evidence that the Mexican-American second generation displays outcomes that adhere to a strict definition of an underclass.

13. See Rutter and Tienda 2005 for a discussion of the use of ethnicity and race in social science research.

14. Appendix B contains a list of respondents and their relevant characteristics.

2. MEXICAN AMERICANS

1. The National Origins Quota Act set a cap on visas from all countries. The caps were set at 2 percent of the foreign-born population in the 1890 U.S. Census. By using the 1890 Census as a basis for the 2 percent cap, the quotas heavily favored northern and western European countries while severely restricting immigration from southern and eastern Europe. The 1924 law also completely barred immigration from Asian countries.

2. See García 1980 for a detailed history of Operation Wetback.

3. The Chicano movement was rife with gender inequality, however. Many Chicanas aimed to carve out a place in the movement through myriad strategies, ranging from a call for the eradication of machismo to resignifying it for a new generation. For an excellent overview and analysis of early Chicana feminist writings, see García 1997.

4. Some have suggested that MEChA is a militant organization with hopes of reconquering the American Southwest (Buchanan 2006). In reality, MEChA functions primarily as a social organization that celebrates Mexican ethnicity and advocates for more Latinos in higher education and greater ethnic representation among faculty and staff on high school and college campuses.

5. Wayne Cornelius (2005: 783) notes that prior to Operation Gatekeeper migrants paid roughly $143 for a coyote's services. By 2004, the average cost had increased to upward of $2,000 in real terms.

6. Massey, Durand, and Malone (2002: 114) calculate that the death rate along the U.S.-Mexico border rose from slightly more than one death per hun-

dred thousand border crossings in 1993 to about six deaths per hundred thousand crossings in 1998.

7. The Val-Agri beef plant burned down in December 2000, some nine months before I arrived in Garden City.

8. The industry has also been accused of engaging in the smuggling of unauthorized workers from Mexico. For example, in 2001 Tyson Foods was accused of smuggling hundreds of workers from Mexico to work in their poultry plants. Managers at the Iowa Beef Packing plant are adamant that they do not engage in such practices.

9. According to the U.S. Census, Hispanics may be of any race and include persons of Mexican, Puerto Rican, Cuban, Spanish, Dominican, Central American, and South American ancestries.

10. The U.S. Census asks only about the birthplace of the respondent. It is thus impossible to know from the census the specific generational status (i.e., first, second, third) of an individual. One can know only if a particular person was born in the United States or abroad.

3. DIMENSIONS OF MEXICAN-AMERICAN ASSIMILATION

1. See Waters and Jiménez 2005 for a discussion of current research related to these measures of assimilation.

2. Within the interview transcriptions, I have used ellipses to signal both faltering speech and omissions. Those that signal omissions are enclosed in square brackets. No such distinction is made in other types of quotations, where ellipses always signal omissions.

3. While aspirations (what one hopes for) and expectations (what one can reasonably expect) are not the same, many students with whom I spoke were well on their way to realizing their aspirations, as was indicated by their status as students, sometimes high-achieving students.

4. I did not interview any school-aged dropouts. The absence of such respondents from my sample is not a result of the techniques I used to find respondents. I used contacts in schools in addition to snowball samples outside schools in order to include any potential school-aged dropouts who would have been excluded from the sample.

5. As Alba and economists Brian Duncan and Stephen Trejo (2007) point out, the remaining gap may have more to do with how data are gathered than straightforward explanations related to intergenerational mobility. Duncan and Trejo show that the gap may be attributable to the choice that upwardly mobile, mixed-ancestry Mexican Americans (those with one parent of Mexican descent

and one Anglo parent) make in not marking themselves as "Mexican" on surveys, effectively "dropping out" of the Mexican-origin population. This attrition from the Mexican-origin population means that the socioeconomic progress made by some people of Mexican ancestry goes unmeasured, producing a downward bias in measures of socioeconomic advancement. Telles and Ortiz (2008) find that the multiethnic Mexican Americans are not driving the data, however. Using data from both parents and children (as opposed to synthetic cohorts), they show intergenerational patterns similar to those found in other research.

6. Logan, Alba, and Zhang (2002) show that in some areas immigrants bypass central cities upon arriving in the United States and instead move directly into suburbs.

7. Fischer and Tienda (2006) show that levels of Hispanic segregation vary a great deal by metropolitan area.

8. I employed the same name generator used in the General Social Survey (GSS) conducted by the National Opinion Research Center. The exact wording of the question is: "From time to time, most people discuss important matters with other people. Looking back over the last six months and excluding your spouse, who are the people with whom you discussed matters important to you? Just list their first name or initials below. List up to five." I then asked respondents to do the following: "Now list the ethnic background of each of the people mentioned next to the person's name or initials." Respondents were allowed to include nonspousal family members.

9. The General Social Survey permitted respondents to include spouses and to list as many individuals as they wished. It is also important to note that the GSS lumps all Hispanic subgroups together and makes no distinction between native- and foreign-born individuals.

10. Sánchez (1993) discusses the implementation of Americanization programs designed specifically to speed the assimilation of Mexican Americans in Los Angeles. According to Sánchez, immigrants' customs and traditions were seen by state officials as an impediment to their becoming American. State agencies, including the California Department of Education, and local organizations tried to expedite the assimilation of Mexicans into a distinctly American way of life.

11. Later-generation Mexican Americans in Ochoa's (2004) study of La Puente, California, reported similar pressures to stop speaking Spanish during their childhood.

12. Another possible explanation has to do with distance from the border. Rubén Rumbaut (2002) shows that the distance one lives from the U.S.-Mexico border is inversely correlated with the ability to speak Spanish.

13. Garden City also celebrates Cinco de Mayo with a parade. I was not in Garden City during that celebration, however.

4. REPLENISHING MEXICAN ETHNICITY

1. In 1998 California voters passed Proposition 227, which eliminated bilingual education and requires all public education to be conducted in English.

2. Anecdotal evidence suggests that the popularity of *quinceañeras* is growing. *Time* magazine reported that *quinceañera* planners now exist. Wal-Mart and a number of other mainstream retail stores stock *quinceañera* dresses, and *quinceañera* courts are increasingly multiethnic (Miranda 2004). Some of the largest corporations in the world have also become involved. Disneyland and Disney World offer *quinceañera* vacation packages.

3. One needs to look no further than the shelves of major bookstores and myriad Latino marketing firms to see how Latinos, and Mexicans in particular, factor into the calculus of firms and organizations looking to expand their customer base or membership roles. Book titles such as *How to Win the Hispanic Gold Rush* (Valle and Mandel 2003) and *The Whole Enchilada: Hispanic Marketing 101* (Faura 2004) are emblems of the ways in which appealing to ethnic identity is a widely invoked strategy for attracting clientele and membership.

4. A number of Protestant churches in each city offer Spanish-language services as well. However, the Catholic churches in both cities offer far more services in Spanish than the Protestant churches do, and these masses are very popular among Mexican immigrants.

5. Sociologist Irene Bloemraad (2006) argues that the United States exhibits multiculturalism in its politics but not as much in its policies, a contrast to Canadian multiculturalism, which emanates from official federal policy.

6. In 1996 California voters approved Proposition 209, which prohibits the state, local governments, districts, public universities, colleges and schools, and other government instrumentalities from using race, sex, color, ethnicity, or national origin as criteria for selection.

7. Nagel (1997) and Padilla (1985) also show how state-run programs that positively recognize ethnicity shape ethnically based political action and individual ethnic identity.

8. Linton and I found that 41 percent of the U.S. municipal governments we surveyed provided additional pay to bilingual employees (Linton and Jiménez 2009).

9. April Linton (2004) shows that the status of Hispanics in a metropolitan area helps to explain the level of bilingualism. Linton demonstrates that more Hispanic elected officials in a metropolitan area yields an increase in the number of native-born bilingual Hispanics.

10. Nericcio (2007) provides a more pessimistic interpretation of historical and modern trends related to the representation of Mexican-origin peoples in American popular culture.

5. THE TIES THAT BIND AND DIVIDE

Findings from this chapter appear in Jiménez 2008.

1. For an excellent discussion of symbolic and social boundaries, see Lamont and Molnar 2002.

2. Filipinos are the second largest immigrant group in Santa Maria, constituting only 7 percent (or 1,794) of the total foreign-born population. In Garden City, Vietnamese immigrants are the second largest immigrant group, also making up only 7 percent (or 451) of the total foreign-born population there.

3. See Sánchez 1997 for a discussion of the relationship between racism and nativism.

4. Since Mexican immigrants in each city tend to take jobs for which there is next to no interethnic competition, there was very little sense among respondents that Mexican immigrants are in competition for jobs with native-born residents or that other forms of direct economic competition exist. Research with Mexican Americans in other settings reports similar findings (Ochoa 2000, 2004).

5. Vato is a Chicano slang term for "man" or "dude." The term is often associated with gang culture.

6. Survey results also suggest that public debates about immigration affect U.S.-born Latinos (Pew Hispanic Center 2007).

7. Although modern-day Portuguese immigration to eastern cities is very much a reality (see Bloemraad 2006), virtually no Portuguese immigrants live in Santa Maria.

8. These boundaries are not new. Fissures have always existed between American-born Mexicans and foreign-born Mexicans. See Gutiérrez 1995 for a detailed history of relations between Mexican Americans and Mexican immigrants.

9. Mexican Americans in Garden City and Santa Maria are not alone in encountering the boundaries that linguistic differences highlight. Ochoa (2004), García Bedolla (2005), and Menchaca (1995) show that Mexican Americans are ridiculed when Mexican immigrants deem their Spanish to be inferior.

6. ASSESSING MEXICAN IMMIGRATION

1. According Sampson, Morenoff, and Raudenbush (2005), Latino immigrants are much less likely to commit crimes than native-born individuals.

2. See Griswold del Castillo and García 1995 for more about César Chávez and the United Farm Workers.

3. Citrin and his colleagues (1997) note similar findings using nationally representative samples. Respondents' opposition to immigrants came from anx-

iety over taxes and the national economy, not from personal economic circumstances.

4. The findings in this section also appear in Jiménez 2007.

5. Sociologists Alejandro Portes and Rubén Rumbaut (2001) describe this adaptation as "dissonant acculturation" and show that Mexicans are the group that most often displays this form of adaptation.

6. During my time in Santa Maria, for example, a number of second-generation Mexican Americans were accepted into Ivy League and elite West Coast colleges and were among the star athletes and campus leaders.

7. Telles and Ortiz (2008) offer a similar explanation for how later-generation Mexican Americans might have been affected had Mexican immigration stopped.

8. Some Mexican Americans may in fact use Mexican immigrants as a point of reference for their belonging in U.S. society. During the immigration protests of 2006–7, some staunch Mexican-American restrictionist leaders emerged on the national scene. Respondents in Garden City and Santa Maria, however, showed no evidence of adopting such a stance.

7. ETHNIC DRAWBRIDGES

1. See Coleman 1990: 13–18 for a discussion of purposive action.

2. See Lacy 2007 and Pattillo-McCoy 1999 for a discussion of the black middle class and identity.

3. Sociologists hotly debate the unsettled question of whether or not an ethnic enclave provides an economic boost or an arena of economic exploitation for newly arrived immigrants (see Sanders and Nee 1987, 1992; and Portes and Bach 1985).

4. According to the United States Census, 84.5 percent of Guadalupe residents were Hispanic in 2000, and 40.6 percent of this city's population was foreign-born.

5. Gutiérrez (1995) shows that Mexican-Americans' organizations in the first half the twentieth century made efforts to assimilate immigrants in order to fend off non-Mexicans' backlash against the entire Mexican-origin population.

6. Although LULAC once distanced itself from Mexican immigrants, even advocating for laws that restricted Mexican immigration, over time it changed its stance and is today an advocate for people of Mexican origin regardless of their nativity and legal status.

7. See Wilson 1987 and Massey and Denton 1993 for a discussion of segregation and social isolation.

8.   According to school district records, in 2000 the high school in the center of town had a total student enrollment of 3,298, of which 2,537, or 77 percent, were Hispanic. The public school in the more affluent southern end of Santa Maria had a total population of 2,614 in 2000, of which 837, or 32 percent, were Hispanic.

9.   On the 2003 California Standards Test, eleventh graders at the high school in Santa Maria had a mean-scaled reading score of 675.3 compared with 694.4 at the high school in Orcutt. Where math is concerned, the pattern was much the same: 706.5 compared with 722.8.

8. CONCLUSION

1.   This rejuvenation may also be changing American conceptions of race in profound ways. Gregory Rodriguez (2007) argues that Mexican immigrants bring with them a five hundred-year-old history of race mixing and a high degree of comfort with racial ambiguity that will help change the rigid understanding of race in the United States.

Bibliography

Acuña, Rodolfo. 1972. *Occupied America: The Chicano's Struggle Toward Liberation*. San Francisco, CA: Canfield Press.

———. 1996. *Anything but Mexican: Chicanos in Contemporary Los Angeles*. New York: Verso.

———. 2000. *Occupied America: A History of Chicanos*. New York: Longman.

Agius, Jody. 2008. "Brown Picket Fences: The Mexican-origin Middle Class in Southern California." PhD dissertation, Sociology, University of California, Irvine, Irvine, CA.

Agius, Jody, and Jennifer Lee. 2009. "Brown Picket Fences: The Immigrant Narrative and Patterns of 'Giving Back' among the Mexican Origin Middle Class." *Ethnicities* 9 (1): 5–31.

Alba, Richard D. 1985. *Italian Americans: Into the Twilight of Ethnicity*. Englewood Cliffs, NJ: Prentice-Hall.

———. 1988. "Cohorts and the Dynamics of Ethnic Change." In *Social Structure and Human Lives*, ed. M. White Riley, 211–28. Newbury Park, CA: Sage Publications.

———. 1990. *Ethnic Identity: The Transformation of White America.* New Haven, CT: Yale University Press.

———. 2005. "Bright vs. Blurred Boundaries: Second-generation Assimilation and Exclusion in France, Germany, and the United States." *Ethnic and Racial Studies* 28 (1): 20–49.

———. 2006. "Mexican Americans and the American Dream." *Perspectives on Politics* 4 (2): 289–96.

Alba, Richard, Dalia Abdel-Hady, Tariquel Islam, and Karen Marotz. Forthcoming. "Downward Assimilation and Mexican Americans: An Examination of Intergenerational Advance and Stagnation in Educational Attainment." In *New Dimensions of Diversity: The Children of Immigrants in North America and Western Europe*, ed. M.C. Waters and R. Alba. Ithaca, NY: Cornell University Press.

Alba, Richard, and Tariq Islam. Forthcoming. "The Case of the Disappearing Mexican Americans: An Ethnic-identity Mystery." *Population Research and Policy Review.*

Alba, Richard, and Victor Nee. 1997. "Rethinking Assimilation Theory for a New Era of Immigration." *International Migration Review* 31 (4): 826–74.

———. 2003. *Remaking the American Mainstream: Assimilation and Contemporary Immigration.* Cambridge, MA: Harvard University Press.

Almaguer, Tomás. 1975. *Class, Race, and Chicano Oppression.* Somerville, MA: New England Free Press.

———. 1994. *Racial Fault Lines: The Historical Origins of White Supremacy in California.* Berkeley: University of California Press.

Alvarez, Luis. 2008. *The Power of the Zoot: Youth Culture and Resistance during World War II.* Berkeley: University of California Press.

Avila, Henry J. 1997. "Immigration and Integration: The Mexican Americans Community in Garden City, Kansas, 1900–1950." *Kansas History* 20 (1): 22–37.

Barrera, Mario. 1979. *Race and Class in the Southwest: A Theory of Racial Inequality.* Notre Dame, IN: University of Notre Dame Press.

Barth, Fredrik. 1969. "Introduction." In *Ethnic Groups and Boundaries*, ed. F. Barth, 9–38 . Boston: Little, Brown.

Basch, Linda G., Nina Glick Schiller, and Cristina Szanton Blanc. 1994. *Nations Unbound: Transnational Projects, Postcolonial Predicaments, and Deterritorialized Nation-States.* Langhorne, PA: Gordon and Breach.

Bean, Frank D., Susan K. Brown, Mark A. Leach, and James Bachmeier. 2007. "Becoming U.S. Stakeholders: Legalization and Integration among Mexican

Immigrants and Their Descendents." Merage Foundation for the American Dream, Newport Beach, CA.

Bean, Frank D., Jorge Chapa, Ruth R. Berg, and Kathryn A. Sowards. 1994. "Educational and Sociodemographic Incorporation among Hispanic Immigrants in the United States." In *Immigration and Ethnicity: The Integration of America's Newest Arrivals,* ed. B. Edmonston and J. Passel, 73–96. Washington DC: Urban Institute.

Bean, Frank D., and Gillian Stevens. 2003. *America's Newcomers and the Dynamics of Diversity.* New York: Russell Sage Foundation.

Binder, Norman E., J.L. Polinard, and Robert D. Wrinkle. 1997. "Mexican American and Anglo Attitudes toward Immigration Reform: A View from the Border." *Social Science Quarterly* 78 (2): 324–37.

Blau, Peter Michael. 1977. *Inequality and Heterogeneity: A Primitive Theory of Social Structure.* New York: Free Press.

Blauner, Robert. 1969. "Internal Colonialism and Ghetto Revolt." *Social Problems* 16 (4): 393–408.

Bloemraad, Irene. 1999. "Portuguese Immigrants and Citizenship in North America." *Lusotopie* 5103–20.

———. 2006. *Becoming a Citizen: Incorporating Immigrants and Refugees in the United States and Canada.* Berkeley, CA: University of California Press.

Bogardus, Emory S. 1970. *The Mexican in the United States.* New York: Arno Press.

Boger, John Charles, and Gary Orfield. 2005. *School Resegregation: Must the South Turn Back?* Chapill Hill: University of North Carolina Press.

Borjas, George J. 1999. *Heaven's Door: Immigration Policy and the American Economy.* Princeton, NJ: Princeton University Press.

Broadway, Michael J. 1994. "Beef Stew: Cattle, Immigrants, and Established Residents in a Kansas Beefpacking Town." In *Newcomers in the Workplace: Immigrants and the Restructuring of the US Economy,* ed. L. Lamphere, A. Stepick, and G. Grenier, 25–43. Philadelphia, PA: Temple University Press.

Brown, Susan K. 2006. "Structural Assimilation Revisited: Mexican-origin Nativity and Cross-ethnic Primary Ties." *Social Forces* 85 (1): 75–92.

———. 2007. "Delayed Spatial Assimilation: Multigenerational Incorporation of the Mexican-origin Population in Los Angeles." *City &Community* 6 (3): 193–209.

Brubaker, Rogers. 2001. "The Return of Assimilation? Changing Perspectives on Immigration and Its Sequels in France, Germany, and the United States." *Ethnic and Racial Studies* 24 (4): 531–48.

Buchanan, Patrick J. 2006. *State of Emergency: The Third World Invasion and Conquest of America.* New York: Thomas Dunne Books.

Calavita, Kitty. 1992. *Inside the State: The Bracero Program, Immigration and the I.N.S.* New York: Routledge.

Camarillo, Albert M. 1971. "Research Note on Chicano Community Leaders: The G.I. Generation." *Aztlán* 2 (1): 145–50.

———. 1996 . *Chicanos in a Changing Society: From Mexican Pueblos to American Barrios in Santa Barbara and Southern California, 1848–1930.* Cambridge, MA: Harvard University Press.

Cardoso, Lawrence A. 1980. *Mexican Emigration to the United States, 1897–1931.* Tucson, AZ: University of Arizona Press.

Carter, Prudence L. 2005. *Keepin' It Real: School Success beyond Black and White.* New York: Oxford University Press.

Cazares, Ralph B., Edward Murguía, and W. Parker Frizbie. 1985. "Mexican American Intermarriage in a Nonmetropolitan Context." In *The Mexican American Experience: An Interdisciplinary Perspective,* ed. R. O. de la Garza, F. D. Bean, C. M. Bonjean, R. Romo, and R. Alvarez, 393–401. Austin: University of Texas Press.

Chavez, Leo R. 1998. *Shadowed Lives: Undocumented Immigrants in American Society.* Fort Worth, TX: Harcourt Brace College Publishers.

Child, Irvin. 1943. *Italian or American? The Second Generation in Conflict.* New Haven, CT: Yale University Press.

Citrin, Jack, Donald P. Green, Christopher Muste, and Cara Wong. 1997. "Public Opinion toward Immigration Reform: The Role of Economic Motivations." *Journal of Politics* 59 (3): 858–81.

Coleman, James S. 1990. *Foundations of Social Theory.* Cambridge, MA: Harvard University Press.

Cook, Philip J., and Jens Ludwig. 1998. "The Burden of Acting White: Do Black Adolescents Disparage Academic Achievement?" In *The Black White Test-score Gap,* ed. C. Jencks and M. Phillips, 375–400. Washington DC: Brookings Institution Press.

Cornelius, Wayne A. 2005. "Controlling 'Unwanted' Immigration: Lessons from the United States, 1993–2004." *Journal of Ethnic and Migration Studies* 31 (4): 775–94.

Cornell, Stephen E. 2000. "That's the Story of Our Life." In *Narrative and Multiplicity in Constructing Ethnic Identities,* ed. P. R. Spickard and W. J. Burroughs, 41–53. Philadelphia, PA: Temple University Press.

Cornell, Stephen E., and Douglas Hartmann. 1998. *Ethnicity and Race: Making Identities in a Changing World.* Thousand Oaks, CA: Pine Forge Press.

Dávila, Arlene M. 2001. *Latinos, Inc.: The Marketing and Making of a People.* Berkeley: University of California Press.

Dawson, Michael C. 1995. *Behind the Mule: Race and Class in African American Politics.* Princeton, NJ: Princeton University Press.

de la Garza, Rodolfo O., and Louis DeSipio. 1998. "Interests Not Passions: Mexican-American Attitudes toward Mexico, Immigration from Mexico, and Other Issues Shaping U.S.-Mexico Relations." *International Migration Review* 32 (2): 401–22.

de la Garza, Rodolfo O., Louis DeSipio, F. Chris García, John García, and Angelo Falcon. 1992. *Latino Voices: Mexican, Puerto Rican, and Cuban Perspectives on American Politics*. Boulder, CO: Westview Press.

de la Garza, Rodolfo O., Angelo Falcon, and F. Chris García. 1996. "Will the Real Americans Please Stand Up? Anglo and Mexican-American Support of Core American Political Values." *American Journal of Political Science* 40 (2): 335–51.

de la Garza, Rodolfo O., Angelo Falcon, F. Chris García, and John A. García. 1993. "Attitudes toward U.S. Immigration Policy: The Case of Mexicans, Puerto Ricans, and Cubans." *Migration World* 21 (2/3): 13–16.

de la Garza, Rodolfo O., Jerry L. Polinard, Robert D. Wrinkle, and Tomás Longoria. 1991. "Understanding Intra-ethnic Attitude Variations: Mexican Origin Population Views of Immigration." *Social Science Quarterly* 72 (2): 379–87.

Dohan, Daniel. 2003. *The Price of Poverty: Money, Work, and Culture in the Mexican-American Barrio*. Berkeley: University of California Press.

Duarte, Cynthia. 2008. "Negotiating 3rd+ Generation Mexican American Identity in Los Angeles, CA." PhD dissertation, Sociology, Columbia University, New York.

Duncan, Brian, and Stephen Trejo. 2007. "Ethnic Identification, Intermarriage, and Unmeasured Progress by Mexican Americans." In *Mexican Immigration to the United States*, ed. G. J. Borjas, 229–67. Cambridge, MA: National Bureau of Economic Research.

Durand, Jorge, Douglas S. Massey, and Fernando Charvet. 2000. "The Changing Geography of Mexican Immigration to the United States: 1910–1996." *Social Science Quarterly* 81 (1): 1–15.

Edmonston, Barry, and Jeffrey S. Passel. 1994. *Immigration and Ethnicity: The Integration of America's New Arrivals*. Washington DC: Urban Institute Press.

Erdmans, Mary Patrice. 1998. *Opposite Poles: Immigrants and Ethnics in Polish Chicago, 1976–1990*. University Park: Pennsylvania State University Press.

Eschbach, Karl, Jacqueline Hagan, Nestor Rodriguez, Rubén Hernández-León, and Stanley Bailey. 1999. "Death on the Border." *International Migration Review* 33 (2): 430–54.

Espenshade, Thomas J., and Charles A. Calhoun. 1993. "An Analysis of Public Opinion toward Undocumented Immigration." *Population Research and Policy Review* 12 (3): 189–224.

Espenshade, Thomas J., and Katherine Hempstead. 1996. "Contemporary American Attitudes toward U.S. Immigration." *International Migration Review* 30 (2): 535–71.

Faura, Juan. 2004. *The Whole Enchilada: Hispanic Marketing 101*. Ithaca, NY: Paramount Market Publishing.

Fischer, Mary J., and Marta Tienda. 2006. "Redrawing Spatial Color Lines: Hispanic Metropolitan Dispersal, Segregration, and Economic Opportunity." In *Hispanics and the Future of America*, ed. M. Tienda and F. Mitchell, 100–137. Washington DC: National Academies Press.

Fishman, Joshua A. 1965. "The Status and Prospects of Bilingualism in the United States." *Modern Language Journal* 49 (3): 143–55.

———. 1972. *The Sociology of Language: An Interdisciplinary Social Science Approach to Language in Society*. Rowley, MA: Newbury House Publishers.

Flores, William V., and Rina Benmayor. 1997. *Latino Cultural Citizenship: Claiming Identity, Space, and Rights*. Boston: Beacon Press.

Foote Whyte, William. 1943. *Street Corner Society: The Social Structure of an Italian Slum*. Chicago: University of Chicago Press.

Fordham, Signithia. 1996. *Blacked Out: Dilemmas of Race, Identity, and Success at Capital High*. Chicago: University of Chicago Press.

Fordham, Signithia, and John U. Ogbu. 1986. "Black Students' School Success: Coping with the 'Burden of "Acting White.""' *Urban Review* 18 (3): 176–206.

Gamio, Manuel. 1930. *Mexican Immigration to the United States: A Study of Human Migration and Adjustment*. Chicago: University of Chicago Press.

———. 1931. *The Mexican Immigrant, His Life-story: Autobiographic Documents*. Chicago: University of Chicago Press.

Gans, Herbert J. 1962. *The Urban Villagers: Group and Class in the Life of Italian-Americans*. New York: Free Press.

———. 1979. "Symbolic Ethnicity: The Future of Ethnic Groups and Cultures in America." *Ethnic and Racial Studies* 2 (January): 1–20.

———. 1992. "Second Generation Decline: Scenarios for the Economic and Ethnic Futures of the Post-1965 American Immigrants." *Ethnic and Racial Studies* 15 (April): 173–92.

García, Alma M. 1997. *Chicana Feminist Thought: The Basic Historical Writings*. New York: Routledge.

———. 2003. *Narratives of Mexican American Women: Emergent Identities of the Second Generation*. Walnut Creek, CA: Alta Mira Press.

García, Juan R. 1996. *Mexicans in the Midwest, 1900–1932*. Tucson: University of Arizona Press.

García, Juan Ramón. 1980. *Operation Wetback: The Mass Deportation f Mexican Undocumented Workers in 1954*. Westport, CT: Greenwood Press.

García, Mario T. 1989. *Mexican Americans: Leadership, Ideology and Identity, 1930–1960*. New Haven, CT: Yale University Press.

García Bedolla, Lisa 2005. *Fluid Borders: Latino Power, Identity, and Politics in Los Angeles*. Berkeley: University of California Press.

Glazer, Nathan. 1997. *We Are All Multiculturalists Now.* Cambridge, MA: Harvard University Press.

Glazer, Nathan, and Daniel Patrick Moynihan. 1970. *Beyond the Melting Pot: The Negroes, Puerto Ricans, Jews, Italians, and Irish of New York City.* Cambridge, MA: MIT University Press.

Gómez-Quiñones, Juan. 1990. *Chicano Politics: Reality and Promise, 1940–1990.* Albuquerque: University of New Mexico Press.

González Baker, Susan, Frank D. Bean, Augustín Escobar Latapi, and Sidney Weintraub. 1998. "Immigration Policies and Trends: The Growing Importance of Migration from Mexico." In *Crossings: Mexican Immigrants in Interdisciplinary Perspectives,* ed. M. M. Suárez-Orozco, 81–109. Cambridge, MA: David Rockefeller Center for Latin American Studies, Harvard University Press.

Gordon, Milton M. 1964. *Assimilation in American Life: The Role of Race, Religion, and National Origins.* New York: Oxford University Press.

Gouveia, Lourdes, and Donald D. Stull. 1995. "Dances with Cows: Beefpacking's Impact on Garden City, Kansas and Lexington, Nebraska." In *Any Way You Cut It: Meat Processing and Small-town America,* ed. D. D. Stull, M. J. Broadway, and D. Griffith, 85–107. Lawrence: University of Kansas Press.

Grebler, Leo, Joan W. Moore, Ralph C. Guzman, and Jeffrey Lionel Berlant. 1970. *The Mexican-American People, the Nation's Second Largest Minority.* New York: Free Press.

Griffith, David. 1995. "Hay Trabajo: Poultry Processing, Rural Industrialization, and the Latinization of Low-wage Labor." In *Any Way You Cut It: Meat Processing and Small-town America,* ed. D. D. Stull, M. J. Broadway, and D. Griffith, 129–51. Lawrence: University of Kansas Press.

Griswold del Castillo, Richard. 1979. *The Los Angeles Barrio, 1850–1890: A Social History.* Berkeley: University of California Press.

Griswold del Castillo, Richard, and Arnoldo de León. 1997. *North to Aztlán: A History of Mexican Americans in the United States.* New York: Twayne Publishers.

Griswold del Castillo, Richard, and Richard A. García. 1995. *César Chávez a Triumph of Spirit.* Norman: University of Oklahoma Press.

Guerín-Gonzáles, Camille. 1994. *Mexican Workers and American Dreams: Immigration, Repatriation, and California Farm Labor, 1900–1939.* New Brunswick, NJ: Rutgers University Press.

Guglielmo, Thomas. 2003. *White on Arrival: Italians, Race, Color and Power in Chicago, 1890–1945.* New York: Oxford University Press.

Gutiérrez, David. 1995. *Walls and Mirrors: Mexican Americans, Mexican Immigrants, and the Politics of Ethnicity.* Berkeley: University of California Press.

Gutiérrez, Ramón. 2004. "Internal Colonialism: An American Theory of Race." *Du Bois Review* 1 (2): 281–95.

Haney-López, Ian. 1996. *White by Law: The Legal Construction of Race.* New York: New York University Press.

———. 2003. *Racism on Trial: The Chicano Fight for Justice.* Cambridge, MA: Belknap Press of Harvard University.

Hansen, Marcus L. 1952. "The Third Generation in America." *Commentary* 14 (November): 492–500.

Harris, David R., and Jeremiah Joseph Sim. 2002. "Who Is Multiracial? Assessing the Complexity of Lived Race." *American Sociological Review* 67 (August): 614–27.

Higham, John. 1963. *Strangers in the Land: Patterns of American Nativism, 1860–1925.* New York: Atheneum.

Hochschild, Jennifer L. 1995. *Facing Up to the American Dream: Race, Class, and the Soul of the Nation.* Princeton, NJ: Princeton University Press.

Hondagneu-Sotelo, Pierrette. 1994. *Gendered Transitions: Mexican Experiences of Immigration.* Berkeley: University of California Press.

Huntington, Samuel P. 2004a. "The Hispanic Challenge." *Foreign Policy* (March/April): 30–45.

———. 2004b. *Who Are We? The Challenges to America's National Identity.* New York: Simon and Schuster.

Ignatiev, Noel. 1995. *How the Irish Became White.* New York: Routledge.

Jacobson, Matthew Frye. 1998. *Whiteness of a Different Color: European Immigrants and the Alchemy of Race.* Cambridge, MA: Harvard University Press.

———. 2006. *Roots Too: White Ethnic Revival in Post–Civil Rights America.* Cambridge, MA: Harvard University Press.

Jaffe, Abram J., Ruth M. Cullen, and Thomas D. Boswell. 1980. *The Changing Demography of Spanish Americans.* New York: Academic Press.

Jiménez, Tomás R. 2004. "Multiethnic Mexican Americans and Ethnic Identity in the United States." *Ethnicities* 4 (1): 75–97.

———. 2007. "Weighing the Costs and Benefits of Mexican Immigration: The Mexican-American Perspective." *Social Science Quarterly* 88 (3): 599–618.

———. 2008. "Mexican-immigrant Replenishment and the Continuing Significance of Ethnicity and Race." *American Journal of Sociology* 113 (6): 1527–567.

Jiménez, Tomás R., and David Fitzgerald. 2007. "Mexican Assimilation: A Temporal and Spatial Reorientation." *Du Bois Review* 4 (2): 337–54.

Kasinitz, Philip, Mary C. Waters, John H. Mollenkopf, and Merih Anil. 2002. *Transnationalism and the Children of Immigrants in Contemporary New York.* New York: Russell Sage Foundation.

Kennedy, John F. 1964. *A Nation of Immigrants.* New York: Harper-Collins.

Krebs, Ronald R. 2006. *Fighting for Rights: Military Service and the Politics of Citizenship.* Ithaca, NY: Cornell University Press.

Lacy, Karyn. 2007. *Blue-chip Black: Division and Unity in the Black Middle Class.* Berkeley: University of California Press.

Lamont, Michele, and V. Molnar. 2002. "The Study of Boundaries in the Social Sciences." *Annual Review of Sociology* 28 (1): 167–95.

Landale, Nancy S., R. Salvador Oropesa, and Cristina Bradatan. 2006. "Hispanic Families in the United States: Family Structure and Process in an Era of Family Change." In *Hispanics and the Future of America,* ed. M. Tienda and F. Mitchell, 138–78. Washington DC: National Academies Press.

Lee, Jennifer, and Frank D. Bean. 2007. "Reinventing the Color Line: Immigration and America's New Racial/Ethnic Divide." *Social Forces* 86 (2): 1–26.

Levitt, Peggy. 2001. *The Transnational Villagers.* Berkeley: University of California Press.

———. 2002. "The Ties That Change: Relations to the Ancestral Home over the Life Cycle." In *The Changing Face of Home: The Transnational Lives of the Second Generation,* ed. P. Levitt and M. C. Waters, 123–44. New York: Russell Sage Foundation.

———. 2007. *God Needs No Passport: Immigrants and the Changing American Religious Landscape.* New York: New Press.

Lieberson, Stanley, and Mary C. Waters. 1988. *From Many Strands: Ethnic and Racial Groups in Contemporary America.* New York: Russell Sage Foundation.

Liebow, Elliot. 1967. *Tally's Corner: A Study of Negro Streetcorner Men.* Boston: Little, Brown.

Linton, April. 2004. "A Critical Mass Model of Bilingualism among U.S.-born Hispanics." *Social Forces* 83 (1): 279–314.

Linton, April, and Tomás R. Jiménez. 2009. "Contexts for Bilingualism among U.S.-born Latinos." www.informaworld.com/smpp/content~content=a90473 3531~db=all~order=pubdate.

Livingston, Gretchen, and John R. Kahn. 2002. "An American Dream Unfulfilled: The Limited Mobility of Mexican Americans." *Social Science Quarterly* 83 (4): 1003–12.

Logan, John R., Richard D. Alba, and Wenquan Zhang. 2002. "Immigrant Enclaves and Ethnic Communities in New York and Los Angeles." *American Sociological Review* 67 (2): 299–322.

López, David E., and Ricardo Stanton-Salazar. 2001. "Mexican Americans: A Second Generation at Risk." In *Ethnicities: Children of Immigrants in America,* ed. R. G. Rumbaut and A. Portes, 57–90. Berkeley: University of California Press.

López-Turley, Ruth N. 2009. "College Proximity: Mapping Access to Opportunity." *Sociology of Education* 82 (2): 126–46.

Macias, Thomas. 2004. "Imaginandose Mexicano: The Symbolic Context of

Mexican American Ethnicity beyond the Second Generation." *Qualitative Sociology* 27 (3): 299–315.

———. 2006. *Mestizo in America: Generations of Mexican Ethnicity in the Suburban Southwest.* Tucson: University of Arizona Press.

Marin, Alexandra. 2004. "Are Respondents More Likely to List Alters with Certain Characteristics? Implications for Name Generator Data." *Social Networks* 26 (4): 289–307.

Marsden, Peter V. 1988. "Homogeneity in Confiding Relations." *Social Networks* 10: 57–76.

Massey, Douglas S. 1985. "Ethnic Residential Segregation: A Theoretical Synthesis and Empirical Review." *Sociology and Social Research* 69 (3): 315–50.

———. 1987. *Return to Aztlán: The Social Process of International Migration from Western Mexico.* Berkeley: University of California Press.

———. 1995. "The New Immigration and Ethnicity in the United States." *Population and Development Review* 21 (3): 631–52.

Massey, Douglas S., and Nancy A. Denton. 1993. *American Apartheid: Segregation and the Making of the Underclass.* Cambridge, MA: Harvard University Press.

Massey, Douglas S., Jorge Durand, and Nolan J. Malone. 2002. *Beyond Smoke and Mirrors: Mexican Immigration in an Era of Free Trade.* New York: Russell Sage Foundation.

Massey, Douglas S., and Garvey Lundy. 2001. "Use of Black English and Racial Discrimination in Urban Housing Markets: New Methods and Findings." *Urban Affairs Review* 36 (4): 470–96.

———. 2008. *New Faces in New Places: The Changing Geography of American Immigration.* New York: Russell Sage Foundation.

Matute-Bianchi, María Eugenia. 1986. "Ethnic Identities and Patterns of School Success and Failure among Mexican Descent and Japanese-American Students in a California High School: An Ethnographic Analysis." *American Journal of Education* 95 (November): 233–55.

Meier, Matt S., and Feliciano Ribera. 1993. *Mexican Americans, American Mexicans: From Conquistadors to Chicanos.* New York: Hill and Wang.

Menchaca, Martha. 1995. *The Mexican Outsiders: A Community History of Marginalization and Discrimination in California.* Austin: University of Texas Press.

Migration Policy Institute. 2008. "2006 American Community Survey and Census Data on the Foreign Born by State." www.migrationinformation.org/DataHub/acscensus.cfm#, retrieved April 2, 2008.

Miranda, Carolina A. 2004. "Fifteen Candles: Quinceañera—Coming-of-age Parties for Latina Girls—Are Going Mainstream." *Time,* July 19, 2004, 83.

Muñoz, Carlos. 1989. *Youth, Identity, Power: The Chicano Movement.* New York: Verso.

Murguía, Edward. 1982. *Chicano Intermarriage: A Theoretical and Empirical Study.* San Antonio, TX: Trinity University Press.

Murguía, Edward, and Edward Telles. 1996. "Phenotype and Schooling among Mexican Americans." *Sociology of Education* 69 (October): 276–89.

Myers, Dowell. 2007. *Immigrants and Boomers: Forging a New Social Contract for the Future of America.* New York: Russell Sage Foundation.

Nagel, Joane. 1995. "American Indian Ethnic Renewal: Politics and the Resurgence of Identity." *American Sociological Review* 60 (6): 947–65.

———. 1997. *American Indian Ethnic Renewal: Red Power and the Resurgence of Identity and Culture.* New York: Oxford University Press.

Nericcio, William A. 2007. *Tex[t]-Mex: Seductive Hallucinations of the "Mexican" in America.* Austin: University of Texas Press.

Newton, Lina Y. 2000. "Why Some Latinos Supported Proposition 187: Testing Economic Threat and Cultural Identity Hypotheses." *Social Science Quarterly* 81 (1): 180–93.

Ngai, Mae M. 2004. *Impossible Subjects: Illegal Aliens and the Making of Modern America.* Princeton, NJ: Princeton University Press.

Novak, Michael. 1973. *The Rise of the Unmeltable Ethnics: Politics and the Culture of the Seventies.* New York: Macmillan.

Ochoa, Gilda. 2000. "Mexican Americans' Attitudes toward and Interactions with Mexican Immigrants: A Qualitative Analysis of Conflict and Cooperation." *Social Science Quarterly* 81 (1): 84–105.

———. 2004. *Becoming Neighbors in a Mexican American Community: Power, Conflict and Solidarity.* Austin: University of Texas Press.

Ogbu, John U. 1991. "Immigrant and Involuntary Minorities in Comparative Perspective." In *Minority Status and School: A Comparative Study of Immigrant and Involuntary Minorities,* ed. M. A. Gibson and J. U. Ogbu, 3–36. New York: Garland Publishing.

Omi, Michael, and Howard Winant. 1994. *Racial Formation in the United States: From the 1960s to the 1990s.* New York: Routledge.

Oppenheimer, Robert. 1985. "Acculturation or Assimilation: Mexican Immigrants in Kansas, 1900 to World War II." *Western Historical Quarterly* 16 (4): 429–48.

Ortiz, Vilma. 1996. "The Mexican-origin Population: Permanent Working Class or Emerging Middle Class?" In *Ethnic Los Angeles,* ed. R. D. Waldinger and M. Bozorgmehr, 247–77. New York: Russell Sage Foundation.

Padilla, Felix. 1985. *Latino Ethnic Consciousness: The Case of Mexican Americans and Puerto Ricans in Chicago.* Notre Dame, IN: University of Notre Dame Press.

Pager, Devah. 2003. "The Mark of a Criminal Record." *American Journal of Sociology* 108 (5): 937–75.

Palerm, Juan-Vicente. 1992. "A Season in the Life of a Migrant Farm Worker in California." *Western Journal of Medicine* 157 (3): 362–66.

———. 1994. "Immigrant and Migrant Farm Workers in the Santa Maria Valley, California." Center for Chicano Studies and Department of Anthropology, University of California, Santa Barbara.

———. 1997. "The Expansion of California Agriculture and the Rise of Peasant-worker Communities." Paper presented at the conference Del pasado al futuro: Nueva dimensiones de la integración México–Estado Unidos, March 17–19, Mexico City.

Park, Robert Ezra. 1950. *Race and Culture.* Edited by R. E. Park. Glencoe, IL: Free Press.

Park, Robert Ezra, Ernest W. Burgess, and Roderick D. McKenzie. 1925. *The City.* Chicago: University of Chicago Press.

Passel, Jeffrey S. 2008. "Trends in Unauthorized Immigration: Undocumented Inflow Now Trails Legal Inflow." Research report, Pew Hispanic Center, Washington DC.

Pattillo-McCoy, Mary. 1999. *Black Picket Fences : Privilege and Peril among the Black Middle Class.* Chicago: University of Chicago Press.

Perlmann, Joel. 2005. *Italians Then, Mexicans Now: Immigrant Origins and Second-generation Progress, 1890–2000.* New York: Russell Sage Foundation.

Perlmann, Joel, and Roger Waldinger. 1997. "Second Generation Decline? Children of Immigrants, Past and Present—a Reconsideration." *International Migration Review* 31 (4): 893–922.

Perlmann, Joel, and Mary C. Waters. 2004. "Intermarriage Then and Now: Race, Generation and the Changing Meaning of Marriage." In *Not Just Black and White: Immigration, Race and Ethnicity in the United States,* ed. N. Foner and G. Frederickson, 262–77. New York: Russell Sage Foundation.

Pew Hispanic Center. 2007. "2007 National Survey of Latinos: As Illegal Immigration Issue Heats Up, Hispanics Feel a Chill." Research report, Pew Hispanic Center, Washington DC.

Portes, Alejandro, and Robert L. Bach. 1985. *Latin Journey: Cuban and Mexican Immigrants in the United States.* Berkeley: University of California Press.

Portes, Alejandro, Luis E. Guarnizo, and Patricia Landolt. 1999. "The Study of Transnationalism: Pitfalls and Promises of an Emergent Research Field." *Ethnic and Racial Studies* 22 (2): 219–35.

Portes, Alejandro, and Rubén G. Rumbaut. 1990. *Immigrant America: A Portrait.* Berkeley: University of California Press.

———. 2001. *Legacies: The Story of the Immigrant Second Generation.* Berkeley and New York: University of California Press and Russell Sage Foundation.

Portes, Alejandro, and Min Zhou. 1993. "The New Second Generation: Segmented Assimilation and Its Variants." *Annals of the American Academy of Political and Social Science* 530 (November): 74–96.

Putnam, Robert D. 2000. *Bowling Alone: The Collapse and Revival of American Community.* New York: Simon and Schuster.

Qian, Zhenchao, and Daniel T. Lichter. 2007. "Social Boundaries and Marital Assimilation: Interpreting Trends in Racial and Ethnic Intermarriage." *American Sociological Review* 72 (1): 68–94.

Ramos, Henry A. J. 1998. *The American GI Forum: In Pursuit of the Dream, 1948–1983.* Houston, TX: Arte Publico Press.

Reed, Deborah, Laura E. Hill, Christopher Jepsen, and Hans P. Johnson. 2005. "Educational Progress across Immigrant Generations in California." Public Policy Institute of California, San Francisco, CA.

Rivas-Rodríguez, Maggie. 1999. *Mexican Americans and World War II.* Austin: University of Texas Press.

Roberts, Bryan R., Reanne Frank, and Fernando Lozano-Ascencio. 1999. "Transnational Migrant Communities and Mexican Migration to the US." *Ethnic and Racial Studies* 22 (2): 238–66.

Rodriguez, Gregory. 1996. "The Emerging Latino Middle Class." Pepperdine Public Policy Institute, Malibu, CA.

———. 2007. *Mongrels, Bastards, Orphans and Vagabonds: Mexican Immigration and the Future of Race in America.* New York: Pantheon.

Roediger, David R. 1991. *The Wages of Whiteness: Race and the Making of the American Working Class.* New York: Verso.

———. 2005. *Working toward Whiteness: How America's Immigrants Become White: The Strange Journey from Ellis Island to the Suburbs.* New York: Basic Books.

Rosenfeld, Michael J. 2002. "Measure of Assimilation in the Marriage Market: Mexican Americans 1970–1990." *Journal of Marriage and the Family* 64 (February): 152–62.

Rumbaut, Rubén G. 2002. "Severed or Sustained Attachments? Language, Identity, and Imagined Communities in the Post-immigrant Generation." In *The Changing Face of Home: Transnational Lives of the Second Generation,* ed. P. Levitt and M. C. Waters, 43–95. New York: Russell Sage Foundation.

Rumbaut, Rubén G., Douglas S. Massey, and Frank D. Bean. 2006. "Linguistic Life Expectancies: Immigrant Language Retention in Southern California." *Population and Development Review* 32 (3): 447–60.

Rumbaut, Rubén G., and Alejandro Portes. 2001. *Ethnicities: Children of Immigrants in America.* Berkeley and New York: University of California Press and Russell Sage Foundation.

Rutter, Michael, and Marta Tienda. 2005. "The Multiple Facets of Ethnicity." In *Ethnicity and Causal Mechanisms,* ed. M. Rutter and M. Tienda, 50–79. New York: Cambridge University Press.

Salgado de Snyder, Nelly, Cynthia M. López, and Amado M. Padilla. 1982. "Ethnic Identity and Cultural Awareness among the Offspring of Mexican Interethnic Marriages." *Journal of Early Adolescence* 2 (3): 277–82.

Sampson, Robert J., Jeffrey D. Morenoff, and Stephen Raudenbush. 2005. "Social Anatomy of Racial and Ethnic Disparities in Violence." *American Journal of Public Health* 95 (2): 224–32.

Sánchez, George J. 1993. *Becoming Mexican American: Ethnicity, Culture, and Identity in Chicano Los Angeles, 1900–1945*. New York: Oxford University Press.

———. 1997. "Face the Nation: Race, Immigration and the Rise of Nativism in Late 20th Century." *International Migration Review* 31 (4): 1009–30.

Sanders, Jimy M. 2002. "Ethnic Boundaries and Identity in Plural Societies." *Annual Review of Sociology* 28: 327–57.

Sanders, Jimy M., and Victor Nee. 1987. "The Limits of Ethnic Solidarity in the Enclave Economy." *American Sociological Review* 52 (6): 745–73.

———. 1992. "Problems in Resolving the Enclave Economy Debate." *American Sociological Review* 57 (3): 415–19.

Selena. 1997. Warner Bros. movie, directed by Gregory Nava.

Skerry, Peter. 1993. *Mexican Americans: The Ambivalent Minority*. New York: Free Press.

Skrentny, John D. 2002. *The Minority Rights Revolution*. Cambridge, MA: Harvard University Press.

———. 2007. "Are America's Civil Rights Law Still Relevant." *Du Bois Review* 4 (1): 119–40.

Smith, James P. 2003. "Assimilation Across the Latino Generations." *American Economic Review* 93 (2): 315–19.

———. 2006. "Immigrants and the Labor Market." *Journal of Labor Economics* 24 (2): 203–33.

Smith, James P., and Barry Edmonston. 1997. *The New Americans: Economic, Demographic, and Fiscal Effects of Immigration*. Washington DC: National Academies Press.

Smith, Robert Courtney. 2005a. *Mexican New York: The Transnational Lives of New Immigrants*. Berkeley: University of California Press.

———. 2005b. "Racialization and Mexicans in New York." In *New Destinations: Mexican Immigrants in the United States*, ed. V. Zúñiga and R. Hernández-León, 220–43. New York: Russell Sage Foundation.

Sparks, Jeanne. 1990. "Hobbs: Illegal Alien Situation Out of Hand." *Santa Maria Times*, July 17, Santa Maria, CA.

Stack, Carol B. 1997. *All Our Kin: Strategies for Survival in a Black Community*. New York: Basic Books.

Stern, Alexandra Minna. 2005. *Eugenic Nation: Faults and Frontiers of Better Breeding in Modern America*. Berkeley: University of California Press.

Stull, Donald D. 1990. "'I come to the Garden': Changing Ethnic Relations in Garden City, Kansas." *Urban Anthropology* 19 (4): 303–20.

———. 2001. "Through the Window Once More: Changing Relations in Garden City, Kansas, 1980–2000." Paper presented at the Tenth Annual Five-state Multicultural Conference, April 5, Garden City, KS.

Suárez-Orozco, Marcelo M. 2000. "Everything You Want to Know about Assimilation but Were Afraid to Ask." *Daedalus* 129 (4): 1–30.

Taylor, Paul S. 1932. *Mexican Labor in the United States: Chicago and the Calmut Region.* Berkeley: University of California Press.

———. 1934. *An American-Mexican Frontier: Nueces County, Texas.* Chapel Hill: University of North Carolina Press.

Telles, Edward, and Edward Murguía. 1990. "Phenotype Discrimination and Income Differences among Mexican Americans." *Social Science Quarterly* 71 (4): 682–96.

Telles, Edward E., and Vilma Ortiz. 2008. *Generations of Exclusion: Mexican Americans, Assimilation, and Race.* New York: Russell Sage Foundation.

Tienda, Marta, and Faith Mitchell. 2006. "Introduction: E Pluribus Plures or E Pluribus Unum?" In *Hispanics and the Future of America*, ed. M. Tienda and F. Mitchell, 1–15. Washington DC: National Academies Press.

Tuan, Mia. 1998. *Forever Foreigners or Honorary Whites? The Asian Ethnic Experience Today.* New Brunswick, NJ: Rutgers University Press.

Tyson, Karolyn, William Darity, and Domini R. Castellino. 2005. "'It's Not a Black Thing': Understanding the Burden of Acting White and Other Dilemmas of High Achievement." *American Sociological Review* 70 (4): 582–605.

Valdez, Avelarado. 1983. "Recent Increases in Intermarriage by Mexican American Males: Bexar County, Texas from 1971 to 1980." *Social Science Quarterly* 64 (March): 136–44.

Valle, Francisco J., and Judy M. Mandel. 2003. *How to Win The Hispanic Gold Rush: Critical Cultural, Demographic, Marketing, and Motivational Factors.* Lincoln, NE: iUniverse, Inc.

Venkatesh, Sudhir Alladi. 2000. *American Project: The Rise and Fall of a Modern Ghetto.* Cambridge, MA: Harvard University Press.

Verba, Sidney, and Norman H. Nie. 1972. *Participation in America: Political Democracy and Social Inequality.* New York: Harper Row.

Vigil, James Diego. 1988. *Barrio Gangs: Street Life and Identity in Southern California.* Austin: University of Texas Press.

———. 2002. "Community Dynamics and the Rise of Street Gangs." In *Latinos: Remaking America*, ed. M. M. Suarez-Orozco and M. Páez, 97–109. Berkeley: University of California Press.

Wacquant, Loïc. 2003. *Body and Soul: Notebooks of an Apprentice Boxer.* New York: Cambridge University Press.

———. 2008. *Urban Outcasts: A Comparative Sociology of Advanced Marginality.* Cambridge, MA: Polity Press.

Waldinger, Roger David. 1996. *Still the Promised City? African-Americans and New Immigrants in Postindustrial New York.* Cambridge, MA: Harvard University Press.

Waldinger, Roger, and Cynthia Feliciano. 2004. "Will the New Second Generation Experience 'Downward Assimilation'? Segmented Assimilation Re-assessed." *Ethnic and Racial Studies* 27 (3): 376–402.

Waldinger, Roger, and Michael I. Lichter. 2003. *How the Other Half Works: Immigration and the Social Organization of Labor.* Berkeley: University of California Press.

Waldinger, Roger, Nelson Lim, and David Cort. 2007. "Bad Jobs, Good Jobs, No Jobs? The Employment Experience of the Mexican American Second Generation." *Journal of Ethnic and Migration Studies* 33 (1): 1–35.

Warikoo, Natasha Kumar. 2007. "Racial Authenticity among Second Generation Youth in Multiethnic New York and London." *Poetics* 35 (6): 388–408.

Warner, W. Lloyd, and Leo Srole. 1945. *The Social Systems of American Ethnic Groups.* New Haven, CT: Yale University Press.

Waters, Mary C. 1990. *Ethnic Options: Choosing Identities in America.* Berkeley: University of California Press.

———. 1998. "Commentary." In *Crossings: Mexican Immigration in Interdisciplinary Perspectives,* ed. M.M. Suárez-Orozco, 107–9. Cambridge, MA: Harvard University Press and David Rockefeller Center Series on Latin American Studies.

———. 1999. *Black Identities: West Indian Immigrant Dreams and American Realities.* New York and Cambridge, MA: Russell Sage Foundation and Harvard University Press.

Waters, Mary C., and Tomás R. Jiménez. 2005. "Assessing Immigrant Assimilation: New Empirical and Theoretical Challenges." *Annual Review of Sociology* 31: 105–25.

Wilson, William J. 1987. *The Truly Disadvantaged: The Inner City, the Underclass, and Public Policy.* Chicago: University of Chicago Press.

Wimmer, Andreas. 2008a. "Elementary Strategies of Ethnic Boundary Making." *Ethnic and Racial Studies* 31 (6): 1025–55.

———. 2008b. "The Making and Unmaking of Ethnic Boundaries: A Multilevel Process Theory." *American Journal of Sociology* 113 (4): 970–1022.

Wirth, Louis. 1928. *The Ghetto.* Chicago: University of Chicago Press.

Wojtkiewicz, Roger A., and Katherine M. Donato. 1995. "Hispanic Educational Attainment: The Effects of Family Background and Nativity." *Social Forces* 74 (2): 559–74.

Wyman, Mark. 1993. *Round-trip to America: The Immigrants Return to Europe, 1880–1930*. Ithaca, NY: Cornell University Press.

Yancey, William L., Eugene P. Erickson, and Richard N. Juliani. 1976. "Emergent Ethnicity: A Review and Reformulation." *American Sociological Review* 41 (3): 391–403.

Yinger, J. Milton. 1985. "Assimilation in the United States: Mexican Americans." In *Mexican Americans in Comparative Perspectives*, ed. W. Conner, 30–55. Washington DC: Urban Institute.

Yinger, John. 1986. "Measuring Racial Discrimination with Fair Housing Audits: Caught in the Act." *American Economic Review* 76 (5): 881–93.

Zhou, Min. 2004. "Coming of Age at the Turn of the Twenty-first Century: A Demographic Profile of Asian American Youth." In *Asian American Youth: Culture, Identity, and Ethnicity*, ed. J. Lee and M. Zhou, 33–50. New York: Routledge.

Zhou, Min, and Jennifer Lee. 2004. "Introduction: The Making of Culture, Identity, and Ethnicity among Asian American Youth." In *Asian American Youth: Culture, Identity, and Ethnicity*, ed. J. Lee and M. Zhou, 1–32. New York: Routledge.

Zolberg, Aristide R., and Litt Woon Long. 1999. "Why Islam Is Like Spanish: Cultural Incorporation in Europe and the United States." *Politics and Society* 27 (1): 5–38.

Zúñiga, Victor, and Rubén Hernández-León. 2005. *New Destinations of Mexican Immigration in the United States: Community Formation, Local Responses and Inter-group Relations*. New York: Russell Sage Foundation.

Index

Note: Italicized page numbers indicate figures.

acculturation: definition of, 134–35; dissonant, 310n5. *See also* Americanization; assimilation

affirmative action: attitudes toward, 263–64; educational attainment and, 75; end of, 132–33, 308n6

African Americans: class differences among, 217–18; discrimination against, 156; indicators of inauthentic, 170; Irish immigrants distinguished from, 209; racist assumptions about, 158–59; WWII service of, 237–38

age: attitudes toward cost of immigration and, 201; of interviewees, 27, 283–88. *See also* birth cohorts; generations; youth

Agius, Jody, 219, 220, 230

agricultural industry: demands for cheap labor, 39–40, 47, 59–60; Mexicanization of, 60. *See also* beef-packing industry; labor market and workplaces

agricultural workers: advice for, 224–25; Chicanos' support for, 45–46; exempt from head tax and literacy test, 35; experience-based understanding of, 229–31; nativist assumptions about, 160; in sugar beet industry, 54, 56–57, 72

Alba, Richard: on assimilation, 10, 17, 21, 241; on cultural resources, 102; on ethnic boundaries, 140; on immigrants' housing choices, 307n6; on immigrants' struggles, 260; on improvements by birth cohort, 77, 306–7n5; on language use, 90–91; on Mexican- American identification, 275

La Alianza de Pueblos Libres, (Alliance of Free Peoples), 46

American: use of term, 303n1

American dream: accommodating views of immigration based on, 185–88, 195–96; immigrants' struggles to attain, 260–62

American G.I. Forum (AGIF), 41, 81, 236–38

defined by, 164–70; in beef-packing industry, 54–56; as beneficial to Mexican Americans, 196–97, 203–11, 239; boom in (1980 onward), 48–51; characteristics of, 4–5, 199–200; Chicanos' views of, 43–44; as cost to Mexican Americans, 198–203; cross-national ties of, 95–97; disincentives for return home, 50–51; economic role of, 191–92; everyday assistance for, 221–27; foreignness linked to, 142; holiday celebrations of, 94; homesickness of, 232–33; information lacking for, 233–34; limits on (1960s and 1970s), 47–48; LULAC stance against, 38; Mexican Americans' casual interactions with, 104–8; Mexican Americans' distancing from, 38, 40–41, 240–48; Mexican Americans' friendships with, 108–14; Mexican Americans' identification with, 151–54; Mexican Americans' intra-marriage and dating of, 114–18; Mexican Americans' social standing impacted by, 197–211; organized efforts to help, 234–40; politicization of issue, 142, 145–47; questions about, 3, 256–57, 296–99; racial attitudes of, 311n1; restrictionist views on, 190–97, 310n8; surnames linked to, 156–57; U.S. debate about, 182, 212–14, 250–51, 262; use of term, 303–4n3; work-related assistance for, 227–33. See also attitudes and opinions of Mexican Americans; authenticity; ethnic raw materials; immigrant replenishment; Spanish-language use
Mexican-origin population: application of lessons from, 264–71; research approach to, 24–28; assumed to be unauthorized immigrants, 154–61; attrition of, 275, 306–7n5; defining event of, 13, 24, 28, 219, 220, 223, 235, 238–39, 262; diversity of, xi–xii, 19, 52–53, 57, 182, 227; double-edged sword for, 262–64; entry points for, 3; European immigrants compared with, 7, 163–64, 251; everyday interactions among, 219–20; exceptional characteristics of, 5–8; as exemplars of segmented assimilation, 16; first significant presence of, 6, 304n5; generational differences among, xiii, 15; ignored in immigration research, 8–12; increased from 1910–30, 3, 11; as minority group, 46, 263; names (labels) for, 303–4n3;

non-Mexicans' distinctions among, 161–64, 208–9, 226; as permanent, unmeltable immigrant group, 23–24, 30, 259–62; political and social clout of, 22; questions about being, 296; similarities among, 209–11; in U.S. racial and ethnic landscape, 23–24, 57, 61, 62, 124, 178, 253–62; as voluntary migrants, 14–15. See also Chicano generation; ethnic identity and ethnicity; Garden City (Kans.); immigrant replenishment; Mexican Americans, first generation (1848–1909); Mexican Americans, second generation; Mexican Americans, later generation; Mexican immigrants (born in Mexico, now in U.S.); Santa Maria (Calif.); unauthorized migrants
Mexican-origin population statistics: on crime, 309n1; death rate along border, 50, 305–6n6; demographic profile, 52, 58, 61, 63; foreign-born, in California, 61; foreign-born, in Kansas, 56; in Garden City composition, 57; in Guadalupe, 310n4; native- vs. foreign-born, compared, 37, 38, 44, 58, 61, 63; number of first Mexican Americans, 274, 304n5; number of foreign-born, 32; number of unauthorized immigrants, 51; as percentage of beef-packing workers, 55; as percentage of foreign-born population, 6–8, 7; in Santa Maria composition, 62; in schools, 311n8; undercounted in censuses, 304n7
Mexican problem: use of term, 144–45
Mexican Revolution, 35–36, 54, 59, 261
Mexico: as cheap labor source, 35–36; economic instability in, 49, 50–51; events celebrated in, 94; percentage of immigrants to U.S. from, 184; U.S. annexation of, 13; visits to, 96, 116, 138–39; wealth disparities in, 34
Miami (Fla.): Cuban enclave in, 218–19, 227
middle and upper classes: African Americans in, 217–18; benefits of immigrants for, 196–97, 203–11, 239; emergence and growth of, 40–42, 48, 51–52; ethnic drawbridges lowered by, 238–39; friendships and ethnic raw materials among, 108–14; historical events aiding move into, 74–75; occupations aiding move into, 73–74, 75–76; residential choices of, 79–81; symbols deployed by, 159–60, 174

Text: 10/14 Palatino
Display: Univers Condensed Light 47; Bauer Bodoni
Indexer: Margie Towery
Illustrator: Bill Nelson
Compositor: BookMatters, Berkeley
Printer and binder: Maple-Vail Book Manufacturing Group